THE CAMBRIDGE
COMPANION TO
LITERATURE ON SCREEN

THE CAMBRIDGE COMPANION TO
LITERATURE ON SCREEN

This *Companion* offers a multi-disciplinary approach to literature on film and television. Writers are drawn from different backgrounds to consider broad topics, such as the issue of adaptation from novels and plays to the screen, canonical and popular literature, fantasy, and adaptations for children. There are also case studies on, for example, Shakespeare, Jane Austen, the nineteenth-century novel, and modernism, which allow the reader to place adaptations of the work of writers within a wider context. An interview with Andrew Davies, whose adaptation work includes *Pride and Prejudice* (1995) and *Bleak House* (2005), reveals the practical choices and challenges that face the professional writer and adaptor. The *Companion*, as a whole, provides an extensive survey of an increasingly popular field of study.

A complete list of books in the series is at the back of this book.

THE CAMBRIDGE
COMPANION TO
LITERATURE ON SCREEN

EDITED BY
DEBORAH CARTMELL

AND

IMELDA WHELEHAN

CAMBRIDGE
UNIVERSITY PRESS

CAMBRIDGE UNIVERSITY PRESS
Cambridge, New York, Melbourne, Madrid, Cape Town, Singapore, São Paulo

Cambridge University Press
The Edinburgh Building, Cambridge CB2 8RU, UK

Published in the United States of America by Cambridge University Press, New York

www.cambridge.org
Information on this title: www.cambridge.org/9780521614863

© Cambridge University Press 2007

First published 2007

Printed in the United Kingdom at the University Press, Cambridge

A catalogue record for this publication is available from the British Library

ISBN 978-0-521-84962-3 hardback
ISBN 978-0-521-61486-3 paperback

CONTENTS

CONTENTS

NOTES ON CONTRIBUTORS

JAN BAETENS teaches at the Institute for Cultural Studies of the University of Leuven. His research areas are: photography, literary theory, and word and image studies. With Marc Lits, he co-edited the bilingual volume *Novelization: From Film to Novel* (2004).

PETER BROOKER is Professor of Literary and Cultural Studies at the University of Nottingham. His recent publications include *Modernity and Metropolis: Writing, Film and Urban Formations* (2002); *Bohemia in London: The Social Scene of Early Modernism* (2004); and *Geographies of Modernism* (as co-editor; 2005). He is co-director of the AHRC-funded (Arts and Humanities Research Council) Modernist Magazines Project and co-editor of a forthcoming three-volume critical and cultural history of modernist magazines. He plans a book on "Newness."

JUDITH BUCHANAN is Senior Lecturer in Film Studies in the Department of English at the University of York. She is the author of *Shakespeare on Film* (2005) and her monograph on *Shakespeare on Silent Film* is forthcoming with Cambridge University Press. Her work on biblical films of the silent era forms the basis of her next project.

SARAH CARDWELL is Senior Lecturer in Film and Television Studies at the University of Kent. She is the author of *Adaptation Revisited: Television and the Classic Novel* (2002) and *Andrew Davies* (2005), as well as many articles and essays within film, television, and adaptation studies.

DEBORAH CARTMELL is Principal Lecturer, Subject Leader of English and Head of the Graduate Centre at De Montfort University. She is author of *Interpreting Shakespeare on Screen* (2000); co-editor of *Adaptations: From Text to Screen, Screen to Text* (1999), the Film/Fiction series (Pluto Books, 1996–2001), and *Shakespeare* (2005–). She is currently working on *Literature on Screen: An Overview* with Imelda Whelehan.

TIMOTHY CORRIGAN is a Professor of Cinema Studies, English, and History of Art, and Director of Cinema Studies at the University of Pennsylvania. His work in film studies has focused on modern American and international cinema, as well as pedagogy and film. Books include *New German Film: The Displaced Image* (1983); *The Films of Werner Herzog: Between Mirage and History* (1986); *Writing about Film* (2001); *A Cinema without Walls: Movies and Culture after Vietnam* (1991); *Film and Literature: An Introduction and Reader* (2000); and *The Film Experience* (co-authored with Patricia White; 2004). He is presently concluding research on a book-length study entitled *The Essay Film*, which examines the films of such filmmakers as Chris Marker, Derek Jarman, and Trinh T. Minh-Ha.

ANDREW DAVIES Andrew Davies is a writer and adaptor for television and cinema; among his many adaptations are *A Very Peculiar Practice* (1986, 1988), *Pride and Prejudice* (1996), *Tipping the Velvet* (2002), *The Way We Live Now* (2004), *Bridget Jones's Diary* (1996), *Bridget Jones: The Edge of Reason* (2004), and *Bleak House* (2005).

ANNETTE DAVISON is a Lecturer in Music at the University of Edinburgh, where she teaches on the history and analysis of film music and sound, twentieth-century music, critical and cultural theory, and contemporary musicology. She recently published *Hollywood Theory, Non-Hollywood Practice: Cinema Soundtracks in the 1980s and 1990s* (2004) and co-edited (with Erica Sheen) a collection of essays on the work of the director, David Lynch, *American Dreams, Nightmare Visions: The Cinema of David Lynch* (2004). She has published on the film music of Hans Werner Henze and David Lynch, soundtrack synergies, and is currently writing a book about Alex North's score for the film adaptation of *A Streetcar Named Desire* (Scarecrow Press) and an article on the soundtrack to the film adaptation of Bret Easton Ellis's *American Psycho*.

MARTIN HALLIWELL is Professor of American Studies and Director of the Centre for American Studies at the University of Leicester. He is the author of five books, including *Images of Idiocy: The Idiot Figure in Modern Fiction and Film* (2004) and *Transatlantic Modernism: Moral Dilemmas in Modernist Fiction* (2006). His next book on American culture in the 1950s will be published in spring 2007 with Edinburgh University Press.

I. Q. HUNTER is Principal Lecturer and Subject Leader in Film Studies at De Montfort University, Leicester. He edited *British Science Fiction Cinema* (1999), co-edited *Pulping Fictions* (1996), *Trash Aesthetics* (1997), *Sisterhoods* (1998), *Alien Identities* (1999), *Classics* (2000), *Retrovisions* (2001), and *Brit-Invaders!* (2005), and has published widely on exploitation, horror, and cult films. He is currently writing a British Film Guide to *A Clockwork Orange*.

DOUGLAS LANIER is Associate Professor of English at the University of New Hampshire, where he specializes in Renaissance drama, film, literary pedagogy, and Shakespeare and contemporary popular culture. In addition to his book,

Shakespeare and Modern Popular Culture (2002), he has published many articles on Shakespeare and the mass media, including Shakespeare in radio, audio recordings, film, television, and popular drama. In addition to his continuing research in Shakespeare and popular culture, he is currently at work on a study of cultural stratification in early modern British drama.

BRIAN McFARLANE an Honorary Associate Professor at Monash University, Melbourne, is compiler, editor, and chief author of *The Encyclopedia of British Film* (2003; 3rd edition 2005). Other books include *Novel to Film: An Introduction to the Theory of Adaptation* (1996); *An Autobiography of British Cinema* (1997); *The Oxford Companion to Australian Film* (as co-editor; 1999); *Lance Comfort* (1999); and *The Cinema of Britain and Ireland* (as editor; 2005).

LINDA V. TROOST is Professor and Chair of English at Washington & Jefferson College in Pennsylvania. In addition to writing on musical theater in eighteenth-century London, she is the co-editor, with Sayre Greenfield, of *Jane Austen in Hollywood* (1998) and founding editor of the annual *Eighteenth-Century Women*.

ECKART VOIGTS-VIRCHOW is currently Deputy Chair of English Literature at the University of Chemnitz, Germany. His *Introduction to Media Studies* was published in 2005. He is also editor of *Janespotting and Beyond: British Heritage Retrovisions since the Mid-1990s* (2004).

PAUL WELLS is Director of the Animation Academy at Loughborough University. He has published widely in the animation field, including *Understanding Animation* (1998), *Animation and America* (2002), *Fundamentals of Animation* (2006), and *Halas & Batchelor Cartoons: An Animated History* (2006).

IMELDA WHELEHAN is Professor in English and Women's Studies and Faculty Head of Research at De Montfort University. She is author of *Modern Feminist Thought* (1995), *Overloaded* (2000), *Helen Fielding's Bridget Jones's Diary: A Reader's Guide* (2002), *The Feminist Bestseller* (2005), co-author of *Fifty Key Concepts in Gender Studies* (2004), co-editor of *Adaptations: From Text to Screen, Screen to Text* (1999) and the Film/Fiction series (Pluto Books, 1996–2001). She is currently working on *Literature on Screen: An Overview* with Deborah Cartmell.

DEBORAH CARTMELL AND IMELDA WHELEHAN

Introduction – Literature on screen: a synoptic view

The publication of *The Cambridge Companion to Literature on Screen* confirms the fact that Literature on Screen has finally arrived. Always a "hybrid" subject, literature on screen was too literary for film studies and too film-based for Literary Studies, and has tended to occupy an uneasy place between the two, perhaps tending towards departments of literature in the main. Literary adaptations have been the subject of much academic discourse in both fields (auteur studies, and Shakespeare on Screen texts are two obvious examples), but until the last decade there have been few attempts to evaluate the process of adaptation itself and even then only some of these investigations attempt to theorize the textual transactions that occur in the process – whether in the mind of the adaptor, the critic, or the reader/viewer.

As early as 1936, Renaissance scholar Allardyce Nicoll, in *Theatre and Film*, considers the potential of film to merit the same status as theatrical texts, while conversely reflecting on how film fails to achieve its potential when it simply copies, or "culls" from literature.[1] Like Nicoll, George Bluestone in 1957, in the first book-length study of adaptation, *Novels into Film*, alludes to Gotthold Ephraim Lessing's essay *The Laocoon* (1766), on the differentiations between poetry and painting. In his opening chapter, Bluestone famously begins his book by looking at connections between film and literature and ends by contemplating their differences, implicitly placing a question mark over the enterprise altogether. Robert Richardson, in 1969, extends this discussion by asserting at the outset of his book that film and literature are essentially different: "what we all know, but what is worth restating, that what makes a good film doesn't make a good novel and what makes a good novel doesn't necessarily make a good film."[2] Taking in novels, short stories, and poetry, Richardson's book is the first devoted to the subject of *literature* and film (although it must be said that many in the discipline use the word "novel" to refer to literature as a whole).[3] For the sake of clarity and definition, it's vital that literature *and* film be distinguished from literature *on* film and the latter, the subject of this book, has historically privileged the literary over the cinematic. Explicit in all of these works is a desire to free our notion of film adaptations from this dependency on literature so that adaptations are not derided as sycophantic, derivative, and therefore inferior to their literary counterparts.

Nonetheless, there have been both filmmakers and writers who believe that, if a film is to be a good adaptation, it needs to be "faithful" to its literary source and that the best adaptations are those that come closest to preserving and revering the literary text. Contemplating degrees of proximity to the text has given rise to a number of taxonomies of adaptation. To mention a few, Jack Jorgens, in 1977, divides Shakespeare adaptations into theatrical, realist, and filmic,[4] Dudley Andrew, in 1984, splits adaptations into "borrowing" (where the film hopes to win an audience because of the reputation of the source), "intersecting" (in which the "cinema records its confrontation with an ultimately intransigent text") and "transforming" (where the adaptation "faithfully" reproduces a literary text to the screen).[5] Kamilla Elliott, in 2003, offers no less than six models of adaptation, consisting of the "psychic," "international," "ventriloquist," "decomposing," "genetic," and "trumping."[6] Hidden in these taxonomies are value judgments and a consequent ranking of types, normally covertly governed by a literary rather than cinematic perspective. What fascinates us here is not so much the taxonomies themselves, which reflect disciplinary preferences and often the privileging of one medium over another, but this *will to taxonomize*, which is symptomatic of how the field has tried to mark out its own territory. These various and sometimes conflicting schemes of categorization show how many directions the field can take, as well as the multitudinous ways in which the field connects with the originary disciplines of literary and film studies, constantly widening its purview and possibly trampling on sacred ground. As Brian McFarlane notes in the seminal *Novel to Film* (1996), such classifications "represent some heartening challenges to the primacy of fidelity as a critical criterion."[7]

This seemingly intractable need for a film to be "true" to or "match" its literary source partially underpins the heritage genre. Adaptations that aspire to be "faithful" to their literary source encapsulate what Andrew Higson, in his work on the heritage genre, has described as the "discourse of authenticity":[8] films that endeavor to give the impression of accuracy in the representation of a literary text, historical event, or period. No matter how good a copy it is, however, it is *qua* "copy" inevitably doomed to be inferior to its original. Explicit and implicit comparisons have been drawn between adaptations and the flickering reflected lights described by Plato in *The Republic*; these lights (unnervingly resembling a cinema), viewed by philistine cave dwellers who have never seen the "real" light, can do as much harm as good and are no substitute for the "ideal" of the original – the unreachable ur-text in the sky. This mindset has given rise to debates about the dilution of English Studies and attacks on Media/Film and Cultural Studies that have contributed to, in Allan Bloom's words, "the impoverishment of the souls of today's students."[9] Adaptation as a pale copy of the real thing is an entrenched belief prevalent in popular press reviews of film adaptations, where the final paragraphs almost always contain an obligatory return to the inevitable "not as good as the book" conclusion. Such conclusions are reached for the most part by an imperfect knowledge of both forms by the critic. As Béla Balázs acutely notes about film criticism in the 1940s, "the most important art of our time is that about which one need know nothing whatever,"[10] and this unselfconscious display of ignorance about film as art has marred adaptations criticism.

Most recent studies of adaptation have thrown water on the reflected light or "not as good as the book" approach, an approach that has, for far too long, as Robert Ray observes, dogged the field of literature on screen studies by a narrow one-sidedness that assumes adaptations are merely cheap imitations of a Platonic ideal that is, by its very nature, inimitable.[11] Robert Stam rises to Ray's challenge and regards film adaptations as "readings," as part of a continuing dialogical process. Eager to distinguish himself from the judgmental and narrow approach of "fidelity" criticism, he regards both literary and film adaptations equally as not about life, but about art, involved in a complex interchange with a range of other texts. Stam finds Genette's "transtextuality," especially the fifth type, "hypertextuality," a useful tool for unpacking film adaptations. "Hypertextuality" refers to one text's relation to its "hypotext" – so that, for instance, the numerous versions of *Hamlet* are hypertextual elaborations, prompted by the same hypotext (i.e. Shakespeare's play).[12] Kamilla Elliott looks at the roots of film adaptations in the tradition of *ut pictura poesis*, especially in relation to the nineteenth-century illustrated novel and divides the study between interart affinities and interart analogies, film's integral connections with the novel as well as the oppositions between novel and film. Her concern is with classic texts that can be read as almost predicting or foreshadowing the relationship between literature and film in their reflections on images and words.[13]

This book looks at literary texts not as primary sources but as "intertexts," one (albeit dominant) of a multiplicity of perspectives, thereby freeing an adaptation from unprofitable "eye for an eye" comparisons. While both Stam and Elliott offer fresh insights into the field of literature on film, these approaches are restricted to words and images, to canonical works of literature, to film (excluding television), and to the genre of the novel, and therefore represent a limited and rarefied segment of the field. A book that opens up the multiple dimensions of adaptations studies is John Desmond and Peter Hawkes's *Adaptation: Studying Film and Literature* (Boston: McGraw, 2006) which includes the usual suspects (the novel, short story, and play) as well as relatively unchartered fields, such as non-fiction, popular fiction, animation, and even failure. Designed as a student textbook, the study can only skim, albeit provocatively, the rich minefield covered by adaptations – however, the authors ultimately limit themselves to a broadly genre-centered approach. This book aims for a more extensive coverage, taking stock of the ever-expanding scope of the subject, which must, firstly, include literature other than the novel. Shakespeare on screen studies, for instance, now a major industry of criticism, seems to exist mysteriously outside the field of literature on film. While there are clear affinities between the form of the novel and film narration, some account needs to be taken of screen adaptations of literature as varied as the Bible to the fairytale, to different genres, such as fantasy, romance, heritage, and to popular (rather than canonical) texts. Secondly, literature on screen studies needs to take on board technical innovations and contributions made in areas such as anima-tion to soundtracks. Thirdly, changing attitudes to film adaptations need to be evaluated in relation to both the history of adaptation and to the repre-sentation of different historical periods on screen. Fourthly, television adap-tations, so often excluded from literature on screen studies, require a more sustained analysis, especially given the exponential popularity of the classic serialization from the late 1970s onwards and the different industrial condi-tions (some indeed more favorable to the transposition of the long multi-layered plots of nineteenth-century realist novels) within which they emerge. Fifthly, extra-cinematic factors (current trends, historical events) are vital to film adaptations but are curiously absent from most studies of the subject. Production values, technological changes, commercial considerations – in short, the film and television industries themselves – are a sixth and vital dimension of literature on screen studies. Finally, some acknowledgment that film can precede a literary text in the reversal of the literature/film translation needs to be made. Indeed, film can and does provide a source text for literature in the form of novelizations, as well as less conspicuous manifestations of this process (such as *Star Wars* being the ur-text for the Harry Potter novels).

This *Companion* aims to paint a picture of literature on screen in a variety of ramifications and is divided into four parts: Theories of literature on screen; History and contexts; Genre, industry, taste; and Beyond the "lit-erary" (which considers sound, vision, and hybridity). The book doesn't aspire to theoretical containment of literature on screen. Rather, it aims to address the different approaches and the range of topics invited by the multi-dimensionality of the discipline itself, seeing adaptation as a field in process which can capitalize on its liminal disciplinary positioning by ever appropriating and reframing critical and theoretical models to suit its own purposes.

The one thing that literature and film have in common is narrative, as Brian McFarlane observes in Chapter 1. McFarlane throws down a gauntlet to literary elitism by arguing that an adaptation doesn't simply counterfeit (and reduce) but adds to the original narrative a battery of codes, both cultural and cinematic; in this he is in agreement with Morris Beja who asserts that "what a film takes from a book matters; but so does what it brings to a book."[14] McFarlane considers the particular challenges that different literary genres pose for adaptors, how "fidelity" criticism can be undermined by intertextual approaches, and the essential necessity to be open to the possibility that adaptations can improve upon their literary originals. It's vital to bear in mind that there is no necessary dominant genre: and this assumption that the literary text *must* be supreme because literature *must* be better than film has undoubtedly blighted much work in the field. In Chapter 2, Timothy Corrigan charts the rise of film adaptation and the strained relationship between literature and film arising from issues of copyright, the introduction of sound, the Hays' Production Code,[15] and the rise of the Hollywood "prestige film" which evolves into the heritage film of the late twentieth century. Corrigan suggests that the battle to rescue film from the clutches of literature, in the earlier part of the twentieth century, has resulted in polarizing Film Studies and Literary Studies, with film adaptation forlornly, "in the gap." Yet from this position, with little need to respect the anxiously policed boundaries of film or literary studies, Corrigan asserts that the richest opportunities for challenging ideas are likely to emerge.

The second part begins with an account of adaptations in the silent era and the appropriation of narrative material in order to supply cultural kudos and moral credibility to what was a cinema in danger of falling victim to its own excesses: commercialism and immorality. In Chapter 3, Judith Buchanan focuses on the Gospel narratives on film and how the portrayal of Christ, in particular, has exacted both zeal and offence which, as she says has "succeeded in making other, purely literary interest groups – Dickensians, fans of Austen, even Shakespeareans – look mild-mannered and unconcerned by comparison" (p. 47). The discussion of the audacity of filmmakers in "making the Word flesh" is continued in Chapter 4 by Douglas Lanier in his survey of Shakespeare on screen. There is a tradition in Shakespeare films to read the Chorus's speech from *Henry V* – "A kingdom for a stage" without irony, that Shakespeare felt confined by the limitations of the stage and that his true appeal is in the images behind the words rather than the words on their own. The derogatory representation of theater, on screen, from Georges Méliès's *Hamlet* (1907) to Richard Eyre's *Stage Beauty* (2005), according to Lanier, reflects a growing tendency to erase all traces of theatricality (and, by implication, Shakespeare's words) in Shakespeare on film. Lanier also notes how these films are often made for a video/DVD and educational market that has historically privileged the more "faithful" adaptation, given the text-based nature of Shakespeare studies within academia.

Certainly video and DVD have increased the shelf-life of classic adaptations and the educational market is far from overlooked in these productions. If the current tendency is to modernize or transform Shakespeare on film, on the whole eighteenth- and nineteenth-century literature on screen tends to dwell on "authentic" period details. While it is evident that early twentieth-century writers drew inspiration from the cinema, "cinematic" writers from the nineteenth century were identified by the likes of the filmmaker, Sergei Eistenstein,[16] in particular, Flaubert, Dickens, and Zola. Linda Troost, in Chapter 5, outlines the popularity of these writers, especially Austen (who, as Andrew Davies comments in this volume, is a "gift" to screenwriters). Troost looks at the adaptability of nineteenth-century novels across film and television and considers Austen's fate in heritage productions as reflective of the author's own fascination with material detail. Austen adaptations themselves are often seen as the template for approaches to literary adaptation, as new versions emerge so often that, as Troost asserts, Jane Austen has become "a household name even in non-bookish households" (see p. 84 in this volume) and hints at the multitudinous ways in which adaptations can increase the cultural capital of a literary text. It is clear that Shakespeare and Austen on screen have become established areas of study within the English curriculum. Where these authors go, others will follow. There is a growing corpus of literature on screen adaptations of Dickens, Trollope, George Eliot, and Hardy, among others.[17]

Martin Halliwell and Peter Brooker, in Chapters 6 and 7, concur that when the two media are contemporary and therefore intertwined (with writers adapting cinematic techniques and often, as in the case of William Faulkner and F. Scott Fitzgerald, becoming screenwriters themselves) there is, paradoxically, less confidence in adapting fiction to screen than that of earlier periods. With few attempts by mainstream cinema to rise to the challenges of modernist fiction, what is lost in these adaptations is formal experimentation (especially use of narrative voice) and symbolic richness, and ultimately literary realism is the favored form for Anglo-American appropriation. Halliwell and Brooker both consider *The Hours* (Stephen Daldry, 2002), a film concerned with modernism and postmodernism, reception and authority, indeed with adaptation itself. For Halliwell, the success of *The Hours* suggests the ripe potentiality for adaptation of further, even "high" modernist texts. For Brooker *The Hours* (as literary text and film) expresses the postmodern potentialities of contemporary adaptation – an act of free exchange between literature, reading, historical moment, and film – which celebrates the ways in which intertextuality can refashion, or even cast as irrelevant the notion of the "original" while engaging us in sometimes complex and always satisfying cultural riddles, where the pleasure of the text is also in finding other texts embedded there. In postmodern adaptation the pleasure is in locating and celebrating an excesss of interpretation, rather than attempting to close off "unauthorized" ones, or suggest a hierarchy of readings (that the book necessarily engenders the film).

Much has been written about the concept of the "auteur" in film theory and, while there may have been a movement away from this concept to a consideration of the collective production of a movie, it is interesting to explore what happens when auteur adapts author. If one can extend the notion of "auteur" beyond the director, Sarah Cardwell in Chapter 12 identifies in Andrew Davies the closest one comes to an "auteur" in the field of television drama, suggesting, as Cardwell observes, the increased emphasis on writing in this area. His career as a scriptwriter has spanned over twenty years and his 1995 *Pride and Prejudice* in particular is a defining moment in the history of classic adaptation. Deborah Cartmell and Imelda Whelehan spoke to him about his work, and particularly the recent acclaimed BBC *Bleak House* (2005). In these conversations, at the close of this volume (Chapter 16), it becomes clear that the process of adaptation itself is influenced by numerous external factors, including previous adaptations, elements in the original text that seem to need "correcting" (he claims that only Austen's plots are utterly reliable and logical) or updating (he cites as one example the portrayal of women – notably Esther Summerson in *Bleak House*), and the need to do something distinctive which challenges the audience's preconceptions about the classic serial (in *Bleak House* this is done via scheduling and episode duration).

Part Three explores genre, selecting heritage, fantasy, romance, and children's fiction. Film expands on established Aristotelian narrative divisions (with specific conventions and rules) in turn, introducing new genres within literature, such as the Western, thriller, horror, and gangster genres. Reading film criticism today, the literary origins of genre criticism are often forgotten or swept aside; for example, notwithstanding Homer, Virgil, Dante, Spenser, or Milton, film genre critic Steve Neale asserts that " 'Epic' is essentially a 1950s and 1960s term."[18] Such has been its dominance within Film Studies (as successor to auteurist approaches that regarded the director as the single creative force behind a film and hence the "author"),[19] that "genre theory" now seems to belong to the movies alone and it's worth stressing here that genre, like narrative, is another point of contact between literature, film, and television.

The pronounced recent phenomenon of "screening the author"– with films such as *Shakespeare in Love* (1998), *Adaptation* (2002), and *Finding Neverland* (2004) – is an example of "writing back," significantly in harmony with the renewed interest in the author and biography within English Studies. The emphasis on the author gives these films an aura of "authenticity," the principal objective of the "heritage" film. The heritage genre is often applied to classic literature on screen, and, on one level, is, as stated earlier, a cinematic manifestation of fidelity criticism, as it seeks to create – what fidelity critics seem to yearn for – an "authentic," historically accurate and therefore faithful reproduction. Eckart Voigts-Virchow in Chapter 8 exposes the many pitfalls in generic categorization and unpacks the "heritage" genre's peculiar English associations by interrogating what "heritage" means in both a British and a German context and what happens when the "past" nostalgically consumed by one national audience is actually located geographically and culturally elsewhere. This chapter offers a breakdown of the components of heritage to identify a much more complex area than often assumed, what Alan Parker dismissed as the "Laura Ashley school of film-making." In addition it charts a phenomenon which underlines this challenge – how a British middlebrow writer has become one of the most adapted writers in Germany in recent years in the creation of an *ersatz* heritage, projecting German actors and production teams into an English heritage space – but also reminds us that adaptations do not occur within a global context without some fascinating local variation. We have chosen to look at genres that are – largely due to their popularity – frequently devalued: the woman's film, the fantasy film, and children's literature on screen. Following from a discussion of heritage, in Chapter 9 Imelda Whelehan excavates the archetypal women's film, *Now, Voyager*; the "stock types," normally dismissed as formulaic or repetitive, are seen to summon to mind and interrogate areas of concern to women, including female consumption, relationships, and oppression. The "normal" dynamic of exchange between literary text and screen version is reversed, seeming to confirm another first principle of adaptations study – that mediocre books make the best films. It is, however, argued that this reversal is less to do with the innate aesthetic "value" (or lack of it) of the text and more to do with the perception that popular fiction is merely fodder for the classic Hollywood treadmill – witnessed by the fact that many of the best known films of the 1940s used recently published books from reliable bestselling writers as their base.

In Chapters 10 and 11, Ian Hunter and Deborah Cartmell comment on the particular problems facing adaptations of popular genres – fantasy and children's literature on screen. Dogged by the demands of the fans for fidelity, both genres reveal a hostility between the screen and literary text, a hostility that the likes of director Peter Jackson is able to overcome in *The Lord of the Rings* films (2001–3). Yet at the same time this quest for the "definitive" version is sent up by the differing demands (and possibilities) of the cinema and DVD marketplace: as Hunter wryly observes, the collectable extended versions of the original film releases force us to ask whether viewing the cinema version is enough and when one can actually claim to have seen the authentic version. Cartmell further pursues Bluestone's observation about the innate hostility between film and literature in an account of children's literature in adaptation where, as discussed by Hunter, fidelity can be demanded by an ardent reading public and where, as Whelehan discussed in relation to the classic "woman's film" of the 1940s, novels can pale into obscurity, massively overshadowed by their screened counterparts. As Cartmell observes, when the adaptation emerges from a clear commercial agenda, such as the products of the Disney corporation, the film is part of a brand, the "magical kingdom" one enters as the film credits roll. In films for children, ideological considerations come to the fore and in the case of Disney, the imposition of "family values" can rob a text of more interesting narrative contradictions or tensions, allowing only the most conservative readings of character and motivation.

The study of literature on screen is opened up to include television, animation, sound, and the previously unthinkable "novelization" (where the source text is now a film). There is, arguably, a prejudice towards TV within literature on screen studies which is challenged by Sarah Cardwell in her account, in Chapter 12, of what is most commonly thought of as an adaptation: the serialized literary classic. The classic serial is marked out chiefly by a shared visual aesthetic and all television adaptations are colored by the ingrained assumption that television is less adventurous, more conservative than film. As Cardwell demonstrates, television was an important factor in the development of the heritage film "look" with pathfinding serials such as *Brideshead Revisited* (1981) establishing a model later emulated by films such as *A Room with a View* (1985). Rather than claim that TV adaptations can be as significant in their impact as film (although this is indeed the case), Cardwell argues for a medium-specific approach which allows for a considered analysis of industry conditions and technological constraints (particularly the dominance of studio filming in adaptations of the seventies, which leads to a much more stagey feel). Add to this the ways in which such adaptations contribute to the mission of public service broadcasters who need to show they further the "public good," in which light "a television adaptation, unlike a film, cannot be regarded as mere entertainment" (see p. 188). Another significant omission within the field, the animated classic, is redressed by Paul Wells in Chapter 13 in which he outlines the painstaking lengths to which animators go, to quote Hamlet, to "suit the word to the picture." Shocking for literary critics, no doubt, Wells finds Eliot's concept of the "objective correlative" – which Eliot applies to *Hamlet* – a useful tool for unpacking the adaptation process in the cartoon. Wells suggests that in animation one may achieve the transition from literature to screen unmediated by the interventions of live actors, location, and costume. Animation's ability to enable shifts between "realism" and "fantasy" without additional special effects underlines Wells's assertion that "only animation can properly facilitate the fullest proposition of the literary text" (p. 204).

Perhaps the most overlooked of all aspects of literature on film studies, which almost always concentrates on word/image debates, is sound. Annette Davison in Chapter 14 demonstrates how music functions as an intermediary presence between spectator and film character, offering a chorus-like insight, functioning along the lines of irony. Whether commissioned for the film, or a well-known piece of music with other associations, music contributes mood, amplifies emotions, emphasizes temporality, culture, or era, and can offer continuity between cuts and editing; regardless of a viewer's specific musical tastes, the audience is adept at decoding musical signification. Her analysis of Carl Davis's score for the 1995 BBC *Pride and Prejudice* illustrates Davis's concern for historical accuracy and at the same time dramatizes the centrality of music to a young woman's social experiences within the middle and upper classes during Austen's time. His fortepiano scoring of the opening credits and the musical motifs attached to individual characters (the latter used to largely comic effect in the 1940 film of *Pride and Prejudice*) reminds us that adaptations, since the beginning of the sound era, can exploit the multi-layering effect of different signifying systems.

In Chapter 15 Jan Baetens offers a history of the phenomenon of the novelization which he reads as anti-adaptation or anti-literature on film. His account of this oft-neglected dimension in the adaptation process exposes the sheer vitality and variability of the field. Those that are most visible – the spin-off novels from Hollywood box office hits – offer little insight into the history of the genre and its purposes, which range from providing the "missing" dialogue in the silent era to enabling experimental forms of writing which are inspired by the fast-developing art of cinema, creative reworkings of the movies, and culminating in the rewritings of fan communities. Here we move from the dominant perspective of the novelization as cynical commercial exploitation to it being a means of empowerment for an audience which can repurpose a narrative to infinite ends. He concludes by posing the dilemma that once we acknowledge the existence of screen to literary text adaptations, the entire field is thrown into disarray and that "novelization forces us to consider cinema and literature in the global (mass) media structure of our time and to tackle the various ways in which media compete and contaminate each other" (see pp. 236–7). The book has come full circle – both McFarlane and Baetens openly declare what could only be spoken of in whispers in most of the twentieth century: that a film can be better than the book it is "based" on and that the film can be the original of the literary text. What Elliott dubbed the literature/film "wars,"[20] where each discipline seeks purity from the other as the guardian of the image or the word, is shown to be a chimera: there is no hallowed ground to which one can retreat unsullied. The history of the connections between literature, popular fiction, cinema, television, animation, music, and novelization is one of appropriation and contamination – this heady mixture of forms co-existing and mutating being symbolic of the progress of narrative in the twentieth and twenty-first centuries. These turf wars, still ongoing, say little about the innate characteristics of any one form, but volumes about the changing social, economic, and historical conditions in which these forms exist.

NOTES

1 (London, Bombay and Sidney: George G. Harrap & Company, 1936).
2 *Literature and Film* (1969; rpt. Bloomington and London: Indiana University Press, 1973).
3 Kamilla Elliott, for example, maintains that theater exerts more influence on cinema than does the novel while entitling her book, *Rethinking the Novel/Film Debate* (Cambridge: Cambridge University Press, 2003).
4 *Shakespeare on Film* (Bloomington: Indiana University Press, 1977), pp. 7–35.
5 *Concepts in Film Theory* (Oxford: Oxford University Press, 1984), p. 99.
6 *Rethinking the Novel/Film Debate.*
7 *Novel to Film: An Introduction to the Theory of Adaptation* (Oxford: Oxford University Press, 1996), p. 11.
8 *English Heritage, English Cinema: Costume Drama since 1980* (Oxford: Oxford University Press, 2003), p. 42.
9 *The Closing of the American Mind: How Higher Education has Failed Democracy and Impoverished the Soul of Today's Students* (Harmondsworth: Penguin, 1987).
10 Béla Balázs, *Theory of the Film: Character and Growth of a New Art* (1948), trans. from the Hungarian by Edith Bone (New York: Dover Publications Inc., 1970), p. 18.

11 *How a Film Theory Got Lost and Other Mysteries in Cultural Studies* (Princeton: Princeton University Press, 1985), pp. 120–31.

12 *Literature Through Film: Realism, Magic, and the Art of Adaptation* (Malden and Oxford: Blackwell, 2005), p. 5. See the discussion of Genette in Chapter 7 in this volume, p. 113.

13 *Rethinking the Novel/Film Debate.* For the relationship between book illustration and animation, see Paul Wells, Chapter 13 in this volume.

14 Morris Beja, *Film and Literature: An Introduction* (New York: Longman, 1979), p. 88.

15 From the early 1930s to the early 1950s, American commercial film was regulated by a code (named after Will Hays, then President of the Motion Picture Producers and Distributors of America) that imposed tight regulation on the content of commercial cinema in a climate of unease about the moral influence of movies on the public.

16 See for instance, "Dickens, Griffiths and the Film Today," *Film Form*, ed. Jay Leyda (London: Dobson, 1963), pp. 195–256. Repeatedly, Eisenstein argues that filmmakers are followers, not imitators, of the likes of Shakespeare and Dickens.

17 See Chapter 16 in this volume for a discussion of Dickens on screen with Andrew Davies.

18 *Genre and Hollywood* (London and New York: Routledge, 2000), p. 85.

19 Neale discusses how genre theory came to displace auteurism (p. 10). Thomas Schatz, in *Hollywood Genres* (Boston, Madison: McGraw Hill, 1981), p. 9, sees the auteurist and genre approaches overlapping: "In fact the *auteur* approach, in asserting a director's consistency of form and expression, effectively translates an auteur into a virtual genre unto himself, into a system of conventions which identify his work."

20 Kamilla Elliott, "Novels, Films and the Word/Image Wars" in Robert Stam and Alessandra Raengo (eds.), *A Companion to Literature and Film* (Oxford: Blackwell, 2004), pp. 1–22.

PART ONE

Theories of literature on screen

I

BRIAN McFARLANE

Reading film and literature

Perhaps no aspect of filmmaking has been so thoroughly canvassed at every level, from cinema-foyer gossip to learned academic exegeses, as the matter of adaptation of literature into film. It is not as though adaptation is the only kind of relationship that might exist between film and literature, but it is the one that most persistently preoccupies the theorist, the critic, the reviewer, the buff, and the ordinary filmgoer alike. No one feels too awed by it to be willing to risk judgments about the latest adaptation, usually to the film's disadvantage; nor do theorists regard the subject as too simple to engage their attention.

So, to start, I should like to do what I can to dispose of some of the shibboleths that hover about the discourse, both popular and scholarly, relating to film–literature connections. First, it shouldn't be necessary after several decades of serious research into the processes and challenges of adaptation to insist that "fidelity" to the original text (however distinguished) is a wholly inappropriate and unhelpful criterion for either understanding or judgment. It may be that, even among the most rigorously high-minded of film viewers confronted with the film version of a cherished novel or play, it is hard to suppress a sort of yearning for a faithful rendering of *one's own vision of the literary text*. My italics are intended to highlight the impossibility of such a venture: that every reading of a literary text is a highly individual act of cognition and interpretation; that every such response involves a kind of personal adaptation on to the screen of one's imaginative faculty as one reads. And how is any film version, drawing on the contributions of numerous collaborators, ever going to produce the same responses except by the merest chance?

In fact one might reasonably have assumed that the "fidelity" factor no longer needed to be addressed in writing about film and literature. By this I mean not only fidelity as criterion but also the very notion that this particular critical battle needs to be refought. Virtually all the books devoted to the subject of adaptation, dating back to George Bluestone's pioneering study,

Novels into Film (1957), have refuted the efficacy of judging the merits of film versions of literary texts by this standard. Nevertheless, one still finds the concept being not merely dismissed but discredited at length. Perhaps this means that the authors of such works have not adequately surveyed the critical field of recent decades; perhaps it also means that no amount of serious discourse ever really disposes of the discontent expressed in "It wasn't like that in the book."

The second misconception, and at this stage the more important one, is that film makes fewer demands on the imagination than a book does. This kind of thinking is based – erroneously, in my view – on the belief that coming to terms with a continuous narrative involving a set of characters operating in a given time and place enjoins a greater effort on the part of the reader than it does on that of the viewer. There it all is, exponents of this view will say, up there on the screen, leaving little for us to have to work on, whereas on the page we have to "translate" those lines of black marks that constitute words, phrases, clauses and sentences into conceptual images. In carrying out this "work," more of our intellectual and emotional resources will necessarily be called into play, and – there is perhaps a touch of Puritanism here – the very effort required will be good for us.

However, it may be just as persuasively argued that in coming to serious terms with a film, much more is being required of us. It is not just a matter of allowing all the perceptual stimuli film offers us to wash over us, any more than the intelligent reading of a book asks no more than that we skim the lines for the gist of the plot. The film, if it is to make any serious impact on us, will require that we pay attention to the intricate interaction of *mise-en-scène* (what is visibly there in the frame at any given moment), the editing (how one shot of a film is joined-to/separated-from the next) and sound (diegetic or non-diegetic, musical or otherwise). Each of these three categories of film's narrational arsenal has numerous subdivisions, and a full response to the film will ask the viewer, at various levels of consciousness, to take them all into account, sometimes separately, more often in concert. There are two utterly different semiotic systems at issue here, and I want to claim that there is at least as much at stake in the informed response to the codes at work in film, both cinema-specific and extra-cinematic codes, as there is in the acts of visualization and comprehension enjoined on the reader.

Third, there has been a pervasive suggestion that some sorts of literature are more susceptible to screen adaptation than others. The Australian novelist Helen Garner, reviewing Bernard Rose's 1997 version of *Anna Karenina*, claims that there is "a class of literature that, by its very nature, is not adaptable to the screen."[1] She goes on to suggest that, in such cases, film-makers are simply out of their league. Her assertion that they lack the capacity to reproduce the "narrative voice" of the original assumes that "narration" in the cinema is no more than incidental voice-over, and fails to grasp that it is the work of film not to replicate the narrating voice of the novel but to find its *own* voice through its own means. The novel, she goes on to say, "can bound through time and space" in ways, she implies, that film can't. She appears not to have thought about the way film can dart from present to past, from here to there, with an immediacy perhaps unparalleled by any other art form.[2] There is, in such views as these, a breath-taking failure to recognize the specificities of the two semiotic systems involved, and simply an implied argument that the newer one should find ways of replicating the achievements of the earlier. Complex and difficult novels and plays are not unamenable to film adaptation, but require the most intelligent and resourceful talents to address the task. No one is denying that to think of adapting *Finnegan's Wake*[3] may call for more obvious cinematic ambition than to take on *Death on the Nile*, but that is not to deny that appropriate ways to tackle it exist.

Fourth, to repeat a clause from the opening paragraph: adaptation is not the only kind of relationship that might exist between film and literature. By this I mean that there is a small but attractive body of films that engages with literature in ways other than conventional adaptation. A film such as Gavin Millar's beautiful and undervalued *Dreamchild* (1985) offers film versions of some scenes from *Alice in Wonderland* but is just as much a study of the relationship between the author, Lewis Carroll/Charles Dodgson, and the real-life Alice; a reflection on age and how it changes perceptions, and a series of explorations of the very nature of narrative. The same kind of connection between the literary creation (*Peter Pan*) and its real-life inspiration underpins *Finding Neverland* (2004), and Stephen Daldry's (adaptation of Michael Cunningham's) *The Hours* (2003) is a sort of fantasia of themes deriving from *Mrs. Dalloway* and its author, Virginia Woolf. Modern-set versions of *Emma* (Amy Heckerling's *Clueless*, 1995) and *Henry IV Parts I and II* (Gus Van Sant's *My Own Private Idaho*, 1991) suggest that the directors had more on their minds than careful adaptation of Jane Austen and Shakespeare: their interest seemed to lie primarily in how far works of earlier centuries might be made to seem relevant to later generations in settings and times far removed from those in which they had their origins. Such films, as well as Patricia Rozema's *Mansfield Park* (1999), drawing on Austen's diaries and a post-colonial reading of the history of the period as well as on the novel itself, all offer recognition of ways in which the interests of literature and film might fruitfully mesh.

Two anecdotes from my recent experience may serve to highlight some of the recurring problems that accrete around the study of the relations between film and literature. In a discussion of Martin Scorsese's glorious film version of *The Age of Innocence* (1993), a colleague of literary background claimed to have liked the film but added "Of course it's not nearly as subtle or complex as the novel." At stake in such a remark are again the semiotic differences *and* the fact that the colleague's literary training had equipped her to recognize subtlety and complexity in the verbal medium but not in the film. In a novel these qualities will be the result of the dextrous, nuanced use of words; in a film, they will derive from the interaction of those aspects of *mise-en-scène*, sound and editing in play at any given moment. The cross-over from the reading of literary texts to the "reading" of a film is more problematic than my colleague had assumed – and notice how this term "reading" is still much used for film, both strengthening the tie to the earlier medium and implying its primacy.

The other anecdote that struck me concerned a woman who had brought Hans Andersen's stories, "The Little Mermaid" and "The Ugly Duckling," to read to her grandchildren. She was taken aback and disappointed to be told that they knew that story because they'd seen a film or video version of it. The source of her disappointment seemed to lie in the ingrained notion that the written word not merely preceded but (invariably) outranked the audio-visual moving image. Was she really expecting these small children to respond to the quality of the prose and, if so, is there never an occasion when the images on the screen might be just as effective? And, effective for what? The point here is that, if she was mainly concerned with bringing the *narrative* to the children's attention, the result might just as easily have been achieved by their exposure to the film. Did those story-tellers at the time of the rise of printing fear that the oral tradition would be lost to the book – and that the new medium, with its capacity for endless replication, would inevitably be inferior in what it required of the imagination and intellect?

There is not much point in merely insisting that a film is a film, whether or not it is adapted from a literary source, and that the latter is of no conse-quence when it comes to our response to the film. The fact is that filmgoers simply *are* interested in how filmmakers have gone about the business and art of transposition from one medium to another – and that this transposition and the processes involved constitute a phenomenon of continuing interest to large numbers of people. This alone would make the relations between film and literature worth serious study, as would the ongoing fascination for filmmakers of literature, whether novels, short stories, plays, or – less often – poems. There is plenty of evidence of this fascination: many of the most popular and most highly regarded films have their roots in literature of one kind and at one level or another.[4] And those filmmakers are, more often than not, more deferential in their attitude to the works they are adapting than the critics are in appraising the filmed results. It may therefore be more helpful to consider what film and literature have in common than either to require film to "reproduce" the experience of the book (however doomed an enterprise that might be) or to insist simply on the autonomy of the film.

To take novels first: these are the most numerously adapted. It would involve more monumental research than is appropriate here to establish exact comparative figures, but even a casual look at the British Film Institute's database, *Film Index International*,[5] confirms this. In the brief synopses accompanying every film listed, the word "novel" in relation to source occurs 2,549 times; similar references to plays occur 1,598 times, to short stories 118 times and to poems 112 (and many of the latter refer to short and/or experimental films). These figures are by no means infallible: there may be many more instances of all of these literary forms if one were (insanely) to count up all the references to the sources in the credits given for each film, for which no search mechanism is readily available. My point is that these figures, rough as they may well be, serve to confirm one's impression that it is the novel above all which has absorbed filmmakers' attention among possible literary sources.

Why should this be so? What have film and the novel in common that so attracts filmmakers to try their hand at rendering in audio-visual moving images what the novelist has achieved in words on the page? Clearly they have not been inhibited by Bluestone's famous assertion about the novel and film being "overtly compatible, secretly hostile."[6] Reduced to the sparest terms, what they share is "narrative"; what seems likely to keep them at arm's length is "narration." By "narrative" I mean here a series of events, sequentially and/or consequentially connected by virtue of their involving a continuing set of characters. By "narration," in this brutally simplified terminology, I imply all the means by which the narrative has been put before reader or viewer. It is, in this reading, narrative that makes the two mediums seem compatible, whereas it is in narration that their secret hostility may lie.

In an earlier study[7] when trying to avoid the subjectivism and impressionism that seemed to bedevil the comparative analysis of novel and film, I used Roland Barthes's taxonomy of narrative functions, accepting his dictum that "A narrative is never made up of anything other than functions: in differing degrees, everything in it signifies."[8] This still seems to me a useful starting point, since it enables a division into those functions of the antecedent text which are conducive to *transfer*, because not dependent on the literary mode (e.g. events, pure information), and those which, intransigently tied, in Barthes's nicely mysterious term, to "the writing" (e.g. matters relating to characterization, "atmosphere"), will require of the filmmaker *adaptation proper*. If, that is, the filmmaker wants to achieve an equivalence in his/her medium for such literary effects, as distinct from scrapping them altogether in the interests of a freer retelling of the adapted fiction. Essentially, those elements of the novel most readily susceptible to transfer exist at the deeper levels of the narrative: the events that reveal or are caused by the implication of characters or which may be more arbitrary than that suggests; the mythic resonances that a narrative may echo or set up; the psychoanalytic patterns which may be exemplified in the chain of events; or the "character functions" (villain, hero, helper etc.) identified by Vladimir Propp in his study of Russian folktales.[9]

In terms other than theoretical, it is probably true to say that for many (most?) people the attraction common to novel and film is that both create "worlds" and "lives" in more amplitude and with potentially more regard for representational realism in their detail than the other literary forms. Drama and poetry (to be referred to below) are more obviously constrained by formal and stylistic characteristics. In semiotic terms, it is perhaps true to say that, in the novel and immeasurably more so in the film, the gap between signifier and signified is narrower than it is in drama and poetry. We expect in novel and film a sense of the "real," a potent sense of diegesis that keeps us aware of the minutiae of a world that is going on beyond the page or the screen's frame. In both cases the imagination of the consumer is kept active in creating this world, whether by a conceptualizing based on the words given on the page or by a conceptualizing based on the diverse *perceptual* information taken in while watching the screen and listening to the soundtrack.

When I write of "perceptual information" in relation to how we respond to screen narrative, I am referring to that battery of codes – some cinema-specific, some more generally cultural – that film draws on in the processes of signification. It is clear that, in responding to the stimuli offered by film, viewers must take cognizance of linguistic codes (including, for instance, the accents and tones of voice employed by actors, which will enable them to reach conclusions relating to, say, class, ethnicity, and temperament), to non-linguistic codes (in matters of musical and other sound effects), to visual codes (we don't merely look; we *see* and interpret what we see), and to cultural codes that have to do with, say, costume and décor. All of these are part of the filmgoer's responsive activity, though they are not peculiar to film. We make assumptions in everyday life on the basis of decoding such signs. Film also has its own codes: we are required to distinguish lengths of shot, distances of action from the camera, angles from which the action is viewed, the kinds of editing employed (ranging from the barely apprehended cut to the fade). These all signify differently; they are not just haphazardly chosen and they are all part of the complex business of film narration. If all this is to be taken on board, with whatever degree of consciousness, it is hard to maintain that accessing the information of film narration is a pushover compared to the serious reading of a literary text.

Having said that both novel and film are adept in the rendering of time and place, one must make some important distinctions between the ways each goes about doing so. Novels are characteristically, but by no means exclusively, narrated in the past tense. There are exceptions, when the novelist employs a present-tense narration, though this can often seem affected after the initial surprise of the enterprise has worn off. Film, on the other hand, is always *happening* in the present tense. There is no filmic equivalent for words like "ran" or "walked": their very inflection signals an act that is complete as it is being described on the page. Film will, instead, show us characters in the act of "running" or "walking." Even when film resorts to flashback to make us aware that the action depicted is meant to be read as happening in the past, there is nothing intrinsic to the image at any given moment to make us think, Ah, this is occurring at some anterior time. Once the filmgoer is transported to this past time, every action in the narrative seems to be happening with the same degree of presentness as the actions pertaining to the sequences set at the later date.

However, film does have at its command limited means of varying the temporality of the image. There is usually no difficulty in registering the fact that the film is engaging in a flashback: any one or more of several codes may be called into play with, for example, the camera moving into close-up, or a dissolve being used, or sound from the "earlier" period being leaked in as the transition is made. That, however, is not the same as registering a past – or future – time at a given moment. To achieve this effect without the inflection of a verb to signify it unambiguously as the novelist may, the filmmaker will generally have recourse to a disjunction between image and sound. Three films from the 1940s have stayed in my mind in recent years for their approach to this matter. In Irving Rapper's *The Gay Sisters* (1942), a cynical Barbara Stanwyck is heard on the soundtrack in the "present" telling her sisters how she had some years earlier seduced George Brent to her purposes: the images of the past seduction are mutely rendered while the voice of the present continues. In David Lean's *Great Expectations* (1946), Pip (John Mills) is reading a letter from Biddy and, as he reads, he hears her voice speaking the words of the letter thus summoning up the "past" in which it was written, as distinct from the present in which he is reading. In Edmund Goulding's *The Razor's Edge* (1946), snobbish Elliot Templeton (Clifton Webb) is telling Somerset Maugham (Herbert Marshall) how he will arrange for Larry (Tyrone Power) to travel to Europe in style and to meet all the right people. As his voice continues in the "present," the film cuts to a "future" in which, ironically, Larry is travelling on a messy cargo boat and talking to disreputable-looking types. These three briefly noted examples (all incidentally from films based on novels) point to how film may achieve a greater mobility in time than is often conceded, but perhaps the fact that these occasions have stayed in the mind points to the comparative rarity of the phenomenon. Films which choose to adopt other than a linear approach to narrative, like David Jones's *Betrayal* (1982, based on a play by Harold Pinter) or Christopher Nolan's *Memento* (2000, based on a short story by Jonathan Nolan), both of which choose to tell their stories in reverse order, starting from the present and working back to reveal motivations and causes, are no more than oddities in the history of the screen's dealings with time (they would be unusual in literary modes as well). They are not to be confused with films – or novels – which dip into the past from some accepted "present" but which will either intermittently or ultimately return to that present.

As for film's capacity to hurtle round the centuries, from the Stone Age to the Space Age, surely no other art form has managed this quite so effortlessly. Think of Stanley Kubrick's *2001: A Space Odyssey* (1968, from Arthur C. Clarke's short story) in which this racing through millennia is literally the case; think most particularly of the celebrated match cut when a hurled bone turns into a space ship aeons later. A novel will need to tell us that we are now going back or forward in time, then will probably require some descriptive prose to relocate us temporally; film may count on the informative powers of *mise-en-scène* to achieve this relocation almost on the instant. In Bruce Beresford's *Driving Miss Daisy* (1989), changing American race relations over twenty-five years are signalled without any obvious verbal cue in the form of, say, a date title or calendar, but through the kinds of shifts in decor and costume, as well as in the kinds of discussion the characters engage in, that signify the passage of years. Whereas the novel will make us privy to the changing lives of the characters through their spoken words and through the discursive prose that surrounds them, the film requires us to attend to the details of the *mise-en-scène* (actors in collaboration with their physical surroundings as manifested to the viewer through camera angle, distance and movement, and lighting), and to how the editing processes and soundtrack are directing our attention.

Mobility in the representation of place is an element shared by novel and film, though they achieve it in different ways. A novel can interrupt a strand of narrative occurring in one place to offer, say, a contrasting or complementary strand taking place elsewhere. *Middlemarch* moves fluidly from provincial town to country seat to Rome and so on, and a novel as recent as Dan Brown's all-conquering *The Da Vinci Code* rackets around Europe, leaving us (if we've been sucked in) breathless before the six words "scrawled

directly across the *Mona Lisa*'s face"[10] in the Louvre at the end of one
chapter, then whisking us off to the Police Lieutenant's desk for the start of
the next, and back again to the Louvre for the following.[11] Even within a
chapter, Brown darts from inside a locked bank vault to "Across town,
[where] Collet was standing in the Gare du Nord train terminal, when his
phone rang."[12] There is surely something very cinematic about that kind of
transition from one place to another, reinforced by a species of aural "match
cut" from the turning of the key in the vault door to the ringing of Collet's
mobile phone. Film, of course, is at least equally flexible about switching
places. It can achieve reorientation to a new location in even less time than it
takes us to read that sentence of Brown's. It is not the function of this chapter
to argue the overall superiority of either medium but to indicate that, if there
are some things novels can do with more facility than film and vice-versa,
there is also a substantial ground that they share. This capacity, via their
separate semiotic systems, to evoke place and to move us from one to another
with astonishing fluidity, is one that they indubitably share. Film early
embraced the representational realism of the nineteenth-century novel; the
novel in the next century, in the hands of, say, James Joyce or Virginia Woolf,
may be said to have absorbed some of the narrative practices of film in
relation to depicting shifts in time and place.

Earlier, I suggested that these two art forms also share an interest in
revealing "lives" in a fullness perhaps denied to others. How? In a novel,
the author can draw his/her characters through what they say, what others
say about them and about what the author him/herself confides in the
discursive prose, those reflections that surround what is contained in
inverted commas. A novelist such as Henry James will make us more than
usually privy to the inner thoughts and emotions of his characters by means
of a sometimes extraordinarily detailed interior analysis, following which we
may feel we know that character more intimately than almost anyone in
everyday life. At the other end of the spectrum, the rigorous English novelist
Ivy Compton-Burnett, whose dialogue may quite often evoke James, rarely
tells the reader anything other than what the characters say to each other, so
that one sometimes wonders if her true métier was the radio play. But
whether it is a matter of dialogue or authorial commentary, it is *always* a
matter for the reader of responding to the words on the page as the lives are
revealed in their varying degrees of complexity and verisimilitude.

The film, as I've been suggesting, must draw on a battery of semiotically
charged tools. There is no film equivalent for the word: if we see the word
"dog" on the page, we may well have many different perceptions of what is
signified; if we see on an otherwise blank screen a dog at rest, the very least it
will convey is not "dog" but "this is (or 'here is') a dog." Once sound and

movement and the possibility of editing are added, the ways in which lives are represented necessarily involves a complex response from the alert viewer. The anguished love of Ellen Olenska and Newland Archer in *The Age of Innocence* is the cause of many heartfelt moments in Martin Scorsese's version of Edith Wharton's romance, but one will suffice here to illustrate my point about the multiplicity of codes that film calls into play at any given occasion to make us privy to the lives of its characters. There is a series of poignant shot-reverse-shots as they talk at a lakeside restaurant on Boston Common. Ellen gently reproves Newland with: "You gave me my first glimpse of a real life, then you told me to carry on with the false one." The words are accompanied by her gesture of laying her hand on his, advising endurance. Then successive shots distance her, then fade her, from the screen, as the soundtrack uses Enya's version of "I dreamt I dwelt in marble halls" to emphasize the oneiric sense of loss while the editorial dissolves, in another register, enact the fleetingness and withdrawal with which the encounter is instinct. To prove the complexity of the demands made on the filmgoer by this brief scene, try listening to its soundtrack with your back to the screen or watching it with the sound turned down to nil.

With the adaptation of novels, the essential process is excision of one kind or other: either a paring down or the surgery that removes whole sections, subplots and sets of characters. The Lean adaptations of Dickens illustrate these different approaches. For the most part *Great Expectations* opts for the shaving down of the events and characters (though it does omit everything to do with the vengeful Orlick), whereas his *Oliver Twist* (1948) takes a much more ruthless scalpel to the original. In the latter, Lean hacks out (greatly to the film's advantage in terms of tightness of plotting and of keeping its protagonist before us) a great hunk of the novel's last third, in which Dickens indulges both his love of complicated relationships and his senti-mental view of the life of rural retreat. In 1996, Douglas McGrath, director and screenwriter of *Emma*, was so bent on including everything that some of the material about Jane Fairfax and Frank Churchill can scarcely have been comprehensible to those unfamiliar with the novel. Hossein Amini, on the other hand, took one of Henry James's most densely textured novels, *The Wings of the Dove*, and prepared a screenplay that focused powerfully on the novel's central trio. He also updated the setting by a decade in the interests of highlighting the sexual imperative underlying the novel's main action, and the 1997 result (the work also of many other very gifted colla-borators) was a lean 102 minutes. No attention was dissipated in pursuing what was conceived of as subsidiary to the central action.

Plays have presented different challenges to the adapting filmmaker. Almost a cliché is the idea that they need to be "opened out," to represent more spaces than could be conveniently suggested on the stages for which they were intended, even if this means no more than moving into other rooms in the house than that in which, in rather old-fashioned conventional plays, the action has been set on stage. The implication seems to be that because it is easier for film to move from place to place, and to imbue each with an effortlessly realistic *mise-en-scène*, then it ought to do so. As a result the claustrophobic power of a play such as *Who's Afraid of Virginia Woolf* (1966) was pointlessly dissipated by a mid-film visit to a roadhouse: the talk continued with no appreciable gain from the shift in setting.

Talk: that is what plays are about; that is virtually *all* they are about, give or take a few stage directions, until they move from page to stage, making the move from literature to theater. And "talk" is often seen as the enemy of film; it is not usually a compliment to a film to describe it as "stagy" or "theatrical." The late film and stage director Karel Reisz once dismissed a lot of British cinema as "photographed radio plays,"[13] implying that they stressed dialogue at the expense of the visual. It is not, however, a matter of talk *per se* that is a problem to film: the quality of the talk is one obvious criterion one would want to apply, but also how it is delivered (by actors who know how to make it *mean*), how it is shot (by a director and cinematographer who know how to reinforce and complement the meaning of the words), and what it reveals. It is as easy for the drama of crucial human interaction to be revealed in discussion at a table (as in Louis Malle's *My Dinner with André*, 1981) or in a motel room (as in *Tape*, 2002, from Stephen Belber's play and screenplay, directed by Richard Linklater[14]), as in more wide-ranging arenas. Words are not necessarily the enemy of the "cinematic"; they are only so if used in conjunction with that inferior filmmaking which disregards the other strategies available to the filmmaker. In even the most "realistic" play the all-but *incessant* talk constitutes a degree of stylization that is perhaps at odds with most kinds of filmmaking, but even then Malle's film showed that film can accommodate this most crucial element of dramatic literature.

Short stories offer, in some respects, problems contrasting with those of the novel. To make a full-length film, they will require expansion of existing incidents and characters or the imagining of new ones. One of the most famous of all such adaptations is surely John Ford's Western, *Stagecoach* (1939), derived from Ernest Haycox's short story, "Stage to Lordsburg," and a film so distinguished *as a film* that one scarcely spares a thought for Haycox's taut original. That Frank Perry's *The Swimmer* (1968), adapted from John Cheever's heavily allegorical story, never found significant audiences outside the art-house is perhaps partly attributable to its retaining a heavily literary sense of the metaphorical undercurrent of the swimmer's cross-country odyssey. In Britain there were three successful "portmanteau" films based on short stories by Somerset Maugham: *Quartet* (1948), *Trio* (1950) and *Encore* (1951). Very popular at the time, these films adapted Maugham's ironic, witty tales with very little invention in terms of plot or character, but they were all skillfully written by the likes of R. C. Sheriff and Eric Ambler, and acted by matchless casts of British character actors, so that they seemed more ambitious than they were. At the time of writing, Clint Eastwood has made something very like a masterpiece from F. X. Toole's short stories in *Million Dollar Baby* (2005).

The novella, pitched somewhere between novel and short story, is probably the filmmaker's obvious material: not long enough to need laborious pruning, not so short as to require much new invention. See for instance, Jack Clayton's *The Innocents* (1961, based on *The Turn of the Screw*) and Peter Bogdanovich's *Daisy Miller* (1974), notable examples of adaptations of novellas by Henry James, the latter film almost a cinematic transliteration of the original. Adaptations from poetry are, unsurprisingly, thin on the ground, and are of minimal interest as adaptations, since they require so much elaboration of incident and setting and character to add up to a feature film. Those that have attracted filmmakers at all have been narrative poems like Alice Duer Miller's famous wartime poem–novella, "The White Cliffs" (glossily and expansively filmed by MGM in 1944), Longfellow's "Hiawatha" (filmed without distinction in 1952) and "The Wreck of the 'Hesperus'" (filmed in 1947), Browning's "The Pied Piper of Hamelin" (the 1972 British film is really based more on the legend than the poem), A. B. Patterson's "The Man from Snowy River" (filmed in 1982, the most popular Australian film to that date), and Alfred Noyes's "The Highwayman" (unrecognizably filmed in 1951). Derek Jarman's *The Angelic Conversation* (1985) puts Shakespeare's sonnets to some unexpected uses. Personally, I'm waiting for someone to realize that Milton's *Paradise Lost* contains a wonderful story told in language of surpassing grandeur; if ever there was a challenge to filmmakers, this is it.[15]

The incidence of adaptation of literature into film continues unabated as I write. Those who repudiate the notion of "fidelity" as an evaluative criterion when talking about the relations between film and literature can bolster their case by invoking the far more productive notion of intertextuality. The way we respond to any film will be in part the result of those other texts and influences we inescapably bring to bear on our viewing. We need to have in mind, for instance, the parameters of cinematic practice at the time of the film's production, the proclivities of the film's director and writer, the auras that attach to the film's stars. When we turn to a film adapted from literature, or in some other way connected to a literary text or texts, we need to realize and allow for the fact that the anterior novel or play or poem is only one element of the film's intertextuality, an element of varying importance to viewers depending on how well or little they know or care about the precursor text. For instance, is it more productive to think of *The Magnificent Ambersons* (1942) as an adaptation of Booth Tarkington's novel or as an Orson Welles film? Surely, at the very least, as both. The 1992 version of *Howards End* similarly needs to be considered not just as a version of E. M. Forster's novel but also as a Merchant Ivory production and as an example of 1990s British "heritage cinema": the other texts one may have in mind in considering it are as likely to be, say, the film of *Room with a View* (also from Forster), *Remains of the Day* (1993), *Carrington* (1994) and *Shakespeare in Love* (1999), all films with some kind of literary/heritage connection.

One last point on the subject of intertextuality seems worth noting. We are used to the idea of viewing an adaptation in the light of what we know of its literary forebear, but it also needs to be kept in mind that the reverse process is also a possibility. To read a novel after seeing a film version of it will inevitably color one's response. An adaptation that has "worked" for a viewer may well be one that has, at least for the time of viewing, displaced the original from one's mind; but to go further I would propose that it is possible that one's later reading of even a novel one has known well can be crucially influenced by the film text. In my own case, I can now no longer read *Women in Love* without seeing, in the character of Gerald Crich, not Lawrence's blond Nordic god but the burly, saturnine figure of Oliver Reed in Ken Russell's film (1969). Not only does the film itself, described – sight unseen of course – by F. R. Leavis as "an obscene undertaking," seem to me one of the great British films, but Reed's performance, his mad macho image subdued to the demands of the tightly controlled Gerald, and to the general sense of his being involved in circumstances more intellectually taxing than he was used to, was the high-water mark of his career. However he arrived at it, his Gerald has for me effaced Lawrence's in all subsequent re-readings of the novel.

No one is suggesting that viewer–readers will not have opinions about whether they prefer the film or the novel. Opinions, though, are private reactions that don't necessarily forward the discourse about film and literature. It is almost certainly more productive to consider the relations between the two as another example of what Keith Cohen has resonantly characterized, in his discussion, *inter alia*, of Impressionist painting, Henry James's "central reflector" technique in the novel, and the cinema, as "the process of convergence" among the arts.[16] More recently, Grahame Smith's "story about Dickens's role in the emergence of film, a narrative of consciousness across different media and across time"[17] reinforces one's sense of the myriad ways in which literature and film might be seen, if not as siblings, at least as first cousins, sometimes bickering but at heart having a good deal of common heritage. Recent films about a composer (*De-Lovely*, 2004, constructed around Cole Porter's music), an architect (*My Architect*, 2004, a son's search for the inspiration of his father, the architect Louis Khan), and an artist (*Girl with a Pearl Earring*, 2004, a study of Vermeer in the grip of art and erotic tension) hint at film's ways of addressing and colluding with other art forms. The literature–film connection may be closer than any of these others: and the most helpful discourse surrounding this may be one which, respecting the specificities of each, is concerned to explore how they deal with each other, rather than which came first and which is "better" than the other.

NOTES

1 *The Australian Review of Books*, October 1997.
2 As an adapted author herself (*Monkey Grip*, *The Last Days of Chez Nous*), she should have known better.
3 In fact adapted by Mary Ellen Bute in *Passages from "Finnegan's Wake"* in 1965.
4 As long ago as 1979, Morris Beja claimed that "more than three-fourths of the ... [Academy Awards] for 'best picture' have gone to adaptations ... [and] that the all-time box-office successes favour novels even more." *Film and Literature* (New York: Longman, 1979), p. 78.
5 My copy of this CD-Rom is dated 1998.
6 Bluestone, *Novels into Film* (Berkeley: University of California Press, 1957), p. 2.
7 Brian McFarlane, *Novel to Film: An Introduction to the Theory of Adaptation* (Oxford: Clarendon Press/OUP), 1996.
8 Roland Barthes, "Introduction to the Structural Analysis of Narratives" (1966), in *Image–Music–Text*, trans. Stephen Heath (Glasgow: Fontana/Collins, 1977), p. 73.
9 V. Propp, *Morphology of the Folktale* (1927), trans. Laurence Scott (Austin and London: University of Texas Press, 1968).
10 Dan Brown, *The Da Vinci Code* (2003) (London: Corgi Books, 2004), p. 169.
11 *The Da Vinci Code* reads like a novel desperate to become a film, with its frantic alternations of place and chapter-lengths that feel like film segments. (It did, of course, become a film in 2006, directed by Ron Howard.)
12 Dan Brown, *The Da Vinci Code*, p. 247.
13 Interview with the author, London, 1992.
14 Linklater's romances, *Before Sunrise* and *Before Sunset*, also reveal a director with faith in words.
15 Since writing this, I have learnt that Derek Jarman was at one point "engaged in discussions about a possible film version of Milton's epic." Rowland Wymer, *Derek Jarman* (Manchester: Manchester University Press, 2005), p. 133.
16 Keith Cohen, *Film and Fiction: The Dynamics of Exchange* (New Haven and London: Yale University Press, 1979), Part One, "Convergence."
17 Grahame Smith, *Dickens and the Dream of Cinema* (Manchester and New York: Manchester University Press, 2003), p. 13.

2

TIMOTHY CORRIGAN

Literature on screen, a history: in the gap

Perhaps more than any other film practices, cinematic adaptations have drawn the attention, scorn, and admiration of movie viewers, historians, and scholars since 1895. Indeed, even before this origin of the movies – with the first public projections of films by Auguste and Louis Lumière in France and Max and Emil Skladanowsky in Germany – critical voices worried about how photography had already encroached on traditional aesthetic terrains and disciplines, recuperating and presumably demeaning pictorial or dramatic subjects by adapting them as mechanical reproductions.[1] After 1895, however, film culture moved quickly to turn this cultural anxiety to its advantage, as filmmakers worked to attract audiences with well-known images from books now brought to life as *Cinderella* (1900), *Gulliver's Travels* (1902), and *The Damnation of Faust* (1904). The plethora of cinematic adaptations in recent decades and the flood of scholarship responding to these films – films like *Bride and Prejudice* (2004), Bollywood's version of Jane Austen's novel, and scholarly projects like Robert Stam's back-to-back anthologies *A Companion to Literature and Film* (2005), *Literature and Film: A Guide to the Theory and Practice of Film Adaptation* (2005) and critical study *Literature through Film: Realism, Magic and the Art of Adaptation* (2005) – indicate that the practice of adaptation and the disciplinary debates about it remain as lively and pressing as ever.

Adaptation describes, of course, multiple textual exchanges besides those involving film. Literary and theatrical works have regularly adapted historical chronicles; paintings have adapted theatrical or literary scenes, and music has converted literary figures into audio motifs and scores. The movies have themselves often turned to other sources than literary texts to adapt to the screen. Early Japanese films inherited the figure of the benshi, an actor commenting on the action on the screen or stage, from Kabuki theatre, and these films often found models for spatial compositions in ukiyo-e prints whose dramatic flat surfaces and planes would often draw attention away from the human figures in them. Even music has a significant tradition within the history of cinematic adaptation, most famously found in movies such as the 1940 *Fantasia* and Ingmar Bergman's 1975 filmic opera, *The Magic Flute*. Finally, the direction of the exchange between the cinema and adaptation does not proceed only from a literary original to a cinematic adaptation but also runs in the other directions whereby novels, poetry, and theater absorb and adapt filmic materials and tropes as prominent thematic and structuring principles. Marcel Duchamp's *Nude Descending the Staircase No. 2* (1912) is a famous example of a painting whose fragmented frames of a moving figure approximate the look of a series of film frames, and Vladimir Nabokov notes about his novel *Laughter in the Dark* (1960) that he wrote "the entire book as if it were a film."[2]

With the cinema, however, the adaptation of literature to film describes the central current in film history with movies commonly turning to novels, short stories, or plays as source material to be transformed into screenplays and then into films. Given the cultural and historical ubiquity of cinematic adaptation, Dudley Andrew has gone so far as to observe that the "study of adaptation is tantamount to the study of cinema as a whole,"[3] a claim that can be expanded and refined to suggest how the changing definitions of the cinema have themselves reflected the changing dynamics of cinematic adaptation over the last 110 years. These definitions of the cinema involve a range of attributes such as the cultural status of the movies (as art or entertainment, for instance) or their formal shapes and organizations (such as the historical preeminence of narrative films), and more often than not, they reflect to some degree how the complexities of film technology, economics, aesthetics, and reception position themselves in relation to the literature of the past, present, and future.

The relationship between two terms, "adaptation" and "discipline," strikes me as an especially useful framework within which to measure these dynamics. On the one hand, adaptation, in its specific and more general sense, suggests alterations, adjustments, and intertextual exchanges, while on the other, discipline denotes and connotes rules, boundaries, and textual restrictions. The changing relationships between literature and film and how viewers and scholars have understood that relationship can, I want to argue, be mapped across this gap between film as an adaptive practice and film as a discipline. The many textual, cultural, and industrial territories inhabiting this gap become the prominent fields where the cinema's textual integrity, its cultural status, and its scholarly and academic boundaries are often hotly contested.

No single film addresses more directly and provocatively these complex currents of film adaptation than Jean-Luc Godard's 1963 *Contempt*. A self-reflexive film about the struggles to adapt Homer's *Odyssey* to the screen, the film describes the efforts of an arrogant American producer, Jeremy Prokosch (Jack Palance), to enlist a French screenwriter, Paul Javal (Michel Piccoli), to doctor the script that German director Fritz Lang (playing himself) has developed and is in the process of filming. While Lang struggles to maintain the aesthetic integrity of the epic poem in adapting it as a film, Prokosch urges Paul to transform it into a more sensational and hence more profitable piece of entertainment. ("When I hear the world culture I reach for my chequebook," Prokosch remarks.) Entwined with this plot is the collapse of Paul's marriage to Camille (Brigitte Bardot) and, while the characters struggle to communicate through four different languages, the metaphoric prostitution of *The Odyssey* and Paul's talents as a writer come to parallel Paul's seeming surrender of his wife to Prokosch's lecherous interests. Here, the story of a cinematic adaptation describes an odyssey and battle of different infidelities, financial greed, personal exploitation, translations and misinterpretations, and the crisis of a professional identity. Tossing and turning through the constant movements of "adapting" (stories, lives, identities, and languages) and the longing for authenticity and professional discipline, *Contempt* adumbrates three dominant motifs in the dialogue between film adaptation and the film discipline: textual fidelity and specificity, the cultural position of film, and the academic and scholarly status of film studies. The film is also, fittingly, an extreme remake of a novel by Alberto Moravia, *A Ghost at Noon* (1954).

Specificity and fidelity

The most common discussions and debates about film adaptation seem generally to focus on the notions of specificity and fidelity. Specificity assumes that different representational practices, such as literature and film, have individual material and formal structures that distinguish and differentiate them from other practices. Conversely, fidelity is a differential notion that purportedly measures the extent to which a work of literature has been accurately recreated (or not) as a movie. Emphasizing the textual specificity of literature and film clearly complicates, if not entirely obstructs, aims to "faithfully" adapt a book as a movie, since it implies a translation between "languages" that will always be only approximate or, at best, capture "the spirit" of the original text. Mediating the grounds between specificity and fidelity, moreover, are the different industrial and commercial structures that reinforce the textual differences dividing a literary work and its filmic adaptation, such as the technologies of production (print versus moving images, for instance) and the mechanisms of reception (reading versus viewing). To the degree that a film is faithful or not to the textual specificity of a literary work (the narrative voice and textual style, as well as characters, settings, and plots) or to the "spirit" of that original, cinematic adaptations will always measure both the power of film – to assimilate, to transform, to distort, or to overcome – the specifics of that source material.

Examples of the sometimes extreme pull and push of the practices and debates surrounding specificity and fidelity pervade the entire history of the cinema from 1898 to today. Eric von Stroheim's 1924 *Greed*, for example, attempts to recreate the complete text of Frank Norris's novel *McTeague* (1899), and the result is a renowned example of the collision between artistic commitments to fidelity and the industrial forces that must adapt film's specificity to economic and commercial restraints. After von Stroheim submitted a final version over nine hours long to Goldwyn Pictures, he grudgingly allowed it to be re-edited to approximately four hours. Eventually taken out of his hands by Irving Thalberg, the only surviving version of the film is about two hours and twenty minutes in length. This remarkable effort to overcome – faithfully – different orders of textual specificity becomes then a reminder of how thoroughly those specificities are subject to industrial forces. With many different aims and outcomes, this showdown would be restaged through the rest of the century and beyond. Kenneth Branagh's 1996 *Hamlet* is a stunning 242-minute film aiming to be the first textually complete and hence faithful cinematic version of the play. Made economically feasible in large part by Branagh's multi-film deal with Miramax Films to adapt a number of Shakespeare's plays, this faithful *Hamlet* is, in context, as much a skillful economic negotiation through the power of independent cinema in the 1990s as it is an artistic achievement.[4]

While the majority of casual responses to film adaptations usually call upon some notion of specificity and fidelity (the movie rarely able to do justice to the book for most viewers), the most important film scholars and critics of the twentieth century have also taken strong positions around these terms, frequently as a way of defending the power and art of cinema. Indeed, three of the most notable classical film theorists have represented both the range and complexity inherent in different position towards these central issues of specificity and fidelity. In his 1933 *Film as Art*, Rudolph Arnheim argues vigorously for the differentiation of film forms and styles from those of other literary and pictorial practices, as a way of valorizing the unique art of film: "In order that the film artist may create a work of art," he observes, "it is important that he consciously stress the peculiarities of his medium."[5] In his famous 1942 essay "Dickens, Griffith, and Film Today," Russian filmmaker Sergei Eisenstein acknowledges the massive contribution of literature to film in the evolution of the language of "viewing" but, for Eisenstein, this "rich cultural heritage" has paved the way for the "unprecedented art" of film as the art (and politics) of modern society.[6] Using a subtle model of a "work" which can materialize in different textual practices, André Bazin claims in his 1948 essay "Cinema as Digest" that cinematic "faithfulness to a form, literary or otherwise, is illusory: what matters is equivalence in the meaning of the forms."[7]

As these and other writers recognize, implicit in the two terms, specificity and fidelity, are notions of authority and morality, suggesting how film adaptations and our perspectives on them can be as much about cultural attitudes and intellectual assumption as about the inherent complexity or achievements of a film adaptation. Arguments about how faithful movies are to books or to what extent one medium can be translated into another can differ significantly, for instance, if the source is considered classical literature or popular literature. Because of the canonical status and the historical longevity of a Shakespeare play or a Dickens novel, cinematic adaptations usually have little chance of usurping their authority and so the cinematic adaptation will normally appear "unfaithful" to some extent. Here, specificity suggests a sense of textual purity revealed especially through and in its proper discipline, and fidelity to a source suggests the rights of the original that must be acknowledged and ideally adhered to.[8] With the adaptation of literary works less celebrated or less culturally privileged, such as minor novels or "pulp fiction," it is far less common to hear arguments about specificity and fidelity, and so the remarkable cinematic achievements of Hitchcock's 1958 *Vertigo* are lauded in terms of filmic specificity, while its fidelity to Thomas Narcejac and Pierre Boileau's *From Among the Dead* (1954) is rarely raised as a concern. In this and so many other cases, specificity and fidelity become more clearly about the authority of both literature and film than about faith in textual specificity.

The cultural status, economics, and laws of adaptation

Commercial and historical circumstances or contexts have always mediated the practices of and debates about cinematic specificity, fidelity, and adaptation. Of the myriad examples throughout film history, I will highlight, at several exemplary historical moments, three of the most prominent and important forces used to control and direct literary adaptations in terms of cultural status, economic power, and legal rights. These three social forces identify, in turn, perspectives on cinematic adaptations in terms of three critical categories: cinematic texts, genres, and authors. Not coincidentally, these critical categories have become the prominent figures in adaptation studies both in the past and in the present.

In the early years of film history, literary adaptations become a quickly recognized panacea for many of the pressures and challenges inherent in this new and seemingly revolutionary entertainment. From 1895 to the turn of the twentieth century, early films and debates about those films question, implicitly and explicitly, whether film should in fact be considered a science or an entertainment: "actualities" present daily and historical events such as *The Corbett and Fitzsimmons Fight* (1897) as if they were newspaper reports and sociological recordings, while trick films and other visual amusements, such as Cecil Hepworth's *The Explosion of a Motor Car* (1901), use films to surprise and delight audiences with their visual magic. At the same time and with increasing regularity, the first cinematic adaptations begin to appear, presenting short scenes from famous plays and novels, such as the 1899 version of Shakespeare's *King John* or the 1903 *Uncle Tom's Cabin*.

By 1903 movies are establishing themselves as an entertainment industry moving definitively out of their vaudevillian heritage towards the promise of the higher cultural position associated with theater and literature. Identified in the early years of the twentieth century primarily with working-class and immigrant audiences of music halls and vaudevillian stages, the movies begin to adapt literary subjects to suggest and promote a kind of cultural uplift that would presumably curb many of the social and moral suspicions about their power over children, women, and the putatively uneducated.[9] One specific and celebrated example of this cultural disciplining is the "film d'art" movement, begun by the Société Film Art in 1908 with the production of *Assassination of the Duc de Guise* and flourishing through the 1912 *Loves of Queen Elizabeth*. Adaptations of Shakespeare, Goethe, Hugo, Dickens, and Wagner would also appear.

More broadly, the widespread shift to classical narrative structures after 1910 describes a crucial turn in the cultural alignment of the movies, whereby the movie's choice of and increasing reliance on narrative literature results in the standardization of so-called classical film narrative. D. W. Griffith is doubtless the best-known filmmaker identified with the importation of a narrative structure inherited from nineteenth-century novels. His 1915 *Birth of a Nation*, adapted from *The Clansman* (1905), Thomas E. Dixon, Jr.'s novel and play, not only establishes the central structures of classical film narrative according to those structures – a linear narrative with a cause-and-effect logic driven by the agency of one or two main characters – but also introduces a new cultural standard for films equipped with grander and more complex stylistics, clearly imitating nineteenth-century novels and theatrical melodramas.

This early cultural reframing and assimilation of nineteenth-century narrative structures has both economic and legal implications that are still operative today. Economically, longer, more artistically ambitious movies will expand audience demographics and the larger box office receipts by offering more lavish movies to an audience base that now extends into the middle and upper classes. While early films before 1903 lasted ten to fifteen minutes and charged their audience a nickel to gather in a store-front nickelodeon, Griffith's 1915 *Birth of a Nation*, as a cinematic epic, would run for over three hours, charge two dollars for admission, and with its elaborate orchestral presentations led the way to movie-palace exhibition. These commercial and cultural gains in the adapting of literature, however, also introduce drawbacks. The 1907 *Ben-Hur* initiates the first copyright lawsuit in film history by Harper & Row, the publisher of Lew Wallace's 1880 novel *Ben-Hur: A Tale of the Christ*.[10] The subsequent emergence of the scriptwriter, and the necessity of scripts and screenplays as key components in the production of films, becomes a central transitional figure and production stage in the entire relationship of film to literature, adding to economic costs and allowing more predictability and control over the film process.

Although the first two decades of film history are an especially active period in the cultural disciplining of film through the adaptation of material and practices from older literary or artistic heritages, similar turns in the cultural currency of adaptation describe different key moments throughout the twentieth century. In the late 1920s and 1930s, adaptations of contemporary literature become more popular than ever before, partly because the introduction of sound in 1927 allows movies to more fully recreate literary and theatrical dialogue, character psychology, and plot complexity found in novels. At the same time, MPPDA (The Motion Picture Producers and Distributors of America) and its censorious arm, Will Hays's Production Code, watched carefully to be sure that sensational literature did not cross over into the more popular realm of film. An illustrious moment in the more repressive dynamics of literary adaptation at this time – and one that offers a suggestive sense of how the connotations of discipline and adaptation interact – is the 1931 adaptation of Theodore Dreiser's *An American Tragedy* by, first, the Russian director Sergei Eisenstein, and, then, the German/American filmmaker Josef von Sternberg. With the Hays Office looking conspicuously over the shoulder of Paramount Studios, Eisenstein's adaptation (favored by Dreiser) was rejected and von Sternberg's accepted. As all parties recognized, Eisenstein's version faithfully but dangerously maintained the political and social complexity behind the attempted murder at the heart of the plot, while von Sternberg remade it as a morality tale about the dangers of sexual obsession. Writing in *Close Up*, Harry Potamkin lambasted the cultural and legal politics of literary adaptation in Hollywood: "The fight for the integrity of this experience [depicted in Dreiser's novel] is not a personal one, nor even for the rights of authorship. It is a struggle against the debasing of the intellectual and social level of an experience."[11]

Conversely, during this same period, Hollywood studios expand and increasingly develop "prestige films," usually adaptations of classical litera- ture, like the 1935 version of Dickens's *David Copperfield* and, the same year, *Becky Sharp*, adapted from Thackeray's nineteenth-century novel *Vanity Fair*, the first Technicolor feature in movie history. Although prestige films exist before the 1930s, the growing power of the Hays Office makes classic literary adaptations more attractive than ever, partly because they offer psychologically and socially complex stories whose canonical status could protect them from too close scrutiny by the censors.[12] In this period when most film genres are developing the classical formulae that would be the economic backbone of the film industry, an exceptionally important genre to the economics and legalities of the film industry becomes "the prestige film."

Related to the prestige films but describing a different sort of cultural positioning are the heritage films of late twentieth-century cinema. This more modern version of the literary genre film appears particularly in France and England since the 1980s and includes films such as Merchant Ivory's *A Room with a View* (1985) and Claude Berri's *Germinal* (1993).[13] The cultural motivations may be less clear for this generic variation on 1930s prestige films in contemporary times, yet for many they are certainly there. Within a contemporary climate of political violence and social multiculturalism (seen, for instance, in the Thatcherite 1980s in England) these comfortable images of a literary past often represent a therapeutic nostalgia for "traditional" national values, while at the same time marketing those values to foreign audiences as a self-contained, stable, and unified vision of another culture.[14]

Against the background of this historical sketch, a sharp pattern appears, a pattern that has dominated most film production and film criticism as the direct result of the economic, stylistic, and industrial prevalence of literary narratives (short stories, drama, and novels) as the heart of cinema and cinema studies. Because literary narratives have dominated film culture, it has meant the marginalization of other dynamic forms of adaptation that have lacked the cultural, economic, and even legal presence offered by film narratives, such as film adaptations of poetry, essays, and other non-narra- tive forms. Since D. W. Griffith's adaptation of a Tennyson poem as *Enoch Arden* in 1911 to Chris Marker's claim that he makes essay films like his 1983 *Sans soleil/Sunless*, these alternative relations with literature have been a regular but largely invisible part of film culture.

Announcing itself as a rebellion against "A Tradition of Quality" built around adaptations of classic literature, the French New Wave of the 1950s and 1960s, identified with directors such as François Truffaut, Agnès Varda and Jean-Luc Godard, represents, after narrative texts and literary genres, a third prominent cultural and critical relationship between film and literature.[15] Suggested as early as 1948 in Alexander Astruc's essay "The Birth of the New Avant-Garde: La Camera-Stylo," this configuration valorizes classical films and many of the new wave films that followed the French (from Italy to, more recently, Iran and Taiwan), as the product of "authors" or auteurs. As Astruc phrased it, the film camera (especially with the introduction of light-weight technologies such as the Eclair camera in the 1940s) would now be comparable to the writer's pen: "the cinema is quite simply becoming a means of expression, just as all other arts have been before it, and particularly painting and the novel."[16] Rather than a precedent literary text, the agency of the filmmaker as author now becomes the measure of cinematic distinction, specificity, and quality, and fidelity now becomes a matter of authorial expression and authenticity.

These claims for cinematic authorship have in fact described a variety of cultural strategies and positions adopted before the 1950s which are still prevalent today. It recalls, for instance, the literary and commercial confrontation suggested earlier by Harry Potamkin in relation to *An American Tragedy* and also the celebrated confrontation in the early 1930s between Bertolt Brecht and German filmmaker G. W. Pabst over the adaptation of Brecht's *Threepenny Opera* where, despite Brecht's angry protest, both the legal and artistic rights of the filmic author superseded those of the literary author once a work had been sold to a filmmaker.[17] In more recent years, auteurism has both maintained and shifted its cultural significance according to exigencies of time and place. Contemporary Iranian cinema, for example, consciously exploits the cultural capital of auteurs like Abbas Kiarostami, allowing him to make films like *10* (2002), meant to undermine the very presence and importance of the director as auteur.

Both film practices and studies of those practices have been dominated, since the 1950s, by models of film genre and film auteurs, both of which spring from and relate to the exchanges between film and literature. While these two critical models are commonly opposed – one representing industrial patterns and the other individual expression – their foundations in the cultural positioning of the film/literature exchange reminds us of the fluid dynamic that binds the categories. One telling example that engages the cultural, economic, and legal dimensions of film and literature is the New German Cinema of the 1970s and early 1980s. This group of filmmakers took conscious advantage of the critical and financial power of a successful auteurist cinema and reshaped it as a more political and cultural tool: auteurs like Wim Wenders, Helke Sanders, and Rainer Werner Fassbinder leveraged their positions as international figures to make films that often explored critically the history and politics of a contemporary Germany that attempted to resist and deny those films. At one point, these auteurs developed their own version of prestige cinema with a spate of classic literary adaptations that included Volker Schlondorff's 1979 *The Tin Drum* and Fassbinder's 1980 *Berlin Alexanderplatz*. In this case, however, adapting literary classics becomes not about prestige or heritage but a way to mount a slightly veiled but critically stinging engagement with a contemporary German political paranoia (and censorship).

Disciplines and academia

Paralleling the changing cultural positions of film adaptation and its primary configurations as specific texts, genres, and auteurs, a century of scholarly debates has both reflected and challenged the many different aesthetic and social relationships between film and literature. Since 1895, responses to adaptation by philosophers, journalists, scholars, and filmmakers describe active and robust testimonies to intellectual openings that occur when questions of the specificity of the medium and the kinds of fidelity possible with film adaptation become recharged within those different historical and cultural contexts.

Even before 1895, debates about adaptation shadowed discussions of art and literature. Most famously, towards the end of the eighteenth century, Gotthold Ephraim Lessing's *Laocoon* (1766) presented a detailed philosophical analysis of how the arts differ in terms of their forms and respective powers to represent the world, and while many of the major educational and intellectual figures of the nineteenth century (notably Matthew Arnold) developed rigorous positions about the shared and distinguishing features of the arts within modern cultures, the major challenge to many of these aesthetic and academic positions emerged quickly in the form of mass entertainments – from theatrical spectacles and dioramas of the early nineteenth century to the photography, musical halls, and cinema projections that followed. Between the high cultural ground being articulated in universities and museums and the low cultural fairgrounds from which the movies would spring, the nineteenth century predicted a long line of anxieties and claims about the relationship of the movies to the other arts.

One early and perceptive writer about the movies, Vachel Lindsay, was an especially articulate voice in these debates. Writing his landmark *The Art of the Moving Picture* in 1915, Lindsay was an active poet with a profound social sense who regarded the new art of film as the medium to bring the spirit of poetry to the democratic masses of America. In their ability to adapt and to serve other arts and professions, movies are able to draw on a wide variety of interdisciplinary fields, in addition to the literary, and so activate those fields as "sculpture-in-motion," "painting-in-motion," and "architecture-in-motion." Indeed, in one of the most prophetic arguments of his early book, Lindsay foresees film as a key tool for linking and communicating the many scholarly disciplines in universities and museums, allowing academic research to be disseminated outside their walls as a "University Extension."[18]

Since that early vision of an interdisciplinary academy promoting film as the new literature, questions of adaptations have continued to function as lightning rods for evolving critical questions about the cinema and the shaping of film studies as an intellectual discipline. Paralleling Eisenstein's arguments about the specificity of film form as it develops out of its theatrical and literary past, various avant-garde movements since the 1920s struggled to release film from the shadow of literature and literary studies and establish its formal and intellectual independence. A decade after Lindsay's utopian visions of movies found a place in the colleges and universities of the world, cine-clubs around the world and the journals that sprang up around them – the new academies for this new art – argued heatedly about the merits of a film art whose technologies of movement have replaced literature and the traditional arts. In England, for instance, the journal *Close Up* (1927–1933), "The Only Magazine Devoted to Film as an Art," featured writings by the poet H. D. and novelist Dorothy Richardson and, despite its literary roots, often fought for a unique art of film, not found in the commercial cinema.[19] In France in the 1940s, Gilbert Cohen-Séat shaped the "filmology movement" specifically as an intellectual field devoted to the study of film in society. Indeed, in all these cases, the insistence on the singularity of film practice as a discipline would remain a consistent motif through the 1950s and, in 1960, experimental filmmaker Maya Deren would announce that the intellectual and creative integrity of film required a complete divorce from its former literary partners. Film "must relinquish the narrative disciplines it has borrowed from literature and in timid imitation of the casual logic of narrative plots" and instead it must "determine the disciplines inherent in the medium, discover its own structural modes, explore the new realms and dimensions accessible to it and so enrich our culture artistically as science has done in its own province."[20]

This insistence on the intellectual and artistic separation of film and literature evolves along a somewhat different path in the 1960s when film studies begins to enter college and university curriculums in full force and, in tandem, begins articulating itself more consciously as a scholarly discipline developing out of the humanities. In the span of years between two seminal works, George Bluestone's 1957 *Novels into Film* and Robert Richardson's

1969 *Literature and Film*, the interdisciplinary exchange of the two practices would be articulated confidently on a broadly humanistic base, addressing topics like "modes of consciousness" (Bluestone) in novels and movies, or "the question of order and coherence in poetry and film" (Richardson). Quite importantly, at this turning point in the 1960s, film courses and scholarship tended to justify their place through work on European auteurs and the related assumption that film form is a "language." This in turn leads to the institutionalization of a kind of film studies immediately associated with authorial and literary models found in English Departments needing, during this turbulent decade, to loosen and expand their academic and scholarly reach. Through this period, film scholarship adapts decidedly literary (usually narrative) and linguistic models which allowed for comfortable transitions between literature and film, while at the same time film studies moves to secure itself a disciplinary place within academia through the presence of an emerging canon of cinematic "authors."

In the 1970s and 1980s, the academic and critical centers of film studies would shift in two principal directions, neither of which is particularly hospitable to adaptation studies: towards medium-specific, neo-formalist studies and towards ideological studies. Whereas the first champions the distinctive difference of film from literature (and other representational practices), the second embraces the broader conceptual grounds for film based in post-structuralism, psychoanalysis, and contemporary ideological models. In an important sense, both directions are attempts to define film as a discipline, the first in terms of its textual specificity and the second within the large field of film theory.

While these contemporary film studies would insist on the discipline of their own forms or on the theoretical specificity of film practices, adaptation studies of a more conventional kind would flourish, almost as a third and separate field on the fringes of the emerging discipline of film studies. As a product of films' early association with language and literature departments (still under the influence of New Criticism and its valorization of single texts), according to Robert Ray, "film and literature scholars could only persist in asking about individual movies the same unproductive layman's question (How does the film compare with the book), getting the same unproductive answer (The book is better). Each article seemed isolated from all the others; its insights apparently stopped at the borders of the specific film or novel selected for analysis."[21]

Ray's argument is especially worth considering since he moves beyond debates about aesthetics of specificity and fidelity to the professional and institutional pressures shaping film studies. He goes on to raise important questions about interdisciplinary recuperation of film studies by various language and literature programs where, following the exigencies of the academic marketplace and a "publish or perish" economy, critical and scholarly engagements with film adaptations have tended to produce an excess of predictably dull close readings of literature adapted as film. Today "the task facing all of us, especially film and literature scholars," Ray concludes, "involves rethinking the media's *fait accompli*, imagining new ways in which words and images can be adapted and combined, as well as new purposes for those combinations."[22]

Since at least the 1990s, I believe, this rethinking has in fact been taking place and producing new energies and significant scholarship in adaptation studies, opening the questions informing the relations of literature and film in larger, less predictable, and more concrete ways. Some of this work springs from more exact cultural and historical investigation, some from the expansion of theoretical boundaries to take into account the hybrid and multi-textual nature of questions about gender, textual authority and priority, or national and transnational formulations of adaptation. This body of recent adaptation studies does not amount to the "poetics of adaptation" that Ray calls for. On the contrary, one positive result of this multiplication and expansion of the field of adaptation study may be precisely the salutary erosion of a traditional longing for cohesion and disciplinarity within film studies.

Indeed it is precisely this potential for adaptation to challenge traditional disciplinary boundaries that has always identified its greatest potential to filmmakers, everyday moviegoers, and academic scholars. Walter Benjamin's 1936 "The Work of Art in the Age of Mechanical Reproduction" is the most renowned argument to identify this ability of film to challenge and overturn the categories and positions that distinguish traditional arts and literatures, claiming that the "auratic" reading and viewing formations of those classical arts must give way before the cinema's radical remakings, transformations, and adaptations. More recently, Rey Chow describes cinema studies as a "phantom discipline" practiced mainly by interdisciplinary "amateurs" (like herself) who approach film studies from outside its disciplinary margins without necessarily any (or much) formal training:

> If, instead of attaining centrality, film has remained phantomlike as an academic discipline, it is because it is inextricably linked to every other type of knowledge production ... [To] the extent that cinema tends to reside in the gap between, on the one hand, tangible and archival products (which necessitate specialized documentation and institutional accommodation) and, on the other, the enthralled but transient experiences of generations of moviegoers (for whom film is integral to the texture and fabric of petty bourgeois life), it will perhaps always remain an ambiguous object of study with unstable, open boundaries – but therein may lie its most interesting intellectual future.[23]

Between disciplinarity and adaptation, between literature and film, adaptation studies provide, I am convinced, especially ambiguous, risky, unstable, and enormously interesting opportunities today. When opened out beyond questions of specificity and fidelity, adaptation studies necessarily and productively trouble and open disciplinary boundaries (both those of literary studies and film studies). It is in that gap that many of the most compelling ideas appear.

NOTES

1 See Charles Baudelaire, "The Salon of 1846: On the Heroism of Modern Life" in Francis Frascina and Charles Harrision, *Modern Art and Modernism: A Critical Anthology* (New York: Harper & Row, 1975).
2 Alfred Appel, Jr., *Nabokov's Dark Cinema* (New York: Oxford University Press, 1974), p. 258.
3 *Concepts in Film Theory* (New York: Oxford University Press, 1984), p. 103.
4 See Timothy Corrigan, "Which Shakespeare to Love? Film, Fidelity, and the Performance of Literature," in Jim Collins (ed.), *High-Pop: Making Culture into Popular Entertainment* (Oxford: Blackwell, 2002), pp. 155–81.
5 Rudolph Arnheim, *Film as Art* (Berkeley: University of California Press, 1957), p. 35.
6 Sergei Eisenstein, "Dickens, Griffith, and Film Today," in Eisenstein, *Film Form: Essays in Film Theory* (New York: Harcourt, Brace, and World, 1949), p. 233.
7 André Bazin, "Cinema as Digest," in James Naremore (ed.), *Film Adaptation* (New Brunswick: Rutgers University Press, 2000), p. 20.
8 See Robert Stam, "Beyond Fidelity: The Dialogics of Adaptation," in *Film Adaptation*, ed. James Naremore (New Brunswick, New Jersey: Rutgers University Press, 2000), pp. 54–78.
9 See Roberta Pearson and William Uricchio, *Reframing Culture* (Princeton: Princeton University Press, 1993).
10 For further discussion of this film, see Chapter 3 in this volume, pp. 54–7.
11 Harry Alan Potamkin, "Novel into Film: A Case Study of Current Practice," in *The Compound Cinema: The Film Writings of Harry Alan Potamkin*, ed. Lewis Jacobs (New York and London: The Teachers College Press, 1977), p. 186.
12 See Marie-Claire Ropars-Wuilleumier, *De la littérature au cinéma: genèse d'une écriture* (Paris: Armand Colin), 1970.
13 See Ginette Vincendeau, *Film/Literature/Heritage: A Sight and Sound Reader* (London: BFI, 2001). Although most critics have been, at the very least, suspicious of the ideological motivations of hertitage films, a recent, quite brilliant re-reading of the ideological potential for heritage cinema can be found in Rosalind Galt, *The New European Cinema: Redrawing the Map*, New York: Columbia University Press, 2006.
14 See Chapter 8 in this volume for a discussion of heritage film and television.
15 It has been shown that despite their anti-literary pronouncements, Truffaut, Godard, and other New Wave filmmakers were regularly dependent on literary texts and references.

16 "The Birth of a New Avant-Garde: Le Camera-Stylo," in Timothy Corrigan (ed.), *Film and Literature: An Introduction and Reader* (Saddle River, New Jersey: Prentice Hall, 1999), p. 159.

17 In *The Threepenny Lawsuit*, Brecht begins his polemic: "We have often been told (and the court expressed the same opinion) that when we sold our work to the film industry we gave up all our right; the buyers even purchased the right to destroy what they bought." "The Film, the Novel, and Epic Theatre," in *Brecht on Theatre* (New York: Hill & Wang, 1964), p. 47.

18 Vachel Lindsay, *The Art of the Moving Picture* (New York: Liveright, 1970), p. 261.

19 See Donald, James, Anne Freidberg, and Laura Marcus (eds.), *Close Up, 1927–1933: Cinema and Modernism* (Princeton: Princeton University Press, 1998).

20 "Cinematography: The Creative Use of Reality," *Film Theory and Criticism*, 6th edn., ed. Leo Braudy and Marshall Cohen (New York: Oxford University Press, 2004), pp. 197–8.

21 Robert Ray, "The Field of 'Literature and Film,'" in *Film Adaptation*, ed. James Naremore (New Brunswick, New Jersey: Rutgers University Press, 2000), p. 44.

22 Ibid., p. 49.

23 Rey Chow, "A Phantom Discipline," *PMLA* 116.5 (2001), 1391–2.

PART TWO

History and contexts

3

JUDITH BUCHANAN

Gospel narratives on silent film

In the silent era, the film industry reached early, eagerly, and repeatedly for literary sources of a more or less reputable character to feed its voracious hunger for narrative material. The authors enlisted to supply a good plot line and some associated cultural kudos included Dickens, Thackeray, Hugo, Pushkin, Racine, Goldsmith, Twain, Wilde and, most frequently of all, Shakespeare. Filmmakers on both sides of the Atlantic gratefully embraced the respectability that adapting the "classics" could bring and were widely applauded for doing so. Impressive claims were made about what a Shakespeare picture, for example, might do both for a viewing public in need of cultural and moral edifying and for an industry in need of rescuing from its own worst impulses. Aligning itself with an established literary pedigree was an economical route towards artistic legitimacy and moral propriety for an industry keenly aware that, initially at least, it lacked both.

If establishment respectability was what was required of a literary source, the Christian Bible did not just offer it, it *was* it. It is, therefore, no surprise that the film industry appropriated biblical material strikingly early in its own development. Making such films was not, however, a project without potential pitfalls. Adapting any known literary work for the screen is a delicate business. It runs the risk of irritating those most intensely invested in the particular character, history and perceived cultural value of the source. Nevertheless, adapting sections of the Bible has proved difficult to rival in the sphere of literary adaptation for the strength of the competing responses it can provoke. Those wedded to the value of screening biblical narrative have, since the earliest days of the medium, been zealous in their enthusiasm for the project. Those offended by the endeavour, by contrast, have been lurid in their condemnation of its presumption in attempting to give cinematic expression to holy writ. The passionate extent of the personal and institutional investment in this particular book (Book) has succeeded in making other, purely literary interest groups – Dickensians, fans of Austen, even Shakespeareans – look mild-mannered and unconcerned by comparison. For

Church lobbyists, there is simply far more at stake in adapting a biblical narrative for the screen in terms of personal belief and spiritual responsibility than could ever be the case in the adaptation of a non-sacred text, however much revered.

The sensitivity of the adaptation project has been felt particularly keenly in relation to the screen presentation of the figure of Christ. In the early cinema period (pre-1912), there were two central anxieties in this respect: the first related to performance, the second to exhibition. In relation to performance, it was thought by many Christians, and in particular by conservative evangelicals, to be not just impertinent but hubristic for an actor to attempt to impersonate God-made-man – a being whose sinlessness and divinity properly placed him beyond the scope of mere acting, however reverently undertaken or impressively accomplished in human terms. The nervousness about exhibition related to the spaces in which the moving picture was subsequently to be projected. For the filmed story of the life and passion of Christ to be taken into the nickelodeons, vaudeville houses and other cheap amusement halls of the period and to unspool in spaces that also played host to less wholesome film subjects and live acts, was thought by some to be inherently demeaning. The challenges of the adaptation project were, therefore, both formalist and socio-cultural in character. How should it be enacted, and in what context should it subsequently engage with the public? Given the lively division of opinion in response to these questions, it is hard to imagine a literary source more fraught with potential hazards for the would-be adaptor than the Christian Gospels.

However potentially daunting in prospect, there has been no shortage of filmmakers to take on the task. The first Gospel-based film was released in the United States in late 1897, just two years after the Lumière brothers' pioneer screening in Paris. It was a one-reel recording of the traditional Passion Play mounted by the local community in Horitz, Bohemia (Austria). Distributed by Edison, it was exhibited as part of a programme that included hymns and a sermon. By 1900 it had already been followed by further Gospel adaptations from Edison, Lumière, Gaumont, and Pathé. The final Gospel-based film of the silent era was Cecil B. DeMille's predictably spectacular feature *The King of Kings*, released in 1927 on the cusp of the advent of commercial sound. In between these diverse end-markers, there were many scores of attempts to film a version of the Gospels, or to absorb a Passion strand into a more expansive, or more complex, film narrative.

This chapter will examine a selection of Gospel-based films that emerged before 1927, considering the appeal of this set of stories to the developing film industry, the accommodations and the interventions it made to the inherited biblical material, the sensitivities aroused by the portrayal of

Christ on screen, the range of ways found to assuage or circumvent these anxieties, and the commercial contexts that surrounded the release of the films. The Gospels constitute a revealing case study of literary adaptation in the period since they lay bare with unsparing clarity a set of cultural prejudices both about the perceived status of the medium and about the desirable degree of allegiance to a source text. Three case-studies will be offered: *From the Manger to the Cross* (Kalem: Sidney Olcott, 1912), *Ben-Hur* (MGM: Fred Niblo, 1925) and *The King of Kings* (DeMille Pictures Corporation: Cecil B. DeMille, 1927).[1] Taken in order, they illustrate well some of the developments and adjustments undergone in the screen presentation of the Gospels. Before turning to individual films, however, it is worth considering why the film industry reached with such enthusiasm for Gospel stories as suitable material for adaptation in the pre-sound era.

The appeal of the Christian Bible to the film industry

In the energetically inventive early days of the industry, Gospel stories served three pressing institutional needs. Firstly, for an industry driven by an almost insatiable hunger for material, they provided a ready-made pool of narratives. Stories about Jesus' life, death and resurrection had the advantage of being familiar enough to early cinematograph audiences to be easily intelligible even in the compressed and largely wordless form that the one- or two-reel format made necessary. After 1911, the appeal of the Bible as a source for cinematic adaptation in the United States became yet more pronounced. That year saw the conclusion to a legal copyright row about Kalem's 1907 film of *Ben-Hur*. The film had traded without permission upon the success of Lewis Wallace's 1880 *Ben-Hur* novel and the subsequently adapted stage play. The suit was passed up the courts to the Supreme Court which ruled that Kalem was indeed guilty of copyright infringement. The company was ordered to destroy all prints of the film and to pay $25,000 in compensation.

This was a ruling that focused the collective mind of the industry. If the ownership of copyrighted literary material had now to be respected, adapting a literary work for the screen took on new costs. Kalem's bloody nose had the inevitable effect of making uncopyrighted, or out of copyright material, the more appealing. It is perhaps noteworthy that after the ruling had gone against them, Kalem and director Sidney Olcott turned swiftly to the Bible as the source for their next major project, the multi-reel Gospel adaptation *From the Manger to the Cross* (1912). Here was material that was unquestionably safe in legal terms. If anyone held the authorship rights to the Bible, he (He) was unlikely to make a claim in law. In amongst its other attractions for the film industry in this period, therefore, the Bible was appealingly unencumbered by costly legal obstacles.

The second attraction of biblical source material for the industry lay in the artistic pedigree it had accrued over the centuries. Visual representations of the life and passion of Christ had long been considered one of the highest forms of Western artistic expression. By attaching itself to a painterly Christographic tradition, the film industry could implicitly claim some of that accumulated cultural capital for itself. Film's appropriation, quotation, and animation of recognizable imagery from the legacy of Western religious art became part of its bid to be considered not just a technological wonder of the modern world but, more weightily, an art form alongside others. It was, in effect, a claim to prestige by association.

Finally, the Bible offered the industry not just artistic but moral legitimacy. If the Bible was edifying for the individual and inspiring for the community, then so, ran the claim, was the industry that rendered it in cinematic form. In 1910 Frank L. Dyer, the then president of the influential Motion Picture Patents Company in the United States, wrote an article designed to counter the charge of degeneracy intermittently thrown at the industry. The most effective way to assert the medium's moral worth, Dyer suggested, was to draw material for motion pictures from literary sources of impeccable repute. It was precisely an association with such sources, Dyer maintained, that would ensure the "development of the art to a position of dignity and importance. When the works of Dickens and Victor Hugo, the poems of Browning, the plays of Shakespeare, and stories from the Bible are used as a basis for moving pictures, no fair-minded man can deny that the art is being developed along the right lines."[2] The Bible, it seemed – along with a pedigree pot of other literary sources – was good for the film industry. It offered an edifying sheen of respectability to a commercial enterprise that was, in some quarters at least, keen to slough off some of the more salacious associations that still rather colorfully clung to it through its early (and ongoing) taste for titillating subjects.

The "picture men," however, were also at pains to point out that in the coming together of Bible and film industry, the beneficial traffic was not all one way. Just as the industry could profit from the artistic and moral weight that the Bible brought to its reputation, so the Bible (and its patron the Church) could benefit from the mass market to which the industry had access. *From the Manger to the Cross*, it was claimed, was "destined to be more far-reaching than the Bible in telling the story of ... the Saviour."[3] Fifteen years later, Cecil B. DeMille, seldom outdone in the ambition of a project or scale of a claim, asserted that *The King of Kings* would not just reach more people than its biblical source but would promote belief in Christ in excess of anything that the printed word could achieve: "If you printed seventy-five million Bibles, ... [audiences'] idea of the life of Jesus Christ is going to be formed by what we give them, this next generation will get its idea of Jesus Christ from this picture."[4] Gospel films moved from defining themselves as humble pointers towards their source to being, in effect, direct competitors to it.

The triple endowment of familiar narratives, artistic pedigree, and moral weight brought in its wake significant commercial possibilities. The making and distributing of Bible films, as filmmakers and their backers quickly realized, was broadly taken as evidence of laudably lofty ambitions, and lofty ambitions meant an expanded market. Trading upon the widely perceived respectability and "artistry" of their biblical products, film companies specifically targeted these films at a "better class" of potential spectators. In many cases, they arranged for the films to be exhibited in the more reputable theatrical venues, in church halls, and even in churches (including Catholic churches until 1910 when Pope Pius X denounced the practice as a desecration of sacred space).[5] These exhibition spaces, adapted from their usual theatrical, social and liturgical purposes, were often considered more seemly for the screening of such subjects from the point of view of the films' dominant market. The debate cinema historian Edward Wagenknecht recalls in his own family about whether to see the 1907 Pathé Passion film at "the nickel show" was not untypical: "My mother at first thought not, and we did not see the picture at the Family Electric Theater; but later when we found the entire film being shown on a single bill at the Bijou Dream, we weakened and went in."[6] The Bijou Dream was, by clear implication, a better class of establishment than the Family Electric Theater. It was still a "weakening" to enter it, but it was at least an acceptable venue, unlike the Family Electric. In these cases, attendance seems to have been bound up as much in the dignity of the venue as in the subject being exhibited.

Early Gospel films

Even before the *Ben-Hur* copyright trial gave an added boost to the appeal of uncopyrighted literary sources for the film industry, the Gospel had already proved popular with filmmakers on both sides of the Atlantic. Before 1907, for example, Pathé alone released three such films (in 1900, 1904, and 1907). The second of these, *La Vie et la Passion de Jésus-Christ* (1904), pragmatically included a short sequence (the initial walking on water) that had also appeared in the 1900 Pathé film. It is testimony to the stability of the iconography of Gospel films in the period (design, choreography, costume, performance styles, shooting conventions, scenic composition) that a "borrowed" sequence from one could be absorbed into another without an undue sense of disruption.

In their pictorializing of episodes from the life of Christ, the most wideranging of these films began with the Annunciation and ended with the Ascension, including slightly clumsy dalliances with special effects of superimposition at intervals throughout. The films made scenic efforts to locate themselves in a Judean, first-century setting through painted backdrops, scenic properties, and costume, and almost always used all four Gospels (the three Synoptics and the Gospel of John) as a composite source. Not uncharacteristically for the period, scenes were composed in long shot from a static camera, with few mid-scene edits. Simple headline inter-titles ("The Massacre of the Innocents," "The Last Supper," "The Resurrection") typically introduced each episode.

The earnest project of many of these early Gospel films was to enshrine the events of the biblical story in lasting, reviewable and accessible form. The Jesus figure could be performed but there was no attempt to invest that performance with psychological interest or complexity. Sacred miracles could be bathetically alluded to through the joyously executed but still slightly clunking processes of trick photography, but it was not appropriate to attempt more than this in relation to a story whose dimensions and significance were thought to be ultimately beyond human telling or showing. These films were not, that is, seeking to stand for the Gospels but, in their most reverential expression, simply to allude respectfully to them. They even, on occasions, alerted the viewer to the pictorial limitations of their own project – for example in the crudely schematized line drawing of a generic, bearded male face on a piece of cloth that is offered as a "representation" of the face of the Christ, a holy relic held aloft in the 1904 *La Vie et la Passion de Jésus-Christ*. The *import* of this image resides in its understood status as the Messianic imprint. In its actual substance, however, it makes little attempt even to resemble the face of the actor playing Jesus here. Its significance lies most pressingly in its allusiveness to something patently beyond its material reach. And the same was true of the films themselves.

From the Manger to the Cross (Kalem: Sidney Olcott, 1912)

Unlike *La Vie et la Passion* which modestly raised a question about the unlikeness, or stylized "untruth" of the image of the Jesus it depicted, Sidney Olcott's *From the Manger to the Cross*, by contrast, was keen to assert its truthfulness and authenticity in relation to Scripture and its attendant traditions at every turn. The film was a high-profile life of Christ, and ran for an almost unprecedented eighty minutes over five reels (making it one of the earliest American features). The film was shot, as its opening title card makes clear, "at Jerusalem, Bethlehem and other authentic locations in Palestine." A celebration of setting was both part of Kalem's promotional strategy and that for which the film was most frequently commended in review. Its chapter headings (for example, "The Flight into Egypt," "Period of Youth," "The Last Supper," "The Crucifixion and Death") are super-imposed over known paintings of the life of Christ. Scenes within these chapters are punctuated at regular intervals with quotations taken directly from the King James Version of all four Gospels. Each quotation is con-scientiously referenced with its biblical point of origin by chapter and verse. The film's Protestant adherence to the specificity of the text of the Bible is, therefore, keenly felt. It is, however, placed alongside an equally strongly expressed taste for painterly composition. The effect (and surely the purpose) of alternating between the frequent use of direct biblical quotation (which even appear in an antiquated Bible-evocative font), and close painterly reference is to simulate the appearance of an illustrated Bible whose illustra-tions happen, in this cinematic instantiation, to have been lightly animated. The film therefore courted the feel of a cinematic Gospel.

Despite the film's title (whose *From … to* formulation misleadingly sug-gests that narrative trajectory might be central to the film's interests), its chief organizing principle seems to be to replace one artistic and largely static vignette with another. Many of these vignettes are recognizable as visual quotations from known religious paintings, chiefly those of James Tissot. Tissot's late nineteenth-century watercolors of the life of Christ were popu-larly disseminated as Bible illustrations. They are geographically and ethno-graphically precise while exhibiting little interest in investigating their principal subject as a knowable psychological being. In adopting Tissot's aesthetics, Olcott also followed suit in keeping anything more intimate about state of mind, psychological dilemma, or human grief largely suppressed.[7] Unlike central characters for other, non-biblical motion pictures in the period, the gracefully performed Jesus that Richard Henderson-Bland gives us in this film is, therefore, spared the intrusive impertinence of a quizzical camera that would search his face, or even presume to approach his person at all.

It is not just emotional interest that is anachronistically kept strategically absent from Olcott's movie. *From the Manger* is so justifiably proud of its location scenery, painterly compositions, and textual fidelity that it also feels little imperative to offer supplementary viewing pleasures in terms of cine-matic technique. Other films emerging from the same transitional moment in the industry's development demonstrated far greater technical inventiveness, camera movement, mid-scene editing, and variety of focal lengths. Olcott himself even showed evidence of being more cinematically adventurous elsewhere in his own work for Kalem.[8] What he seems to have subjected himself to for the purposes of this film, however, is, in Charles Keil's formulation, a deliberate "stylistic retardation."[9] It is as if he believed that it was only legitimate for cinema to dare to treat such elevated subject matter at all if it played down its own technical capacities and tried not to draw undue attention to its interpretive role in the production. If it is more respectful to be less intrusive, then this film is certainly respectful. It couches itself, for large sections of the film, as a series of minimally animated *tableaux*.

The overall result is a film that feels effortful in its insistent trailing of its aspirations (for textual fidelity, location authenticity, and artistic reference) and of its anxieties (to resist the cinematic). As a viewing experience now, therefore, it seems burdened by the number of agendas it feels bound to pursue in order to prove a worthy vehicle of transmission for its elevated subject. Its first audiences, however, were struck by the reverential beauty of the picture, not by signs of strain. It premiered to enthusiastic reviews in New York City in October 1912 before receiving its international distribution; it opened at both the Albert Hall and the Queen's Hall in London in December 1912 where it ran for three months.

In January 1913, the British Board of Film Censors (BBFC) was formed. Since the English Reformation, there has been a cultural nervousness about figurative depictions of Christ on these shores. As testimony to the ongoing legacy of Reformist sensitivities, the BBFC prohibited the figurative depiction of Christ on screen as one of its two founding principles (the other was a ban on the depiction of nudity). From 1913 onwards, any film that contravened the ban on the "materialization of the conventional figure of Christ" was automatically denied a certificate for exhibition in Britain.[10] The BBFC's ruling related only to films that would seek a British release in the future, not to ones that had already secured one. *From the Manger*, having just slipped under the wire in this respect, was able to continue its London run undisturbed. Future productions, however, would have to be more circumspect in how they told a Gospel story if they wished to secure a British release.

Ben-Hur (MGM: Fred Niblo, 1925)

Although *From the Manger* offers a figurative depiction of Jesus, it is less direct in its presentation of angels, replacing the halo-ed actresses of the early Gospel films with a simple, strategically placed shaft of light. In later films, this more abstract approach to character would be extended to include the treatment of the Jesus figure himself. MGM's 1925 *Ben-Hur*, directed by Fred Niblo (and, unlike the 1907 Kalem version, in possession of all necessary copyright permissions), is strikingly self-denying in its treatment of Jesus.[11] Wallace's 1880 source novel *Ben-Hur* is an epic tale about the turbulent fortunes of a first century man, Judah Ben-Hur, whose life intermittently intersects with and is profoundly touched by that of Jesus of Nazareth. Despite the crucial role Jesus plays in the story (both novel and film are subtitled "A Tale of the Christ"), in the film a series of impediments to vision are strategically deployed, and other techniques of visual evasion teasingly adopted in order to ensure we never see him directly. He is potently evoked by the sly shot of a hand, a footprint, the corner of a robe, a shaft of light falling upon a space just occluded from view and, above all, by the transfiguring effect he has on other characters. The appearance of his person, however, is left in the realm of suggestion only.[12]

In keeping Jesus as the constantly implied but never quite seen presence just beyond the frame's edge, the film was abiding by the contractual stipulations of Wallace himself. When he eventually agreed to sell the rights to his hugely successful novel for a stage adaptation, he had it written into the contract that there would be no figurative depiction of Jesus on stage at all in order not to offend good taste.[13] In the production that was duly mounted first on the New York stage in 1899 and subsequently, with unparalleled theatrical success, across the Anglophone world, a beam of light only was invited to stand for the Jesus figure who touches and inspires Judah's life and cures his mother and sister of leprosy.[14] MGM were sold the rights for the *Ben-Hur* franchise on condition that they too respected the wishes of its author in this respect.

The principal motivation for placing Jesus permanently just out of reach of the camera was, therefore, in the first instance legal necessity. Inevitably, though, it also had an effect on narrative structure and commercial appeal. Firstly, Jesus' absence allowed Judah (screen idol Ramon Navarro) narrative, visual, and performative space in which to be an uncompromising flesh and blood hero. Wrapping the scriptural account into another story (which could carry the onus of narrative excitement) made it easier to sustain an appropriate range in the emotional cadences and a desirable pace in the plotting. D. W. Griffith had done something similar in *Intolerance* (1916) by intercutting his Passion narrative with three other stories (the fall of Babylon, the St Bartholomew's Day massacre, and a contemporary melodrama). Cecil B. DeMille and screenwriter Jeanie MacPherson had energized a weighty Old Testament biblical story by juxtaposing it with a zippy contemporary narrative in *The Ten Commandments* (1923). Equally, the story of the admirable but flawed hero of *Ben-Hur* provided the narrative and emotional peaks and troughs that movie audiences had come to expect of their motion pictures but which the scriptural account alone might have struggled to provide. By keeping Christ at the level of suggestion, the film is thus able to enjoy both the winning human energy of its non-Messianic hero, *and* the evocative power and sustained mystery of the implied godly presence who is always, and on occasions movingly, kept coyly just out of sight. The two narrative pillars of the film – the one visualized, the other not – occupy different dimensions in the film and need never, therefore, compete with each other for audience attention or sympathy.

As a film in which Christ was never literally configured, *Ben-Hur* had no trouble securing a British exhibition certificate. In Britain, it proved a sensation – and reportedly did better business in London even than it had in New York.[15] It received a twice daily screening at London's 3,000-seat Tivoli Theatre for an unprecedented run of fifty-one weeks. At the Super Cinema in Birkenhead, it was screened thrice daily for a more modest two weeks but, unusually, with full orchestra and effects. It was even shown, by special arrangement with the King, at a royal screening in the Waterloo Chamber in Windsor Castle, after which the Dean of Windsor reported that he was "much impressed . . . by the delicacy with which the Christ history in the film was depicted."[16]

The Dean of Windsor's appreciation of the film was widely shared by ecclesiasts. Even R. G. Burnett and E. D. Martell, two conservatives who in 1932 published a piece of anti-cinema polemic entitled *The Devil's Camera*, were magnanimously willing to exempt *Ben-Hur* from the "scores of sinister exploitations of vice and crime and blasphemy" that characterized the bulk of contemporary cinema as they saw it.[17] *Ben-Hur* therefore succeeded in being that rare thing – an uncompromisingly commercial film that nevertheless won respect in even the most uncommercial quarters.

Its commercial status was beyond doubt. It cost over \$4 m to make (the most expensive film of its moment) and managed to turn itself into a global cinematic event in order to recoup its outlay. A plethora of commercial tie-ins (among other things for Palmolive soap and a specially commissioned perfume called "Ben-Hur") and an extensive range of photo postcards of its stars (Navarro, Francis X. Bushman as Messala, May McAvoy as Esther, Carmel Myers as Iras the "vamp") were produced to accompany its release. A market-savvy new edition of the novel which included photo stills from the film was brought out by Harpers in order to re-energize book sales, and this also helped to fuel interest in the film, not only as a spectacular picture but also as a literary adaptation. Several different lavish souvenir programmes full of film stills and anecdotal articles about the production and its history were produced for sale at the classier exhibition venues worldwide. The range and ubiquity of the related merchandise and publicity helped to keep the film in the public eye for an unprecedented length of time. *Ben-Hur* was not only, therefore, as one of its many attractive programmes proclaimed it, "An exquisite romance of Sacred and Profane love" but also, in its simultaneous courting of the Dean of Windsor and of profitable perfume sales, of sacred and profane vested interests.[18]

The King of Kings (DeMille Pictures Corporation: Cecil B. DeMille, 1927)

Cecil B. DeMille's lavish Gospel adaptation, *The King of Kings*, was released just sixteen months after *Ben-Hur*, supplanting in the process the earlier film as the most expensive film yet made. Officially, *The King of Kings*, in Jeanie MacPherson's adapted screenplay, took a less tangential approach to biblical interpretation than *Ben-Hur* (whose relationship to the Gospel accounts was mediated through a biblical offshoot novel). In practice, however, the nature of *The King of Kings'* engagements with the Gospel accounts is on occasions also freely creative in interpretive approach. It is an emotionally charged and visually beautiful film stamped with all the well-known DeMille signature traits – high sentiment, emotional intensity, impressive spectacle, charming detail, a taste for the overblown, a celebration of the decadently sexual, and a high-minded rhetoric in all public discussion of its aims.

As if remembering the representational strategy of *Ben-Hur*, DeMille's film has a purposeful flirtation with the possibility that it too will withhold the face of Christ from cinematic view. Certainly the arrival of that face on screen is strikingly delayed beyond the point at which it might simply count as an anticipated entrance. It is worth charting the film's progress towards that strategically deferred moment of revelation.

The film's opening sequence is set in the palatial home of Mary Magdalene (Jacqueline Logan), who in DeMille's version has been reconfigured as the extravagantly vampish, but now neglected lover of Judas Iscariot. As an economical pointer to her dangerous loucheness, she is seen reclining on a couch wearing provocatively little and cuddling a pet leopard. As further evidence of the sybaritic indulgence of both Mary and, behind her, the production's design department, her zebra-drawn chariot appears amidst the marble columns in order to take her to the Nazarene carpenter in search of Judas. In the context of the film as a whole, the sexualized, even deviant excess of Mary Magdalene's lifestyle is clearly being held up for judgment. As it unfolds through the early moments of the film, however, it is undoubtedly being joyously milked for titillating visual pleasure and hyperbolic cinematic energy.

When the scene shifts from Mary Magdalene's palace, we are then introduced, in a leisurely way, to the community gathered around the Nazarene. The context is mapped in detail for us, from the amassed crowds waiting to see him to the boy Mark whose leg has just been healed; from the Roman soldiers listening in on the seemingly revolutionary talk about a "new King" to the scribes and Pharisees irritated by the crowd's enthusiasm for this provincial rabbi; from a donkey tethered outside to Mary the mother weaving at a loom inside; from the disciples picked out and introduced in turn to the little blind girl who seeks the healer. It is only after lengthy sections of wheeling teasingly around the space in which we can infer Jesus is situated, that the film, some nineteen minutes in, finally succumbs to the draw to turn the camera on him. And when his face eventually appears on screen, the moment is given as much weighty significance as possible by being filtered through the emerging perceptions of the blind girl who, having been given her sight by Jesus, is now learning to see. Like a stylized rehearsal of the coming of cinema itself, light miraculously leaks into her world (an experience the film invites us to share through subjectivized camera work). The sight that swims in to her, and our, vision through the dispersing mists is the face of Jesus (played here with generous humanity by H. B. Warner). As it eases itself into focus amidst a halo of light, that face is invested with both an irradiating power and the slight suggestion of a twinkle, the effect of both of which is enhanced by the strategic delay in its arrival on screen.

The film's direct counterbalance to this beatific face are the grotesque features of the High Priest Caiaphas. In a transparent attempt to sidestep a more general charge of anti-Semitism, the film damns, even demonizes, Caiaphas personally by action, word, and image: the guilt in this production is all his. This might legitimately have provoked objections.[19] In this period in Britain, however, the most vocal sensitivities were still more Christocentric than this: it was not, therefore, the grossly cartooned presentation of Caiaphas that absorbed the critical attention in its early British run.

The BBFC's ruling prohibiting the materialization of the figure of Christ on screen meant than a British distribution was far from being assured, despite the film's enormous success and enthusiastic reviews in the United States. Undeflected, the American distributors set to work circumventing the ban in imaginative and, as it turned out, effective ways. Without applying for an exhibition certificate from the BBFC they initially showed the picture to private gatherings of invited clergy to win over some key support. They subsequently ran a series of screenings for representatives from local county councils, in the pursuit of a series of individual exhibition licences to be issued authority by authority. Just as county councils reserved the right to ban films passed for national exhibition by the BBFC, so it was also in their gift to pass films for local exhibition that had not been given a BBFC certificate. On this basis, by 1931 *King of Kings* had been exhibited in 153 of the 160 British local authorities applied to, without ever having been presented to the BBFC. It was a backdoor distribution route whose striking effectiveness contributed in time to the cumulative undermining of the BBFC's resolution to stand firm against the perceived impertinence of such films.[20]

In the institutional encounter between the Bible (and its ecclesiastical patron) on the one hand and the film industry on the other that biblical films implicitly represented, there was a reciprocal trade-off of both benefits and costs. On the beneficial side, Bible and film industry exchanged cultural elevation for market penetration. Less favorably, biblical films brought not just moral approbation but also significant religious controversy to the industry and, for those wedded to the unalterable sanctity of Scripture, the same films risked displacing the inspired word (Word) of God in public life in diminished and uninspired form.

Film adaptations of the Gospels have always been precariously poised between the concerns of the faithful and the demands of commerce. The ability of these films to slip between secular and sacred exhibition spaces exemplifies well their dual, or competing, allegiances. The body of spectators who could be won over to moving pictures through a judicious combination of a morally respectable picture and a socially respectable exhibition venue has always constituted a significant potential market. The 1907 Pathé Passion film, for example, was probably seen by more people in the United States in the years 1907–8 than any other single film;[21] the 1925 *Ben-Hur* and 1927 *King of Kings* each in turn broke records not only of budget but also of worldwide attendance. From the industry's point of view, therefore, Gospel-inspired films represented a rare point of profitable encounter between spiritual and commercial interests. Where religious education, moral uplift, and financial gain could be found making common cause, it is no surprise that there proved to be, and continues to be, a lively concentration of filmmaking interest.

NOTES

A draft of this chapter was given as part of the Ethics series in the Divinity School of the University of Edinburgh in March 2005. I am grateful to the audience there on that occasion for their helpful responses and in particular to Jolyon Mitchell for his judicious and welcome suggestions for areas of related reading.

1 At the time of writing, each of these films is commercially available on video or DVD in American formats (NTSC video tapes and Region 1 DVD). Where there is any difference of opinion about the release date, I follow that given in Magliozzi, R. S.,

Treasures from the Film Archives: A Catalog of Short Silent Fiction Films held by FIAF Archives, (Metuchen, New Jersey and London: The Scarecrow Press, 1988).

2 Frank L. Dyer, "The Moral Development of the Silent Drama" *Edison Kinetogram* (15 April 1910), p. 11. Quoted in Uricchio, W., and Pearson, R. E., *Reframing Culture: The Case of the Vitagraph Quality Films* (Princeton, New Jersey: Princeton University Press, 1993), p. 48.

3 Quoted in Keil, C., "*From the Manger to the Cross*: The New Testament Narrative and the Question of Stylistic Retardation," in *Une invention du Diable? Cinéma des premiers temps et religion*, ed. Cosandey, R., Gaudreault, A., and Gunning, T. (Sainte-Foy: Les Presses de l'Université Laval, 1992), p. 116.

4 DeMille quoted in Birchard, R. S., *Cecil B. DeMille's Hollywood* (Lexington: The University Press of Kentucky, 2004), p. 222.

5 See Holloway, R., *Beyond the Image: Approaches to the Religious Dimension in the Cinema* (Geneva: World Council of Churches, 1977), p. 26.

6 Wagenknecht, E., *Movies in the Age of Innocence* (Norman: Oklahoma Press, 1962), p. 20.

7 For a discussion of Olcott's debt to Tissot, see Reynolds, H., "From the Palette to the Screen; the Tissot Bible as Sourcebook for *From the Manger to the Cross*" in Cosandey, Gaudreault, and Gunning (eds.), *Une Invention du Diable?* (Sainte-Foy: Les Presses de l'Université Laval, 1992), pp. 275–310.

8 Keil, "*From the Manger to the Cross*," p. 113.

9 Keil, "*From the Manger to the Cross*," p. 112.

10 See Robertson, J. C., *The Hidden Camera: British Film Censorship in Action, 1913–1975* (London and New York: Routledge), p. 163.

11 The film took three years to make, was shot in Italy and California and premiered on 30 December 1925 at the George M. Cohan Theatre in New York.

12 Jesus was also kept out of frame in MGM's equally spectacular but less charming William Wyler/Charlton Heston 1959 remake.

13 McMillen, W., "A Century of Lew Wallace and a Half Century of 'Ben-Hur'," *The Mentor* (May 1927), p. 35.

14 In its first twenty years (1899–1919), the play became the most successful stage show ever, being seen by approximately 25,000,000 people worldwide. See Kreitzer, L. J., *The New Testament in Fiction and Film* (Sheffield: Sheffield Academic Press, 1993), p. 55.

15 Cinema Programme for the Tivoli Strand, London, David Allen and Sons, undated, p. 5. Author's collection.

16 Tivoli programme, p. 17.

17 Burnett, R. G. and Martell, E. D., *The Devil's Camera: Menace of a Film-Ridden World* (London: Epworth, 1932), p. 11.

18 Cinema program for the Van Curler Theatre in Schenectady, 2–5 December 1926, p. 5. Author's collection.

19 See Pamela Grace, "Gospel Truth?" in Stam, R., and Raengo, A. (eds.), *A Companion to Literature and Film*, (Oxford: Blackwell, 2004), pp. 46–57.

20 The BBFC compromised its ruling against the screen depiction of Christ in stages and finally abandoned it in 1961 for the remake of *King of Kings*. See Robertson, *The Hidden Camera*, pp. 15–16, 32–3.

21 Abel, R., *Red Rooster Scare: Making Cinema American, 1900–1910* (Berkeley, Los Angeles: London, University of California Press, 1999), p. 61.

4

DOUGLAS LANIER

William Shakespeare, filmmaker

It has become a popular commonplace that had Shakespeare been born in the twentieth century, he would have been a filmmaker. This idea has had a long history, stretching back at least as far as George Méliès's 1907 film *La Mort de Jules César*. In it, Shakespeare, suffering from writer's block, falls asleep. As he does, he dreams of the assassination scene from *Julius Caesar*, presented behind him in one of the double-exposure shots for which Méliès was renowned. His writing problems solved, Shakespeare awakes with delight and even stabs a loaf of bread, imitating what he has just seen.[1] The effect is to reverse the usual relationship between Shakespeare's theatrical script and the cinematic image of Caesar's murder. As Méliès presents the writing process, one of Shakespeare's most famous scenes springs from an imagination not bound to the stage, an imagination fundamentally visual not verbal. The final shot, of Shakespeare's face surrounded by the flags of many nations, suggests that his international appeal springs not from his words but from the moving images that lie behind them. It suggests that the essentially visual – and thus panlinguistic – nature of Shakespeare's imagination, like that of silent film, makes his work capable of crossing cultural boundaries. Shakespeare and film, Méliès argues, are conjoined at an essential level. Something of this same idea appears in the final moments of *Shakespeare in Love* (John Madden, 1998). Again, the scene is of Shakespeare composing. Having lost his love but gained a royal commission, Shakespeare sits down to write *Twelfth Night*. We see what Shakespeare imagines: dreamy images of Viola's shipwreck, the drowning of Shakespeare's rival Lord Wessex, and Viola's arrival on a vast, sandy beach, all cross-faded with Shakespeare's upturned face, his pen poised to begin. Shakespeare imagines the opening scenes of his *Twelfth Night*, that is, as a movie, one which he only afterward records as a playscript. This moment in the film follows Shakespeare's triumphal stage presentation of *Romeo and Juliet*, a play also rooted in Shakespeare's erotic experience but which has pointedly crude, unrealistic stage effects (note Juliet's red handkerchief for blood, for example). It is as if in finding his footing as an artist Shakespeare's imagination has become cinematic – pointedly he does not imagine *Twelfth Night* as a stage performance, and the final image of the film, in which Shakespeare imagines Viola walking on a pristine beach, emphasizes with its white expanse the cinematic screen itself. If in the film's ending Viola has slipped the shackles of the marriage market, so Shakespeare has transcended the primitive mechanics of Elizabethan playhouse practice in favor of the cinema of the mind.

I begin with the commonplace of Shakespeare as filmmaker because it articulates a persistent desire of filmmakers and producers throughout the last century, a desire somehow to appropriate Shakespeare's accrued cultural authority for the institution of the cinema, a desire that lies behind the enormous array of Shakespeare films produced since the inception of Shakespeare on film in 1899. That desire begs to be parsed closely. On the one hand, to claim Shakespeare as a filmmaker is to (re)claim him as a fundamentally popular artist, working unashamedly in a commercial medium directed at mass audiences. Such a claim runs counter to a dominant perception of Shakespeare – that his work is high culture, appreciated best by intellectuals, academics, and bluebloods. Both *La Mort de Jules César* and *Shakespeare in Love* insist upon Shakespeare's status as a popular artist, *La Mort* with its final shot and its choice of scene (the assassination of a potential emperor), *Shakespeare in Love* with Shakespeare's dual burden throughout the film, to capture the true nature of love free of stage convention while creating a bankable hit, something he does with *Romeo and Juliet*. The primary beneficiary of this conception is typically not Shakespeare at all but rather the commercial film industry, which can then use Shakespeare, (re)defined as both "popular" and "artistic," to legitimize its own pursuit of mass commercial appeal.

This strategy emerged early in the history of screen Shakespeare when, in the face of claims that silent film was eroding cultural standards, studios like Vitagraph produced silents on Shakespearean topics to demonstrate film's morally – and culturally – uplifting potential and to assert the compatibility of traditional high art with the new medium.[2] But the strategy persisted well into the age of talkies. The three major Shakespearean films of the 1930s, Paramount's *Cleopatra* (1934, a free adaptation), Warner Brothers' *A Midsummer Night's Dream* (1935), and MGM's *Romeo and Juliet* (1936) were all designed as artistic showcases for the Hollywood studios in which they were made. Olivier's *Henry V* opens with a theatrical performance at the Globe Theatre to which the onscreen audience responds enthusiastically, a reminder of Shakespeare's status as a popular playwright, before Olivier moves eventually to a conventional cinematic presentation of the Battle of Agincourt. Branagh's Shakespeare films of the 1990s have consistently featured metadramatic sequences that celebrate what Branagh sees as the communal or populist orientation of Shakespeare's works and the communalism of Shakespearean players and their audience.[3] Indeed, a recurrent motif in Shakespeare films, faithful and free, is of an enthusiastic popular reception for a Shakespeare adapted to modern cinematic tastes. Even when this motif bears an ironic charge, it voices a powerful, persistent cultural fantasy of the twentieth century: if Shakespeare's work could only be brought into accord with the protocols of mass culture, particularly those of film, he might be wrested from the hands of cultural elitists and handed (back) to "the people." Such a fantasy, promoted within popular culture and by Shakespearean filmmakers alike (though in quite different forms), serves far more to reinforce the perception that film is a culturally democratizing medium than it does to describe the effects of adapting Shakespeare to the screen.

On the other hand, to reconceive of Shakespeare's imagination as fundamentally cinematic is to relocate Shakespeare's quintessence not in his language – the altar at which bardolaters have traditionally worshipped – but in those elements most central to the cinema – plot action, character, and most importantly photorealistic images. It is to posit that Shakespeare settled for (rather than chose) dramatic poetry because he lacked a camera to convey the fevered creations of his mind. This conception has roots in film's competition with the stage throughout the twentieth century. So long as Shakespeare is identified with his language, the argument runs, his works remain localized, situated firmly in the British past, hobbled by an antique idiom, tied to stage conventions both artificial and outmoded. To think of Shakespeare as a filmmaker, not as a theatrical wordsmith, then, is to treat his relationship to dramatic poetry and the Elizabethan stage as a matter of historical accident rather than creative synergy, and thus to locate his essence in an image-driven media form which, putatively, is more universal and timeless. It is also to separate Shakespeare from the literary, for so reconceived he is not a writer engaged primarily with other books or poetic or theatrical traditions, but one who writes from direct personal experience, experience to which the camera can supposedly give more direct access. The claim that Shakespeare is fundamentally cinematic also implies its converse – that filmmaking is in some way fundamentally Shakespearean, that is, potentially artistic rather than just entertainment, global in its reach and universal in its appeal. Such is the implication, for example, of Méliès casting himself as Shakespeare in *La Mort de Jules César*. Linking Shakespeare to film becomes a means for articulating (or simply accepting) the cinema's considerable ambitions as a media form.

The earliest examples of screen Shakespeare were closely tied to the theatre, offering viewers records of stage performances to which they otherwise had no access. Within a decade a new strain of Shakespearean filmmaking, first emergent in the later films of Vitagraph's American film series of 1908–12, broke with the stage and created productions conceived specifically for the camera. These films used real locations rather than stage sets and took advantage of such cinematic techniques as intercutting lines of action, using closeups to reveal character or emphasize narrative detail, tracking action with the camera, and substituting a telling image or tableau for a speech. These films asserted an ideal of photorealism that would come to dominate Shakespearean filmmaking. The growing divide between stage and screen Shakespeare can be seen in Shakespearean film burlesques, which first appear in significant numbers in the mid-1910s. Unlike nineteenth-century stage burlesques, which transposed Shakespeare into an inappropriate (usually working-class) social register, these films typically featured a disastrous Shakespearean stage performance, often performed by amateurs. These films make their parodic object specifically *theatrical* Shakespeare, demonstrating how easily stage performance lapses into absurdity. Equally telling are films that chronicle the corrupting or murderous power of Shakespeare over stage actors. *The Mad Lover* (also known as *A Modern Othello*; Léonce Perret, 1917) and *Carnival* (Harley Knoles, 1921) feature performances of *Othello* which an actor threatens to act out in reality what is merely a play, presenting stage performance as seductively dangerous and stage Shakespeareans as suspiciously unstable. Film's hostile treatment of theatrical Shakespeare continued into the age of the talkies. For Shakespearean film, the advent of sound technology threatened to bring a return to the theatricality of the past, since it necessarily foregrounded Shakespeare's language. Notably, the three major Shakespeare films of the early talkies era – *The Taming of the Shrew* (Sam Taylor, 1929), *A Midsummer Night's Dream* (William Dieterle and Max Reinhardt, 1935), and *Romeo and Juliet* (George Cukor, 1936) – were, despite all their considerable star power, box-office and critical disappointments.

The definitive work to address the relationship between Shakespearean stage and screen in the era of sound, most critics agree, was Olivier's *Henry V* (1944). Olivier acknowledges Shakespeare's theatrical roots by staging the play's first three scenes in the Globe before he makes a transition to a conventionally cinematic (and comparatively wordless) treatment of the battle of Agincourt. Olivier's film registers the pressure to shift the narrative from stage to screen, and, given that the play's prologue focuses on Shakespeare's seeming dissatisfaction with the resources of Renaissance playmaking, his film seems to affirm the superiority of cinematic representation and

Shakespearean drama's potential congruity with it. When Kenneth Branagh returned *Henry V* to the screen in 1989, he excised all traces of theatricality. The opening sequence moves almost instantly from primitive fire to modern electricity (on the word "invention," no less), and the Prologue offers his critique of the "wooden O" on a film soundstage, making explicit the argument implicit in Olivier's film. Indeed, the modern Prologue, anachronistically walking through scenes of fourteenth-century history, lends the film a documentary, "you are there" quality, as if film gives unmediated access to the past Shakespeare presents. More recently, the pressure to erase Shakespearean theatricality has extended to its most famous example, Hamlet's play-within-the-play. In Michael Almereyda's *Hamlet* (2000), the Danish prince becomes a Gen-X independent filmmaker and his "Mousetrap," an avant-garde video.

If popular culture has sometimes sought to present Shakespeare's adaptation to the screen as a liberation from the shackles of the stage, an apotheosis of his heretofore unrealized imaginative intent, until relatively recently Shakespeare film criticism has fixated upon the problem of transposing Shakespeare between media. Speaking broadly, until the 1980s critics addressed Shakespearean film adaptations through one of two models, script-centered and film-centered. With its roots in earlier forms of performance criticism, script-centered criticism begins with the Shakespearean script and measures the film at hand against it, typically with an eye toward specifying its degree of fidelity. This entails not merely analyzing the patterns of textual cuts and additions by the filmmaker and identifying the principles that lie behind them, but also adducing key images and themes in the Shakespearean text and examining how they are translated into visual terms. With a faithful rendering of Shakespeare's script as the ideal, the governing critical assumption is that a good Shakespearean film is one that best or most completely "realizes" the Shakespearean script. By contrast, film-centered criticism embraces cinematic integrity as its key criterion of value; its interest is in the extent to which Shakespeare has been fully converted from stage to screen. Jack J. Jorgens's influential typology of Shakespearean film adaptations exemplifies this approach.[4] Jorgens posits a continuum of three adaptational modes – theatrical, realist, and filmic – within which any given Shakespeare film might be situated. Theatrical adaptations transfer stage performances to the screen with minimal accommodation to cinematic convention; realist adaptations recast Shakespeare in terms of traditional cinematic realism, with emphasis on naturalistic *mise-en-scène*, continuity editing, conventional camera placement, and photographic "objectivity"; filmic adaptations emphasize the camera's expressive possibilities, foregrounding non-illusionistic, deliberately stylized or "poetic" lighting, editing, sound, and production design. Jorgens's typology, we should note, is also an evaluative scheme. We should value a Shakespeare film, he implies, insofar as it leaves the theatre behind, an assumption which in practice tends to privilege arthouse Shakespeare over mainstream adaptations. Despite their differences, however, both script-centered and film-centered criticism conceive of Shakespearean film adaptation primarily as a formal issue.

In the 1980s there emerged a new mode of Shakespearean film criticism, what we might call ideology-centered criticism. Leaving behind the notion that film adaptation should passively "realize" Shakespeare, this critical mode conceived of film adaptation as an ideological process. Shakespeare films actively recast Shakespeare's text in the service of particular political or ideological ends, ends which the critic teases out for critique. Ideology-centered criticism has a specific and general horizon. In the act of re-interpreting a Shakespearean play, each Shakespearean film appropriates Shakespeare's considerable cultural authority for a director's or producer's particular political vision – in Olivier's 1944 *Henry V*, to bolster the war effort, and in Zeffirelli's 1968 *Romeo and Juliet*, to mythologize the "make love, not war" movement. But by their very nature, Shakespearean films also transfer (or at least duplicate) Shakespeare's cultural authority from stage and page to the film medium, an operation which has perhaps far-reaching consequences given the corporate, commercial, and global nature of film production. Ideological critics have tended to accept the postmodern premise that the Shakespearean script cannot be erected as a norm against which to judge individual films; "Shakespeare" no longer refers to an established text or ideal performance but to a set of variants without a norm. The critics have also tended to reject film-centered criticism's primary interest in format, preferring instead to focus on the content of Shakespearean films, analyzing their acknowledged and unacknowledged agenda. Even so, ideology-centered criticism is not value-free, for in practice films are often measured against the ideological norms – stated or unstated – of the critic. The most productive recent criticism of Shakespeare on film has taken up this approach, asking not only "how have the formal features of Shakespeare's script been adapted to film?" but also "to what end(s) is Shakespeare being used in this film?" and "how does this film (re)produce, change, or contest Shakespeare's cultural authority?"

Ideological criticism came of age in the shadow of the political conservatism of the Reagan and Thatcher eras, and it was followed by an extraordinary revival of Shakespeare on film in the 1990s in which Shakespearean filmmakers actively courted the mass market by reshaping the plays in terms of popular genres, most notably action film, teen romance, and nineteenth-century costume drama. These filmmakers, Branagh in particular, presented the movies as a means for giving Shakespeare's work back to "the people." This claim has posed a difficult problem for ideological critics. On the one hand, ideological critics have been concerned not only with unmasking the cultural politics of Shakespearean films but also with highlighting their progressive potential – in Alan Sinfield's words, laying out "the complex interplay of the dominant with residual, emergent, subordinate and oppositional forces" with an eye toward finding "space for socialist *intervention*."[5] In addition to providing greater access to Shakespeare in performance, film might offer the possibility of a Shakespeare aligned with populist values or a Shakespeare that exposes the mechanisms of dominant ideology.[6] On the other hand, most ideological critics have remained deeply sceptical about the newly "popularized" screen Shakespeare. Recent critical discussion has focused on whether the Shakespeare films of the last decade, aimed at a mass audience and financed by mainstream studios, are a progressive or conservative development in the history of Shakespearean performance. This debate reminds us how complex the question of Shakespeare's popularity on film is, and the ease with which quite different notions of Shakespearean popularity can be confused or conflated.

The issue is especially vexed in the Shakespeare classroom, where recent changes in video technology have made it possible – indeed *de rigeur* – for teachers to integrate Shakespeare on film into their pedagogical routines. Since the introduction of the VCR in the 1980s and DVD in the 1990s, instructors regularly teach the Shakespearean script alongside video performances, using the same regimens of close analysis for each, so that students now expect to be introduced to Shakespeare through film. Without doubt video offers students greater access to Shakespeare performances and places questions of performance front and center in classrooms once dominated exclusively by literary and historical approaches. It also holds out the promise of stimulating students' appreciation and taste for Shakespeare by recasting the Bard as contemporary and hip, a figure of pop, not elite, culture. This hope was particularly sparked by the extraordinary success of Baz Luhrmann's *Romeo + Juliet* (1996), the film that spawned the concerted "teening" of Shakespeare in a cycle of youth-oriented Shakespeare films and spin-offs throughout the next several years. Since the mid-1980s, Shakespeare teachers and filmmakers have developed an increasingly symbiotic relationship, both using film as an instrument of popularization: teachers have come to depend on film to spur student interest in Shakespeare, while filmmakers depend upon the educational market for their work's financial viability. Even in the classroom, it would seem, Shakespeare is now regularly introduced to youth as a filmmaker *manqué*, so much so that they find it difficult to imagine him otherwise.

The triumph of Shakespeare film in the classroom has widespread ideological implications, not merely for pedagogical and critical practice but also for the (re)conception of Shakespeare in coming generations. Screen Shakespeare would seem to liberate students from an excessive reverence for the Shakespearean text and to reinforce the notion that Shakespeare's plays have their life in performance, not on the page. Indisputably, these films have garnered an interest in Shakespeare among many students, in and outside the classroom. Even so, the exact nature of that interest demands critical scrutiny, particularly when it is linked with ubiquitous axioms of contemporary popular culture that are hardly ideologically neutral. A major risk is that uncritically using Shakespeare on film simply naturalizes Shakespeare's relationship to the film medium rather than drawing attention to the screen's ideological transformation – for good or ill – of Shakespeare. This risk is magnified by the aura of celebrity surrounding the cinema, but also by instructors' preference for films that use Shakespeare's language rather than modern idioms. Paradoxically, fidelity to Shakespeare's language in film adaptations can mask the ideological work of the filmmaker, even when Shakespeare's narrative is transposed to a different era or setting, because it allows for the illusion that the filmmaker is passively "realizing" the Shakespearean script, the "essential" Shakespeare. Reinforced is the sense that Shakespearean content is freely commutable from medium to medium, period to period, and is not media- or historically specific, but also that film is Shakespeare's "proper" medium rather than one of several media forms – all associated with particular social orders – to which his work has been retrofitted. To put this another way, the popularity of Shakespeare offered by film often comes at the price of engaging the ideological nature of adapting Shakespeare to the screen, and it risks turning the classroom into yet another promotional arena for the protocols of contemporary media culture.

Despite the introduction of film into the Shakespeare classroom and changes in pedagogical and critical fashion, text-centered criticism continues to reign supreme, partly because assessment regimes continue to stress mastery of the Shakespearean text as an academic skill. In practice textual fidelity remains a primary concern – those films perceived to be most faithful to the Shakespearean script, those most useful for teaching the text, are those most frequently taught and written about. The danger is that discussion of the ideological nature of Shakespearean film adaptation becomes subordinated to or obliterated by other premises: that some films more accurately or correctly reproduce their Shakespearean sources, that cinematic fidelity to Shakespeare is possible or desirable. The truth is that all film performances by their cinematic nature must radically reinvent their Shakespeare. The great virtue of unfaithful or free adaptations – beside the strengths of individual films themselves – is that they foreground issues of remediation and ideological recoding often tacit in many Shakespeare films. The changes free adaptations make in the language, genre, narrative, characters, and tone of their Shakespearean sources reveal lines of cultural force at play in their so-called "faithful" counterparts.

To illustrate this proposition, consider two very different "free" adaptations of *Romeo and Juliet* produced during the 1990s Shakespeare film boom: *Tromeo and Juliet* (Lloyd Kaufman, 1996) and *Shakespeare in Love* (John Madden, 1998). *Tromeo and Juliet* is an example of that time-honored genre, the Shakespearean burlesque, produced by Troma Studios, specializing in low-budget exploitation films for the teen market. Typical of burlesque, emphasis falls on the gap between the "high" register of the source material and the "low" idiom or social class into which it is transposed; in *Tromeo*'s case, that idiom includes gleefully vulgar language and action, gratuitous sexual titillation, comically graphic violence, and deliberately crude production values, in the words of the film's promotional tag, "Body Piercing, Kinky Sex, Dismemberment. The Things That Made Shakespeare Great." In this version, Tromeo is the working-class son of down-and-out Monty Que, a former softcore artfilm maker cuckolded and swindled out of his business by "Cappy" Capulet, a viciously puritanical hypocrite anxious to marry off his daughter Juliet to London Arbuckle, heir to a meat-packing fortune and a lovelorn fool. *Tromeo* includes a number of motifs from Shakespeare's play, each perversely twisted: Juliet's close relationship with her Nurse becomes a lesbian tryst with Ness, her live-in caretaker; Tromeo and Juliet meet at a costume party at which Tromeo is dressed as a cow; Juliet's anxious soliloquies about Romeo are transformed into bizarre dreams about eroticism and pregnancy; the potion Juliet receives from the priest does not simulate death but transforms her temporarily into an ugly human-pig mutant calculated to horrify Arbuckle (he commits suicide rather than marry her); in the end, instead of dying the couple discover that they are brother and sister and choose to marry anyway.

Produced within a year of *Romeo + Juliet*, the film which became the template for the teen Shakespeare boomlet to follow, *Tromeo* satirically targets not Shakespeare *per se* but the implicit sensibilities of Luhrmann's adaptation and through it the mass-market screen Shakespeare of the 1990s. Most obvious among the elements it satirizes is the relationship between social class and "popularization." The film parodically weds Shakespeare to American trash culture, a world presented as primarily urban working-class and rabidly anti-highbrow in its orientation. Notably the film's villain,

Cappy Capulet, is a social climber, anxious to be accepted into polite society even though he lacks the taste and savoir-faire to present himself properly; his near-psychotic desire to control his daughter's sexuality and wed her to the wealthy but boorish Arbuckle spring from his entirely hypocritical social aspirations. *Tromeo and Juliet* targets the bourgeois, leisure-class romanticism of *Romeo + Juliet*, this despite Luhrmann's veneer of urban grit and knowing uses of youth culture. Luhrmann's lovers certainly identify with "the people" – Romeo slums with his friends at seedy Verona Beach's Globe, a run-down pool hall, and Juliet's closest confidante is her working-class Latino nurse – but they do so from the security of their parents' prosperity, with ready access to designer clothes, cool cars, and fab parties. Alienation from their parents Luhrmann's teen lovers may feel deeply, but the production's dominant register is upper class. This sensibility operates too in its treatment of the urban setting. Whereas Luhrmann's metropolitan Verona is an urban fantasyscape modeled on a media image of Los Angeles, its street life experienced largely from great heights or distances (in the establishing shots) and in video bites (in the riot scenes), Kaufmann's effects-unenhanced New York is a world of trash-strewn, photographically ugly streets, empty lots, and seedy dives where Tromeo and his friends actually live rather than just visit. For Luhrmann, the street serves a hip signifier; for Kaufmann, it functions as a social determinant.

Kaufmann's handling of setting accords with *Tromeo*'s lampooning of other stylistic elements of *Romeo + Juliet*. The physical violence of *Tromeo* is not conducted from within the safety of stylized choreography, as is the case with the opening gun battle in *Romeo + Juliet*, but rather is graphic, cruel, and gratuitously excessive to the point of uneasy comedy. Whereas Luhrmann's Romeo and Juliet are unusually chaste teenagers, perhaps a mark of decorum and a nod in the direction of the educational market, Kaufmann's film acknowledges, even celebrates sexuality (in all its polymorphous possibility) as a driving force for the lovers' romance and treats Cappy's brutal attempts to regulate Juliet's sex-life as far more perverse than the urges they target. Indeed, Kaufmann everywhere reasserts the primacy of the body in various carnivalesque and grotesque forms, in the theme of meat, in bodies tattooed or pierced (sometimes on camera), in mutations or various blendings of animal and human. As a counter *Romeo + Juliet*, *Tromeo* targets the bourgeois–idealist decorum that tacitly governs Luhrmann's adaptation, a polite, finally high-cultural (re)vision of Shakespeare on film that keeps a strategic distance from those "popular" elements that give the film its street credibility. Contributing to the critique is *Tromeo*'s deliberately crude production values and shoddy special effects, a stark contrast to the glossily photographed, MTV-style edited, and cinematically allusive style of Luhrmann's film. *Romeo + Juliet* assumes and rewards sophisticated pop and high cultural literacies, a quality Jostein Gripsrud has dubbed "double access,"[7] one he identifies as a newly emergent form of class privilege; Luhrmann addresses the kind of viewer who can appreciate both Elizabethan verse and allusions to spaghetti westerns and Prince ballads. Rather than presenting Shakespeare as seamlessly congruent with pop culture, *Tromeo* insists upon their comic incommensurability, something particularly apparent in the gap between Shakespearean dialogue and contemporary teenspeak. To Juliet's observation that "Parting is such sweet sorrow," for example, Tromeo replies, "Yeah, it totally sucks." In short, *Tromeo* highlights and critiques the tacit decorum cast over Shakespeare by its cinematic "teening," a film style it presents as "popular" but which is in fact characteristic of an educated class-fraction capable of navigating freely between two registers of cultural literacy. The sardonic ending of *Tromeo and Juliet* makes its skewering of bourgeoisified Shakespeare particularly clear. Instead of Luhrmann's tragic ending in which the lovers are beatified by an ascending camera, Kaufmann pictures Tromeo and Juliet married, living in suburban New Jersey in the shadow of chemical plants with their mutant children, a savage parody of the middle-class happy ending.

Shakespeare in Love engages a rather different issue precipitated by the cinematic mainstreaming of Shakespeare in the 1990s. If that mainstreaming sought to transform Shakespeare's long-standing reputation as box-office poison, his new status as a commercial entertainer potentially jeopardized his status as an icon of Authorship – the "Bard" – and with it the very source of cultural authority that made Shakespeare an attractive object for film adaptation. *Shakespeare in Love* acknowledges – albeit ironically – Shakespeare's new home in the cinematic marketplace by recasting the Elizabethan world as a half-timbered Hollywood where the demand for a blockbuster breeds conventionalized writing, "love and a bit with a dog." As the film opens, Shakespeare is caught between the need for a hit and his desire to produce art on par with that of Marlowe, a double-bind that has rendered him creatively and physically impotent. His challenge is to pursue commercial success with a popular audience without compromising his potential to create "authentic" art capable of showing, in the words of Queen Elizabeth, "the very truth and nature of love." That authenticity he finds with Viola de Lessups, a poetry-loving beauty who is contracted by her father to marry Lord Wessex but who loves Shakespeare. Their passionate, doomed affair provides the basis for *Romeo and Juliet*, pushing Will out of formula comedies into the realm of romantic tragedy where, the film suggests, he finds his distinctive voice. Viola's dilemma doubles

Shakespeare's: she finds herself trapped by the marriage market that renders her artistic aspirations – her desire to act – inert and regards her as little more than chattel. If *Romeo and Juliet* has been rendered overfamiliar by seemingly endless citations, parodic and straight, of the balcony scene and the basic narrative of lovers divided by feuding, *Shakespeare in Love* seeks to revivify the play by giving it a biographical backstory, one more in line with contemporary romance and one which shuttles freely between two horizons of allusion, highbrow and pop cultural. But, additionally, using the *Romeo and Juliet* narrative as a parallel to the playwright's artistic plight suggests that Shakespeare's own play uncannily anticipates the problem of his unsettled cultural status in the age of the multiplex. Like Juliet and Viola, Shakespeare risks losing his authority to the demands of commerce.

Shakespeare in Love offers a spectacular recuperation of Shakespeare's artistic status with its presentation of a fictional opening performance of *Romeo and Juliet*, pictured as a runaway popular success with everyone from prostitutes and puritan preachers to the Queen herself. What gives the performance its power, the film suggests, is not only Shakespeare's writing but a novel element of the production, a woman (Viola) rather than a boy in the role of Juliet. For the film audience, that power is deepened by our knowledge that the lines Will and Viola exchange as Romeo and Juliet express their otherwise forbidden passion for each other. Unlike the Elizabethan audience, we filmgoers are able to witness the "real" romantic tragedy that lies behind the fictional stage narrative. To put this another way, this performance of *Romeo and Juliet* gains its authenticity and thus artistic authority to the extent that we perceive it leaves behind that distinctive mark of English Renaissance theatricality, the cross-dressed nature of women's roles, and instead accords with distinctive canons of mainstream cinematic performance: photographic naturalism (women in women's roles) and method acting (channeling "real" emotions through the fictional narrative).[8] Within the film, Queen Elizabeth stands in for the film spectator, aware, as the stage audience isn't, of Will and Viola's romance and of Viola's desire to break the stultifying limits on women's lives symbolized by cross-dressing. Elizabeth legitimizes Will as Author by recognizing that the power of his writing springs from his truthfulness to his own deeply felt experience, "reality" rather than stage convention or commercial formula. This embedded stage performance transmutes what has become the most clichéd and stagy of Shakespeare's plays into terms that (re)affirm Shakespeare's authority as a poet of love and that render his work more compatible with cinematic naturalism. It prepares for a more complete transmutation in the film's coda where the playwright's imagination is presented as fundamentally cinematic, the to-be-written opening page of *Twelfth Night* fading directly into the final widescreen shot of Viola striding westward, toward Hollywood.

The reinvention of Shakespeare as a filmmaker I've discussed here is part of a longer history of reinventing Shakespeare in each age's various self-images and favored media.[9] It is a process which began as early as the publication of Shakespeare's collected works in the 1623 First Folio, a volume boldly claiming that Shakespeare's stageplays could exist as a book for readers and that its author could be counted as a literary classic. For nearly 300 years since that publication, the Shakespeares of page and stage co-existed and competed on a variety of fronts for cultural primacy. That dynamic has been altered by last century's reinvention of Shakespeare as a filmmaker, a reinvention which by the 1990s came to seem decisive. The adaptation of Shakespeare to film is thus not simply another in a long line of reinventions, but a more fundamental alteration of his work and cultural meaning. Certainly the filming of Shakespeare promises to guarantee his continued cultural vigor in an arguably increasingly post-theatrical, post-literary age, and it may provide a means, as Méliès hoped it would at the beginning of the screen Shakespeare era, for gaining the Bard a genuinely global popularity. We should, however, reflect upon the potential limits and losses of this latest Shakespearean avatar, not out of nostalgia for some lost golden age of Shakespearean performance, but in recognition that the undeniable power of Shakespeare on film may contribute to the decline of the very medium – and with it certain notions of the "public" and particular forms of public culture – that makes Shakespeare Shakespeare. In the classroom we might make visible to students the ideological implications of film adaptation, highlighting larger-scale cultural and political processes of mediatization within which they are enmeshed. Shakespeare's adaptation to the screen testifies to modern popular culture's continued, albeit ambivalent, attraction to the resilient cultural authority of his works. But if Shakespeare has entered the twenty-first century reborn as a filmmaker, it behooves us not just to celebrate his cinematic popularity but to scrutinize it closely.

NOTES

1 Méliès's film is lost, though a detailed description of it, produced for the *Star* Film catalog, survives. See Robert Hamilton Ball, *Shakespeare on Silent Film: A Strange Eventful History* (New York: Theatre Arts Books, 1968), pp. 36–7.
2 See William Uricchio and Roberta E. Pearson, *Reframing Culture: The Case of the Vitagraph Quality Films*, Princeton: Princeton University Press, 1993, pp. 65–95, and Kennet Rothwell, *A History of Shakespeare on Screen*, 2nd edn. (Cambridge: Cambridge University Press, 2004), pp. 5–11. See Chapter 3 for a discussion of early cinema's desire to enhance the cultural value of the genre.

3 See Douglas Lanier, " 'Art thou base, common, and popular?': The Cultural Politics of Kenneth Branagh's *Hamlet*," in *Spectacular Shakespeare: Critical Theory and Popular Cinema*, ed. Lisa S. Starks and Courtney Lehmann (Madison, New Jersey: Fairleigh Dickinson University Press, 2002), pp. 149–71.

4 *Shakespeare on Film* (Bloomington: Indiana University Press, 1977), pp. 7–35.

5 Alan Sinfield, "Introduction: Reproductions, interventions," in *Political Shakespeare: New Essays in Cultural Materialism*, ed. Jonathan Dollimore and Alan Sinfield (Manchester: Manchester University Press, 1985), p. 131.

6 Whether the film medium can accomplish these goals is debatable. See Catherine Belsey, "Shakespeare and Film," *Literature/Film Quarterly* 11 (Spring 1983), 152–7; and Graham Holderness, "Radical Potentiality and Institutional Closure: Shakespeare in Film and Television," in *Political Shakespeare*, pp. 182–201.

7 " 'High Culture' Revisited," in *Cultural Theory and Popular Culture: A Reader*, ed. John Storey (Athens, Georgia: University of Georgia Press, 1998), pp. 536–7.

8 The link between cross-dressed women's roles and the purging of Shakespearean theatricality surfaces in two other films of the period, Michael Hoffman's *A Midsummer Night's Dream* (1999), where Francis Flute's doffing of his wig wins the day for the mechanicals in their performance before the Athenians, and Richard Eyre's *Stage Beauty* (2004), where an actress's performance of Desdemona's death sheds its source in cross-dressed artificiality when she and her co-star channel their antagonisms through the scene.

9 See Gary Taylor's *Reinventing Shakespeare: A Cultural History from the Restoration to the Present* (Oxford: Oxford University Press, 1991). Oddly, Taylor's discussion almost entirely excludes Shakespeare on screen.

5

LINDA V. TROOST

The nineteenth-century novel on film: Jane Austen

The nineteenth-century novel has been a staple of twentieth-century enter-tainment. For decades, film companies have been producing adaptations of novels by Charles Dickens, Emily and Charlotte Brontë, Jane Austen, Wilkie Collins, George Eliot, William Makepeace Thackeray, Anthony Trollope, and Henry James, as have television companies like the BBC and ITV. Why are these authors so popular? First of all, they tell good stories. They also have name recognition and prestigious cultural associations. They provide good visuals. Finally, their works are out of copyright.

Judging by the rate of production and consumption, both American and British audiences have an insatiable hunger for films with historical settings and films based on great books. For some, historical films and serials provide entertainment, allowing a temporary escape from a modern world of care, predictability, or dullness. For others, they provide fare more intellectual than the blockbuster films that dominate at the multiplex cinema. In parti-cular, they appeal to women (an audience that film companies have often neglected) with their foregrounding of relationships and women's issues. With the development of home VCR and DVD players, films and television serials have gained an extended life. No longer does a television adaptation vanish from the cultural consciousness after its broadcast. The success of newer adaptations even means a release on DVD of older versions, too. Thanks to the phenomenal reception of the 1995 *Pride and Prejudice* and *Sense and Sensibility*, the BBC and ITV Austen adaptations from the 1970s and early 1980s have been released in inexpensive DVD versions.

The approaches that screenwriters and directors take when adapting nineteenth-century novels to a large or small screen vary. These adaptations can be sorted into three general categories: (1) Hollywood-style adaptations, (2) Heritage-style adaptations, and (3) Fusion adaptations. Since Jane Austen's six novels have received a multitude of film and television treatments over the decades, examples drawn from various dramatizations of her novels will form the center of my discussion, with particular attention paid to *Pride and*

Prejudice, which provides examples in all categories. Had I more space, I would examine a fourth category, the Imitation. The Imitation uses a novel's plot and character but updates the setting to focus on a modern-day highly structured society. *Clueless* (1995) is the most notable example of this genre, but there are also recent versions of *Pride and Prejudice* set in modern India and Mormon Utah.

Hollywood-style adaptations

Early Hollywood films took incredible liberties with the plots and settings of classic novels, as if the book's audience and the film's audience had no overlap. For example, the silent version of Tolstoy's *Anna Karenina*, entitled *Love* (1927), limited by the strictures of production codes, featured an alternative ending for Americans in which Anna (Greta Garbo) marries Vronsky (John Gilbert). Such revisionist screenwriting is still with us, although the reasons for wholesale changes are different. Hawthorne's *The Scarlet Letter* underwent significant changes in 1995 to emerge as a politically correct film starring Demi Moore. Thackeray's *Vanity Fair* got sentimentalized in 2004 so that Becky Sharp, played by Reese Witherspoon, would seem more sympathetic.

MGM's 1940 film of *Pride and Prejudice* reveals Hollywood's cavalier tendency clearly. It was the first Austen work to reach the screen, and British novelist Aldous Huxley and American playwright Jane Murfin wrote the script.[1] Appearing as it did at the start of World War II and with British actors and a British screenwriter, it becomes a film designed to strengthen the British and American alliance at a fragile moment. Huxley and Murfin aim to make the England of the film into a world worth protecting and the characters of the film into people Americans can identify with (and eventually fight alongside). The director relocated the film to the 1830s so that costumes by noted designer Adrian would look more opulent and *Gone-with-the-Wind*-like. In the film, petticoats and giant bonnets abound. The overall impression is one of modest exuberance, a long way from the European decadence that scanty Regency garb might evoke. These are costumes that evoke solid morals and a strong character.

Filmed in a studio in black and white, the exterior shots were heavily decorated with paper flowers to give the romantic impression of "Britain as a garden perpetually in bloom."[2] The score evokes Olde England by excerpting tunes like the sixteenth-century madrigal "Now is the Month of Maying" and the eighteenth-century song "Flow Gently Sweet Afton" to evoke a pleasant, rural past. The May Day party at Netherfield (a scene fabricated for the film) also "idealizes the British common people and reminds the spectator of common British pastimes," such as dancing around a maypole and shooting a longbow, and reminds the viewer of "the charm of British rural traditions."[3] This is not an England full of arrogant rich snobs, but a delightful place peopled with madcap, non-threatening characters.

The class problem is also defused. Elizabeth Bennet describes herself as middle class (and therefore a typical American), and we never see Pemberley, which would make Darcy's upper-class background very obvious. He gets over his snobbery very quickly, of course, to show us that rich Brits are plain folks just like Yanks and have a sense of humor, too. Lady Catherine de Bourgh's role also is radically altered for this reason. (Actress Edna Mae Oliver also stipulated in all her contracts that she play only sympathetic characters.) Reshaped into a romantic representative of egalitarian democracy, Lady Catherine only tries to thwart Elizabeth's possible marriage to Darcy to test her affection for him – Lady Catherine is fully behind the marriage of her aristocratic nephew to Mr. Bennet's middle-class daughter and is anxious to do whatever needs to be done to advance it.

The 1996 Miramax *Emma* is very much the same kind of jolly film as the MGM *Pride and Prejudice*. Hollywood style requires beautiful stars, and it is hard to find a more beautiful Emma than Gwyneth Paltrow or a younger Mr. Knightley than Jeremy Northam. The film is eye and ear candy: lush lawns, elegant interiors and exteriors, Vermeer-like pictorial shots, highly expressive music, and witty dialogue. However, this world is just as much a fantasy England as that portrayed in the MGM Garson–Olivier film fifty-five years earlier.

The fantasy is not that of Merrie England; rather it is the England of Laura Ashley. The costumes are impressionistic versions of Regency style designed by Ruth Myers, not usually associated with period films. The dresses, especially those worn by the star, look stunning, but they are not modeled on contemporary fashion prints of the time. Emma and Harriet frequently go outside hatless, gloveless, and in short-sleeved dresses, behavior that would have astonished Austen, raised in an era when ladies guarded their skin from the sun. The locations are chosen more for their impact on a wide cinema screen than for their authenticity. The large tent on the Westons' lawn, complete with two outdoor fishbowls on Chinese red stands, is highly amusing and attractive, but unlikely. The elegant Adams interiors at Hartfield would be more appropriate in a Duke's house than Mr. Woodhouse's (in fact, some of Hartfield's interiors were filmed at Syon House).

The general mood of the film also marks its Hollywood style. It is exuberant, with clever editing and juxtaposing of scenes, quick cuts, fast-paced dialogue, and a delightful musical score that manages to sound neither anachronistic nor period – it creates its own time. As in many older films, *Emma*'s score tells the viewer how to interpret a character or scene. It substitutes for the omniscient narrator.[4] For example, woodwind instruments signal the arrival of comic characters such as the Eltons. We know, therefore, not to take them seriously. Music also projects emotion. During the ball at the Crown Inn, we hear dance music as Emma looks anxiously at Harriet, the wallflower. However, the moment Mr. Knightley asks Harriet to join him in the set, the music of the five-member band swells into that of a much larger and richer symphony. One cannot fail to interpret Emma's happiness at that moment. It is not subtle, but it works.

Most important, Hollywood style requires the showcasing of a star. The camera favors Paltrow in most shots, and the plot focuses almost entirely on Emma's concerns and point of view. Jane Fairfax almost disappears, and many minor characters either vanish or turn into comic caricatures, especially Miss Bates, Mr. Elton, and Harriet. The portrait of a community that Austen presented turns into a film about one member of that community. Looks matter, too. Although the novel describes Harriet as radiantly beautiful and Emma as merely "handsome," Toni Collette as Harriet is distinctly plain. She is plump, freckled, and clumsy, a foil for the slim, pale, and elegant Paltrow. The Miramax *Emma* is no ensemble piece striving for an authentic interpretation of a great novel; it is a star vehicle in the best Hollywood tradition.

Heritage-style adaptations

At the other extreme from Hollywood-style fantasy worlds are the British television serials that pride themselves on their historical authenticity. For many novel readers, the serials are the most satisfying examples of books on film. The form has many advantages. A film can run only about two hours; a TV serial can occupy five or six hours, thereby allowing more of the plot to be retained. A film needs a three-act structure; a serial can incorporate the many climaxes that naturally mark a multi-volume nineteenth-century novel. Most people think first of BBC Television when it comes to serials, and for good reason. The BBC started broadcasting The Classic Serial starting in 1951, an offshoot of their radio dramatizations.[5] In fact, this origin hints at the dialogue-heavy nature of the serials and their concern with fidelity to the original works. In 1967, with *The Forsyte Saga*, BBC dramatizations moved from live broadcast to videotape, which opened up a lucrative overseas market for the BBC and for the commercial television companies who also produced serials.[6] In time, this overseas market would become a major force behind the production of new serials.

These early dramatizations, to use the term preferred in the early years, were especially noted for their meticulous adherence to plot, characterization, and setting, but they lack sparkle, partly because of this fidelity. The BBC did extensive research, so the sets, props and costumes were historically accurate and have a distinctive look. In the 1972 BBC adaptation of Austen's *Emma*, for example, the characters had what looked like unwashed hair, all in an attempt to simulate Regency hygiene – bouncy, shiny hair is a modern development.[7] The costumes in this serial are beautifully made, but the authentic color combinations sometimes look garish to modern eyes. Also, the early productions use very conservative filming techniques. Shot largely on sets with fixed cameras, BBC serials mostly show interior scenes, straying only rarely to location. For the same reason, they are thin on wide-angle shots (as for landscapes or crowd scenes), tracking shots (those that follow a character as he or she moves), and long shots (for distant objects). Since they do not use background music and the pacing is very slow, there are numerous long silences. Takes are longer than we are accustomed to, and contribute to the leisurely pace of the narrative. Granada Television produced a version of *Persuasion* in 1971 that was equally relaxed in pace but occasionally used moving cameras and location shots (in Lyme Regis and Bath), which gives their serial a bit more vibrancy than a BBC production. But Granada did not always get the period details right. For example, Anne Elliot's hairstyle is noticeably contemporary, not period. In short, viewers had two choices: accurate, authentic, and slightly dull dramatizations or more filmic but less accurate ones.

It was not long, though, before film directors began to adopt the serials' standards for historical correctness and strive for a period feel. Stanley Kubrick's adaptation of Thackeray's *Barry Lyndon* in 1975 was notable for using only real locations, not sets, and for shooting all scenes with natural light – candles or sunlight only – in an effort to recreate the eighteenth century. This necessitated the use of special camera lenses, but his innovation changed the way costume drama would be filmed in the future. Merchant Ivory Productions became a household name when, in 1979, it adopted some of these production values for James's *The Europeans*. James Ivory, the director, recognized that this was a landmark film for the company:

> Most of the talented, highly disciplined, and extremely knowledgeable crew ... had been trained at the BBC ... [They] had taken almost an archaeological, or a scientifically detached approach to the film's overall design, which made it stand out at a time when most period films – particularly ones made in America – looked pretty sloppy. For instance, in this film the actresses, as a matter of course, were required to be tightly laced up into corsets with stays (which made them stand, walk, and sit right), and were not allowed to fiddle with their own makeup, or to surreptitiously put on lipstick or eye shadow, etc. or dictate how

their hair would be dressed … I heard the costume designer and hairdressers collaboratively discussing "the line" – that all-important silhouette that ran from the top of an actor's (or actress's) correctly coiffed head, to the tips of his (or her) shoes, which defined the historical period exactly to within a year or two.[8]

With *The Europeans*, Merchant Ivory Productions established a new era in adaptations of novels on film and went on to dominate this style of historical film for over a decade. They combined historical accuracy and artistic filming, something that not been done before in novel adaptations.

In the same year as the first Merchant Ivory period film, the BBC, who had been losing ground to commercial stations like Granada, produced, in tandem with the Australian Broadcasting Commission, a serial in the Merchant Ivory style. *Pride and Prejudice*, with screenplay by Fay Weldon, was broadcast in January 1980, just after the rise of Margaret Thatcher and the establishment of the first National Heritage Act. This serial is often seen as the start of "heritage drama" even though it was only following established BBC methods with regard to period style. It does, however, adopt many filmic techniques that give the production a greater visual sophistication. Cyril Coke, the director, had access to cameras that could track, pan, and zoom, and the moving camera gives this serial an energy the earlier ones lack. An original musical score underlies many of the scenes without dialogue, eliminating the long silences of past. Most significant, this production has many scenes filmed on location in Lincolnshire and Derbyshire that showcase the English landscape and period house, inside and out.

In the past several years, there has been some debate on whether heritage drama has been good or bad for England's image.[9] Many critics have complained that serials like *Pride and Prejudice* give a skewed view of English life by privileging the upper class, showing a monocultural society, indulging in nostalgia for an England that never existed, and espousing conservative, Thatcherite values. Others complain that problems result from commercialization, that Austen becomes a mere marketer of "heritage products."[10] Unlike the earlier Austen serials, the 1979 *Pride and Prejudice* is the first to be filmed largely on location, so many of its props and sets are genuine heritage artifacts, not reproductions from the BBC scene shop. As a result, they have an aura about them that cannot help but attract the director's and viewer's eye.

The disadvantage of such authenticity, however, is that the objects and possessions can become disproportionately important, displacing characters or ideas. Andrew Higson observes that

> Many of the films include set-piece celebratory events, lavish dinner parties or balls, for instance, which provide plenty of opportunities for filling the frame

with splendid costumes and hair-dos, tableware and food. Equally frequently, conversations take place against a backdrop of picturesque semi-rural southern English scenery, or the frontage of some magnificent castle, stately home, or quaint cottage, the types of ancient architectural and landscape properties conserved by the National Trust and English Heritage.[11]

What is wrong with this? It distracts from the story: "Though narrative meaning and narratorial clarity are rarely sacrificed, these shots, angles and camera movements frequently seem to exceed narrative motivation. The effect is to transform narrative space into heritage space: that is, a space for the display of heritage properties rather than for the enactment of dramas."[12]

Surface cannot help but seem like substance when the camera lingers lovingly over period houses, wineglasses, china, food, and costumes, as if these objects conferred moral value upon their possessors through the power of age, beauty, and association with upper-class culture. However, Austen does exactly this in her novel. Just as Rosings, with its garish furniture and expensive mantelpiece exemplifies Lady Catherine's moral worth – or rather, lack of it – so does Pemberley exemplify Darcy's moral value. The visit to Pemberley is a key moment in the novel, and it depends on examining heritage space – there is no avoiding it. Elizabeth's tour of the estate and its gardens brings her face to face with Darcy's heritage: "brother, a landlord, a master ... how many people's happiness were in his guardianship! – How much of pleasure or pain it was in his power to bestow! – How much of good or evil must be done by him!"[13]

Although Austen's novel hints that Pemberley is probably in the eighteenth-century style, the 1979 production makes Pemberley a Jacobean house (Renishaw Hall, home of the Sitwells). In fact, the filmed version does not fit especially well with what Austen presents in the novel. This ancient space – old even to tourists in the Regency – with its ancient contents and loyal retainers, helps explicate Darcy for Elizabeth, but the explication is different to the viewer. The gardeners, housekeepers, and footmen in powdered wigs remind us of the staff that stately homes require. The suit of armor in the front hall underscores the age of the house and speaks of service to the Tudor/Stuart court and the nation – before the days of constitutional monarchy and other advances. We are never allowed to forget that Darcy is aristocratic. Although there are some rooms in Pemberley that exhibit a more modern style, the overall effect of the house is serious; it is overwhelmed and weighed down with "heritage products" to make a point.

Nor do the Italian gardens of Renishaw match Austen's description of Pemberley's Capability Brown grounds. Instead, the serial shows us a formal garden, with tightly clipped yews and geometric shapes. The viewer only receives reinforcement about Darcy as a stiff, stern man and misses much of his softer side. This may explain why the director gave Darcy a large, soulful-eyed dog, which can project an image of his lovableness, and with which Elizabeth can interact, but on the whole, the entire Pemberley sequence sends mixed signals to the viewer. Even as it seems to display English heritage to us, it simultaneously critiques it.[14]

Fusion adaptations

By 1995 and 1996, however, when a great wave of Austen adaptations appeared, British life and values had changed a great deal. Thatcher's government left its mark and Blair's tried to bring Britain down a new path. The BBC expanded its mission beyond providing education and culture to the nation – it now needed to be financially self-sufficient. And television companies discovered that there was money to be made in selling British Heritage to overseas markets. Like Britain, the serials and telefilms also changed. Faithfulness to the novel was no longer paramount. What mattered now was an ability to connect with a broad range of viewers, tell a good story and show compelling images. In short, Hollywood style and British heritage style fused.

The BBC first tried such a fusion in 1986 on Austen's *Northanger Abbey*, with limited success. Instead of doing a faithful dramatization with strong heritage values and conservative filming techniques, they tackled something more edgy. First of all, *Northanger Abbey* is a two-hour telefilm, not a serial. The costuming is a mixture of authentic style and 1980s punk, and the characters often veer into the surreal. Isabella and John Thorpe, in particular, seem menacing in overblown costumes, strong colors, and blowzy wigs. The film story is dominated by the Gothic material that only forms a small part of the novel, and it all seems much less Catherine's imaginings than reality. The film seems to have missed some of the satire of the novel to become a horror picture, complete with masochistic dream sequences and filming worthy of Expressionist cinema. Bizarre characters appear, such as a heavily made-up foreign marquesa with a black page. Historical accuracy goes out the window, as Catherine and John Thorpe indulge in mixed-sex bathing in the Roman Baths and General Tilney keeps a Harris's hawk (an American bird) as a pet. This production was a departure for the BBC and ahead of its time. For those viewers used to staid serials, it must have been quite a shock.

After *Pride and Prejudice*, Hollywood did not pick up Jane Austen until Emma Thompson's 1995 adaptation of *Sense and Sensibility* for Columbia Pictures, a fusion production directed by Ang Lee. It was studded with stars, and those who were not already stars soon became them. The script departs from the novel in many ways, exaggerating social difference for the benefit of viewers not familiar with the book. In the film, the Dashwood women are much poorer than they are in the novel. In the film, Marianne gives up her pianoforte out of poverty but Colonel Brandon sends it to her later as an anonymous gift (a scene borrowed from *Emma*). Most obviously, Thompson remakes several major characters. Of the four main characters, only Elinor Dashwood maintains a sense of Austen's original. Marianne, the voice of sensibility, is made sympathetic instead of an object of satire; Edward Ferrars, one of Austen's dullest heroes, becomes witty and charming; and Colonel Brandon, a most unprepossessing man in the novel, becomes a Byronic hero to die for. Even minor characters get a rewrite: the novel's Mrs. Dashwood and little Margaret are very silly; in the film, both become voices of optimism. Radical feminist and economic issues are prominently foregrounded even as the film paradoxically endorses the conservative concept of marriage as a woman's goal in life.[15]

Despite its mixed political agenda, *Sense and Sensibility* remains true to the tradition of heritage drama in spite of its American producers. For example, all the locations are appropriate and the livestock are historic breeds. No modern plants flower in the background.[16] Costumers Jenny Beavan and John Bright characterize effectively through accurate period clothing. For example, Fanny Dashwood's flashy, colorful costumes reveal her shallowness, just as Marianne's simple but elegant dresses reveal her good taste. In the London ball scene, each of the 100 extras has a distinct characterization, "from soldiers and lawyers to fops and dowagers."[17] The location shift from grand Norland Park to humble Barton Cottage makes quite obvious how much these women have come down in the world through no fault of their own. Costume and location do much to delineate class and status in this film.

But the film really succeeds because the focus of the movie stays on the relationships the characters have with each other, not on social commentary. Thompson's revisions make us feel the anguish of Marianne, Willoughby, and Colonel Brandon, something Austen's novel keeps at a distance. We feel for the plight of the Dashwood women as they lose their home and learn to live on a few hundred pounds a year, sometimes without heat or meat. We weep with Elinor as she tries to coax her sister back from the edge of death. The film demands an emotional investment from the viewer.

1995 was a full year for Austen adaptations. The BBC came out with two adaptations in the same year that *Sense and Sensibility* was released. Both were successful because they, too, found the right balance between heritage values and entertainment needs. *Persuasion*, a telefilm, is the more traditional, somewhat in the style of the 1979 *Pride and Prejudice*. Except for the ending, it is faithful to the novel and thick with authenticity: candlelight, unwashed hair, heritage livestock, rain, blood sports. The ending, however is peculiar and breaks the tone of the film. As the lovers kiss in public (something that even Lindsay Doran dared not introduce in *Sense and Sensibility*), a Fellini-esque circus parade inexplicably appears in the middle of Bath. Just before the credits, we see Anne on board ship with Frederick Wentworth, belying his comment in the novel that wives do not belong on ships (in this film world, apparently, women get their way). The BBC had learned its lesson with *Northanger Abbey* and toned down the unfaithful material, but they kept enough to heighten the emotional impact that a good film needs.

The other BBC production from the same year outshone the small-scale *Persuasion* and made Jane Austen a household name even in non-bookish households. *Pride and Prejudice*, as adapted by Andrew Davies, ignited Darcymania in Britain, to the benefit of both Austen and purveyors of heritage products.[18] Also following the newer tradition of looser links to fidelity, Davies brought to the surface Darcy's smouldering passion for Elizabeth, always kept in the background of the novel itself. The camera often lingers on Darcy, now the object of the gaze – standing on a staircase, by a window, in a bathtub, pulling off his neckcloth – and we sense the sexual frustration he feels. His emotion climaxes in the most famous invented scene in the serial, when Darcy dives into a pond at Pemberley as if to cool his ardour.

The summer after the serial aired, Lyme Park, the National Trust property that served as Pemberley, was jammed with hundreds of paying visitors, anxious to see that pond. The earlier production of *Pride and Prejudice* showcased heritage objects; this adaptation instead showcased southern England's green and pleasant landscape, Derbyshire's rugged and wind-blown one and Pemberley's ponds. Ironically, the success of both *Pride and Prejudice* and *Sense and Sensibility* rested on their *infidelity* to Austen's novels and departure from traditional "adaptation" filming methods. Both attracted larger audiences than others had done precisely because they reconceived the books as highly visual films rather than chatty dramatizations of novels – but they knew just how far to push things.

For *Pride and Prejudice*, costuming, editing, and dialogue were central to the serial's appeal. Both Darcy and Elizabeth dressed to enhance their sexuality, not something BBC viewers were accustomed to in dramatizations. Jennifer Ehle as Elizabeth had a voluptuous charm enhanced by a corset; Colin Firth had the famous breeches. The quick cuts and lavish use of locations also gives the film a great deal of life. For example, the opening 120 seconds of the serial depict, to a lively piano accompaniment and minimal dialogue, at least twelve different scenes: Bingley and Darcy riding, Bingley and Darcy admiring Netherfield from horseback, a shot of

Netherfield, Lizzy admiring them, Lizzy running down a path, Lizzy walking past a mare and colt, Lizzy walking in a lane, the exterior of Longbourne, three different interiors of Longbourne, and the exterior of the Meryton church. The montage we see as Darcy reads his letter contains fourteen different locations, quite a dense visual treat. The dialogue is also fast paced, largely because, unlike earlier screenwriters, Davies does not use much of the novel's dialogue. Instead, he writes lines that *sound* as though they came from the novel, such as Elizabeth's comment to Jane: "I'll end an old maid and teach your ten children to embroider cushions and play their instruments very ill." It sounds like Austen, but it isn't Austen. The adaptation succeeded largely because it was not an adaptation in the old style; it incorporates filmic elements and broke the obsession with fidelity that had dominated Austen serials for decades.

Another adaptation came out in 1999 that carried the fusion style to an extreme. Patricia Rozema's *Mansfield Park*, jointly produced by Miramax and the BBC, presents a version of the novel filtered through the lens of postcolonial literary criticism. It offers up all the expected heritage features, but with a twist. We see the Price residence in Portsmouth, complete with bugs, reminding us that not all lived in fine period houses. Mansfield Park itself (Kirby Hall) is cold and inhospitable, like its family, lacking much furniture or any drapes, carpets, or paintings. One of the earliest scenes shows a ship seen in the harbor carrying slaves, a reminder of the source of the Bertram family's wealth: a sugar plantation in Antigua. Other scenes bring the brutality of British colonialism to the fore as Fanny looks with horror through Tom's sketchbook of Antigua life and recoils from scenes depicting Sir Thomas raping and beating slaves.[19] Since Edward Said's publication in 1993 of *Culture and Imperialism*, the issue of slavery in Austen's novel has been a central topic among literary critics, and the film underscores this critical concern, determined to be up to date.

The film's biggest challenge is making the protagonist likable. Rozema ends up doing to Fanny Price what Emma Thompson did to Edward Ferrars: she remakes the character into someone more appealing. Meek Fanny Price is now a satirist, rebel, and writer, modeled on Jane Austen herself, a character who directly addresses the camera as the author of her own tale. The modern filmic techniques go beyond anything seen before in an Austen adaptation. Rozema uses the camera symbolically, in modernist style. Movement itself represents freedom: we see birds flying and cameras swooping, complementing the ideas in the film that emphasize the freedom of a woman to choose her own life and mate. Chiaroscuro plays a large role in the look of the film, underlying the darkness of Mansfield Park and, by extension, the moral darkness of its patriarch Sir Thomas Bertram, slave-owner. But despite the heavy political agenda the film carries, Austen's satiric wit is, if anything, stronger in the film than in the novel. Fanny's cheeky comments to the viewing audience keep the tone from sinking into earnestness, but it is precisely this mixed tone that may have disturbed audiences. Admittedly, the book has always been problematic, treating Fanny at times with a satiric touch, and at other times positioning her as the exemplar of moral clarity. There is no reason to think that a film version would be any less problematic.

In keeping with the revolutionary tone of the production, Andrea Galer's costumes show "the Regency without poofiness." Frivolous characters like Maria and Julia wear overtrimmed, fussy dresses, and the glamorous, amoral Crawfords wear high-fashion clothes that push the edge of propriety: Mary's necklines are a bit lower than everyone else's and Henry's breeches a bit tighter than strictly required. Fanny herself often dresses in severe, dark riding habits, setting herself apart from the rest of the group and establishing her identity as an independent spirit. None of the costumes are incorrect, however, and in her quest for authenticity to the period, if not to Austen, Rozema even hired researchers to check the dialogue for anachronism and a protocol expert "to assure that no niceties of the time were too severely trampled."[20] But there is no denying that Rozema's film trampled on the protocol of Austen adaptations by introducing a heavy-handed political message and, therefore, had some trouble finding an audience. Those who loved the heritage aspects of *Pride and Prejudice* recoiled from the stark grittiness of this film; those who liked stark grittiness tended not to watch costume drama.

Joe Wright's 2005 *Pride and Prejudice* for Working Title Films, a production company better known for contemporary ensemble pieces like *Four Weddings and a Funeral* and *Love Actually* than historical drama, also evokes this slightly gritty, more realist style. In the first feature film of *Pride and Prejudice* since 1940, the *mise-en-scène* is moved to 1797, the year Austen wrote *First Impressions*, no doubt to avoid comparison with the very famous costumes (and cleavages) in the 1995 BBC serial. The camera angles and use of zoom lenses are, the director notes, "in the tradition of British realism" and are designed to give a sense of "movement" and to avoid the feeling of a painting, of the "picturesque."[21] Despite the period dress and the obligatory location shots, the look of the film is contemporary: Elizabeth slouches around in dark frocks instead of standing erect in pale gowns, and her hair is constantly mussed, thereby minimizing the fussy, dandified look that some associate with Regency England. The director has aimed for "the mess of real life" instead of "the chocolate-box."[22] Even the men have modern hair, also untidy. "This is the muddy-hem version," notes screenwriter Deborah Moggach.[23] This *Pride and Prejudice* aims to attract a very different audience – teenagers – who will gravitate toward a film that looks superficially like *Pirates of the Caribbean* crossed with *Wuthering Heights*: an edgy heroine in stays (Keira Knightley) meets a broody hero in a long coat (Matthew Macfadyen) – the music swells as emotions boil and the fog thickens. It is, of course, peopled with stars of stage and screen, such as Dame Judi Dench and Donald Sutherland, who will interest older viewers, but its style hopes to attract the youthful audience that loved *The Princess Bride*, the audience that actually goes to movie theaters, rather than the older audience more likely to stay at home and watch, for the hundredth time, a DVD of Colin Firth diving into the pond.

To appeal to this new demographic, one largely unfamiliar with the novels and even the 1995 adaptation, Austen's verbal satire vanishes, to be replaced by jokey or naughty one-liners from the mouths of comic or minor characters. For example, the trailer teases us with impropriety. A voice states "The Bennet sisters were looking for husbands – " and the film cuts to the Rev. Collins in a pulpit saying "– which are only to be obtained through intercourse." Obviously, teenagers viewing this film will be safe from "high culture"; they can expect just "fun." The low humor coexists with PG-rated romantic angst, exemplified by lovers in the rain or fog, looking earnest and tortured but never kissing. It is a different fantasy version of England than that projected in the Miramax *Emma*, but it is also obviously another vehicle designed to showcase a very young, photogenic star. It may not be a very complex adaptation, but it still may bring a few new readers to the novel.

Conclusion

As the world moves toward greater complexity and impersonality, we have begun to rediscover the delights and uses of the past. Serial and film versions of nineteenth-century novels have helped feed that interest, showing a time when things were different – not necessarily better, merely different. The heritage business has also fed into this new interest. National Trust and English Heritage properties have enjoyed a surge of visitors, largely because of expanded ideas about heritage and also because of the appearance of their properties in filmed versions of great British novels. But heritage is no longer just period wine glasses, elegant gowns and stately homes; it now includes the life and work of the serving classes, rural life and industrial sites. The serials and films reflect that change, too. The new fusion style of novel adaptation does more than combine Hollywood's needs for entertainment with heritage drama's preoccupation with accuracy of presentation. Fusion film incorporates a larger and more complex picture of a novel's world than even the novelist may have considered and thereby allows modern viewers a safe arena in which to explore difficult ideas that still have relevance: "contemporary anxieties and fantasies of national identity, sexuality, class, and power."[24] And, to paraphrase Horace, if it can entertain us at the same time, so much the better.

NOTES

1 Kenneth Turan, "*Pride and Prejudice*: An Informal History of the Garson–Olivier Motion Picture," *Persuasions* 11 (1989), 140–3.
2 Ellen Belton, "Reimagining Jane Austen: The 1940 and 1995 Film Versions of *Pride and Prejudice*" in *Jane Austen on Screen*, ed. Gina and Andrew Macdonald (Cambridge: Cambridge University Press, 2003), p. 182.
3 Belton, "Reimagining Jane Austen," p. 182.
4 For a further discussion of the function of music, see Chapter 14 in this volume.
5 For a thorough history of the classic serial, see Robert Giddings and Keith Selby, *The Classic Serial on Television and Radio* (London: Palgrave Macmillan, 2001).
6 Giddings and Selby, *The Classic Serial*, p. 27.
7 For a study of this serial's production and methods, see Monica Lauritzen, *Jane Austen's Emma on Television: A Study of a BBC Classic Serial* (Göteborg: Acta Universitatis Gothoburgensis, 1981).
8 James Ivory, "Director's Comments: *The Europeans*," *Merchant Ivory Productions: Filmography*, www.merchantivory.com/europeans.html.
9 A good summary of the arguments on both sides can be found in the first two chapters of Andrew Higson's *English Cinema, English Heritage: Costume Drama Since 1980* (Oxford: Oxford University Press, 2003).
10 Roger Sales, *Jane Austen and Representations of Regency England* (London: Routledge, 1994), pp. 17–27.
11 Higson, *English Cinema*, p. 40.
12 Ibid., p. 39.
13 Jane Austen, *Pride and Prejudice*, ed. Vivien Jones (London: Penguin, 1996), p. 240.
14 See my "Filming Tourism, Filming Pemberley," *Eighteenth-Century Fiction* 18.4 (Summer 2006), 477–98, for a discussion of Weldon's adaptation.
15 For discussions on the conservative–radical debate in Austen's fiction and the films, especially in *Sense and Sensibility*, see Julian North's "Conservative Austen, Radical Austen: *Sense and Sensibility*" in *Adaptations: From Text to Screen, Screen to Text*, ed. Deborah Cartmell and Imelda Whelehan (London: Routledge, 1999), pp. 38–50, and the following essays from *Jane Austen in Hollywood*, ed. Linda Troost and Sayre Greenfield (Lexington: University Press of Kentucky, 1998, 2001): Rebecca Dickson, "Misrepresenting Jane Austen's Ladies: Revising Texts (and History) to Sell Films," pp. 44–57, Kristin Flieger Samuelian, " 'Piracy is Our Only Option': Postfeminist Intervention in *Sense and Sensibility*," pp. 148–58, and Devoney Looser, "Feminist Implications of the Silver Screen Austen," pp. 159–76.
16 A field chosen in the autumn proved to be full of yellow flowers in the spring, when filming started. The plant (probably canola) was identified as "not period,"

but producer Lindsay Doran saw no problem with this. Only when Hugh Grant refused to do the scene because of the plants did she reluctantly concede and change the location. (L. Doran, talk given at the Jane Austen Society of North American annual meeting, Los Angeles, 9 October 2004.)

17 Emma Thompson, *The Sense and Sensibility Diaries* (New York: Newmarket; London: Bloomsbury, 1996), p. 258.

18 See Andrew Davies on his view of Darcymania in Chapter 16 in this volume.

19 Interested readers should see Joseph Lew's essay "'That Abominable Traffic': *Mansfield Park* and the Dynamics of Slavery" in *History, Gender, and Eighteenth-Century Literature*, ed. Beth Fowkes Tobin (Athens: University of Georgia Press, 1994), pp. 271–300. In particular, his discussion of connections drawn in 1802 between slave ownership and moral/sexual degeneracy suggests to me that Austen may very well have understood what Rozema was trying to convey through Tom's violent artworks.

20 *"Mansfield Park* Press Pack," New York: Miramax Pictures, 1999, pp. 29–30.

21 Joe Wright, quoted in Joanna Briscoe, "A Costume Drama with Muddy Hems," *Times Online*, 31 July 2005, www.thetimes.co.uk.

22 Joe Wright, quoted in Caroline McGhie, "A house in want of a fortune," *Telegraph Online*, 24 August 2005, www.telegraph.co.uk.

23 Quoted in Briscoe, "A costume drama with muddy hems."

24 Higson, *English Cinema*, p. 28.

6

MARTIN HALLIWELL

Modernism and adaptation

Film adaptation has always had a love–hate relationship with literary modernism. A creative union seemed almost certain in the 1910s and 1920s, though. Modernist writers were fascinated with visual media; German theorist Walter Benjamin proclaimed film the definitive modern form; and the modernist magazine *Close Up* (1927–33) was forging aesthetic links between film and literary culture "from the angles of art, experiment, and possibility."[1] The energies of literary and cinematic modernism in the years either side of World War I promised an imaginative movement beyond the limits of written and visual forms. Many modernist writers could be "profoundly cinematic even when not fully cognizant of it"; filmmakers such as D. W. Griffith, Georges Méliès and Eric von Stroheim were drawn to the written word because it lent early cinema aesthetic validity; and two 1928 versions of *The Fall of the House of Usher* by French director Jean Epstein and American team James Sibley Watson Jr. and Melville Webber showed what could be achieved by transforming Edgar Allan Poe's gothic tale into visually provocative cinema.[2]

However, when it comes to cinematic adaptations of modernist fiction filmmakers have often found themselves faced with major technical problems. Critics Gilberto Perez and Sam Girgus have argued that these problems derive from the way in which modernist culture exacerbates the tension between film as a "reflective" form (representing and documenting) and a "creative" medium (reworking and transforming).[3] This tension is true of all adaptations, but is particularly acute within the framework of modernism for three main reasons. First, the commercial pressures on mainstream cinematic production have historically (at least since the early 1930s) demanded slick products that do not challenge viewers, whereas high literary modernism demands scrupulous attention from readers. Second, the interest among modernist writers in unreliable narrators, psychologically complex characters, fragmented perceptions, and mythical allusions are devices that rarely translate smoothly into film without technical complication or dilution of creative intent. And, third, the modernist disdain of bourgeois culture does not sit comfortably with the liberal ideology that is usually upheld in commercial film.

In order to explore these issues, this chapter will discuss a range of examples from both sides of the Atlantic which demonstrates the problems and creative risks that have arisen in adapting modernist fiction. Historically the solution to the problems of adapting modernist texts has been the tactic of general avoidance, with the nineteenth-century realist novel, naturalistic drama, and genre-based fiction offering easier routes to adaptation. This has been more prevalent in the United States than in Europe, where the dominant tenets of classical Hollywood film – seamless worlds, linear narratives, a stable hierarchy of characters, humanist ideology, and tidy resolutions – have offered quite a different trajectory to that taken by most modernist writers. Even though the American modernists William Faulkner, Nathanael West, and John Steinbeck were employed by Hollywood studios as screenwriters in the 1930s and 1940s, adaptations of their most challenging novels were rare, with producers and directors more often excited by the prospect of adapting realist fiction.

Adapting modernist fiction

William Faulkner offers a classic illustration of the stand-off between the US film industry and literary modernism. Following two decades as a published novelist, Faulkner was drawn to Hollywood in 1932, where he worked periodically through the 1930s and 1940s as a screenwriter, initially for MGM and later for Twentieth-Century Fox and Warner Brothers, with credits for films such as *To Have and Have Not* (1944) and *The Big Sleep* (1946). The first film that Faulkner worked on at MGM with director Howard Hawks, *Today We Live* (1933), was an adaptation of his own short story "Turn About," but most of his work was strictly of a contractual nature. Tom Dardis notes that Faulkner's fiction was not in high demand in the 1940s; only after he received the Nobel Prize for Literature in 1949 were studios drawn to adapting his work.[4] Even then, the big studios were interested in his more realistic fiction such as his 1948 novel *Intruder in the Dust* (Clarence Brown, 1949) and *The Hamlet* (1940), adapted as *The Long Hot Summer* (Martin Ritt, 1958), rather than his experimental phase of modernist writing from 1929 to 1936.

Twentieth-Century Fox did make one attempt to adapt the most technically difficult of Faulkner's novels, *The Sound and the Fury* (Martin Ritt, 1959), but the studio shied away from its most challenging elements, with producer Jerry Wald striving for narrative economy and screenwriters Irving

Ravetch and Harriet Frank Jr. reordering events and editing out the psychologically complex sections. The screenwriters also ensured that two of the
chief characters have redeeming qualities: unlike Faulkner's novel the tor-
mented brother Quentin Compson (John Beal) does not commit suicide and
the sadistic Jason (Yul Brynner) is granted the capacity to love.

The chief difficulty in this adaptation is that Faulkner's *The Sound and the
Fury* is told from four different perspectives (three sections are in the first-
person and the last in the third-person), with the idiot brother Benjy's "voice"
the first that the reader encounters. This perspectival technique is avoided in
the film because it makes for a disorienting sequence of events, with very
little establishing material. Not only this, but Benjy's voice is entirely muted
in the film, in contrast to the novel where the reader has access to his sense
impressions and his frustrated attempts to speak. Actor Jack Warden
struggled to render Benjy's psychic confusion and resorted to heavy-handed
techniques such as wearing a placard advertising a local freak-show to
emphasize his character's idiocy. As such, it is hard to detect Faulkner's
modernist novel as the source text of Martin Ritt's film. This is not a problem
in its own right, but critic Bruce Kawain argues that the studio missed a trick
with the adaptation. Whereas Faulkner was forced to translate Benjy's
interior thoughts into words, Kawain argues that the film might have conveyed his sense impressions through "visual montage."[5] On this argument
Faulkner's problem of finding words for Benjy's unspoken thoughts would
not have arisen: "the viewer could simply *see* that Benjy was young or old,
near a pasture or outside a barn."[6]

When Hollywood has worked within the terms of the modernist novel it
has often led to uneven responses, such as the three cinematic adaptations of
Fitzgerald's *The Great Gatsby* (1926, 1949, and 1974). Critic Wheeler
Dixon argues that "not one of Fitzgerald's novels has been brought to the
screen with a true sense of fidelity to the original source material" and
without losing "the intensity and power" of his fiction.[7] Dixon mourns the
loss of the 1926 silent Paramount adaptation directed by Herbert Brenon,
which he estimates was probably the most faithful of the three adaptations.[8]
Dixon is arguably too preoccupied with the issue of fidelity, but his reading
of director Elliot Nugent's 1949 adaptation of *The Great Gatsby* is illumi-
nating. This was in part a novelistic adaptation, and in part a reworking of
Owen Davis's 1926 stage play, which Fitzgerald had commented read
"pretty badly." Paramount initially bought the rights for the novel for
$16,000, but (in contrast to Dixon's view) this first adaptation was thought
to be over-theatrical, was criticized for using extensive intertitles, and for
lacking imaginative direction. In 1949 Paramount released a second adaptation that attempted to redeem some of the novel's visual qualities (with a

screenplay by Cyril Hume and Richard Maibaum), but it remained theatrical in its self-contained scenes and it modulated the narrative perspective to lessen the subjectivism of Nick Caraway's cynical view of Long Island in the 1920s.

The 1949 adaptation reworks Fitzgerald's novel along the lines of classical Hollywood realism. Rather than having the past revealed in snatches, the film fills in the back story through three carefully orchestrated flashbacks given in historical sequence. To ensure that the stable hierarchy of characters is established from the outset, Jay Gatsby (Allan Ladd) is introduced as the chief character in an opening montage in which he is portrayed in archetypal gangster role, whereas in the novel there is a long delay before he appears enigmatically as a guest at his own party. And the symbolic texture of the novel also suffers in adaptation, with localities such as the Valley of the Ashes losing their dramatic impact (it is quite obviously a film set) and Gatsby's attempt to reclaim lost time (in Fitzgerald's narrative the clock falls from the mantelpiece as Gatsby nervously waits for Daisy, and Nick ruminates on Gatsby's attempt to "beat back time" in the final epic lines) is reduced to the clichéd line "it's time to start over," moments before Gatsby is shot. Rather than an extended epilogue that conveys crucial information about Gatsby's past, the film is bookended by scenes in which Nick and Jordan Baker reflect on Gatsby's life as they visit his grave. This provides a fatalistic account of an individual with vaulting ambition and prevents the viewer from sharing Nick's begrudging respect for Gatsby in the novel.

Wheeler Dixon concludes that "the result was a curiously tedious, flat, and unimaginative film, with little visual or thematic resonance."[9] In fact, such are the multiple changes that Nugent and screenwriters make to the novel that it is only the storyline and the reputation of the author (a pair of spectacles and an image of Fitzgerald's novel accompany the opening credits) which identify it as an adaptation. Echoing director Martin Ritt's reservations about his hand in adapting Faulkner's *The Sound and the Fury*, Elliot Nugent admitted that his 1949 adaptation did not live up to his cinematic expectations. This was one of the reasons why Paramount commissioned a third color version with a much more lavish budget in 1974, directed by Jack Clayton with a screenplay by Francis Ford Coppola.[10]

There were other modernist adaptations in postwar America, particularly focusing on the vogue of "American in Paris" movies such as *The Last Time I Saw Paris* (Richard Brooks, 1954), adapted from Fitzgerald's short story "Babylon Revisited" (1931), and *The Sun Also Rises* (Henry King, 1957) from Hemingway's 1926 novel. But neither of these films could be considered modernist along the lines of the two writers' experiments with form, perspective, and symbol. At mid-century one had to look outside the United

States to find filmmakers interested in the aesthetic possibilities of the modernist novel, with the Japanese director Akira Kurosawa intensifying the modernist qualities of Dostoevsky's *The Idiot* in 1951 and French director Pierre Chanel directing a low-budget adaptation of *Native Son* (also 1951), starring the author Richard Wright in the lead role as the angry Bigger Thomas. *Native Son* is an interesting case in point of what could not be done in the Hollywood studio system at mid-century, but in this instance it was less to do with formal qualities and more with racial politics. MGM showed interest in adapting Wright's *Native Son* in 1941, following the success of the stage adaptation where the African American actor Canada Lee played Bigger Thomas, but the studio wanted a white actor in blackface for the lead role. Director Orson Welles reacted to this demand by planning to shoot the film in Mexico where a mixed cast would be tolerated, but the project ended in defeat when Welles could find no financial backers.[11]

In the 1950s isolated cases of modernist adaptation emerged in France with director Alain Resnais's visually stunning collaborations with Marguerite Duras in *Hiroshima, Mon Amour* (1959) and with Alain Robbe-Grillet in *Last Year In Marienbad* (1961). But it was not really until the 1960s and 1970s that they began to appear with some degree of regularity, including adaptations of Franz Kafka's *The Trial* (Orson Welles, 1962), James Joyce's *Ulysses* (Joseph Strick, 1967), Thomas Mann's *Death in Venice* (Luchino Visconti, 1971), Nathanael West's *The Day of the Locust* (John Schlesinger, 1974), and Herman Hesse's *Steppenwolf* (Fred Haines, 1974). But even in the 1970s when the tenets of classical filmmaking had undergone a decade of transition stimulated by the French New Wave and the emergence of "New Hollywood," modernist adaptations were rare, with a movement back to the realist novels of Jane Austen, E. M. Forster, and Henry James in the 1980s signalling a return to a more parochial Anglo-American literary heritage. There have been some recent attempts to adapt modernist fiction such as *Mrs. Dalloway* (Marleen Gorris, 1997), but filmmakers are still more comfortable adapting turn-of-the-century novels such as *The Golden Bowl* (James Ivory, 2000) and *House of Mirth* (Terence Davies, 2000) rather than high modernist texts from the 1920s, toning down the more experimental qualities of Henry James's late fiction and the irony of Edith Wharton's narrative voice.

We should not just look to "straight" adaptations though, or transpositions of fiction to film, to gauge the relationship between literary and cinematic modernism. Part of the problem is that modernism in the film industry cannot be as clearly periodized as it can in terms of literary production. The period 1890–1940 saw an intensification of modernist experimentation for writers on both sides of the Atlantic, whereas the same period marked an extended cycle in the history of filmmaking, taking in its birth, development, and maturity as an aesthetic and commercial form.

Scott Eyman has argued that the introduction of sound in 1928 represented a fall from the aesthetic possibilities and universal language of silent cinema, making film material "less malleable" where "allusion and metaphor" were replaced by standardized dialogue that did not sit easily with the psychological interiority of modernist fiction.[12] The coming of sound certainly brought with it a stricter demarcation between commercial and experimental film, and when the magazine *Close Up* shifted from monthly to quarterly format in early 1931 it seemed as if the modernist moment of creative possibility had been lost. For this reason critics usually return most regularly to silent filmmakers Sergei Eisenstein, Dziga Vertov, and Walter Ruttmann to identify the modernist style. For example, Sam Girgus hails Vertov's *Man with a Movie Camera* as a supreme blend of "artistic creativity and technical innovation with social and cultural consciousness," while Michael Wood reads it as "a celebration of film, shown as miraculously able to capture motion."[13]

But even before the coming of sound the modernist novel was problematic for filmmakers. Vertov and Eisenstein were either not interested or did not have the technical resources to adapt modernist novels; instead they were keen to make "cinematographic poems" that absorbed the kinetic energies of modernism.[14] Even pioneering émigré adapters of the silent period such as Erich von Stroheim in *Greed* (1923) and Victor Sjöström in *The Scarlet Letter* (1926) returned to realist and naturalist novels to develop their cinematic art. This is not to say that modernism has no place in the development of film, but simply that the transactions between literary modernism and modernist filmmaking are complex and cannot be easily approached by looking at isolated case studies. To this end, the next two sections will consider two key modernist preoccupations – space and time – which open up a set of thematic exchanges between modernist literature and film, before the discussion turns to a recent adaptation, *The Hours* (Stephen Daldry, 2002), as a means for exploring the problematic modernist interface between fiction and film.

Modernist space

In his two-part philosophical meditation *Cinema 1* (1983) and *Cinema 2* (1985) French theorist Gilles Deleuze identifies the "movement-image" and the "time-image" as the two fundamental parameters of film, arguing that there was a general transition from "movement" to "time" following World War II. Deleuze rarely refers to modernism in his two books, perhaps because modernity complicates this historical separation of spatiality and temporality. Instead, he associates classical cinema with the movement-image and post-classical cinema with the time-image as a shift from fixed spatial coordinates towards a cinematic aesthetic "which tends to overflow the real" and "organizes itself into a travelling spectacle."[15] In *Cinema 2* he looks to postwar Italian filmmakers Federico Fellini, Michelangelo Antonioni, and Luchino Visconti to most clearly demonstrate this shift. But the truth is that they and other European directors were only reviving the spirit of early modernism that had been marginalized by the functional filmmaking that dominated the 1930s and 1940s.

Deleuze also underestimates the space of modernity as an urban culture of movement, with the growth of metropolitan centres in Paris, Zurich, London, St. Petersburg, and New York providing a fertile climate for experimentation across a number of cultural forms. The most significant example of this urban concentration was the "city symphony." Films such as *Berlin: Symphony of a City* (Walter Ruttmann, 1927), *Rain* (Joris Ivens, 1929), and *Man with a Movie Camera* (Dziga Vertov, 1929) focused on Berlin, Rotterdam, and Moscow respectively to document the dynamism of modern urban culture.

But the form of the city symphony was established on the other side of the Atlantic by the American photographer Paul Strand and painter Charles Sheeler in *Manhatta* (1921), a film that has no single source text, but can still be considered an early example of adaptation. In this short seven-minute film of a working day in Manhattan, Strand and Sheeler use a variety of modernist techniques further developed in the city symphonies which followed *Manhatta*, including crosscutting, tracking, abstraction, and perspectival shots to convey multiple views of urban modernity. Despite their training in static visual forms, Strand and Sheeler were drawn to moving images to capture city rhythms, interposing the images of Manhattan with lyrics taken from Walt Whitman's New York poems, "Crossing Brooklyn Ferry" (1881) and "Mannahatta" (1888). In these two poems Whitman fuses documentary realism with a lyrical vision of the democratic pulse of urban culture, with lines such as: "on the ferry-boats the hundreds and hundreds that cross, returning home, are more curious to me than you suppose."[16]

This mixture of forms is also evident in the literary and cinematic idioms of *Manhatta*, suggesting that Strand and Sheeler viewed filmmaking as a hybrid form combining both visual and narrative technologies. *Manhatta* is entranced by Whitman's poetry, even though there is no simple correlation between lyrics and images. Whitman's lyrics can either be seen as reinforcing the impression of New York as "the city of ambition" (as Alfred Stieglitz dubbed it in his 1910 photograph) or they offer ironic juxtaposition to a city full of smoke and industry that facilitates working life at the expense of community and leisure. Critics are also divided on this issue: Jan-Christopher Horak claims that the lyrics were used as an integral part of the film (reflecting the interest in Whitman among other modernist painters such as Joseph Stella), but Scott Hammen asserts that the lines were added after completion at the Rialto Theatre, where the film was premiered with the alternative title *New York the Magnificent* in July 1921.[17] Whatever the provenance of the Whitman lyrics, as Miles Orvell argues, they serve to "soften the effect of the actual modern city, a city that as pictured is far beyond what even Whitman might have imagined."[18]

On the other side of the film/fiction divide, the American modernist John Dos Passos was drawn to cinematic techniques to nuance the formal qualities of his fiction, using montage and cross-cutting as an aesthetic feature of his *U.S.A.* trilogy (1930–6). In this way he developed his interest in the Soviet filmmaker Sergei Eisenstein from his earlier novel *Manhattan Transfer* (1925), which charts the rapid development of the US from an agrarian to an urban nation. In *Manhattan Transfer* the critic David Minter sees a similar ambivalence to that displayed in *Manhatta*: "the city consists not only of patterns and systems – marvels of architectural design, civil engineering, social planning, and human governance – but also of noisy, disordered, congested, conflicted scenes in which repressed anxieties and animosities return."[19] *U.S.A.* intensifies the formal experimentation of *Manhattan Transfer*, tracing the series of events over thirty years that led up to the stock market crash of October 1929. Rather than concentrating on plot and characters, the trilogy explores the social, economic, and cultural forces that shaped the nation in the early century. Some sections are conventionally naturalistic, but even here multiple viewpoints are deployed and oral elements jostle for attention amongst scraps of print culture. The first volume of Dos Passos's trilogy, *The 42nd Parallel* (1930), also uses newsreel and cinematic technique. Biographies of "great men" (Andrew Carnegie, Henry Ford, and Woodrow Wilson) are juxtaposed with advertisements and factual headlines, while the "camera eye" sections (reminiscent of Dziga Vertov's 1923 description of the "kino-eye") mimic an unfixed camera shifting dynamically between perspectives.

Dos Passos's use of the "camera eye" technique was influential on loosening narrative from the control of conventional first-person or third-person narrators, but it was not adopted widely by other American writers in the 1930s because (although *U.S.A.* was a proletariat novel) as a formal technique it was criticized for evading ideological commitment. One author who did echo Dos Passos's interest in the montage city was the Jewish American writer Henry Roth in his immigrant New York novel *Call It Sleep* (1934), but Roth did not draw explicitly on a film aesthetic.

On the other side of the Atlantic, however, *Manhattan Transfer* did have a direct influence on the German modernist Alfred Döblin in *Berlin Alexanderplatz* (1929; trans. 1931; adapted by Rainer Fassbinder into a fifteen-hour epic in 1980). In this novel Döblin uses similar techniques to Dos Passos for capturing the chaotic crosscurrents of Berlin, focusing on Alexanderplatz as a gathering point for multiple narrative lines. Döblin shared with Dos Passos an interest in juxtaposing a plethora of cultural forms, including songs, advertisements, timetables, weather forecasts, court hearings, election speeches, and urban noises. The fragmentation of images, texts, and sounds revealed a new urban aesthetic in which the hierarchy between high and low culture was no longer stable. There are differences between Döblin and Dos Passos though. For one, Döblin uses a more consistent narrative perspective (despite a number of unidentified voices) and he focuses more closely on a central character, Franz Biberkopf. In this way Döblin developed an interest in charting the movement of an urban collective while maintaining focus on a single protagonist, which echoes James Joyce's fusion of personal, public, and mythic narratives in *Ulysses* (1922).

Modernist time

When Gilles Deleuze turns his attention to early filmmaking in *Cinema 2* he argues that many films contain internal tensions between concrete and abstract elements, or as he calls it a "cinema of the body" and a "cinema of the brain."[20] While it is tempting to demote spatial movement to that of unthinking bodies, Deleuze points out that for modernist filmmakers such as Dziga Vertov and Sergei Eisenstein these tensions are played out in different ways. Even though temporality is both visceral and cerebral for both film-makers, Vertov's sustained camera shots reveal temporality as continuous and dynamic in its flow, whereas Eisenstein's use of montage and cutting suggests that moments of time overlap or occur simultaneously.

In Walter Ruttman's *Berlin: Symphony of a City*, for example, the space of modernity is defined not just by urban topography, but also by the temporal changes of a day in the life of Berlin. The five acts of the film are signalled by periodic images of a public clock, which we first see at five in morning and last see at midnight. But clock time is just one mode of temporality and is juxtaposed with other processes: machine time, transport time, recreation time, and one woman's attempt to defeat time by jumping from a bridge. Experiential time (what Henri Bergson called *la durée*) was often in conflict with clock time, with modernists developing a range of techniques to explore this tension, and some such as Vertov arguing that machine time and human time should be brought into a more dynamic relationship.

More important than the different literary and cinematic techniques used to represent rival conceptions of temporality was a reorientation towards the past, with modernity frequently seen as a rupture from nineteenth-century concerns. In modernist texts the past is frequently depicted as an irretrievable place from a previous century with different traditions and conflicting cultural priorities. Some extreme modernists such as the Futurists celebrated unreservedly the emerging technologies of the new century, but the past most often re-emerged as a revenant that haunts and disrupts the present, with many modernists troubled about the direction in which modern culture was heading. This is evident in the ambivalent treatment of New York City in *Manhatta* and the fragmentation of cultural artefacts in *Berlin Alexanderplatz* and T. S. Eliot's *The Waste Land* (1922), encapsulating what Leo Charney calls the "drift" of modernity in which "self-present identity is lost" and replaced by ungovernable "moments, fragments, and absent presents."[21]

Two of the most iconic modernist literary texts to deal with changing conceptions of temporality are Thomas Mann's novella *Der Tod in Venedig* (*Death in Venice*, 1912; trans. 1925) and Marcel Proust's epic *A la recherche du temps perdu* (*Remembrance of Things Past*, 1913–27; trans. 1922–31), both the subject of adaptations in the 1970s and 1980s. The two texts are at the opposite ends of the modernist spectrum in terms of length: *Death in Venice* is a short novella in which time is shown to be running out for the respected German writer Gustav von Aschenbach, while *Remembrance of Things Past* is a sprawling epic that elongates moments of time and demonstrates the ways in which chance encounters involuntarily transport an individual into the past. Despite their manifest differences, both texts treat time with a seriousness of intent that propels Mann's Aschenbach and Proust's Swann into worlds in which chronological time is seen as an imposition on the more chaotic flux of experience and desire. Aschenbach has spent too much of his life with a clenched fist writing moral and edifying works for an expecting audience; when he is advised to take a vacation in Venice and becomes fascinated by the young Polish boy Tadzio he finds time falling in on him as desire and a cholera epidemic attack his very being. In contrast, the aristocratic Swann remains in control of his outer world, but finds that in the various episodes of his life, such as his affair with Odette de Crécy in *Swann in Love*, he is often consumed by feelings which he cannot control and which awaken his "passion for truth" that transcends temporality and social etiquette.[22] On this basis, as Deleuze identifies, the temporal forces of decomposition, history, and revelation are intertwined with aesthetics for Proust and Visconti.[23]

Visconti's adaptation of *Death in Venice* (*Morte a Venezia*, It, 1971) and Volker Schlöndorff's *Swann in Love* (*Un Amour de Swann*, Fr, 1984) focus on the way in which overwhelming desire collapses the everyday experience of time. Both films emphasize the visuality of desire, with Swann (Jeremy Irons) fascinated by every sensual gesture of Odette (Ornella Muti), while Aschenbach (Dirk Bogarde) is entranced by the ethereal beauty of Tadzio (Bjorn Andresen) as he follows him around the streets of Venice and is transfixed by him as he plays on the beach. Both adaptations modify the love objects as presented in the fiction: Tadzio does not have the gothic traits that mark him out in Mann's novella (with his "jagged and pale" teeth of "brittle transparency"), and Odette in Schlöndorff's film is much more classically beautiful than the exaggerated characteristics she is given in Proust: "her eyes were beautiful, but so large they seemed to droop beneath their own weight, strained the rest of her face and always made her appear unwell or in a bad mood."[24]

Critics of the two adaptations agree about their powerful visual qualities. Stuart Burrows argues that Visconti's film is all about "watching" in which the cinema viewer is caught in the protagonist's homoerotic gaze, but also the camera that focuses in on Aschenbach's increasingly idiosyncratic behavior as he plays out the role of unrequited lover. The camera not only enhances Tadzio's painterly qualities (at one moment he is framed by a stained-glass window), but it lingers on Aschenbach's visage, and records scenes after he has departed or to which he is insensible.[25] This technique of visual lingering and juxtaposition of perspectives appears to stem from Visconti's close engagement with Proust (although his script for *Remembrance of Things Past* was never made as a film), serving to elongate time at those very instants when the viewer realizes that it is quickly running out for Aschenbach. Melissa Anderson is much more critical of Schlöndorff's *Swann in Love*, preferring two more recent adaptations, *Le Temps retrouvé* (Raúl Ruiz, Fr, 1999) and *La Captive* (Chantal Ackerman, Fr/Bel, 2000), as well as Harold Pinter's unfilmed *The Proust Screenplay*, for developing the novel's themes. Anderson argues that *Swann in Love* does not capture the subjective voice of the text, choosing instead to focus in on the visual minutiae of the conventional costume drama and the more obvious signs of desire such as the cattleya orchids Swann adjusts in Odette's cleavage.[26] Other critics such as Paul Arthur also argue that Ruiz's film *Le Temps retrouvé* is better at conveying "Proustian structures of consciousness" with "gliding camera movements evoking the ephemerality and instability of memory."[27] But what Schlöndorff does do well is to contract the temporality of the 200-page section of Proust's first volume (narrated largely in the third person) into a twenty-four hour period in which the capaciousness of Swann's desire is in tension with the clock time that marks out the stages of his day.

In fact it is not so much in the visual qualities of the two adaptations, but the musical elements that signal the filmmakers' attempts to deal with the modernist qualities of the source texts. Bogarde's character is an amalgam of Mann's Aschenbach and Gustav Mahler, the Adagietto from Mahler's 5th Symphony (1902) lending the film an epic and emotional expansiveness that the visual gaze and circumscribed locality of Venice do not. As such, Aschenbach's flashbacks collapse aesthetic distinctions into general meditations on modernist art and its assault on nineteenth-century cultural values. Although some critics were unhappy about the obtrusive presence of Mahler's score, in a film largely devoid of dialogue, music is the primary element that develops the narrative and temporal lines.[28] It also suggests that the dissolution of one writer on vacation in Venice is actually symbolic of a decaying civilization with which time has caught up.

The music in *Swann's Way* is less impressive, mainly because there is no equivalent refrain to Mahler's Adagietto. But the music nevertheless serves both literary and cinematic functions, offering a direct route to Proust's primary theme of "lost time" as well as providing aural pleasure. This double function is particularly evident early on in the film when Swann is gripped by one of his involuntary memory spasms at a chamber concert. Seconds after he has asked "what time is it?" and prepares to leave the concert he becomes entranced by Vinteuil's sonata, which plays "the national anthem" of his love for Odette and renders him motionless, unable to break away from his internal drama. Melissa Anderson is right in her assessment that we have no access to Swann's subjectivity at these moments in the film (unlike Proust's manifold psychological insights), but such is the rigidity of his body and intensity of his look that it speaks almost as much as the novel's longer description, in which the music suggests to him "a world of inexpressible delights, of whose existence, before hearing it, he had never dreamed, into which he felt that nothing else could initiate him; and he had been filled with love for it, as with a new and strange desire."[29] Rather than Proust's *la durée* being a smooth uninterrupted stream of consciousness, Leo Charney argues that it is an "erratic vagrancy" full of lapses and moments of arrest.[30] And rather than Visconti and Schlöndorff resorting to voiceover to render these internal states (a technique which would be dramatically risky and much too literary), they use the motionless state of the characters as they watch and listen to dramatize those epiphanic moments so common in modernist novels when time fades away, only to re-emerge seconds later in the tedium of prosaic reality or in the frustrations of desire.

Lost spaces/lost time in *The Hours*

Whereas Deleuze in *Cinema 1* and *Cinema 2* suggests a historical shift from movement to temporality as the *modus operandi* of filmmaking (with World

War II as the turning point), I would argue that the two parameters are always intertwined within modernist texts. We can see the intertwining of these forces very clearly in a recent film that revisits some key modernist ideas: Stephen Daldry's *The Hours* (2002), adapted from Michael Cunningham's Pulitzer Prize winning novel of 1998. As Peter Brooker discusses in Chapter 7 there are a number of aspects of Cunningham's novel that could be labeled postmodern (including its intertextuality and impersonation of literary styles), but the fact that the primary historical figure behind the text is Virginia Woolf and that the three-part narrative is a reworking of Woolf's *Mrs. Dalloway* (1925) is significant in terms of signalling a modernist continuum. And these connections are not solely literary: Woolf wrote an essay on "The Cinema" in 1926 in which she argues that cinematic reality takes on a fluid life of its own ("we see life as it is when we have no part in it"), and her major novels *To the Lighthouse* (1926) and *The Waves* (1931) engage with the intricacies of "life" in very cinematic ways.[31] But, while Cunningham's novel can also be read as a piece of fledgling cinema, he admits that his research focused on the modernist novel, with epigraphs from Woolf and Jorge Luis Borges indicating that *The Hours* is poised between modernism and a postmodern reworking of modernist motifs.

The Hours moves between three different stories, separated in space and time, but interlinked through the subject matter of *Mrs. Dalloway*. Woolf's novel focuses on a day in the life of Clarissa Dalloway as she prepares for a party in the West End of London while she contemplates her anxieties and the sacrifices she has felt compelled to make. Cunningham's rendering of the story is rather different as it is inflected through three alternating perspectives and three different worlds: first, Woolf's struggle to write *Mrs. Dalloway* in dreary 1920s Richmond; second, the reading of the novel by depressed Los Angeles housewife Laura Brown in the early 1950s; and, third, the acting out of the *Mrs. Dalloway* story by late 1990s New York literary editor Clarissa Vaughan. Adapted by dramatist David Hare, the film retains Cunningham's alternating perspectives, using well-known actresses – Nicole Kidman, Julianne Moore, and Meryl Streep – to play the three characters. Despite wearing a prosthetic nose to play Woolf (making her virtually unrecognizable), Kidman was the star of the film, primarily because the writer's story occupies more than a third of the narrative space in Cunningham's novel and gives birth to the other two stories.

An interesting graphic was used to promote the film in which images of the three characters – Virginia/Laura/Clarissa or Kidman/Moore/Streep – slowly morph into each other, as if this is a clue to the aesthetics of the adaptation. Certainly the three tales reflect and even blur into each other at times, but they focus on three aspects of writing, dealing in turn with author, reader, and fictional restaging. The film improves on the transitions in the novel, by cutting between them when a certain image (such as fresh flowers) or a particular sound reverberates into another of the character's lives. This technique lends the film more fluidity than Cunningham's novel, with fast cutting providing a wave-like motion that is developed in the water imagery of the film, amplified by Philip Glass's haunting score, in which he uses serial refrains to accent the circularity of the three characters' lives.

The central tension of *The Hours* is how to have meaningful relationships while also securing material independence and a place in which one can create: the hallmarks of Woolf's "room of one's own." This central tension is creative, but also potentially tragic. In the writing of *Mrs. Dalloway* (the working title of which was "The Hours") Woolf considered making Clarissa commit suicide, but realized that the death of another character (the shell-shocked war veteran Septimus Warren Smith) would enable her to live: a point that is carried through to the suicide of Clarissa Vaughan's AIDS-suffering friend Richard (Ed Harris). The central character Laura Brown – the depressed counterpart of the 1950s serene housewife played by Julianne Moore in *Far From Heaven* (Todd Haynes, US, 2002) – also contemplates suicide, but instead opts for escape from her ordinary but loveless marriage. She is herself a manifestation of an invented character "Mrs. Brown," from two essays Woolf wrote in 1924 – "Mr. Bennett and Mrs. Brown" and "Character in Fiction" – a seemingly ordinary figure that is often overlooked by writers because they cannot discern her rich inner world. On this point, Woolf attacked the Staffordshire writer Arnold Bennett for creating ill-formed and shallow characters and having "never once looked at Mrs. Brown in her corner." As examples of the intertwining of the space and time of modernity, if one aspect of Cunningham's novel and Daldry's film explores the temporal threads that connect three different moments (1923, 1951, 2001), then the texts are also interested in the spaces, rooms, and corners in which the characters live.

Marleen Gorris's earlier 1997 adaptation of *Mrs. Dalloway* struggled to render the interiority of Woolf's novel, and *The Hours* works through this by projecting the interior world onto two different characters separated by time and space – what Peter Brooker calls the "refunctioning" of the modernist author and source text. *The Hours* suggests a series of temporal and spatial layers that do not add up to a final cut, or a definitive re-writing of Woolf's novel. Instead resonances and connections abound. Just before Richard's suicide he comments to Clarissa "I still have to face the hours ... the hours after the party and the hours after that." We later learn that Richard is Laura Brown's son whom she abandoned along with her husband shortly after her attempted suicide; but although Laura escaped to a new life in Toronto, she herself has to face "the hours after that" and the guilt of leaving her son. There is some relief from the weight of time though. At the end of the novel Clarissa thinks to herself that the consolation of being "devoured by time itself" is "an hour here or there when our lives seem, against all odds and expectations, to burst open and give us everything we've ever imagined."[32] Even though time will come to obliterate these moments, the possibility of future epiphanies signals the end of Cunningham's novel which fuses together two separate worlds: Clarissa welcomes into her apartment the fugitive from the past, Mrs. Brown, and gives voice to the Woolfian words: "Everything's ready."[33]

Daldry's film opts for a very different ending, stressing the permanence rather than the transitory nature of time. At the end we are taken back to the film's beginning with Woolf's desperate walk to the river. Whereas the opening shot cuts away from the figure before she drowns, at the end Woolf walks all the way into the river, her head slowly disappearing as Kidman's voiceover stresses the weight of time: "always the years, always the love, always the hours." What the alternative endings of *The Hours* show us is that, in both its literary and cinematic forms, imaginative modernist adaptations are still possible. As a late modernist adaptation, *The Hours* suggests that just as Woolf's death is replayed so, paradoxically, she and the spectre of modernity are brought back to life.

NOTES

1 This statement appears on the cover of the fourth issue of *Close Up* from October 1927: the cover is reprinted in *Close Up 1927–1933: Cinema and Modernism*, ed. James Donald, Anne Friedberg, and Laura Marcus (London: Cassell, 1998), p. 2.

2 Susan McCabe, *Cinematic Modernism: Modernist Poetry and Film* (Cambridge: Cambridge University Press, 2005), p. 2.

3 See Sam Girgus, *America on Film: Modernism, Documentary, and a Changing America* (Cambridge: Cambridge University Press, 2002), pp. 1–13.

4 Tom Dardis, *Some Time in the Sun: The Hollywood Years of Fitzgerald, Faulkner, Nathanael West, Aldous Huxley, and James Agee* (New York: Scribner's, 1976), p. 104.

5 Bruce F. Kawain, *Faulkner and Film* (New York: Frederick Ungar, 1977), p. 28.

6 Kawain, *Faulkner and Film*, p. 21.

7 Wheeler Winston Dixon, "The Three Film Versions of *The Great Gatsby*: A Vision Deferred," *Literature/Film Quarterly* (2003), p. 289.

8 The trailer for the 1926 version of *The Great Gatsby* is all that remains: a 35 mm print of the trailer is held in The Library of Congress and is available on the DVD collection *More Treasures from American Film Archives* (National Film Preservation Foundation, 2004).

9 Dixon, "The Three Film Versions of *The Great Gatsby*," p. 290.

10 The 1974 adaptation is little better than the 1949 version in terms of telling the story from Nick Carraway's perspective, so crucial to Fitzgerald's novel: see Joy

Gould Boyum, *Double Exposure: Fiction into Film* (New York: New American Library, 1985), p. 117.

11 Mona Z. Smith, *Becoming Something: The Story of Canada Lee* (New York: Faber & Faber, 2004), p. 108.

12 Scott Eyman, *The Speed of Sound: Hollywood and the Talkie Revolution, 1926–1930* (Baltimore: Johns Hopkins University Press, 1997), p. 10.

13 Girgus, *America on Film*, p. 5. Michael Wood, "Modernism and Film," in *The Cambridge Companion to Modernism*, ed. Michael Levenson (Cambridge: Cambridge University Press, 1999), p. 227.

14 As James Chapman notes, Eisenstein was interested in the filmic qualities of fiction. For example, in a 1944 essay he praised the "plasticity" and "optical quality" of Dickens's prose: Chapman, *Cinemas of the World* (London: Reaktion, 2003), pp. 60–1.

15 Gilles Deleuze, *Cinema 2: The Time Image*, trans. Hugh Tomlinson and Robert Galeta (London: Athlone [1985], 1989), p. 5.

16 Walt Whitman, "Crossing Brooklyn Ferry," *Walt Whitman: The Complete Poems* (Harmondsworth: Penguin, 1983), p. 190.

17 See Jan-Christopher Horak, "Paul Strand and Charles Sheeler's *Manhatta*," in *Lovers of Cinema: The First American Film Avant-Garde, 1919–1945*, ed. Jan-Christopher Horak (Madison: University of Wisconsin Press, 1995), pp. 267–8 and Scott Hammen, "Sheeler and Strand's 'Manhatta': A Neglected Masterpiece," *Afterimage*, 6.6 (January 1979), 6–7.

18 Miles Orvell, "The Artist Looks at the Machine: Whitman, Sheeler and American Modernism," in *After the Machine: Visual Arts and the Erasing of Cultural Boundaries* (Jackson: University Press of Mississippi, 1995), pp. 3–27.

19 David Minter, *A Cultural History of the American Novel* (Cambridge: Cambridge University Press, 1996), p. 130.

20 Deleuze, *Cinema 2*, p. 204.

21 Leo Charney, *Empty Moments: Cinema, Modernity, and Drift* (Durham, North Carolina: Duke University Press, 1998), pp. 6–7.

22 Marcel Proust, *Remembrance of Things Past*, Volume I, trans. C. K. Scott Moncrieff and Terence Kilmartin (London: Penguin, 1989), p. 298.

23 Deleuze, *Cinema 2*, pp. 94–7.

24 Thomas Mann, *Death in Venice and Other Stories*, trans. David Luke (London: Minerva, 1996), p. 228. Proust, *Remembrance of Things Past*, Volume I, p. 213.

25 Stuart Burrows, " 'Desire Projected Itself Visually': Watching *Death in Venice*," in *Classics in Film and Fiction*, ed. Deborah Cartmell et al. (London: Pluto, 2000), pp. 143–4.

26 Melissa Anderson, "In Search of Adaptation: Proust and Film," in *Literature and Film*, ed. Robert Stam and Alessandra Raengo (Oxford: Blackwell, 2005), pp. 102–4.

27 Paul Arthur, "The Written Scene: Writers as Figures of Cinematic Redemption," in *Literature and Film*, ed. Stam and Raengo, p. 339.

28 For a critical overview of Visconti's *Death in Venice* see Joy Gould Boyum, *Double Exposure*, pp. 215–21. See Chapter 14 in this volume for a further discussion of the use of music as a replacement for literary devices and techniques.

29 Proust, *Remembrance of Things Past*, Volume I, p. 228. It can be argued that Schlöndorff's camera does not linger on Swann long enough during the Vinteuil

sonata, cutting to others in the room who observe his reaction: see Boyum, *Double Exposure*, p. 263.

30 Charney, *Empty Moments*, p. 10.

31 Woolf, "The Cinema" (1926), *The Crowded Dance of Modern Life*, ed. Rachel Bowlby (Harmondsworth: Penguin, 1993), p. 54. Here Woolf offers an opposite view to Jean Epstein's theory of *photogénie* from the early 1920s, in which he argues that film is intimately bound up with the viewer's perception: see Charney, *Empty Moments*, pp. 150–6.

32 Michael Cunningham, *The Hours* (London: Fourth Estate, 2000), p. 225.

33 Cunningham, *The Hours*, p. 226.

7

PETER BROOKER

Postmodern adaptation: pastiche, intertextuality and re-functioning

Average film-goers probably take more notice of a film's stars than of its director. Stars or actors are, after all, visible on screen for approximately two hours whereas the director merely fronts or ends the credits. How many viewers, for example, know the directors of the *Bridget Jones* films (Sharon Maguire and Beeban Kidron) compared with those who know its stars, Colin Firth, Hugh Grant, and Renée Zellweger? When you read a novel you hold the author's name in your hands, touching it with your finger-tips, and what you see in reading are their words. But when a film is "based on the book, story or play by ...," then the author's name tends also to recede along with their text, even such a one as Helen Fielding, J. R R. Tolkien, Jane Austen, or Shakespeare. The process is, we might say, a technologically-induced version of the "death of the author" theorized by Roland Barthes in the 1960s. Barthes's intention was to demote the godlike figure of the (usually male designated) "Author" to the figure of a "scriptor" working laterally across texts, and to activate the reader, similarly, as a figure who cruised, antennae bristling, across this layered textuality, but did not pause to dig below or look behind this surface for a book's single authorized meaning.[1] Barthes's essay, along with other theoretical essays in the same decade, by Julia Kristeva,[2] for example, inaugurated the concept of intertextuality and the practice of intertextual reading. This was one of the major strategic features of post-structuralism and is a continuing touchstone in the Humanities. At the same time, we cannot fail to notice, almost fifty years after Barthes's essay, that in the world of everyday reading, book reviews, as well as much academic criticism, the author is as strong a presence as ever.

In cinema theory and criticism, there had been an earlier move the other way, and a correspondingly contrary set of popular habits and attitudes. For here under the influence of "auteur theory," promoted chiefly by contributors to the magazine *Cahiers du Cinema* in the 1950s, the work of individual Hollywood and subsequently French "New Wave" directors was elevated above any written fictional source or generic conventions in a bid to earn those directors and the medium of cinema artistic respect. Though this tendency ran counter to the customary denigration of American commercialized culture, it depended, much like traditional literary criticism, on the notion of the creative individual who could bring a distinctive and overriding signature to a varied range of work across different genres. The notion has of course survived in interpretations of the work not only of earlier examples (Alfred Hitchcock, Howard Hawks, Douglas Sirk, and others) but of directors such as Woody Allen, Steven Spielberg, Martin Scorsese, or David Cronenberg. This has been a somewhat anomalous perspective upon film however. For not only is filmmaking an evidently collaborative endeavor and a more clearly technologically advanced industry than book publishing, it has also depended on scripts adapted from novels, whether of "high" or "low" cultural status, and this practice, along with re-makes, cross-genre films, blockbuster series, and the migration of stars and actors from picture to picture and between TV, theater, and cinema, has arguably made the experience of variegated intertextuality, and not authorship, the more immediate one for viewers. The example of Colin Firth, above, whose character Mark Darcy in *Bridget Jones's Diary* (2001) and *Bridget Jones: The Edge of Reason* (2004) is modeled on his TV role as Darcy in the adaptation of Jane Austen's novel *Pride and Prejudice* (1995) would be a case in point.

These differences have something to do with differences in media and modes of production and reception, but they are also informed by habits of cultural value and these are most exposed when book and film, especially "literary" fiction and film, are considered together. The kinds of hierarchical distinctions, often noted in critical study, between literature and film, creativity and commerce, the individual and the mass, or the original and copy, then come relentlessly into play and continue to bedevil this comparison. The criterion of "fidelity to the original" is perhaps the most stubborn, and most futile and deluded of these attitudes – futile because, strictly speaking, fidelity can only mean literal repetition, and deluded because a judgment of success or failure is clearly dependent on differently situated strategies of interpretation.

Academic study has tirelessly returned to the criterion of fidelity and its other associated binary distinctions of type and value to critique their inconsistencies and implications.[3] Most convincingly they have been deconstructed in favor of a preferred emphasis upon relations of difference or dialogue, not of hierarchy, between texts and media. In its broader application this emphasis should include the influence of the differently situated experiences of reading novels and viewing films, sketched above, including the experience of video and down-loaded computer texts, and the different cultural contexts and chronologies in which these occur. The Hollywood adaptations of European film texts (Godard's *Un Bout de Souffle*, 1960, as *Breathless* [Jim McBride, 1983], Wim Wenders's *Wings of Desire*, as *City of Angels* [Brad Siberling, 1998], *Nikita* [Luc Besson, 1990] as *The Assassin or Point of No Return* [John Badham, 1993] – the inspiration in turn of a US TV series) entail these often taken-for-granted cultural exchanges across film and cultural history. More recently there has been a more self-conscious, two-way exchange between American and Asian cinema, in the work of Quentin Tarantino, Wayne Wang, and Wong Kar-Wai, amongst others.

There are points, too, it should be said, when relations of textual difference should be understood in terms of broader and long-term relations of cultural dominance, dependency, and subordination. We cannot ignore, that is to say, the global hegemony of Western literature or American film. Adaptations in literature such as Jean Rhys's *Wide Sargasso Sea* of *Jane Eyre* and J. M. Coetzee's *Foe* of Daniel Defoe's *Robinson Crusoe* (of which there have also been play and film adaptations) are well-known examples of the way later texts reveal the colonial and patriarchal attitudes determining their originals. The recent film versions of Jane Austen's *Mansfield Park* (1999) and Thackeray's *Vanity Fair* (2004) "write back" in this way to their originals. In turn they expose the sadistic sexual abuse of slaves on the Antigua sugar plantation which is the source of Sir Thomas Bertram's wealth in Austen's novel, and foreground the tension between the Imperial rule and the enchantment of India in Thackeray. These films have attracted disparate reviews. What is plain, however, to anticipate some of the discussion below, is that while adaptations are invariably commercial propositions, which might succeed or fail artistically, they can be informed by a committed re-reading, interested in more than an unmotivated recycling of existing stories.

I want to develop the case for this kind of multi-relational critical perspective below, but firstly I shall set the present discussion in a particular context. Postmodernism made its explicit appearance in critical and cultural studies in the early 1980s and brought with it a new vocabulary and perspective upon relations between the real and the image, and the present and past. It did so in response to the newer reproductive media and information technologies and to trends in film and TV which seemed increasingly to feed off repeats and remakes. Both tendencies undermined the concept of the original and therefore had clear implications for the study of adaptations.

Fredric Jameson's celebrated essay "Postmodernism and Consumer Society" (1983), expanded as "Postmodernism or the Cultural Logic of Late Capitalism" (1984), effectively set the agenda for future debate on these themes. Thus with the absence in postmodernism of stable norms, the mocking parody or satire of an earlier age became no longer possible. Nor, with "the transformation of reality into images, the fragmentation of time into a series of perpetual presents" was it possible to access an authentic view of the past or in writing and art "to invent new styles and worlds" since "– they've already been invented."[4] Instead there was pastiche, the practice of neutral and humorless imitation: "speech in a dead language," at best "blank parody."[5] In film this tendency was evidenced, Jameson argued, by the prevalence of the "nostalgia mode," the superficial reproduction or re-styling in films such as *American Graffiti* (1973), *Star Wars* (1977), or *Raiders of the Lost Ark* (1981) of a past decade in American life or of its associated iconography. Even a film such as *Body Heat* (1981) ostensibly set in its own time, blurs this reference, Jameson contends, in the haze of "some indefinable nostalgic past, an eternal 1930s, say, beyond history."[6]

It is easy to multiply subsequent examples of Jameson's types: in the literal shot-by-shot remake of *Psycho* (1998), or the freer remakes *Ocean's 11* (2001) and *Solaris* (2002); in films evoking an earlier period, frequently still of the 1950s, such as *Pleasantville* (1998), *Mulholland Drive* (2001), and *Far From Heaven* (2002), along with the Coen Brothers' *O Brother – Where Art Thou?* (2000) and *The Man Who Wasn't There* (2001), and the fabulously extravagant martial arts derived films, *Hero* (2002) and *House of the Flying Daggers* (2004) by Zhang Yimou, which imagine periods in ancient China. The last twenty years have also seen any number of adaptations of literary texts: by Jane Austen, most obviously, Edith Wharton, Thackeray, Shakespeare, and J. R. R. Tolkien. These examples represent less "more of the same" than *more* of the same; that is to say, the emergence of a more intensively palimpsestic, ironic, and self-reflexive film culture, extending, in company with broader cultural trends, into an enthusiasm for fantasy. The *Star Wars* series is evidence of this increasingly layered complexity. For Jameson in the 1980s, the first *Star Wars* film induced a particular type of nostalgia, "a deep ... longing" to relive the experience of viewing "Saturday afternoon serials of the Buck Rogers type" screened two decades earlier.[7] If some viewers can still see the film this way, the later *Star Wars* films have recruited new, younger audiences and fans and arguably shifted this nostalgia to the moment in 1977 of the screening and first viewing of the opening instalment (Episode IV) in the series.[8]

Indirectly, Jameson's twin notions of pastiche and nostalgia are indebted to the scenario of a hyperreal world of simulacra (the copy of a copy without reference or original in the real world) theorized by Jean Baudrillard. This has proved a deeply controversial proposition in the political realm. Meanwhile, the idea of simulation and the loss of the real finds very clear endorsement in the world of material and cultural production, where neither Levis nor laptops, CDs or books are copies of a single original. Baudrillard's findings have also fed into a continuing debate on the changing conception of the human in its relation, by turns, to the natural world and advanced computer technology. We think in this connection of discussions of cloning, of cyborgs and cyperpunk fiction, and of course of the different texts of *Blade Runner* in some combination of Philip K. Dick's *Do Androids Dream of Electric Sheep?* (1968), Ridley Scott's film versions (1981, 1991), and the later spin-off novels. Dick has proved a fertile source for adaptations to film and a number of his stories, notably *Time Out of Joint* (1959) and *The Simulacra* (1964), as well as those made into films including "We Can Remember It For You Wholesale" (1987), filmed as *Total Recall* (1990), and *Do Androids Dream of Electric Sheep?* deal with the themes of pastiche and authenticity, slippages in time, and the loss of the past which came to characterize academic and popular debate on postmodernism. More recently, Steven Spielberg's 2002 adaptation of Dick's short story, "The Minority Report" (1956) sets these themes in a spectacularly computerized future where, as in Dick's story, crime is anticipated by three mutant "pre-cogs." This system, termed "Precrime," would seem to administer to a perfect, crime-free world, but goes into crisis when the commissioner of police, John Anderton (Tom Cruise in the film) is himself named as a future murderer. This shared narrative nucleus is played out quite differently in story and film, according to the kinds of intertexts indicated above: the respective predilections of author Philip K. Dick (where the system is restored) and *auteur* Steven Spielberg (where it is abandoned and family life is restored); the extra-textual associations with Tom Cruise; the plainly incompatible technologies of the short story and Hollywood production; and the cultural import of crime in Dick's 1960s and Spielberg's millennial America. Thus, where Dick's story strikes the period note of paranoia, the film's audiences might find reason to associate the regime of "Precrime" with the contemporary language of "zero tolerance" and "pre-emptive strikes." A notable further difference is that in Dick the precogs are "... idiots ... deformed and retarded"[9] and are little more than catalysts, whereas, in Spielberg, the story of one of the precogs, re-named Agatha, is highly developed. In the film she is an unusually sensitized and disturbed young woman who has repressed the death of her mother, but, aided by the Tom Cruise figure, is recalled to human society. The film adaptation therefore makes more of the notion of "minority" in the story's title and this too accords with Spielberg's humanist sensibility and his response to other submerged texts or "paratexts" making up the surrounding debates on the non- or post-human.

For Jameson, the uncomprehended reach of globalization and the recycling of styles as pastiche and simulation have obstructed our access to an authentic past and frustrated alike political understanding and genuine artistic novelty. It is not Jameson's intention, however, to defend a betrayed or traduced original, human or otherwise. Rather, he is concerned, unlike the more fatalistic Baudrillard, with the extent to which postmodernist intertextuality merely replicates the circulation of goods and "logic of consumer capitalism," and with how "the disappearance of a sense of history" frustrates the making of a "critical ... contestatory ... oppositional" postmodern art and culture.[10]

Amongst many responses to Jameson's analysis, Linda Hutcheon argued (in 1989) that both the postmodern historical novel and film engage in a critical and still parodic dialogue with the past and therefore produce more than a facile imitation or pastiche of it. This is a more positive way certainly of viewing what Hutcheon suggests is a changed and more self-consciously knowing historical sense – which would embrace adaptations as well as historical fictions. A cultural history of the kind Jameson evokes which operates in one episode by norms (enabling parody) and in another without them (resulting in pastiche) surely rests on too absolute and simplistic a distinction. Indeed, while postmodernism, in league with post-structualism or deconstruction, is credited with challenging the distinction between high and low or popular culture, it has ironically often been marked by persistent binaries of which parody and pastiche and, more broadly, an absolute division between modernism and postmodernism are examples. The result is a melancholy refrain of loss: whether of reference and historicity, or of the subject, or of political agency and critique. To contest this, as Hutcheon does, in order to affirm that parody remains an option, presents us with a "double-coded" postmodernism which at once inhabits the conventions it subverts, but does not, all the same, entirely release us from the limitations of the initial binary configuration.

The concepts of dialogics and intertextuality, as theorized by Mikhail Bakhtin and adopted in film studies, notably by Robert Stam, can help us move beyond the stark choice of "either ... or" to a thoroughly open appreciation of art as, in Stam's words, the "endless permutation of textual traces."[11] Bakhtin viewed all utterances as inherently dialogic: "Each utterance", he wrote, "is filled with echoes and reverberations of other utterances," it "refutes, affirms, supplements, and relies on the others, presupposes them to be known, and somehow takes them into account."[12] Stam argues further that the idea of "intertextual dialogism" undermines the hierarchies and prejudice governing the common response to adaptations and, as he puts it, helps "us transcend the *aporias* of 'fidelity'"[13]. His view of art as a "palimpsestic multi-trace" operating "both within and across cultures"[14] is a particularly salutary one. However, the evident degrees and types of adaptation and different relations between even two core texts, calls for a correspondingly focused but flexible vocabulary able to distinguish types of intertextuality. Stam refers us in this respect to the taxonomy developed in Gérard Genette's *Palimpsests* (1997). Here Genette identifies a general category of "transtextuality" and five subtypes: "intertextuality" (quotation, plagiarism, and allusion), paratextuality (titles, prefaces, interviews, reviews), "metatextuality" (the commentary by one text on another), architextuality (the features assigning a text to a genre) and the most relevant type in the present context, "hypertexuality" concerning the relation between a first "hypotext" and a second, "hypertext" in some way derived from the first.

If Genette helps us distinguish the kinds of transtextuality necessary to a systematic poetics, his terms do not in themselves help us understand the important "process" of adaptation. Nor do they represent a significant advance on the existing, already extensive vocabulary describing this relation: for example, "editing," "substitution," "amplification," "transcoding," "transposition," "re-reading," "re-writing," "bricolage," "imitation," and "mockery," as well as "pastiche" and "parody." Two such concepts are, I suggest, worth some further attention: "translation" and "refunctioning." The concept and practice of translation have a history in which privilege and dominance is conferred upon one language and culture over another – where the first is invariably Western and most often English. Recent thinking, however, not only critiques such assumptions but argues that neither the "original" text and culture, nor its translation and corresponding culture can be deemed homogeneous entities. Rather, the practice of translation, contends Naoki Sakai, is "radically heterogeneous."[15] Sakai adds that "the translator is also the interpreter" and in an "extremely ambiguous and unstable" relation to both the original author (addresser) and reader (addressee).[16] Such thinking undermines any essentialized notion of either prior or subsequent texts and participants and the traditional assumption that a level of underlying sameness exists between them. Rather, translation becomes a "hybridizing instance"[17] marked by disparity, gaps, and indeterminacy rather than equivalence.

If translation can in this way provide a suggestive model for adaptation we have to consider how, in the present instance, this occurs across media and genres and recognize too that the adaptation places no obligation on the viewer to know or acquaint themselves with the source text. In an obvious example, we do not need to know Jane Austen's *Emma* when we watch *Clueless* (1995) – a film which itself became the "original" for a TV series. It is indeed one of the features of postmodernism that texts exploit precisely this kind of dispersed, free-ranging intertextuality. An adaptation, that is to say, will stand in a set of potential intertextual or dialogic relations, not all of which will be realized or need be realized at any given time in order to afford pleasure and understanding. They may also become increasingly distanced from their "original" while entering different transtextual worlds with other synchronically related texts. The moment of reading or viewing, moreover, can and frequently will reverse the chronology of source text and its adaptation, putting the second before the first. In which case the consequence of reading or viewing back to the source text will inevitably be to resituate and transform the supposedly fixed and authentic original.

What none of this discussion broaches, however, is the question of evaluation. How, if we reject the standard of "fidelity" for the analytic vocabulary of "intertextual dialogue" or "translation" are we to assess the interest and quality of an adaptation? We might, in this respect, recall the concept of "refunctioning" (German: *Umfunktionierung*) coined by the theorist and playwright, Bertolt Brecht, himself a frequent adaptor of earlier texts, in response to the film adaptation of his play *The Threepenny Opera*.[18] Brecht had in mind a transformation of artistic form and the means of cultural production in the interests of working-class democracy. The postmodern has distanced us from Brecht's revolutionary cultural politics yet we might consider how, in "translating" Brecht, an adaptation simultaneously "re-functions" both the form and content of its source text so as critically to address the changed cultural and political circumstances of its own time. Such a criterion would enable us to respond to the supposed lack of invention and newness implied in Jameson's account of postmodernism: not at all so as to defend the "original" or its priority, but to restore the possibility of "originality," understood as the practice of an imaginative re-making which edits, echoes, borrows from, recomposes and "re-functions" existing narratives or images; that is to say, makes them work in a different medium with an invigorated social and artistic purpose – what Brecht termed art's "critical attitude to the social world."[19]

I want, with these thoughts in mind, to turn here to a more extended discussion of a particular example. Michael Cunningham's novel *The Hours* transplants, or translates, the double icon of modernist literature, Virginia Woolf and her novel *Mrs. Dalloway* (1925) into a postmodern present in ways that raise questions about style, narrative, and identity, as well as about historical reconstruction and originality. It was made into a film directed by Stephen Daldry in 2002. On first viewing the film I was acquainted with Woolf's career and writing, including *Mrs. Dalloway* but not with *The Hours*. *The New York Times* commented that there was no need to have read *Mrs. Dalloway* before reading *The Hours*, but not to do so would deny readers "a readily available pleasure." Of ten reviews cited in the frontispiece to Cunningham's book only one of any length does not mention Virginia Woolf. Cunningham's novel is said to "shadow and echo," to be "inspired by," to "re-voice" and "emulate" Woolf's.[20] The assumption is that Woolf's text comes first and sets off these later echoes, but clearly this cannot be the case if we enter Woolf's novel after reading Cunningham's, or read Cunningham's after viewing the film. The echoes will in fact circulate through all three texts, possibly embracing the film of *Mrs. Dalloway* (1989) too, and in so doing reconstitute our sense of them.

It is Cunningham's novel, however, not Woolf's, nor the film, which generates the intricate dialogic relationship between these texts. Woolf's *Mrs. Dalloway* was set in its own intertextual relations, of course. She began the novel with the working title of "The Hours" and planned initially that the character Clarissa would commit suicide. She had recently read James Joyce's *Ulysses* which arguably provides the idea of a novel of the day in the life of Mrs. Dalloway, and had delivered a talk on the modern novel (the famous essay "Mr. Bennett and Mrs. Brown") eight days before she wrote in her diary that she had begun "The Hours." A different Clarissa Dalloway appears in the earlier *The Voyage Out* (1915) and there was a short story, "Mrs. Dalloway in Bond Street." These intertexts drop away from her novel, with the result that it acquires the signature of the single author, along with the modernist concern with unity in the midst of, or as transcending, the multifariousness of modern metropolitan life, in one of the marks, says Jameson, of the modernist text. Cunningham's taking over Woolf's working title is in keeping with his novel's amplified sense of time's immediacy and duration and the foregrounded theme of age, memory, illness, and suicide. He also extends Woolf's English location to the USA and multiplies her novel's plot lines. Thus *The Hours* intercuts the story of Woolf's novel-writing, personal circumstances, and mental health with a second which follows Clarissa Vaughan (nicknamed "Mrs. D." in recognition of Woolf's novel) on a day in late twentieth-century New York; and a third which presents the day in the life of Mrs. Brown (the name borrowed from Woolf's essay) in post-World War II suburban Los Angeles.

The novel conforms in these ways to much that would be said of the postmodernist text: in its crossing the genres of biography and fiction, its dislocated time sequence, and also in its style. Thus the novel directly quotes from Woolf's suicide note and *Mrs. Dalloway* and pastiches her novel's idiom and the syntax of free indirect discourse in describing her. Thus:

> She washes her face and does not look, certainly not this morning, not when the work is waiting for her and she is anxious to join it the way she might join a party that had already started downstairs, a party full of wit and beauty certainly but full, too, of something finer than wit or beauty; something mysterious and golden; a spark of profound celebration, of life itself, as silks

rustle across polished floors and secrets are whispered under the music. She, Virginia, could be a girl in a new dress, about to go down to a party, about to appear on the stairs, fresh and full of hope. (p. 31)

Fredric Jameson, once more, characterizes pastiche as "blank parody," the imitation of "dead styles," and the eclipse of the authorial signature. Certainly we do not identify a uniquely personal authorial voice here, but rather a postmodern facility to move laterally across available styles and idioms. Cunningham, in other words, can write like Woolf, but she would not have written like him. We would do better, however, to think of Cunningham's prose as at once an impersonation and homage; far from blank, and far from a rejection of its modernist precursor. Indeed the novel demonstrates the continuing life of a modernist author, "refunctioned" in Cunningham's own prose, in the easy reference to Clarissa Vaughan as "Mrs. D." and in Laura Brown's avid reading of all Woolf's works.

In Cunningham's novel, the character Richard (whose surname we learn shortly before the end is "Brown") is a prize-winning author who is dying of AIDS. He is therefore less the Richard Dalloway who is a version of Leonard Woolf in Woolf's novel than the homosexual Lytton Strachey who once proposed to Virginia Stephen, just as Clarissa and Richard Brown once shared a fleeting kiss and short-lived affair. Cunningham incorporates the story of Woolf's main male character, the shell-shocked Septimus Smith, into the story of Richard who, like Smith, commits suicide by falling from a window. But in its main narrative drive, his novel follows the inter-laced stories of three women across the twentieth century from an opening re-enactment of Woolf's suicide through stories about writing, giving parties, depression, and survival. Crucially all the women are conscious of parallel or alternate worlds. Woolf, stuck in the stolid routines of Richmond, yearns for the dangerous "life" of London; Clarissa's mind turns repeatedly on what might have been between herself and Richard; and Mrs. Brown finally abandons her unfulfilled life as suburban wife and mother for an undefined something else. In the process Cunningham evokes the nascent lesbianism in Woolf's own relationships, expressed in Mrs. Dalloway in Clarissa's youth-ful infatuation with Sally Seton. In New York, Clarissa lives openly with her Sally; and in Los Angeles Laura Brown is awoken by a kiss with her friend to the possibility of her own bisexuality.

The film collaborates with Cunningham's text in its elaborations upon Mrs. Dalloway and in bringing us to rethink the circumstances of Woolf's life and suicide. It supplies the Woolf biography and Cunningham's locations with the period realism of the 1920s and the "authentic" dress and décor of this and the latter settings in post-war and end-of-century America (updated to 2001 in the film). In addition, it brings the strong Hollywood cast of Nicole Kidman, Meryl Streep, and Julianne Moore, known for several other roles, to this story. We might appreciate the joke, too, if we remember the moment in Cunningham's novel where Clarissa Vaughan thinks she spots Vanessa Redgrave or Meryl Streep (the two "Clarissa Dalloways" of the two films of Woolf's novel) on a New York street (p. 27).

The result, however, is more than the "faithful" nostalgia film and knowing star vehicle this might suggest. In particular, David Hare's screenplay radically edits, re-arranges, and supplements Cunningham's text, and the rapid intercutting of the film's opening sets the stories in a more immediate intertextual (spoken and visual) dialogue with each other. The film also introduces four significant additions. The first and third additions concern the Mrs. Brown character and strengthen a sense of her affinity with Woolf. In the first, clearly contemplating suicide, she books into a hotel where she reads *Mrs. Dalloway* (a passage affirming "it is possible to die") and in a sequence, intercut with Woolf's thoughts on her Mrs. Dalloway but which show us Mrs. Brown, dreams that she all but drowns as she knows Woolf did. She henceforth determines to live, as Woolf simultaneously determines Mrs. Dalloway will live. The second addition is an intense exchange between the Leonard and Virginia Woolf characters on Richmond railway station which allows him to explain the background of her mental illness, attempted suicides, and their retreat to the London suburbs, and allows her a speech in which she defends her right to determine her own fate and principally to return to the "life ... the violent jolt" of London. She is dying in Richmond, and "If it is a choice," she says, "between Richmond and death, I choose death." In the third addition, which builds fragmented information in the novel into a conversation between Laura Brown and Clarissa Vaughan after her son Richard's suicide, Mrs. Brown explains her decision to abandon her children and marriage and to determine her own life: "It was death," she says, "I chose life."

The film in this way discovers an emphasis on women's self-determination and links these examples across the century especially through a figure who is at once Woolf's reader, her virtual character, and a surviving actor in the drama of later years. At the same time, while retaining and reworking its intertextual relation to Woolf and Cunningham, it belongs to a further, latter-day and non-literary context as a film about AIDS and as "a woman's picture." In this respect it promotes sympathy for an AIDS sufferer and a positive attitude towards being lesbian; it tells us how what Woolf barely dared contemplate is boldly realized two generations on, but also reveals the profound tensions in a woman's decision to choose her own life. These difficulties are concentrated once again in the middle figure Laura Brown who commits "the worst thing a mother can do" in abandoning her children. Julianne Moore's role in this film and in *Far from Heaven* (2002) in the same year, reinforce this theme in respectively exposing the stifling conformity and racial prejudice of 1950s suburban America. Both characters seek something other than the supposed, male-defined heaven of a standard marriage and domestic family life. In *Far from Heaven* the character cannot make the choice to quit this world for an inter-racial relationship. In *The Hours* Laura Brown's decision to lead an independent life tortured her son and invites opprobrium but re-inspires Clarissa Vaughan's commitment to her lover. Also, in the fourth addition to Cunningham's text, before a closing image of Woolf's drowning, Clarissa's daughter embraces Mrs. Brown. Thus the film confirms how the sisterhood it has evoked, across narratives of independent choice, whether of life or death, continues into a new generation. Thus, as a 'woman's picture' and in more of a pedagogic than nostalgic relation to women's history, the film 'refunctions' its source text, finding a pertinent transposition of Cunningham's reading of Woolf's own legacy.

What general conclusions can we draw from the above? Firstly, adaptation always implies a process of change and not an alignment of two fixed objects. At its most straightforward, this process may be confined to one medium and take the form of the rewriting in one book of another book or the remake of one film in another film. However, this process may involve a combination of book(s) and film(s) in no prescribed chronological order or assumed hierarchy. Secondly, to understand the process of adaptation as one of translation or, at its fullest, of a stratified dialogic and cross-cultural transformation over time, simultaneously undermines the predetermined status of the "original" and the idea of a unilinear reference back and forward down one channel. An adaptation may remove itself from its source text, edit or amplify a part of it, or transpose the whole, in a spirit of deference, homage, critique, opportunism, or indifference. In any case it will inevitably contract a supplementary set of relations with other texts. If there is one primary source text and the adaptation remains in significant textual contact with it, then it will not only present a changed version of its source but transform our understanding and valuation of that primary source too. Michael Cunningham's *The Hours* and the film of his book have, in this way, changed *Mrs. Dalloway* for its readers.

I've wanted to broaden an account of these operations to some consideration of the variations in a viewer's experience. This is an argument which has properly, of course, to take account of variations by age, class, sex, ethnicity, and culture. It also soon spirals away from any systematic description. We can, however, make two simple points: that the source text may not be the chronologically first text in a reader's or viewer's experience; and, secondly, that an "adaptation" may not be experienced as this. *Ocean's 11* (2001), for example, may exist in an actually experienced, potential, or no more than acknowledged relation to the 1960s "original" film and to the sequel *Ocean's 12* (2004). Viewing the three films will produce countless other possible textual and cultural connections. However, *Ocean's 11* may be a one-off viewing experience and known therefore as a "passive" adaptation – though it may be known in relation to other films directed by Steven Soderbergh and/ or starring George Clooney (for example *Solaris*, 2002). This film, the remake *Solaris*, may itself similarly stand in a contemporary setting either in a comparative or again independent relation to the "earlier" film and/or earlier book by Stanislaw Lem.

Adaptations, in short, wait to be realized. Their intertextual and transtextual meanings are inactive, manifest, or potential. The chronologies of our reading and viewing biographies shift back and forth and will on occasion meet up with the production line of books and films, but some (even most) of these texts will pass by as if on a distant track in a parallel world. Adaptations do require an order of events, a before and after, and I have reconstituted this sequence in the discussion of *The Hours* above. But history, *pace* Fredric Jameson, turns out to be less lost than out of joint, suspended or running in reverse. Not only, then, are the author/auteur and the text decentered, as announced by post-structuralism, but so too is the reader/viewer. That this indeterminacy, or "endless permutation of textual traces" has acquired an extra-textual reach into our lives and destinies is surely a feature of the continuing postmodern. The fact that the two-way compound narrative of adaptation from Virginia Woolf to Michael Cunningham's and Nicole Kidman's Virginia Woolf catches at these daily perplexities and yearnings for being someone, somewhere else "through the looking glass ... in another realm altogether; another time"[22] makes these texts both an exhibit of and a reflection upon this sensibility. In this way, adaptation can, as in this case, open out an alternative, undeveloped, or suppressed trace: demonstrating how we too might "refuse the future that's been offered and demand another, far grander and stranger".[23] And this too, surely, where in "refunctioning" its source it addresses its own times, is the answer to Jameson's doubts at the onset of the postmodern debate on "the critical value of the newer art."[21]

NOTES

1 Roland Barthes, *Image–Music–Text* (London: Fontana, 1977), pp. 142–8.
2 Julia Kristeva, *Desire in Language; A Semiotic Approach to Literature and Art*, trans. Thomas Gora, Alice Jardine, and Leon S. Roudiez ; ed. Leon. S. Roudiez (New York: Columbia University Press 1980), pp. 36–63; 64–91.
3 See James Naremore (ed.), *Film Adaptation* (London: Athlone, 2000).

4 Fredric Jameson, *The Cultural Turn: Selected Writings on the Postmodern* (London: Verso, 1998), pp. 20, 7.

5 Ibid., p 5.

6 Ibid., p. 6.

7 Ibid., p. 8.

8 Will Brooker, *Using the Force: Creativity, Community and "Star Wars" Fans* (London: Continuum, 2002). For a fuller discussion of fantasy literature on screen, see Chapter 10 in this volume.

9 Philip K. Dick, *Minority Report* (London: Gollancz, 2002), pp. 3, 4.

10 Ibid., p. 20.

11 Robert Stam, *Literature through Film: Realism, Magic and the Art of Adaptation* (Oxford: Blackwell, 2005), p. 4.

12 Mikhail M. Bakhtin, *Speech Genres and Other Late Essays*, ed. Caryl Emerson and Michael Holquist (Austin: University of Texas Press, 1986), p. 91.

13 Stam, *Literature through Film*, p. 4.

14 Ibid., p. 15.

15 Naoki Sakai, *Translation and Subjectivity: On "Japan" and Cultural Nationalism* (University of Minnesota Press: Minneapolis 1997), p. 15.

16 Ibid., p. 11.

17 Ibid., p. 3.

18 See Walter Benjamin, *Understanding Brecht* (London: Verso 1973), p. 93, and Elizabeth Wright, *Postmodern Brecht: A Re-Presentation* (London: Routledge, 1989), p. 45.

19 Bertolt Brecht, *Journals 1934–1955*, ed. John Willett, trans. Hugh Rorrison (London: Methuen, 1993), p. 392.

20 Michael Cunningham, *The Hours* (London: Fourth Estate, 1999), frontispiece. Subsequent references are included in parenthesis in the text and are to this edition.

21 *The Cultural Turn*, p. 20.

22 Cunningham, *The Hours*, p. 56.

23 Ibid., p. 81.

PART THREE

Genre, industry, taste

8

ECKART VOIGTS-VIRCHOW

Heritage and literature on screen: *Heimat* and heritage

Heritage film, costume film, period film, literary adaptation – often these terms address an overlapping corpus of films. For a long time it has been unfashionable to view these films primarily as adaptations, in spite of the fact that even today the presumably long-dead fidelity criticism is still regularly evoked as a straw man in semiotic and narrative film studies.[1] There is clearly an automatic difference between film and literature in terms of semiotic appearance and the widely different apparatus of production and reception. The adjective "literary" adaptation, as well as the recurrence of authors in titles (*Bram Stoker's Dracula*, 1992; *Mary Shelley's Frankenstein*, 1994), however, invoke the (untenable) primacy of literature as a cultural norm. In the medium-unspecific term "heritage" the transmedial cultural function of film, tourism, literature, educational and historical discourse emerges. All of these terms converge in the idea of a secondary, even subservient pastness of these films – a pastness which is divulged by costume, signalled by the "period" quality and implied in the canonized literary precursor. It follows that the terms "literary adaptation" and "heritage film" also converge in the idea of the canonical, in the body of cultural works accepted by consensus as valid and meaningful to a given community. Because of this, the term heritage film is useful in addressing issues of national, ethnic, cultural, class, and gender identities that are crucial in analyses of these films. This chapter attempts to account for the curious transnational and transcultural migration of heritage concepts which were originally and uniquely formulated in Britain, and are, for instance, largely absent from American research into adaptations and from period and costume films.

The *Oxford English Dictionary* definition of "heritage" includes "any property, and esp. land, which devolves by right of inheritance" and "the condition or state transmitted from ancestors." Heritage industries (films, novels, tourism, theme parks, etc.) re-establish the past as a property or possession, which, by "natural," or better, "naturalized" right of birth, "belongs" to the present, or, to be more precise, to certain interests or concerns active in the present.

Heritage is not history (which seeks knowledge about the past), it is "modern-day use of elements of the past."[2] Thus, heritage is a shared cultural memory prone to be abused for nationalist or ethnocentrist purposes unless rendered decentered. As Julia Kristeva, Antony Easthope, Homi Bhabha, and others have frequently argued, heritage activities revisit the past because memory generates an imaginary identity. In order to prevent variants of nationalism unacceptable to differentiated and particular markets, the idea of a nation must be de-centered and "heteroglossic." As Mikhail Bakhtin stated in "Discourse in the Novel," "this verbal–ideological decentering will occur only when a national culture loses 'its sealed off and self-sufficient character, when it becomes conscious of itself as only one among *other* cultures and languages."[3]

As a recent introduction to heritage tourism points out, heritage comes in a number of guises, both tangible objects (for example buildings, landscapes, museum pieces, and archived documents) and intangible practices (actualizations and performances in festivals, arts, cultural events; films cut across this boundary). In scope, one may differentiate between personal, local, national, and world heritage. A heritage location may encompass natural, cultural, rural as well as urban landscapes, ranging from national parks to castles to factories, and from war memorials to museums to theme parks.[4]

Communities of "worldmates" are created through shared experience, norms, values knowledge, and, of course, media usage. Following the pioneering theories of cultural memory (Pierre Nora, Maurice Halbwachs, Aby Warburg, Jan and Aleida Assmann), one may wish to replace the term "heritage" by the less exclusionary "collective" and "cultural" memory. Heritage is a very restrictive notion of cultural memory; it is diachronic, the preservation of a desirable past. One may speak of a crystallized past which remains a stable utopia across the centuries. It is also a metonymic past because, in general, only part of a given space is loaded with the defining features of a community's heritage. Thus, heritage space and heritage time amalgamate in leisurely pre-industrial gentry life, a feel-good utopia.

Heritage products invariably make reference to the country house, the stately mansion, the gentrified life-style of a neo-pastoral southern Englishness which has come to represent all of the British Isles.[5] The stereotype, known in Germany as "die feine englische Art," features the understated but proud English gentleman (rather than the boorish John Bull), public school norms of conduct embodied in the Earl of Chesterfield's correspondence to his son, self-discipline, and the proverbial "stiff upper lip" of politeness, fair play, and good sportsmanship (as domesticated medieval duelling), slightly splenetic conservatism, exquisite taste and sensibility in the vein of the Earl of Shaftesbury, and liberal republicanism ("the free-born Englishman") in advance of the backward European mainland.

In England, nationalism may be noted since Renaissance trends towards a civic nationalism, specifically in Tudor and Elizabethan times. Englishness and English national identities are thus to some extent founded on ideal images, mainly derived from the gentry of the Augustan Age. It is a civic, elite and class-based rather than ethnic nationalism (which emerged in the nineteenth century in England and throughout Europe, but more intensely in Germany).[6]

Probably the decisive point about the stereotypes of Englishness and England is this: it is an old country in the sense that it was not subjected to the same upheavals, newnesses, and rebirths as post-revolutionary France, post-World War II Germany, or post-Perestroika Russia. As Tom Nairn argues, being first, the English revolutions could be perceived as slow, conventional, non-theoretical, pragmatic, and organic – as opposed to the abstract theory of revolution elsewhere.[7] This has contributed to the *Biedermeier* version of "Deep England," which was severely attacked in the 1980s,[8] and which is excellently parodied in Julian Barnes's *England, England* (1998) as well as in the metahistorical TV sitcom *Blackadder* (1983–9).

Even films set in the twentieth century may be easily compatible with the quest to preserve eighteenth-century ideals or nineteenth-century repression, and the Austen-formula ("Three or four families in a country village is the very thing to work on") still operates in the formulaic romances of publishers Mills and Boon and has done since the 1920s, the ideological origin of trash heritage à la Rosamunde Pilcher et al. The example of Pilcher suggests that the heritage formula may work without the literary pedigree, but canonical nineteenth-century novels have been a clear focus in heritage adaptations. Key texts have seen multiple adaptations, occasionally between 20 and 100, and, as Kamilla Elliott found, there have been more than 1,500 film and television adaptations of British Victorian prose fiction. Elliott concludes that "British Victorian novels and novellas have been more frequently adapted to film than any other body of literature, including Shakespeare plays."[9] Some reasons are clear: film and TV have taken over the role of dominating mass-media discourse from the nineteenth-century novel (as argued by Metz and Eisenstein); storytelling conventions constitute obvious parallels that Colin MacCabe homogenized as the "classic realist text"; the nineteenth century emphasizes a harmonious national and ethnic identity, evoking the centrist values of England as synecdochally pervasive throughout the Empire. It also reflects greatness and moral stability as well as socio-cultural norms, hinged on the family as central social unit. The feminine dominance in both heritage/costume films and Victorian prose fiction is obvious and the Victorian novel provides a wealthy reservoir of powerful heroines enmeshed in, and fighting against clearly established patriarchal strictures.

The seemingly organic attitude towards heritage in Britain is highlighted by the fact that the preservation of cultural memory is organized largely as a private grassroots endeavor. The government agency, English Heritage, operates many of its 500 sites in public–private partnerships. The National Trust, a private charity founded in 1895, gained its mass membership (now over 3 million) only after World War II. The National Trust now runs more than 200 buildings and oversees more than 600,000 acres of countryside in Britain, whereas in Germany such preservation is considered a responsibility of the state (and publicly funded agencies such as the *Stiftung Preussischer Kulturbesitz*).

Heimat and heritage

By way of comparison, one may briefly look at the German term *Heimat* and the Austro-German word for heritage film, *Heimatfilm*. The term *Heimat* (home, home town, native country) is difficult to translate from the German. When German schoolchildren were asked in 1984 what *Heimat* meant to them, they came up with the terms "timeless," "truthful," "pleasant," and "intimate." Home is where you feel at home and what you know to be home – and film and television clearly play a part in providing this emotional homeliness. Just like the gender differences in the roughly parallel terms "mother country" and *Vaterland* (fatherland), the term *Heimat* has different shades of meaning to the term "heritage" in England. The English heritage concept appears more elitist, feminine, regional, and historical than the German Austro-Prussian *Heimat* which is more ethnic, masculine, national, and spatial. Of course, the term *Heimat* has been tainted by its use in fascist and Nazi ideologies. The Nazi ideology of Eduard Spranger, for instance, is partially based on an apotheosis of rural rootedness, conflating concepts of ethnicity and nation (*Blut und Boden*, "blood and soil"). Thus, at least in Germany, the term *Heimat* smacks of anti-internationalism, anti-Marxism, anti-Enlightenment, anti-capitalism, anti-urbanism, and military aggression, particularly towards eastern Europe. Contemporary heritage-film audiences, therefore, seem to respond better to the modest scope of the English heritage construction – domestic, regional, feminine, elitist. In spite of the conflation of ethnicity and nationalism in the fascist version of *Heimat*, it is often thought to relate to the immediate region, the close-knit community of a village rather than the British "home" which is said to refer to all of the British Isles. The status of this British "island *Heimat*," however, is currently unclear. Does it refer to the political entity the United Kingdom of Britain and Northern Ireland, or to Great Britain, or to the mix of nation, ethnicity, and culture that composes the four nations or regions (Irish, Scottish, Welsh, English). Tom Nairn has frequently ridiculed the idea of a British identity as

"*Ukania*," adapting Musil's *Mann ohne Eigenschaften* (*The Man Without Qualities*), which cast the Austro-Hungarian Empire as *Kakania*. According to Nairn, this island's identity bears:

> ... a variety of titles having different functions and nuances – the U.K. (or 'Yookay', as Raymond Williams re-labeled it), Great Britain (imperial robes), Britain (boring lounge-suit), England (poetic but troublesome), the British Isles (too geographical), "This Country" (all-purpose within the Family), or "This Small Country of Ours" (defensive-Shakespearian).[10]

In addition, Britain is marked by ethnic diversity. There is, after all, still no black in the Union Jack; as Bhabha put it, "the bastion of Englishness crumbles at the sight of immigrants and factory workers."[11] A false, or at least myopic sense of ethnic homogeneity, may be regarded as one of the chief attractions in the "homeliness" of heritage films, somewhat equivalent to the ill-defined, but supposedly homogeneous German *Leitkultur* (i.e., guiding, mainstream, or hegemonic culture).

The Austro-German *Heimatfilm* is marked by landscapes untainted by industrialization, revolution, or war. Key regions include rural Bavaria and Austria, the Alps, the Northern heaths and moors, and the seacoasts, the Bodensee or the Rhine valley. This is very similar to the heritage film seeking out landscapes construed as unaffected by the industrial revolution – islands and highlands, the Yorkshire moors (projected as Brontë country), the West Country, especially the coastlines of Devon, Cornwall, and Kent (the latter marketed as the garden of England). Sheep (particularly in England) and horses (particularly in Germany) people the landscapes, which remain free of human exploitation. Carriages, vintage cars, and antique steam trains provide a sense of stable pastness even to heritage films set in modern times.

Plots typically revolve around saving the traditional family seat from financial peril. In general, safeguarding, stabilizing, and reinvigorating the family are pivotal themes to these films. Threats to conjugal bliss and generational equilibrium are variously supplied by divorcees, intruding *femmes fatales*, tempters and temptresses, women and men with a past. Sons and daughters supply filial disobedience and generational conflict.

The German *Heimatfilm* had its heyday in the 1950s, clearly reducing the strain, guilt, and complexity of the post-war years, in the wake of *Schwarzwaldmädel* (1950) and the Karlheinz Böhm/Romy Schneider vehicle *Sissi* (1955). In the 1960s and 1970s, there were alternative and critical variants, the anti-*Heimatfilm*, and finally, the 1980s and 1990s have contributed a few genre revisions best described as post-*Heimatfilm*. Edgar Reitz's magnificent trilogy *Heimat* (1984, 1992, 2004) is set in the provincial Hunsrück village, Schabbach, in Munich during the student revolt of the

1960s, and in post-unification Hunsrück, 1990s, spanning the entire twentieth century. Reitz's *Heimat* trilogy is neither a critical revision of the nostalgic *Heimatfilm* nor does it uncritically embrace the idea of *Heimat*, as it portrays its corruption and insists on the regional and temporal rather than the national dimension. Reitz successfully escapes and redefines the established German heritage formula with the aesthetics of a film *auteur*, setting a new standard for the post-*Heimatfilm*.

The "feel good" factor: heritage – definitions and recyclings

Both concepts, *Heimat* and heritage, emotionalize space and time by constructing a cultural memory. How, then, may we define "heritage film," which is readily recognizable by its high production values, its exuding historicity, its period authenticity? Andrew Higson specifies that he is concerned with "English costume dramas" of the 1980s and 1990s that "articulate a nostalgic and conservative celebration of the values and lifestyles of the privileged classes" and in doing so, reinvent "an England that no longer existed [...] as something fondly remembered and desirable."[12]

Charles Barr first introduced the term "heritage film" with respect to "British understatement and the rich British heritage" in wartime films such as Laurence Olivier's *Henry V*.[13] Since then, basically two phases can be distinguished as heritage heydays. The 1980s films by David Lean (*A Passage to India*, 1984) as well as those of the late Ismail Merchant and James Ivory (*A Room with a View*, 1985; *Howards End*, 1992; *The Remains of the Day*, 1993) were, at best, seen as catering to an individual, nostalgic desire to be part of a non-organic, indirect community. Director Alan Parker famously derided this as the "Laura Ashley school of filmmaking." These films were marked by a number of formal, social, and ideological traits, the key characteristics of which were:

- Small to medium budgets, with a clear dependence on the classic TV serial and other heritage and history formats on TV (the Reithian ethos of betterment and relevance to the traditionally and predominantly national TV audience).[14]
- An appeal to relatively mature, feminine, or gay middle-class audiences, drawn to films exuding warmth and emotionality.
- Reference to traditional quality (decorum, moderation, harmony) beyond the experiments of modernism, stylistic excess, crude low comedy, or the action and horror in movies addressed to male teenagers.
- The use of the implicit values of a literary canon, authorship, and (British, theater-trained) quality acting.

- A showcasing of landscapes (often the rural south) and costume props in an occupational vacuum or a state of permanent recreation.
- An adherence to conventional generic formulas (mimesis, tradition, classics), stylistic means such as long takes and deep focus.
- A focus on domestic issues – historical matters are either absent, ignored, or relegated to personalized and private spheres.

In the 1990s, a second phase of heritage films emerged, including adaptations of Forster, Austen, the Brontës, Hardy, Dickens, Gaskell, Thackeray, James, and Wharton, to mention the most popular authors. This second phase sparked the so-called heritage film debate between Higson and his critics Claire Monk, Stella Bruzzi, and Pamela Church Gibson, often inspired by Raphael Samuel's more benign revision of heritage culture and re-enacted history.[15] Pamela Church Gibson argued that the visual style of 1990s heritage films departs from the canonical Merchant Ivory pattern of the 1980s. According to Monk, 1990s heritage films attempt to go beyond the category in both content and marketing, while some "contemporary" films (such as The Full Monty [1997] and Notting Hill [1999]) might be equally denounced as conservative and nostalgic. Today, both "trashed" and "recycled" heritage concepts circulate within the proliferating genre (e.g. Jude [1996] and Bridget Jones's Diary [2001]). Regardless of whether one interprets this as an innovative or a tried and true formula, the presumed canon of generic formulae has been splintered to include the terms "alternative," "revisionist" heritage, or even heritage films projected as "not-heritage" films, such as Elizabeth (1998) and The Wings of the Dove (1997).[16]

Higson, however, remains unconvinced and continues to reject Monk's argument for a "post-heritage" film: "[...] there is no clear break between these films and, say, Merchant Ivory's Forster adaptations."[17] Following Monk, one might be tempted to abandon the term "heritage film" entirely, but the terms "period film," "literary adaptation,"[18] "historical film,"[19] "retrovision,"[20] or "costume film"[21] open up different cans of worms. The very fact that the categories stimulated so much criticism illustrates how productive and problematic they continue to be.

Heritage films are crucially determined by creating heritage space through location hunting, through "authentifying" period settings and through lavish but "correct" costumes. In the case of Pride and Prejudice, directed by Simon Langton (1995), location hunting was the initial and in some ways, most essential part of the production process. The dimension of "heritage space," therefore, is twofold: it is an "authentified" space and it displays high production values that stimulate the heritage imagination, invigorating ancillary markets, leading to book purchases and readings or re-readings of the novel. In this sense, watching a heritage film may be an inexpensive substitute to visiting a literary heritage site (as a media equivalent to, or *Ersatz* for, real heritage spaces such as Haworth). As Dallen and Boyd hold, with respect to the heritage tourist, real and imagined places merge. Dallen and Boyd do not regard this as critical because literary tourists are not concerned with authenticity, but with exciting their imagination and their interest in literature.[22] Heritage space in movies is by definition staged and invented. Its myopic pastness frequently may be regarded as sanitizing and distorting the past, but audiences seem to respond to the feel-good factor and the "good" memory images they experience. Lyme Park as Pemberley in *Pride and Prejudice*, among other things, says: this is a splendid, expensive place in an equally splendid, expensive, and high profile BBC production which will safeguard the institution's renown. Viewers ascribe "authenticity" to heritage films to some degree because of the presence of "authority," that is canonical literary authors, such as Jane Austen, but to a considerably higher degree, because of their "heritage space." Gerry Scott has commented on his production design for *Pride and Prejudice*: "our aim was to film as much as possible on location because we wanted to use the English landscape as a player in the film."[23] According to Emma Thompson's shooting diary, Ang Lee felt similarly about Flete Estate (representing Barton Cottage in *Sense and Sensibility*): "for Ang, the house is as important a character as the women." Thompson's diary concentrates on the English weather, on Ang Lee wanting sheep in every exterior shot, on pulling "boobs up as far as they'd go" and on getting the season right by having onlookers picking daisies from the lawn when they wouldn't have been flowering at that time of year.[24]

Core heritage films, then, are about both reading and showcasing the token nature of landscapes and costume props, about ruralist nostalgia that harks back to the neo-Romantic "picturesque" ideal developed in response to the threats posed by revolutions and industrialism since the beginning of the nineteenth century. The main function of period authenticity is to avoid dissonance in savoring the past utopia.

The recent case of Mira Nair's *Vanity Fair* (2004), with Gurinder Chada's *Bride & Prejudice* (2004), part of a mini-trend of merging heritage film and Bollywood, is exemplary in exposing the multiple identifications and contradictions within the genre. On the filmmaker's commentary track of the DVD, Nair exhibits a revisionist sensibility: "I wanted *Vanity Fair* to be as far from a stuffy period genteel frock drama as possible." She appropriately introduces ethnic diversity and urban poverty to her heritage space. On the other hand, she proudly mentions ninety stately homes and the Regency streets of Bath that supplied sumptuous and flamboyant locations. Nair seems also aware of the tension between Thackeray's astringent satire and the standard heritage formula based on the romantic comedy. This awareness results in an uneasy marriage of incompatible genres that takes the bite out of the satire in a beautiful *mise-en-scène*.

Nair's mellow treatment turns the plotting upstart Becky into a proto-feminist (but almost devoted wife) and romantic heroine. Not once do we hear, see, or read the authoritative voice of Thackeray's narrator passing judgment on her follies from a vantage point, recounting the "horrid, sarcastic, demoniacal laughter" of the ill-treated Becky who, however, "deserve[s] entirely the treatment [she] gets."[25] Nair explicitly rejects the caricature in her title character (largely deprived of its devious scheming) as well as in the Sir Pitts or Lord Steyne, or the feeble do-gooders Amelia Osborne or Major Dobbin. Nair explicitly praises actors Douglas Hodge (Pitt) and Gabriel Byrne (Steyne) for contributing emotional facets to characters whose caricatures might have more clearly undermined the heritage formula. In this film, dedicated to the late Edward Said in the credits, India is an additional source of exotic extravaganza and the colonized territory holds a Utopian promise of escape from the social strictures of the colonizer as Becky finally escapes with Jos to India. This Bollywood-inspired fairytale of reverse colonization, however, comes with the inevitable American lead (Reese Witherspoon), with a cast of mostly theater-trained British heritage actors such as Romola Garai (cast because of her role in Andrew Davies's *Daniel Deronda*), Douglas Hodge, Bob Hoskins, Geraldine McEwan, or Eileen Atkins (and only McEwan and Atkins succeed in delivering wonderfully sharp caricatures). Miss Swartz (German for "black"), a half-Jewish, "untamed" racial negro stereotype, both in Thackeray's text and vignettes (which Nair claims to have played a major part in the adaptive process) is turned into a fully restrained and assimilated ballroom beauty.

In spite of these clear allegiances to the rom-com heritage formula (rather than to the adapted text), Nair's DVD commentary ends on the inevitable nod to literary authority and fidelity: "I hope that I have done some justice to Thackeray's great banquet of a novel." The adapted screenplay was written by actor–writer Julian Fellowes (*Gosford Park*), who had earlier commented on the inevitable anachronism in shooting heritage films in his novel *Snobs*: "The rest of the cast has to sit in endless restaurants on location hearing how hard they've tried to get the right candlesticks or mobcabs when they know as well as you do that the central characters do not [...] bear the slightest semblance of reality."[26] This is especially true of the cognitive dissonance resulting from Witherspoon as Becky Sharp, who was pregnant during almost the entire shooting. Heritage convention tailored to contemporary markets, not authenticity, provide the yardstick criterion for heritage films, as *Vanity Fair*'s producer Donna Gigliotti makes clear in the DVD package *Making Of*, when she describes Becky Sharp in anti-heritage terms as a Regency Madonna. The title "The Women behind *Vanity Fair*," the pride in a production team dominated by women, and the clear focus on a streamlined Becky Sharp as a proto-feminist and contemporary woman make clear that the film addresses the heritage of female emancipation. In *Vanity Fair*, this emancipation has an un-English locale, the colourful, fashionable India. Post-colonial Bollywood is showcased, for instance, in the choreographed bared-midriff slave dance that replaces Thackeray's charade. The seductive musical esprit borrowed from Bollywood clearly seeks to preserve the heritage feel-good factor threatened by the naturalism of flea-infested wigs, too much mud on the clothes, disruptive *mise-en-scène*, or the spoilsport nineteenth-century social criticism and social satire (inevitable in Thackeray) that is occasionally highlighted in the movie.

The increased viability of marketing heritage movies for DVD sale and rental clearly speaks for the continuing appeal of films created for the heritage audience beyond the adolescent multiplex crowd. Even if the heritage market has reached the point of saturation and the "Austenmania" of the mid-1990s has abated,[27] heritage films continue to appear in various formats and particularly as TV mini-series. The "heritage industry" did not simply vanish into thin air when the new Labour government renamed the Department of National Heritage the Department of Culture, Media, and Sport. In the cinema, *Girl with a Pearl Earring*, *I Capture the Castle* and *Nicholas Nickleby* were released in 2003, Michael Radford's *The Merchant of Venice* in 2004, Roman Polanski's adaptation of *Oliver Twist* in October 2005 and Branagh's *As You Like It* is in post-production. On TV, the quintessential heritage adaptor Andrew Davies has another adaptation of *Brideshead Revisited* in the pipeline. His recent work indicates a move towards generic hybridity by adapting lesser-known Eliot novels (*Daniel Deronda* 2002), lesser-known novelists such as Anthony Trollope (*The Way We Live Now* 2001, *He Knew He Was Right* 2004), non-English novels (*Dr. Zhivago* 2002), "sexier" contemporary recreations of Victorianism, like the Sarah Waters adaptations *Tipping the Velvet* (BBC, 2002) and *Fingersmith* (without Davies, BBC, 2005), "sexier" ancient British history (*Boudica*, ITV, 2003) and, finally, heritage soap-opera (the sixteen-episode *Bleak House*, BBC, 2005).[28]

The migrating fantasy heritage of Rosamunde Pilcher TV

The German nineteenth-century heritage (diminished by fragmented political units and Prussian militarism since the eighteenth century) has been *kaputt*, arguably since 1914, but definitely since 1945. After the retrogressive post-World War II *Heimatfilm* was rendered obsolete by the 1960s student revolt and the *Autorenfilm*, Germany needed an *Ersatz*-heritage. In the climate of global consumerism, audiences tend to appropriate other heritages – and if one is not happy with one's Germanness, then one attempts to appropriate fantasies of Anglo-British heritage. The fact that this new *Heimat* for the German heritage tourist is less authentic than a distinct "German" heritage and not supported by an indigenous literary pedigree (such as Theodor Fontane) seems largely irrelevant because, again, its "feel-good" factor is essential. It simply gives to the German public an emotional stability in the absence of the defunct German tradition of rooted emotionality. The ethnically homogeneous English elite nationalism is particularly attractive because it provides the sophistication of the West Country mansion house which more "authentic," ethnically rooted, backward, and boorish scenarios of provincialism and parochialism cannot supply for contemporary German consumers. The definition of heritage/*Heimat* is clearly regional rather than national, and private rather than public. In addition, German viewers may be unaware of, or less affected by, the class implications of this stately country house. German TV, therefore, assembles a cast of indigenous German TV actors in an English heritage space, a heritage space the traditional *Heimatfilm* cannot afford. The Rosamunde Pilcher adaptations are part of a globalized heritage industry which circulates geographies according to consumer demand. Identity tourism gives German audiences and travellers an *Ersatz*-heritage.

The German cycle of Pilcher adaptations was screened by the public service broadcasting channel ZDF whose public image in Germany suggests that it specializes in catering to mature audiences. The first adaptation was broadcast in 1993, with a piece called *Stürmische Begegnung* (clearly reminiscent of *Stürmische Höhen*, the German translation of *Wuthering Heights*) and with more than 7 million viewers. Since then, audiences have averaged over 8 million – very satisfactory for ZDF, particularly as it was shown at the same time on a Sunday night as the most prestigious German crime show, *Tatort*. In fact, the rating is higher than that of recent British heritage TV productions.

Rosamunde Pilcher (1924–) is a Mills and Boon novelist, formerly writing under the *nom de plume* Jane Fraser and nicknamed the "Queen of Kitsch." She was brought up in Cornwall and sets her novels regularly either at the country mansion "Nancherrow" on the Cornish coast or in Scotland, "where life jogs on at a slower pace, people do stay and live in small communities and take care of each other" as Pilcher is on record to have said. Pilcher has sold more than 30 million books worldwide, more than one third of these, 11 million, in Germany. In 2002 she was awarded an OBE and in the same year both she and her editor at the ZDF, Dr. Claus Beling, jointly received the British Tourism Award. Beling reported that, at first, the German productions were not too well received in Devon and Cornwall, but after busloads of German tourists have been discharged in St. Ives and elsewhere on the Rosamunde Pilcher trail, the British Tourism Authority has discovered the potential of German heritage tourism. In a recent interview I was granted by Beling (14 February 2005 in Mainz) he made some interesting comments on the cycle of 57(!) Pilcher productions since 1993. He ventured that Pilcher's name contributed to her success in Germany because it is not necessarily decoded as "British" – in fact many viewers seem to perceive her as German. The ZDF has stopped commissioning audience research because ratings are stable and because they know their audience segments – female and mature rather than male and adolescent. Having outbid an American rival for the rights to Pilcher's works, the ZDF commissions the productions, which are invariably shot on location in the south-west of England, for instance in St. Ives or Devon. The first productions by Portman Hannibal and Rikolt von Gagern were co-produced with ITV and BSkyB. Since then, the production company Tele-München has fully taken over. The 1998 production *Das große Erbe* (literally "The great inheritance," English title: *Nancherrow*) is an interesting case, because director Simon Langton (of *Pride and Prejudice* fame) guarantees the quintessential ingredients of showcasing the country house, because it has a mixed Anglo-German cast (Lara Joy Körner, Christian Kohlund, Philipp Moog/Joanna Lumley, Robert Hardy, and Patrick MacNee), and because it involves a scenario which has a mixed Anglo-German love story in a post-war depression setting. Pilcher productions with an Anglo-American cast (for instance, *September*, produced in 1995, set in the Scottish highlands and starring Jacqueline Bisset, Michael York, Mariel Hemingway, Peter O'Toole, and Edward Fox) regularly scored lower ratings on German TV. A typical contemporary Pilcher production, therefore, involves an all-German cast and the production language is German (although words on, for example, documents and signboards are invariably in English in the film). These productions have never been aired in Britain because there is no infrastructure for dubbing, Beling suggested, but also because the German *mise-en-scène* of heritage Englishness would hardly go down well with audiences in the British Isles. The Pilcher "trash heritage" has been successfully sold, however, all across Europe, and even to South America. It follows that the global image of Britain is, in part, determined by German heritage TV.

As Coelsch-Foisner, who, regrettably, does not address the TV productions, has recently argued, "wellbeing" (English) or "wellness" (German) are the chief attractions of consuming Pilcher[29] – and these are precisely the terms that do not immediately spring to mind with reference to German history. As opposed to Pilcherland, German heritage offers militarism and villains galore; the bombing of Dresden may be briefly mentioned in Pilcher TV (*Das große Erbe*), but it is not nice enough to remain there long. In fact, Pilcherland is offering the predominantly feminine German target audience a space to enact the great reconciliation with Britain, the former enemy, because, as a reviewer put it:

> This is a world where there is no problem that can't be solved by a strong cup of tea, a nice fire and a good meal. A place where the biggest villains are ex-wives and lovers – and even these aren't terribly bad and mostly end up having redeeming qualities.[30]

To sum up, we all know that the *pars pro toto*, the crystallized past of the heritage film never existed. One should rather focus on investigations into how Germans or Britons design their new, globalized fantasies of national identity: remembering private pasts without history and regional pasts rather than nations. Englishness does not crumble (as Bhabha suggested), it migrates.

NOTES

1 For example, Robert Stam, "Introduction: The Theory and Practice of Adaptation," in, *Literature and Film: A Guide to the Theory and Practice of Film Adaptation*, ed. Robert Stam and Alessandra Raengo (Malden, Massachusetts and Oxford: Blackwell, 2005), pp. 14–16; Brian McFarlane, *Novel into Film: An Introduction to the Theory of Adaptation* (Oxford: Clarendon Press, 1996), pp. 8–10.

2 J. Timothy Dallen and Stephen W. Boyd, *Heritage Tourism* (Harlow: Pearson, 2003), p. 4.

3 Mikhail Bakhtin, "Discourse in the Novel" [1934/35], in Bakhtin, *The Dialogic Imagination*, trans. Caryl Emerson and Michael Holquist (Austin: University of Texas Press, 1992), p. 370.

4 Dallen and Boyd, *Heritage Tourism*, pp. 3–17.

5 On Englishness, see John Lucas, *England and Englishness: Ideas of Nationhood in English Poetry 1688–1900* (Iowa City: University of Iowa Press, 1990); David Gervais, *Literary Englands: Versions of "Englishness" in Modern Writing* (Cambridge: Cambridge University Press, 1993); Simon Gikandi, *Maps of Englishness: Writing Identity in the Culture of Colonialism* (New York: Columbia University Press, 1996); Antony Easthope, *Englishness and National Culture* (London and New York: Routledge, 1998); Jeremy Paxman, *The English: A Portrait of a People* (London: Penguin, 1999); Krishan Kumar, *The Making of English National Identity* (Cambridge: Cambridge University Press, 2003); Alun Howkins, "Rurality and English Identity," in *British Cultural Studies. Geography, Nationality, and Identity*, ed. Morley, David and Kevin Robins (Oxford: Oxford University Press, 2001), pp. 145–56.

6 Lia Greenfield, *Nationalism: Five Roads to Modernity* (Cambridge Massachusetts: Harvard University Press, 1992), pp. 14–17.
7 See Tom Nairn, *The Break-up of Britain* (London: New Left Books, 1977), pp. 16–17.
8 See Patrick Wright, *On Living in an Old Country: The National Past in Contemporary Britain* (London: Verso, 1985); Robert Hewison, *The Heritage Industry: Britain in a Climate of Decline* (London: Methuen, 1987).
9 Kamilla Elliott, *Rethinking the Novel/Film Debate* (Cambridge: Cambridge University Press, 2003), p. 3.
10 Tom Nairn, quoted in Kumar, *English National Identity*, p. 3.
11 Homi Bhabha, "Introduction: Narrating the Nation" in *Nation and Narration*, ed. Homi Bhabha (London: Routledge, 1990), p. 7; see also Stuart Hall, "Racism and Reaction," in *Five Views on Multi-Racial Britain* (London: Commission for Racial Equality, 1978), pp. 23–35; Paul Gilroy, *There Ain't No Black in the Union Jack: The Cultural Politics of Race and Nation* (London: Hutchinson, 1987).
12 Andrew Higson, *English Heritage, English Cinema: Costume Drama since 1980* (Oxford: Oxford University Press, 2003), p. 12.
13 Charles Barr, "Introduction: Amnesia and Schizophrenia," in *All Our Yesterdays: 90 Years of British Cinema*, ed. Charles Barr (London: British Film Institute, 1986), p. 12.
14 Lord Reith was the first director-general of the BBC (founded in 1927). He conceived of radio (and later television) as tools for civilizing and educating the nation. On the classic TV serial see Sarah Cardwell, *Adaptation Revisited: Television and the Classic Novel* (Manchester and New York: Manchester University Press, 2002); Robert Giddings and Keith Selby (eds.), *The Classic Serial on Television and Radio* (Basingstoke: Palgrave, 2001).
15 See Raphael Samuel, *Theatres of Memory* (London and New York: Verso, 1994).
16 See Pamela Church Gibson, "Fewer Weddings and More Funerals: Changes in the Heritage Film," in *British Cinema of the 90s*, ed. Robert Murphy (London: British Film Institute, 2000), pp. 115–24; Claire Monk, "The British Heritage-Film Debate Revisited," in *British Historical Cinema. The History, Heritage and Costume Film*, ed. Claire Monk and Amy Sargeant (London and New York: Routledge, 2002), pp. 176–98, esp. p. 195. For collections on this debate see also Ginette Vincendeau (ed.), *Film, Literature, Heritage: A Sight and Sound Reader* (London: British Film Institute, 2001), and Eckart Voigts-Virchow (ed.), *Janespotting and Beyond: British Heritage Retrovisions since the Mid-1990s* (Tübingen: Narr, 2004).
17 Andrew Higson, *English Heritage, English Cinema*, pp. 44–5.
18 See, e.g., Stam and Raengo (eds.), *Literature and Film*; Elliott, *Rethinking the Novel/Film Debate*; Cardwell, *Adaptation Revisited*; James Naremore (ed.), *Film Adaptation* (New Brunswick, New Jersey: Rutgers University Press, 2000).
19 See, e.g., Monk and Sargeant (ed.), *British Historical Cinema*; Marcia Landy, *Cinematic Uses of the Past* (Minneapolis: University of Minnesota Press, 1997); Marcia Landy (ed.), *The Historical Film: History and Memory in Media* (New Brunswick, New Jersey: Rutgers University Press, 2001).
20 See Deborah Cartmell, I. Q. Hunter, and Imelda Whelehan (eds.), *Retrovisions: Reinventing the Past in Film and Fiction* (London: Pluto Press, 2001).

21 See, e.g., Sue Harper, *Picturing the Past: The Rise and Fall of the British Costume Film* (London: British Film Institute, 1994); Julianne Pidduck, *Contemporary Costume Film: Space, Place and the Past* (London: British Film Institute, 2004).

22 Dallen and Boyd, *Heritage Tourism*, p. 40.

23 In Sue Birtwistle and Susie Conklin, *The Making of "Pride and Prejudice"* (London: Penguin Books/BBC Books, 1995), p. 37.

24 Emma Thompson, *The Sense and Sensibility Screenplay and Diaries* (New York: Newmarket Press, 1996), pp. 228, 237, 255, 259.

25 *Vanity Fair*, ch. 2.

26 Quoted in Lynn Barber, "Jolly Good Fellowes," *The Observer* (28 November 2004).

27 See Higson, *English Heritage, English Cinema*, pp. 138–41.

28 See Andrew Davies, Chapter 16 in this volume.

29 Sabine Coelsch-Foisner, "Reading Rosamunde Pilcher from a Consumer Perspective," *Consumer Cultures: Journal for the Study of British Cultures* 11.2 (2004), 155–167.

30 www.januarymagazine.com (accessed January 2004).

9

IMELDA WHELEHAN

"Don't let's ask for the moon!": reading and viewing the woman's film

When examining popular fiction and its metamorphosis into film it is immediately clear that we are not just concerned with the relationship between an
individual book and its cinematic interpretation, but with the history of
genre fiction in the two media, and the place it is accorded in literary and
film studies respectively. Popular romantic fiction is assigned the position of
a "debased" genre and most commonly spoken about in terms of the mass
market romance, which nonetheless claims its inspiration from some canonical classics, including *Pamela*, *Pride and Prejudice*, and *Jane Eyre*. In commercial terms it is a lucrative market, but critics regard its content as
predictable, ideologically conservative, and undemanding of its reader.
With very few nods to historical change, it has a formula which requires
little adjustment to maintain its momentum; it has not matured into a literary
form with active defenders (such as the fields of science fiction or the crime
novel), and even now very few readers are keen to publicize their love of the
genre. Romance assumes women are its readers and at the "bottom end" of
the market – Mills & Boon or Harlequin – the publishers' market research
has allowed them to consistently produce bestsellers, albeit those where the
author's name is of little consequence. Critical attention was mainly negative
until feminist critics reviewed their initial hostility to the manipulativeness of
the form and turned their gaze on the woman as reader. From this perspective, and represented by pathfinding texts such as Tania Modleski's *Loving
with a Vengeance* (1982) and Janice Radway's *Reading the Romance* (1987),
there evolved some acute insights into the way women use popular cultural
forms to negotiate their own life certainties and to endorse choices that can,
without much interrogation, be shown to have little to do with the vicissi-
tudes of relationships and romantic love.

The "woman's film" indicates a similar identification of a gendered market within the film industry and the films in this broad category "treat
problems defined as 'female' (problems revolving around domestic life, the
family, children, self-sacrifice, and the relationship between women and

production vs. that between women and reproduction), and, most critically, are directed toward a female audience."[1] Films in this grouping largely come under the categories of melodrama and romance, but can also stretch to horror and comedy; the main issue being that they anticipate a woman's eye and tastes and incorporate an assumption that this is necessarily always markedly different from a man's. *Now, Voyager*, has come to be a template for "the woman's film." *Now, Voyager*, a text that was first published as a novel in 1941 and released as a film in late 1942, represents a reversal of the usual economy of exchange between novel and adaptation (the film has become the definitive text) and the success of the film over the novel is characteristic of the fate of much popular fiction during the so-called Classic Hollywood period; the film rights sold on publication so that the novels appear as "tie-ins" to the more slickly publicized film versions. It has been said, too, that the early 1940s was an interesting era for film history because it was assumed that wartime film audiences would be largely comprised of women (although that was not the case).

Romantic film and melodrama consistently experienced high levels of commercial success during this period and, in critical terms, their place as an object of study within feminist film studies and the explorations of spectatorship, psychoanalysis, and consumerism, to name a few key themes, has given the "woman's film" a primary place in understanding the history of Hollywood, particularly during the 1930s and 1940s. The woman's film of this period set up standards and established conventions still beloved and emulated today. Unlike the authors of a Mills & Boon or Harlequin novel, whose names always appear in much smaller type than the title of the book, directors such as Lubitsch are acclaimed as having made huge artistic contributions to film in the era of Classic Hollywood.

Twentieth-century women's popular fiction has been often derided because its focus on the woman reader has, in common with the woman's film, suggested to some a narrowness of approach, a partial vision. What readers often sought in such fiction, however, was a difference of view, a validation of the domestic and the sphere of the maternal; and as often, they desired subversion of the patriarchal narrative of passivity and sacrifice in characters such as Amber St. Clare (*Forever Amber*). Critics of such fiction have moved beyond an analysis of the aesthetic limitations of such work and focus on the needs they meet in the expression of hidden longings and deep contradictions in the experience of femininity – especially at times of massive social change, such as during and after World War II. The books which remained popular classics yield deeper contradictions on repeated readings and make different kinds of sense when viewed in relation to other cultural forms of the period. One of the key aims of this chapter is to suggest that film adaptations of such texts can also be read as part of a continuum of women's texts – part of a circulation of discourses about femininity in novels, films, and advertising, to name three core areas – which gain momentum if read as a cluster. Women's texts then and now have always been set aside derogatively as representing a tendency – whether it be pulp romance, weepies, chick lit, or chick flicks – and of containing scant aesthetic value because they are marked by repetition of plot, imagery, and incident. Looked at another way, though, these repetitions are the most interesting aspect of such texts, as is the question of why women (covertly) enjoy such repetition. Scrutinized further it suggests core anxieties about the space women supposedly inhabit in the world, and their enjoyment of the restaging of these anxieties drama-tized. The films mark themselves out for their focus on the domestic and, in particular, their drive to expose the realities of the inequities of women's lives – not, in the case of Classic Hollywood, to present any credible means of escape, but to make use of the theme's melodramatic possibilities. Nonetheless through this depiction of cruel disempowerment and unrecog-nized potential, the audience, it is suggested, live out their own frustration and disempowerment in the act of consuming film.

There are numerous essays on the "woman's film," spectatorship, and psychoanalysis in relation to feminist film theory and I only have time to touch on these throughout the course of this chapter, yet they underpin the critical assumptions I shall make. I am most concerned, however, to look at another articulation of the adaptations and have chosen to focus on one novel and its film adaptation in the hope that it will serve to raise appropriate questions across the genre. Olive Higgins Prouty, already known as the author of *Stella Dallas* (1923), published *Now, Voyager* in 1941 and the film, starring Bette Davis, Paul Henreid, Gladys Cooper, and Claude Rains and directed by Irving Rapper was released the following year – the Warner Brothers contract having been agreed when the first advance copy of the novel was available. In common with some of the most outstanding and memorable films of the period such as *Random Harvest* (LeRoy, 1942; James Hilton, 1941), *Rebecca* (Hitchcock, 1940; Daphne Du Maurier 1938) and *Mrs. Miniver* (Wyler, 1942; Jan Struthers, 1939) the novel operated almost as a tie-in with the film and was in danger of being overwhelmed by it. It isn't surprising, perhaps, that in all cases except Du Maurier, the authors' names have faded into virtual obscurity (in common with Booth Tarkington, another immensely popular novelist whose *The Magnificent Ambersons* (1918) was made into a hugely successful film released in 1942, directed by Orson Welles). Film companies were exploiting the success of well-known popular authors; and uniquely this allows for a kind of balance between film and source text, where the primacy of the "literary" is not a consideration.

In the main the films are the classics upon which the novels can only bask in reflected glory. In the case of *Now, Voyager*, much has been written about the film, not least because it contains a number of the characteristic ingredients of the "woman's film" and because of a number of striking performances, but little has been written about the novel. It is an attractive text for adaptation because it celebrates women's potentiality for freedom by emerging from the stifling shadows of social expectations and, in this case, from an oppressive matriarch. Though not sexually frank, the novel is imbued with reflections on female sexual desire and the heroine is repressed by forces external to herself: part of her "voyage" is an acceptance of this fact. Prouty, like Hilton and Tarkington, was a prolific popular writer of her time; in addition to the famous *Stella Dallas* she would go on to write five novels which in common with *Now, Voyager* chart the fortunes of the fictional Vale family of Boston. Charlotte Vale, the chief protagonist of *Now, Voyager*, occupies the distinctive familial position of maiden aunt and physically as well as psychologically lives up to that role until a nervous breakdown in adulthood causes her to be sent for treatment and then on a cruise, separated from her domineering mother for the first time.

Prouty wrote of mental illness from experience. She herself had had a breakdown and her treatment left her with her a positive view of modern psychiatry (the therapist in the novel is emphatically not a psychoanalyst). She is better known to some as the patron of Sylvia Plath, since Prouty, herself a graduate of Smith College, funded Plath's education and also supported her through private psychiatric treatment after an attempted suicide, only to be hideously sent up as Philomena Guinea in *The Bell Jar* (1963). Plath's characterization of both Prouty and her prose says everything about the relationship of "literature" to "trash" and the chasm between them:

> I had read of Mrs Guinea's books in the town library – the college library didn't stock them for some reason – and it was crammed from beginning to end with long suspenseful questions: "Would Evelyn discern that Gladys knew Roger in her past? wondered Hector feverishly" and "How could Donald marry her when he learned of the child Elsie, hidden away with Mrs Rollmop on the secluded country farm? Griselda demanded of her bleak, moonlit pillow." These books earned Philomena Guinea, who later told me she had been very stupid at college, millions and millions of dollars.[2]

Despite Plath's casual dismissal of Prouty and her deeply inaccurate parody of her prose, Prouty's Charlotte Vale anticipates concerns that Esther Greenwood in *The Bell Jar* will share – fear of becoming her mother (in both cases a controlling widow), fear of being absorbed by the man and ultimately resentment and rejection of the sexual double standard. Yet Prouty's novel fits all the requirements of a stock melodrama and as such provides the perfect raw material for the woman's film of the 1940s, whereas Plath's novel is raw, self-consciously challenging – the one attempt at adaptation in 1979 resulted in critical oblivion.

The core of the romance plot of this novel is straightforward: Charlotte, regarded by her mother as the "child of my old age"[3] is kept under strict scrutiny by her repressive, domineering mother. Her one early experience of romance is with a ship's officer on a cruise when "Charlotte hadn't been sure what he expected. In the novels she'd read, men didn't like prudes ... The third time [he kissed her] Charlotte had felt the response which the first time she had only pretended. By the end of the fourth day she was deeply in love with Leslie Trotter" (pp. 34–5). While she belongs to an old prosperous Boston family, Trotter is an Englishman from a modest background and her mother takes steps to prevent the engagement (later Leslie marries another heiress from the cruise, suggesting Mrs. Vale's protectiveness could have been well-founded). The novel begins with Charlotte lunching with Jerry in Gilbraltar and a series of flashbacks inform us that she is now in her mid-thirties, has suffered a breakdown which has physically transformed her and is on a cruise, alone this time, for her health. Jerry, like Leslie, is of a lower social class and is married, unhappily, to a woman who, like Charlotte's mother, had her youngest child late in life and resents the child bitterly for this. They become constant companions; a car accident in Naples means that Charlotte misses her boat, and it is in Naples where their brief love affair, we presume, is consummated. When they part, their mutual understanding is that they will never contact each other again, but once back in the States they meet accidentally at a social event, just as Charlotte has agreed to marry widower Elliot Livingstone. She later breaks off this engagement and, after the sudden death of her mother, seems to be heading for another breakdown. Later she comes to care for Tina, Jerry's youngest daughter, who also suffers a breakdown and is treated at the same sanatorium as Charlotte. Through Tina and in Charlotte's role as honorary mother, Charlotte and Jerry are united and their illicit love can be continued by proxy. It is this latter plot twist that surprises and in a sense frustrates the romance plot because Jerry does not leave his wife: Charlotte realizes a "wifely" role as the long term guardian and mentor of his child.

Perhaps Prouty had more in common with Plath than the latter would acknowledge or understand. Prouty had literary ambitions from an early age and her most memorable experiences at Smith were of her creative writing classes. In her memoirs she characterizes herself as a poor student in other respects, but asserts "I'd rather be a mediocre writer than no writer at all."[4]

Her memoir is coy, patrician and largely unrevealing, on the surface cele-brating her successes as a wife and mother as much as it does her work, but her commitment to her writing is evident in every chapter. She consciously summons Virginia Woolf when she speaks of the "room of one's own" she attained in her second year at college (and her quest for such a room in later life becomes crucial to the development of her writing career), yet her feminism must be excavated from between the lines of her prose. In Plath's novel we have a searing and affecting first-person narrative; we share the stifling confines of Esther's bell jar to the extent that external reality is entirely mediated through her own pychosis. In Prouty we understand Charlotte's motivations and anxieties but there is no dwelling on inner torment. These torments are played out on the exterior of the female body, through the spaces women inhabit and through the places in which they are inserted by men.

Now, Voyager is a surprisingly visceral novel: Charlotte's most notable experiences are mediated through the senses first and then through the emotions. From the perfume Jerry gives her on their first outing to the shared cigarette at the novel's denouement, the novel embraces female experiences of the self through the senses. The novel starts with Charlotte "keenly conscious ... of the clothes she was wearing" (p. 1) and closes with her just as keenly aware of the rhythmical music playing in an adjoining room as Jerry attempts a snatched moment of intimacy with her: "The beat of the rumba grew louder. Jerry leaned nearer. If she let him kiss her now, all her resolutions would be swept away" (p. 261). All pivotal scenes in the novel are accompanied by this strong sense of sensory experience, so that food, weather, environment all encroach upon emotion; it is perhaps this visceral and visual quality which allowed such a smooth passage to screen adaptation and which facilitated that essential quality of the classic Hollywood film – the to-be-looked-at-ness of the screen heroine. In addition, dramatic high-points are further wrought with emotion by Max Steiners's score and, at the point where Charlotte finds herself sitting between Elliot and Jerry at a concert, by strains from Tchaikovsky's Symphony No. 6 in B minor, "Pathétique."

In other ways this "romance" text does not seem propitious for adaptation into classic Hollywood, because the ending does not allow for the removal of all obstacles in order to give center stage to the lovers, and instead reaffirms the impossibility of their union – a feature, perhaps surprisingly, retained in the film. In many ways this is the romance of the lost child rather than the spinster aunt – Charlotte is the much-resented child of her mother's old age and Tina is similarly resented and, more than this, the butt of her mother's sexual jealousy. Charlotte is given the child she can never have with Jerry but in return Jerry's love must become a secondary consideration. The film follows the novel so closely that in many cases it is impossible to distinguish the dialogue – for some critics of adaptation this will confirm the theory that a mediocre literary text can have the makings of a superlative film. In this case it is true that the film endures over and above the fiction; but this increases the sense that one is a continuation of the other, and both offer a unique insight into wartime discourses of femininity.

Judith Mayne, in her Afterword to the recent Feminist Press edition of the novel, suggests that the enduring power of the novel is that it "simultaneously elevates and undercuts stereotypes about women's desires" (p. 266). One example she gives is the transformation from ugly duckling in Charlotte's physical metamorphosis from maiden aunt to confident, mature, desiring woman via weight-loss, someone else's *haute couture* clothes, a haircut, and a facial: on the face of it this novel merely continues symbolic traditions of the make-over common to women's fiction and film. Its striking difference lies in its rich sensory structure and in Charlotte's determination to be her own "mother" in this complex rebirthing plot; in classic pulp romance the hero's rite of passage is when he can act as mother to the heroine, and though in a sense Jerry achieves this in their night spent together on a hillside in Naples, it is Charlotte who ultimately heals him through her love for Tina and through finding her own destiny as a benefactor of sick children in the money she gives to the sanatorium, Cascades. The dark, brownstone family house is transformed by Charlotte into a welcoming home where nephews and nieces drop in unannounced for supper. The book's title, taken from the Whitman poem "Untold want" that her psychiatrist Dr. Jaquith gives her before the cruise, affirms Charlotte's quest for self-identity:

> The untold want by life and land ne'er granted,
> Now, voyager sail thou forth to seek and find.

Although Prouty's Dr. Jaquith is emphatically not a psychoanalyst and his cures are deeply pragmatic, including lots of fresh air, independent action, and the deflection of guilt, there are numerous ways in which the text is conducive to a psychoanalytical reading. E. Ann Kaplan notes in *Now, Voyager* the presence of Karen Horney's notion of the "masculine mother" who stunts the daughter's ability to achieve an independent self and crushes any evidence of sexual desire.[5] This sympathetic view of Jaquith in the novel, which indicates Prouty's own response to the life-changing intervention of her own psychiatrist, Dr. Rigg, is carried over into the film in Rains's portrayal and offers a measure of the extent of the popularization of psycho-analytical themes in Hollywood where, as Jeanne Allen points out, "the function of the flashback became increasingly identified with presenting the original trauma, which must be resolved and amended for the protagonist to be 'cured' and the narrative resolved."[6] A key part of the triumph of the film is in Charlotte's own triumph over her mother, but whereas in the book this reflects her own struggle to reinvent herself, in the film it is explained by Jaquith who offers a Freudian interpretation of the mother for us in the opening scenes. From her dour physical appearance to her mannerisms (particularly the fidgeting hands, mirrored by Charlotte before her transformation), to the dark and austere setting of the house, we are given a conventional view of a "Victorian" woman – repressed, unfeminine, and after her husband's early death, the embodied phallic mother.

The stellar line-up in the film of *Now, Voyager* encourages an intertextual viewing and, given the regularity with which such stars would pop up in their studio's latest releases, maybe twice or three times a year, some blurring of roles is to be expected.[7] We imagine that on its release, the audience would expect to see Davis at her arch and ruthless best as in *Jezebel* (1938) and *The Little Foxes* (1941); Claude Rains was to appear memorably in *Casablanca* (1942) in the same year and had been in *Mr. Smith Goes to Washington* (1939); Gladys Cooper had played Beatrice Lacey in *Rebecca* (1940) and had a career stretching back into the silent era. The film streamlines the book's numerous flashbacks so that it is almost chronological except for one flashback to Charlotte as a young woman and her frisson with Leslie Trotter and another brief one involving Jaquith's instructions to her prior to the cruise.[8] This has the effect of offering a seamless transformation, exploiting the key visual interest of the opening scenes – the metamorphosis of Bette Davis from ugly duckling to society sophisticate – and celebrating the power of Hollywood to offer glamour and wealth as symbols of female freedom. These memorable first scenes also act to reinforce Davis's position as a formidable serious actress, who is willing to appear in such an unflattering form. The film creates suspense via Davis's changing physical appearance, in the introduction to Aunt Charlotte as languishing spinster, the intercut flashback of the young Charlotte in plaits and girlish dress and finally in the grand entrance of the transformed "Camille" on the cruise ship. In each case the shot of her face is deferred by showing fragmented parts of the body, in *film noir* style, such as the hands, the legs, or in the case of young Charlotte, the back of the head. In the first scene suspense is built up by the entrance of Dr. Jaquith and a discussion of Charlotte's declining mental health. This then cuts to a disembodied pair of hands working on an inlaid ivory box, then hiding cigarette butts and finally to a stocky pair of legs clad in sensible shoes descending the stairs. Davis, made up to look stocky and plain with an impressive near-monobrow and thick glasses, is barely recognizable; the flashback of her as a younger woman shows her in understated make-up so that while she is more definitely the Davis we recognize, there is still scope for the full make-over in the cruise ship scene. Again, we encounter her legs first – now shapely and tastefully clad in feminine high heels – and then her face, at first tantalizingly shielded by a broad-brimmed hat, but free of spectacles. The device of the spectacle-wearing woman as plain and bookish is exploited by Prouty in the novel and translates easily into one of the enduring stereotypes of classic Hollywood. The bespectacled woman is plain, repressed, intellectual – the removal of glasses signifying attractiveness and desirability. The rejection of femininity in the wearing of glasses is also an implied threat, as Doane observes: "Glasses worn by a woman in the cinema do not generally signify a deficiency in seeing but an active looking."[9]

Seated at lunch with Jerry Durrance (Henreid) Charlotte looks at her reflection in the window, and as all good romance heroines do, she appraises her transformation, encouraging the audience to do the same. This moment recaptures the second chapter of the novel where Charlotte confronts her mirror image in her stateroom: "the profile was looking away from her which gave her the odd sensation of gazing at someone else. So *that* was how she looked! For years she had avoided all such painful speculation and shunned mirrors, schooling herself never to study her reflection in order to see herself as others saw her" (p. 10). This scene in both film and novel marks a shift in Charlotte's self-perception – put another way she engages in the contract that women have entered into almost unconsciously – to accept that they are constantly being scrutinized and therefore must police their own appearance. John Berger drew attention to this explanation for female narcissism in *Ways of Seeing* (1973) and feminist critics have further explored mirror scenes in romance ever since. Such images, where the heroine regards and appraises herself, will chime with the female audience at a number of levels, not least the way they are supposed to encounter themselves in advertisements – "from the field of social psychology, advertising had borrowed the notion of the *social self* as a prime weapon in its arsenal. Here people defined themselves in terms set by the approval or disapproval of others ... Women were being educated to look at themselves as things to be created competitively against other women: painted and sculpted with the aids of the modern market."[10] While the film presents this transformation as spectacle, moving swiftly from old maid to socialite, positioning Davis as object of desire central to the romance plot's motivation, the novel offers a more detailed description of the process of transformation, and in this context it is part of the healing process begun with therapy but not complete until Charlotte engages in full mas-querade, the modeling of the ideal feminine. As Doane says "the masquerade, in flaunting femininity, holds it at a distance. Womanliness is a mask which can be worn or removed. The masquerade's resistance to patriarchal positioning would therefore lie in its denial of the production of femininity as closeness, as presence-to-itself, as, precisely, imagistic."[11]

The helpful notes that her sister-in-law Lisa pins on to Charlotte's borrowed finery further underline the proposition that femininity is to be worked at in order to gain patriarchy's glittering prizes, and the glorious butterfly evening cloak emphasizes the imagery of transformation. Much later in the novel, when she has inherited her mother's wealth and taken Tina into her home, the physical description of Charlotte is more fulsome; "Her black sleek head, black far-separated brows, ivory coloured complexion with changing shadows in the hollows beneath her high cheekbones, and brilliant red lips, made her stand out in any group" (p. 249). The film makes a spectacle of the transformation of Charlotte's temperament too, so that after Charlotte breaks off her engagement to Elliot much to her mother's disgust, she angrily rebukes her: "Dr Jaquith says that tyranny is sometimes the expression of the maternal instinct. If that's a mother's love, I want no part of it!" This scene, a prelude to her mother's death, announces Charlotte's full accession to her self; in the film Jaquith's guiding hand is more obviously in evidence, not least because of Rains's consistent screen presence. Jaquith's role in general undergoes some subtle shifts from novel to film. In the novel he is a kind of spiritual twin for Charlotte; himself unmarried, he recommends meaningful employment in worthwhile activities as an alternative substitute for the "sex instinct" and offers the most feminist account of the value of female independence available in the novel, which legitimizes Charlotte's pursuit of a new path with her own extended family of young relatives and her ward Tina.

In the film Jaquith's influence on Charlotte is more direct, the appearance of the charismatic Rains more likely to place him as rival suitor than benevolent friend, emphasized by the fact she gives him one of her precious ivory boxes. His inclusion in the closing scene of the film as a physical embodiment of her moral conscience endorses this. Prior to her famous shared cigarette with Jerry, Charlotte is shown looking over some blueprints for the new sanatorium building with Jaquith; their exchange of glances when she goes to Jerry acts as a caution not to resume her affair, whereas in the novel she simply reminds Jerry of this promise. The romantic closure is frustrated and yet paradoxically satisfied by the sharing of a cigarette looking out to the stars, and the audience is at liberty to construct themselves more than one happy ending. The film's ending baldly reminds us that "her narrative end is, in fact, little improved from the beginning."[12] Foregrounding the final, fatal confrontation with her mother and Jaquith's absolving of her "New England conscience" arguably dilutes some of the implicit feminist messages of the novel. Charlotte is posed as her mother's adversary and reacts against her

Victorian view of social manners. The nascent conservatism of the novel is transformed by the film to an aspirational vision of wealth and freedom. In the novel Charlotte accepts degrees of informality in opening up the Vale residence to her extended family but essentially she still speaks for privilege and tradition, so that Tina becomes a well-rounded version of her younger self, with the added ingredient of unconditional nurturing love. Just as in *The Bell Jar* Esther's breakthrough takes place when she is given "permission" to hate her mother, so here in the film version of *Now, Voyager*, the repressive mother becomes the fulcrum for the entire plot, overshadowing the distance that Charlotte herself travels on her voyage and, as Allen suggests, precluding "a discussion of the patriarchal social systems which shaped and limited her options."[13] Perhaps its wartime release, less than a year after America joined the allied forces in World War II, was another reason for the deflection of any critique of men or male power, encouraging women to look inwards as "ultimately, only through the imagination can the untold want be granted."[14]

As I've hinted earlier the differences between novel and film at the level of plot are very small. Presumably as a result of its wartime production, in the film the cruise moves from Europe to South America and Jerry's character is more "masculine" in a conventional sense, his own history of mental illness as described in the novel erased. Nonetheless Prouty herself was skeptical about the adaptation, perhaps because she so disliked those of *Stella Dallas* (1923), first adapted as a play, then a silent film, and then as a sound film starring Barbara Stanwyck. She claimed that in her writing, she avoided "sentimentality and melodrama"[15] and therefore would not have appreciated Stanwyck's rendition of Dallas as the heroine of the "weepie" par excellence. The film versions would be later followed by a long-running radio spin-off series which Prouty tried her best to stop and by the film *Stella* (appearing in 1990, long after Prouty's death) starring Bette Midler. Even though Prouty preferred the adaptation of *Now, Voyager*, few of her own suggestions for the film (except concerning Dr. Jaquith) were heeded and in Bette Davis's interpretation of Charlotte, the film is a star vehicle with the image of the independent woman who, to a wartime audience, can be seen to endure and conventionally maintain the home front.

Although this film makes no obvious reference to the ongoing War, unlike *Casablanca*, released in the same year, there are other ways in which its social context is embodied: in the mode of representation of women and the assumption that the main consumers are also women. The "woman's film" was probably vulnerable to more self-conscious manipulation than fiction of the period in the desire to focus on women's lives and on their relationships. As

LaPlace argues, the woman's film is read by female spectators in the light of other examples of female discourse found in women's magazines, advertising and in pulp romance and she reflects on "how this circuit, almost completely ignored by patriarchal scholarship, has functioned for women."[16] The woman's film is of course bound by commercial considerations and the film can sell products just as products can sell the film. Some consumer goods connote choice and liberation, and cigarettes in *Now, Voyager* specifically take on multiple resonances – as symbolic of Charlotte's nascent rebelliousness in the opening scene, as affirmation of her secret intimacy with Jerry and as indicative of the New Woman she represents. As LaPlace observes, "Hollywood cinema, especially in the 1930s, was structured, in part, around the presentation of women as glamorous objects to be emulated and consumed, and around the creation of a *mise-en-scène* that 'fetishises' consumer objects and a consumerist lifestyle."[17] It isn't only goods that are to be consumed, but the star presence itself is manufactured and manipulated to fit the screened glamour and mystique. The significance of Davis's star persona to the role of Charlotte Vale is unmistakable and her "private life" as narrated in the fan magazines of the 1940s adds piquancy to her taking this role. At the time of the film, Bette Davis was one of the top grossing artists in Hollywood and her acting style suggested "assertiveness, intelligence, internal emotional conflict and strength."[18]

Feminist critics of both popular fiction and film have assiduously explored the social, historical, and commercial context in which women's texts are produced, and it is at this level that the woman's film-as-adaptation yields rich insights and ironically throws up similarities in the ambitions of Bette Davis and Olive Higgins Prouty. As I have previously remarked, both romance novels and the woman's film affirm and celebrate intertexuality in their repeating of stock types and their summoning of women's knowledge – of consumption, or relationships, or oppression from a multitude of sources. In the ways they are consumed and in the confused, but ultimately conservative messages they convey, spectators presumably seek both endorsement and challenge to women's domestic and economic roles. Aside from the commercial demand that such texts repeat the successful formulae of their forebears, we can see both Davis and Prouty as "producers" of texts of *Now, Voyager* (if one accepts that stars become auteurs in their ownership of key roles) and in different ways they aim for uniqueness and superior control over the product.

Prouty, from the evidence of her (admittedly unrevealing) memoirs seems uncomfortable with the nature of her literary success which was financial far more than aesthetic. She was extremely discomfited to find that 450,000 of the 763,000 sales of *Now, Voyager* were in the Dell paperback 25 cent edition, retailing at "drugstores and railroad stations."[19] Davis, at the height of her powers and as one of Hollywood's top earners, is looking for acknowledgment of her artistic skill, yet for some critics the *product*, as being infinitely repeatable and replaceable, obscures the acts of the producer. Writing in *The Commonweal*, Philip T. Hartung regards the film as so similar to the "tripe dished up in women's magazines that it is difficult to imagine men having the patience to watch it through,"[20] and identifies the key success of the film (its immersion in such discourses of femininity) while condemning it. Davis struggled against potential obscurity in the 1930s, at the mercy of the mediocre films she was offered and had, earlier in her career, been suspended for refusing certain scripts at Warner Brothers. Prouty, essentially, thought her own talents mediocre and only able to flower with a great deal of editorial support and nurturing and yet had a dread of "popularity" as further devaluing her work. Her writing career, though spread out over time to incorporate busy periods of childcare and domestic responsibilities, becomes increasingly important – to the point where she implicitly declares it a "profession" by taking a room away from her house in which she can write. Davis's star image offers a schizophrenic view of her as at once tough and independent yet deeply feminine and glad to play second fiddle as the wife. In one fan magazine article, she's characterized as the simple, down-to-earth figure who snatches quiet moments with her (first) husband away from the Hollywood treadmill: " 'I think you have to get away from Hollywood and the pictures occasionally,' she says firmly, 'You get into such a terrific rut if you don't'."[21] A later article speculating on the breakdown of this marriage snipes that "it's asking a lot of a man to expect him to be the lesser half of a marital partnership indefinitely – the lesser in income, the lesser in prestige. No matter how much a man loves his wife, it's almost too much to expect him to be happy in the role of just-a-husband . . . and call him by her name with a 'Mr.' attached."[22] Prouty's memoir exposes her own anxieties about literary fame in her impatience with people who provocatively asked her husband what it was like to be married to a famous writer. From early hints that she deferred her marriage to Lewis Prouty until she felt she was in danger of losing him to another woman, and until his suggestion that he take a job in Boston so that she could take creative writing courses at Radcliffe, it is clear that she was profoundly aware of the potential clash between her two desired identities. When she had a nervous breakdown as an adult two years after a second daughter had died, she admits confessing to her doctor (a Jaquith figure in so many respects) of "the difficulties I found in being a mother and a housewife and at the same time writing a novel . . . I was filled with a constant sense of guilt and deception."[23] It was he who prescribed a room outside the home for work and like Jaquith, cured her of her "New England conscience."

I have tried in this chapter to show the points of contrast and interception between the two texts of *Now, Voyager* as well as demonstrating that they are as much constructed by the dominant discourses on femininity which surround them. As Judith Mayne observes, "In the middle-class novel and later the cinema, narrative functions as an encounter with the spheres of private and public life, an encounter which emulates *and* problematizes the division of public and private, as well as the oppositions upon which that division draws – particularly those of gender and class."[24] Certainly, reading both texts from such a perspective lends another dimension to our reception of them, particularly in the way Charlotte Vale, a wealthy heiress by the end, negotiates perceptions of her lack of value to the public sphere, just as Bette Davis was to encounter the seemingly intractable tension between two spheres, so that while she appears as the ultimate feminine in masquerade in the films, she is the "man" in her private relationships. The frustrated romance in *Now, Voyager* dramatizes such tensions further, but also ironically sustains the fiction of romance more powerfully – "The woman is neither fully possessed by the man nor taken for granted; she must continually be wooed and courted; romantic love is kept outside the mundanity of the everyday"[25] – maintaining a space for imaginative resistance on the part of the spectator.

Joy Gould Boyum characterizes adaptations as occupying "a no-man's land, caught somewhere between a series of conflicting aesthetic claims and rivalries. For if film threatens literature, literature threatens film, and nowhere so powerfully, in either instance, as in the form of adaptation."[26] In this chapter I've explored the hypothesis that paradoxically lesser novels make better films and the possibility that texts such as *Now, Voyager* add weight to this claim. As Balázs stated, this is much to do with the theoretical assumption that "good" art can only appear to its best advantage in the form in which it originated, as if "there is an organic connection between form and content in every art and that a certain art form always offers the most adequate expression for a certain content. Thus the adaptation of a content to a different art form can only be detrimental to a work of art, if that work of art was good. In other words, one may perhaps make a good film out of a bad novel, but never out of a good one."[27] Boyum's take on this assumption is that it has much to do with the dominant interpretive community and "that an adaptation will be considered faithful to the extent that its interpretation remains consistent with those put forth by the interpretive community; with the interpretation . . . of that classic work, then, that made it classic in the first place."[28] This creates a circular logic which can only be broken by the text that remains beyond the purview of such an interpretive community because of its status as "trash." *Now, Voyager* becomes the consummate woman's film for all the qualities that Prouty disliked about the categorization of her work – not least that it sold in cheap editions by the truckload. The film version enters an interpretive community more nuanced and multivalent than the literary one as part of a narrative continuum, which gives us a unique insight into the construction and reproduction of gender at a time of enormous social change, and gives weight to the view that "literary forms do not by their very nature resist conversion to the screen; to the contrary, they often both invite and flourish from it."[29]

NOTES

1 Mary Ann Doane, *The Desire to Desire: The Woman's Film of the 1940s* (Basingstoke: Macmillan, 1987), p. 3.
2 Sylvia Plath, *The Bell Jar* (1963; London: Faber, 1966), p. 42.
3 Olive Higgins Prouty, *Now, Voyager* (1941; New York: The Feminist Press, 2004), p. 13. All subsequent references are cited in parenthesis in the text and are to this edition.
4 Olive Higgins Prouty, *Pencil Shavings: Memoirs* (Cambridge, Massachusetts: The Riverside Press, 1961), p. 101.
5 See E. Ann Kaplan, *Motherhood and Representation: The Mother in Popular Culture and Melodrama* (London: Routledge, 1992), p. 109.
6 Jeanne Thomas Allen (ed.), Introduction, *Now, Voyager* (screenplay) (Madison, Wisconsin: The University of Wisconsin Press, 1984), p. 26.
7 Extraordinarily, in *The Old Maid* released three years earlier, Davis plays an "Aunt Charlotte" who this time conceals her real daughter Tina as an orphan.
8 The first flashback is naturalized into the narrative by having Jaquith look at Charlotte's journal of her earlier voyage over her shoulder. The scene dissolves and the journal changes to the pages of a novel – recalling a classic adaptive device.
9 Mary Anne Doane, "Film and the Masquerade: Theorising the Female Spectator," in *Hollywood: Critical Concepts in Media and Cultural Studies*, Volume IV, ed. Thomas Schatz (London: Routledge, 2004), p. 104.
10 Stuart Ewen, *Captains of Consciousness: Advertising and the Social Roots of the Consumer Culture* (1976; New York: Basic Books, 2001), pp. 179–80.
11 Mary Anne Doane, "Film and the Masquerade: Theorising the Female Spectator," p. 103.
12 M. L. Ely, "The Untold Want: Representation and Transformation Echoes of Walt Whitman's *Passage to India* in *Now, Voyager*," *Literature/Film Quarterly* 29.1 (2001), 49.
13 Introduction, *Now, Voyager* (screenplay), p. 39.
14 M. L. Ely, "The Untold Want," p. 43.
15 Prouty, *Pencil Shavings*, p. 154.
16 Maria LaPlace, "Producing and Consuming the Woman's Film: Discursive Struggle in *Now, Voyager*," in *Home is Where the Heart is: Studies in Melodrama and the Woman's Film*, ed. Christine Gledhill (London: BFI Books, 1987), p. 139.
17 Ibid., p. 141.

18 Ibid., p. 147.
19 Prouty, *Pencil Shavings*, p. 199.
20 Quoted in Introduction to *Now, Voyager* (the screenplay), ed. and intro. Jeanne Thomas Allen, p. 36.
21 Quoted in Martin Levin (ed.), *Hollywood and the Great Fan Magazines* (London: Ian Allan, 1970), p. 109 (this article seems to date from 1935 when Davis won an Academy Award, but dates and names of magazines are not given).
22 Quoted in Martin Levin (ed.) *Hollywood and the Great Fan Magazines*, p. 112.
23 Prouty, *Pencil Shavings*, p. 180.
24 Judith Mayne, *Private Novels, Public Films* (Athens, Georgia: University of Georgia Press 1988), pp. 1–2.
25 Maria LaPlace, "Producing and Consuming the Woman's Film: Discursive Struggle in *Now, Voyager*," p. 161.
26 Joy Gould Boyum, *Double Exposure: Fiction into Film* (New York: New America Library, 1985), p. 15.
27 Béla Balázs, *Theory of the Film: Character and Growth of a New Art*, trans. Edith Bone (New York: Dover Publications Inc, 1970), p. 259.
28 Boyum, *Double Exposure*, p. 77.
29 Ibid., p. 242.

10

I. Q. HUNTER

Post-classical fantasy cinema: *The Lord of the Rings*

I

Since the late 1970s the dominant genre of Hollywood blockbusters has been fantasy, and it is not hard to see why. Science fiction extravaganzas, comic book adaptations, and epic series like *Star Wars* (1977–2005), Harry Potter (2001 ongoing), *The Chronicles of Narnia* (2005 ongoing) and *The Lord of the Rings* trilogy (2001–2003) appeal internationally to the crucial teenage demographic; encourage fannish absorption in their expandable universes; showcase advances in special effects; and lend themselves readily to sequels, spin-offs and other commercially essential tie-ins.

Although *Star Wars* (1977) and *Close Encounters of the Third Kind* (1977), which inspired the continuing wave of fantasy, were original stories, fantasy films nowadays more usually derive from pre-existing novels, films, comic books, and video games with some built-in guarantee of audience recognition and cult interest. But the process is not one of simple "adaptation." A film like *The Lord of the Rings* is a starting place as much as an end product of adaptation: just one reference point in a matrix of intertextual relations created by synergic cross-promotion. Video games, graphic and literary novelizations, CD soundtracks, multiple Director's Cuts and DVD versions, prequels, sequels, and franchises – such ostensibly secondary productions, included among what Gérard Genette called "paratexts," not only extend the boundaries of contemporary Hollywood fantasy films but also increasingly determine their form and narrative.[1] The interminable pod-racing scenes in *Star Wars Episode 1: The Phantom Menace* (1999) were essentially previews of the spin-off *Episode 1 Racer* video game; while narrative gaps were deliberately left in *The Matrix: Reloaded* (2003) for the spin-off video game to fill in, and its back-story was fleshed out in *The Animatrix* (2003), a straight-to-DVD collection of *anime* shorts. This is adaptation understood not as fidelity to a controlling original but as dissemination – the commodification of valuable textual material across numerous media. As Deborah Cartmell argues, "instead of worrying about whether a film is 'faithful' to the original literary text (founded in the logocentric belief that there is a single meaning), we read adaptations for their generation of a plurality of meanings. Thus the intertextuality of the adaptation is our primary concern."[2]

It is in this spirit that I shall look at Peter Jackson's films of *The Lord of the Rings* as examples of contemporary fantasy cinema. I shall not work through a point-by-point comparison of the novel and films; for this, see Tom Shippey's chapter in *Understanding The Lord of the Rings*, Brian Rosebury's *Tolkien: A Cultural Phenomenon*, and the comprehensive film guide by Smith and Matthews.[3] A good deal of writing on the films, especially within Tolkien fandom and in the small, intensely author-centered world of Tolkien criticism, has been pitched as studies in betrayal. The focus is on Jackson's deviations from Tolkien – "sins of commission ... that gravely change the character of Tolkien's text," as Jane Chance, one of the better-known Tolkien scholars, complains.[4] Rather than judge the films against the original novel – a profoundly dull undertaking – I shall attend to the various contexts that determined how a cult novel, of uncertain literary standing, was turned into an epic fantasy action film.

In any case, as other contributors to this volume insist, fidelity is rarely a useful criterion when exploring a film's relation to its intertexts. "Fidelity to its source text," as Thomas Leitch puts it elsewhere, "whether it is conceived as success in re-creating specific textual details or the effect of the whole – is a hopelessly fallacious measure of a given adaptation's value because it is unattainable, undesirable, and theoretically possible only in a trivial sense ... [The] source texts will always be better at being themselves."[5] But while, in theory, it is liberating to dismiss fidelity, this doesn't really work in the case of *The Lord of the Rings*. The film-makers could not simply jettison the book, even if they had wanted to, because many viewers of the films would have an investment in seeing it faithfully reproduced on screen; for the book's fans this made the prospect of a film version equally thrilling and anxiety-inducing. *The Lord of the Rings* films *had* to stay faithful to the novel – or rather work within a discourse of fidelity – because of its extraordinary and paradoxical standing in modern popular culture.

The novel is far and away one of the most popular ever written, in terms not only of its breadth of readership (there seem to be no Tolkien readers, only re-readers), but the enthusiasm of its fan-base, which is global, cross-generational, and highly productive in fanzines, small press publications, and online fan fiction. At the same time the novel, since its publication in 1954–5, has attracted the scorn of "the British literary establishment." The "official" line on Tolkien remains a toxic mix of contempt for his Catholicism and conservative politics, disapproval of the fantasy genre as a deviation from the true path of modernism, and snobbish distaste for Tolkien's readership, who are typically constructed as childish, regressed, and nerdish devotees of escapism. In 1997, when a British poll voted *The Lord of the Rings* the "book of the century," there followed an astonishing outpouring of loathing for it in the quality press as a symbol of the public's philistinism and inability to grow up.[6] These discourses about Tolkien and his readership cropped up again with the release of the first film in the trilogy, *The Fellowship of the Ring*. Jenny Turner claimed, for example, that "The strange power of his book casts a spell over readers, as children, as pubescents, as adolescents, as adults, a spell some of them grow out of and others don't."[7] The book, she goes on to say, is "tit in some way, it's an infantile comfort. It's an infantile comfort that's also a black pit."[8] Significantly, the same sort of imagery (infantile, nerdish, irredeemably Other) is often attached to *Star Wars* and its fandom. *Star Wars* is demonized within "serious" film culture much as *Lord of the Rings* is within literary circles. Their popularity is taken as a sign of mass geekery and ideological compliance, and the disdain for Tolkien and *Star Wars* has become a display of cultural capital; proof not only of one's maturity but also of inoculation against regressive Englishness (Tolkien), dumbed down Hollywood (*Star Wars*) and the virus of fantasy itself.

In other words, for all its popularity, *The Lord of the Rings* was a controversial book and would be a tricky adaptation to get right. A cult item, it was nevertheless widely despised and had uncertain appeal to general film audiences. Although fantasy and science fiction were extremely popular film genres, the type of fantasy to which *The Lord of the Rings* belonged was not especially commercial – namely, sword and sorcery. *Star Wars* – sword and sorcery dressed up as science fiction and itself highly indebted to Tolkien – had briefly inspired a spate of heroic adventures in supernatural lands of fable. *Dragonslayer* (1981), *The Beastmaster* (1982), *Conan the Barbarian* (1982), *The Sword and the Sorcerer* (1982), and *Red Sonya* (1985) were high-camp mixtures of pulp, comic strip violence, and the *peplum* (Italian sword and sandal movies), sometimes beefed up with anarcho-individualist politics; while *Willow* (1988) slavishly reworked *Star Wars*'s formula with additions from the stories of Christ and Moses. But this sub-genre petered out in the late 1980s, finding a more permanent niche in role-playing and video games, and until *The Lord of the Rings*, few efforts were made to revive it on screen. *Star Wars* itself would remain the most important template for the adaptation of *The Lord of the Rings*.

Jackson and his co-adaptors were constrained not only to satisfy Tolkien readers by capturing "the essence" of the novel, but also to produce a blockbuster action movie accessible to viewers with no emotional investment in the novel. But the novel's wide fan base, while not sufficient, as Kristin Thompson remarks, to make the film a hit, was certainly large enough to cause damage if the film was felt to be inauthentic, "Hollywoodized" and out of alignment with readers' expectations: "the book's fans were important disproportionately to their numbers, for many of them were vociferous and had either their own websites or at least a niche within a larger site."[9] Success with the fans guaranteed invaluable word of mouth and lucrative repeat viewings. Bertha Chin and Jonathan Gray studied the postings on internet discussion boards of "pre-viewers" of the *The Fellowship*, and found that overwhelmingly they were "devoted fans *of the books*."[10] Although they were anxious about the films, they were willing to see changes and looked forward to the films as a way of continuing the experience of the books and validating their devotion to them. The "pre-viewers," according to Chin and Gray, "regard the films as *correlates* of the book, and not as unitary, independent entities, not as texts in the traditional sense of the word ... [They] regard the films as accessories to the product that is the book." To keep the fans onside, it was crucial not only that the films (or at least the first one) stuck closely to the novel, but that Jackson and his team display credentials as fans themselves. The Tolkien estate, luckily, had no control over the films, but convenient links were emphasized between Tolkien and the film-makers – for example, the fact that Christopher Lee, who plays Saruman, had actually met Tolkien. Jackson himself was opportunistically spun in publicity material as a genial, tubby, bare-footed hobbit. Even so, while mollifying the fans ensured some sort of audience for the film, pandering exclusively to them was aesthetically constricting and commercially perilous. As with the first Harry Potter film, trying to photocopy the novel on screen might stifle the adaptation process completely.[11] Furthermore, for a minority of film fans (like me), *The Lord of the Rings* was not simply an adaptation of Tolkien: it was the latest film by the *auteur* Peter Jackson, an accomplished director of fantasy movies from the splatter-comedy *Bad Taste* (1987) to the psychological drama *Heavenly Creatures* (1994). How would *Lord of the Rings* adapt to and extend *his* distinctive vision? Was the quirkily subversive New Zealander at last selling out to Hollywood?

II

In film terms, the novel of *The Lord of the Rings* is badly put together. There is no villain, except, as Jackson notes several times on the audio commentaries, a lighthouse topped with Sauron's flaming eyeball; to compensate, Saruman and, in *The Return of the King*, an Orc captain are promoted to chief villains and active antagonists to the Fellowship. Some narrative climaxes seem out of place in the book, such as Boromir's death, which occurs at the start of *The Two Towers* novel but is sensibly moved to the end of the film of *The Fellowship*. And the novel's story wanders, especially in *The Fellowship of the Ring*, where it is continuously sidetracked by songs, poems, and irrelevancies such as the episode with the insufferable Tom Bombadil, the novel's Jar Jar Binks. In other words, and quite unsurprisingly, the novel is not remotely like a screen treatment.

The films reorganized it into a relatively classical narrative that draws on established Hollywood genres (the action film, the buddy movie, the war film). The solution with *The Fellowship of the Ring* was to make the story "Frodo-centric," as Jackson and his collaborators explain in the audio commentary, and streamline it as a quest or road movie narrative; events are focalized through Frodo, who, like Luke Skywalker and Harry Potter, becomes the source of most of the story information. The second and third films also reshape the books into more propulsive and linear plots. The story of *The Two Towers*, which in the book is hewn into blocks of self-contained narrative that relate, in turn, to different groups of protagonists, is straightened out into chronological, cross-cut parallel story-arcs; these climax with the action sequences of Helm's Deep, the Ents' attack on Isengard, and Frodo and Sam's sojourn in Osgiliath (invented for the film), which are spliced together like the finale of *The Empire Strikes Back* (1980). This default linearity makes for some awkwardness, notably in the sudden abandonment of Saruman at the end of the theatrical cut of *The Two Towers*. On the other hand, cross-cutting pays off superbly when Gandalf and Pippin, in Minas Tirith, and Sam, Frodo, and Gollum, at the foot of the stairs of Cirith Ungol, simultaneously watch a column of green fire explode from Minas Morgul; this brilliantly unites storylines otherwise separated by many miles and, in the book, by many chapters. Crucially, restructuring the novel ensures that each film is anchored by extended set-piece scenes of peril or war – the Mines of Moria; Helm's Deep (barely a dozen pages in the book); and the Battle of the Pelennor Fields.

Fans – who may accept changes to the plot – might nevertheless expect the filmmakers to respect "the spirit" of Tolkien, but that spirit is often controversial and unhelpful. Some aspects of the story might be hard to put over to a modern audience – the healing power of kings, for example, or the master–servant relationship between Frodo and Sam – but what are often regarded as Tolkien's misogyny and right-wing politics are equally uncomfortable material for a popular film. Elsewhere I have discussed the degree to which the Jackson films know about the "repressed" and misogynistic elements of *The Lord of the Rings*, and correct them.[12] The issue of race is more troubling. The book rests on an opposition of white and black, West and East that is easily interpreted as unthinkingly racist. Admittedly, white–black dichotomies are built into the novel's mythopoeic sources. It is arguable too that, color aside, the novel is intensely multicultural in celebrating the coming together of many peoples against an evil monoculture. But, transferred to screen, *The Lord of the Rings* becomes one of the most racially suspect films of recent years, with its Aryan Elves and pitch-black Orcs and Uruk-Hai (acted much of the time by Maoris). The films deal with race largely by ignoring the problem of skin color, and by emphasizing regional (Scottish, Welsh, and mid-Atlantic) and class accents as markers of difference; the races of Middle Earth are variations within a British diaspora, so that rather than "black" the Orcs are also squaddies speaking guttural Cockney.

The filmmakers latch onto ways to make the film connect to modern audiences, especially the all-important teenagers. The hobbit protagonists are more youthful than in the book. Orlando Bloom as Legolas is turned into a teen idol along the lines of Leonardo di Caprio in *Titanic* (1997). Gross comic relief is introduced, centered mostly on Gimli, and there is some crowd-pleasingly anachronistic dialogue and action (dwarf-tossing, skateboarding with shields). More significant is the Aragorn and Arwen romance. Relegated to an appendix of *The Return of the King*, it is expanded into a key plot development; this alleviates the unrelenting maleness of the story as well as reaching out to young women, who, post-*Titanic* and *Gladiator* (2000), have become target audiences for action blockbusters.

Certain themes in the book, especially those highlighted by Tolkien criticism and in fandom, are drawn out in the films because of their contemporary resonance and applicability (a term Tolkien favored). While esoteric readings of the novel as a Catholic fable or Cold War allegory are unlikely to strike chords with young audiences, its anti-industrialism and ecological concerns seem remarkably up to date. Saruman is a symbol of globalization out of control as he tears up forests and genetically modifies Orcs into Uruk-Hai; Treebeard becomes the mouthpiece of nature against its despoliation by science and power; while the touristic, digitally manipulated images of New Zealand's landscapes rebuke the degradation of the Old World and prompt nostalgia for the pre-industrial West.[13]

The films pay homage throughout not only to Tolkien but to his interpreters and adaptors. After all, Jackson's film was a remake as well as an adaptation. Following aborted efforts by, among others, the British director John Boorman, Ralph Bakshi's long but severely condensed animated version of *The Lord of the Rings* was released in 1978. Widely despised among Tolkien fans, Bakshi's film ends mid-way through *The Two Towers* because funding failed for the proposed second part (in 1980 the producers released a made-for-TV cartoon of *The Return of the King*, which is in the style of a children's musical). Bakshi's film has a psychedelic tone, as might be expected from the director of *Fritz the Cat* (1972), which dates it as a film made for the 1960s generation that had turned the book into an underground cult. Unlike Jackson's version, it is strikingly untroubled by the need to appeal to a teen audience, for example with young protagonists; its Frodo and Sam are potato-faced yokels, while Aragorn is as middle-aged, unprepossessing, and "foul" as he is initially described in the book. Jackson directly quotes Bakshi's film in two shots: in the opening prologue of *The Fellowship*, when the ring bounces in silhouette down a rock, and, in the party scene, with a looming close-up of Odo Proudfoot's feet. But Bakshi's film was not the only precursor adaptation, though it perhaps stood as a model of what not to do. Homage is paid to the highly regarded BBC radio adaptation (1981): Ian Holm, who played Frodo on radio, is Bilbo in Jackson's films. Reassuring appropriations of previous versions of Middle Earth further ensure continuity between the novel, previous visualizations, and Jackson's films – for example, as well as featuring Tolkien's illustrations, the films owed much of their design to the Tolkien illustrators Alan Lee and John Howe. As a result, the films are a compendium of allusions both to earlier versions of the novel and to widely disseminated interpretations of it, which Jackson and his colleagues discuss on the audio commentaries. The mushroom cloud explosion when Sauron is defeated in the prologue nods to readings of the One Ring as a symbol of the atom bomb, and of the novel as a Cold War allegory (this Tolkien much disputed). Recent interpretations of the novel as a meditation on World War I inflect not only the sequence in the battlefield of Dead Marshes, but also the final scene of homecoming when the hobbit veterans sit silently in the Green Dragon, distanced from the rest of the Shire by their incommunicable experience of war.[14] Inspiration is even drawn from irreverent fan readings of Sam and Frodo as a gay couple.

But the films' references go well beyond Tolkien and his interpreters. There is fidelity in the films' promiscuous allusiveness, since the novel itself is a recombinant pastiche of mythology, Anglo-Saxon poetry, Shakespeare, and religious fairy-tale. (At moments the films neatly reference Tolkien's own sources, as when Theoden, before the battle of Helm's Deep, recites a poem [in the novel it is given to Aragorn] in the valedictory *ubi sunt* form of Old English poems such as *Beowulf* and "The Wanderer"). Jackson's films are faithful in many ways to the novel and the discourses around it, but they ultimately inhabit generic and intertextual worlds well beyond Tolkien. This is unavoidable, given the films' need to work as contemporary fantasies rather than antiquarian pastiches of those of the 1950s. By the time of *The Return of the King*, which takes the most "liberties" with the novel, the essential texts to which Jackson had to remain faithful were the preceding two in the trilogy; it was the fans of those films, an entirely new constituency, who must now be satisfied and appeased.

The rain-drenched battle scenes in *The Two Towers* recall the Japanese director, Akira Kurosawa; the fight in *Fellowship* between Gandalf and Saruman is staged as if for a martial arts film; Kristin Thompson notes an allusion to the "Stargate" sequence in *2001: A Space Odyssey* (1968) when Gandalf passes beyond time and space in *The Two Towers*.[15] More ambiguous are echoes of *Marathon Man* (1976) in Gandalf's asking "Is it safe?" and *Jaws* (1975) in Gimli's toast to bow-legged women. Christopher Lee's casting as Saruman links the films with both horror, a genre to which many scenes unquestionably belong, and *Star Wars*, Lee featuring as Count Dooku in *Episode II* (2002) and *III* (2005). *Star Wars* is the films' acknowledged precursor and rival, as scattered allusions to it attest. Theoden's death scene exchange with Eowyn ("I have to save you," "You already have") repeats the last words between Luke and Darth Vader in *Return of the Jedi* (1983).[16] The defeat of the Oliphaunts at the Battle of Pelannor Fields replays the Battle of Hoth in *The Empire Strikes Back*: the giant elephants are brought down with tripwires just like AT-AT Imperial Walkers.

The Lord of the Rings, with its aesthetic of something for everyone (romance, action, queer subtexts), was solidly in the tradition of the post-*Star Wars* revival of the family film. As Peter Krämer has shown, the key films in the ten years after *Star Wars* returned to the epic form of the pre-New Hollywood era and also to spiritual matters, albeit now in the guise of science fiction and fantasy.[17] Mark Cousins noted that since the blockbuster period of the late 1970s films have increasingly aspired to mythic status:

> For nearly sixty years ... American movies had been about people and what they do – fall in love, explore the mid-west, commit crimes, drive cars, sing, etc. Many of the new blockbuster films also had strong characters but they drew more from comic books, the ideas of psychoanalyst Sigmund Freud, and from myth. Like early, pre-psychological cinema, they used the promise of sensation, thrill and fear to lure people back to the cinema.[18]

Hollywood's mythic pretensions accelerated further when Chris Vogler, a script analyst for the Walt Disney Company in the 1980s, wrote a famous memo arguing that successful screenplays were variations on a twelve-stage Hero's Journey model. A good film reworked this Jungian ur-narrative within the standard Three Act structure promulgated by screenwriting manuals. The perfect screenplay was *Star Wars* and the ideal genre was fantasy, in which archetypes could gambol freely and spirituality was untouched by religious dogma. If *The Lord of the Rings* reminds us of *Star Wars*, this is not only because *Star Wars* borrowed heavily from Tolkien's novel, or even that both happened to mine identical archetypes: *all* Hollywood films now draw inspiration from *Star Wars*'s Joseph Campbell-influenced pseudo-myth of individual liberation, sacrifice, and enlightenment. Nowadays, as Tom Shone acidly remarks, it is no longer enough for a film's hero to be human; he must be supremely archetypal, at the very least a messiah (Neo in *The Matrix* trilogy) or Chosen One (Harry Potter, Anakin Skywalker) and preferably God himself (*The Passion of the Christ* (2004)).[19]

This intoxication with universal archetypes invites a more sinister ideological interpretation. Ken Gelder has suggested that *The Lord of the Rings*, like other recent epics, is compensatory fantasy of the most serious, imaginatively disabling, and politically reactionary kind.[20] For him its lurid "clash of civilizations" encourages the projection of simplistic moral and cultural divisions onto world politics, divisions with straightforward heroic solutions. The recent efflorescence of the fantasy genre, which most openly indulges ideological daydreams, is therefore symptomatic of a dangerously mythic understanding of the present. But I suspect Gelder is too pessimistic. If the films had been made in the 1980s, Sauron's evil Empire would have an obvious signified and their politics might be as unambiguous as *Conan the Barbarian*'s. But (judging anecdotally from commentary on the internet) the films are capable of quite different political applications. *The Return of the King* is widely read as an inadvertent commentary on the Iraq War, with Sauron standing in for George W. Bush.[21]

III

Especially in contemporary Hollywood, adaptation is caught up in interminable processes of allusion, homage, commentary, and appropriation. Some critics argue that this compulsive referentiality, along with the predominance of special effects and action sequences, signal a new stage in Hollywood film, a development (or regression) away from the virtues of classical narrative. According to this argument, since the late 1960s American cinema has entered a post-classical period in which films increasingly deviate from classical narrative's flexible guidelines, which ensured that stories were character driven, had a conventional structure of beginning – middle – end, with clearly motivated events linked by chains of causes and effects, and, thanks to the rules of continuity editing, were easy for spectators to follow. In post-classical Hollywood films, these guidelines are either weakened or overturned, above all in the "high concept" blockbuster action film pioneered by *Jaws* and *Star Wars*. High concept films, whose essential elements can be pitched in thirty seconds, "can be considered as one central development – and perhaps *the* central development – within post-classical cinema, a style of filmmaking molded by economic and institutional forces."[22] In such films, some critics maintain, coherent plot development and characterization have broken down and there is an increasing dominance of spectacular action sequences and special effects; as Warren Buckland explains, they are not "structured in terms of a psychologically motivated cause-and-effect narrative logic, but in terms of loosely-linked, self-sustaining action sequences often built around spectacular stunts, stars, and special effects ... Narrative complexity is sacrificed on the altar of spectacle."[23]

However, this is an overstatement, a rhetorically sweeping dismissal of dumbed-down Hollywood rather than an accurate description of its characteristic products. Kristin Thompson notes that in any case blockbusters do not make up the majority of Hollywood films, which still adhere to classical norms:

> Why has the notion of fragmented, incoherent, spectacle-and-action-laden films taken such hold in academia recently? For one thing, most commentators have too quickly equated all of Hollywood cinema with its blockbusters. Most films made in any given year are medium-budget comedies, romances, action pictures and children's fare ... [Such] genres tend to be built on principles of classical construction. Even if special-effects extravaganzas were as fragmentary as critics claim, they would not constitute the norm.[24]

And, as we have seen, even a blockbuster like *The Lord of the Rings* attempts to follow established classical principles. For all its post-classical delight in special effects, hyperreal locations and characters like Gollum, and set-piece action sequences, *The Lord of the Rings* is a sequential character-driven quest narrative (albeit a quest to dispose of rather than discover something); it is filmed in a style of unemphatic realism in which the staggering special effects are subordinated to the needs of the story; and the plot resolution, while exhausting, at length achieves the resounding closure of "The End." Indeed some of the difficulties of adaptation were caused by the novel's being so resolutely non-classical in its construction. Like most recent Hollywood cinema, in Thompson's words, the film trilogy "continues to succeed through its skill in telling strong stories based on fast-paced action and characters with clear psychological traits. The ideal American film still centers around a well-structured, carefully motivated series of events that the spectator can comprehend relatively easily."[25]

The post-classicism of the *The Lord of the Rings* has less to do with details of its narrative structure than with the textual instability created by the extended DVD versions, which were, Jackson said, "for the fans."[26] The extended DVDs (which to some extent replicate the "expanded universe" of the novel as well as its more sprawling qualities) are curious texts, both more satisfying and more shambolic than the theatrical prints, neither unpolished rough cuts nor final and definitive Director's Editions (there is an inviting parallel with *The History of Middle Earth*, the series of drafts, false steps, and early versions edited by Christopher Tolkien). Some of the material is even "wrong" in classical terms; the scenes of the Mouth of Sauron and the arrival of the Corsairs in the Extended *Return of the King* are indefensible as storytelling, as Jackson admits on the commentary, because their narrative information is redundant. Across twelve DVDs the Extended Versions seem to lay bare the film-making process and the choices involved in adapting the novel. They encourage multiple viewings, absorption into the details of adaptation and film production, and allow consumers a sense of participation in the phenomenon of *The Lord of the Rings* – all of which help turn a blockbuster into a mass cult film. The DVDs also incorporate parallel competitor narratives to the film itself, such as the heroic struggle, recalled in the "making of" documentary, to edit *The Return of the King* in time for its premiere, and the forging of the fellowship of the actors themselves, which, according to the cast commentary on the Extended *Fellowship*, was sealed by their all getting identical Elvish tattoos. As writers of *Lord of the Rings* Real Person Slash – fan stories about imaginary erotic relationships between the male actors – have been quick to realize, this adds new dimensions to a text already teeming with homoerotic possibilities.[27] The leisurely (novelistic?) pace of the Extended Versions, as well as their longeurs and diversions, loosen the classical linearity of the theatrical cuts and elaborate on their style of allusive shorthand to "missing" scenes and thematic contexts of the novel. So in the Extended *Two Towers*, when Treebeard admonishes an oak tree for trying to devour Merry, his words are those, in the novel, of Tom Bombadil to Old Man Willow; the scene works as an injoke and homage to Bombadil, who has been dropped from the story. The shot in the Extended *Fellowship* of a statue of Aragorn's mother, which resembles one of the Virgin Mary, plays to fans' extratextual knowledge of Tolkien's Catholicism; it is not a theme the film can do much with but the shot at least installs it as an interpretative possibility.

The Extended Versions, in fact, raise questions about what it means to have actually seen *The Lord of the Rings*. Has one authentically *experienced* the film, in its full intertextuality, if one has not seen all the versions, listened to the commentaries, and imagined the ideal cut towards which the "finished" movies only gesture? One might think that this "ideal cut" might, in some Borgsian manner, perfectly reproduce the "original" novel. Yet, paradoxically, the more closely one examines Jackson's *The Lord of the Rings*, and the more interesting they becomes as *films*, the less relevant Tolkien's novel seems to their meaning, context, and aesthetic success.

NOTES

1 Gérard Genette, *Paratexts: Thresholds of Interpretation*, trans. Jane E. Lewin (Cambridge: Cambridge University Press, 1997). On Genette's useful categories, see Robert Stam and Alessandra Raengo (eds.), *Literature and Film: A Guide to the Theory and Practice of Film Adaptation* (Malden, Massachusetts; Oxford, and Carlton: Blackwell Publishing, 2005), pp. 26–31.

2 See Deborah Cartmell and Imelda Whelehan (eds.), *Adaptations: From Text to Screen, Screen to Text* (London: Routledge, 1999), p. 28.

3 Tom Shippey, "Another Road to Middle Earth: Jackson's Movie Trilogy" in Rose A. Zimbardo and Neil D. Isaacs (eds.), *Understanding* The Lord of the Rings: *The Best of Tolkien Criticism* (New York: Houghton Mifflin, 2004), pp. 233–54); Brian Rosebury, *Tolkien: A Cultural Phenomenon* (London: Palgrave Macmillan, 2003); Jim Smith and J. Clive Matthews, *The Lord of the Rings: The Films, The Books, The Radio Series* (London: Virgin Books, 2004).

4 Jane Chance, "Is There a Text in This Hobbit? Peter Jackson's *Fellowship of the Ring*," *Literature/Film Quarterly* (2002: 2), 82.

5 Thomas Leitch, "Twelve Fallacies in Contemporary Adaptation Theory," *Criticism* 45.2 (Spring 2003), 161.

6 On critical disdain for Tolkien and the scandal of the 1997 poll, see Tom Shippey, *J. R. R. Tolkien: Author of the Century* (London: HarperCollins, 2001), pp. xx–xxiv; Patrick Curry, *Defending Middle Earth: Tolkien, Myth and Modernity* (1997; London: HarperCollins, 1998), pp. 15–20; and Joseph Pearce, *Tolkien: Man and Myth* (London: HarperCollins, 1998), pp. 21–2.

7 Jenny Turner, "Reasons for Liking Tolkien," *London Review of Books* 15 November 2001, 16.

8 Ibid., p. 15.

9 Kristin Thompson, "Fantasy, Franchises, and Frodo Baggins: *The Lord of the Rings* and Modern Hollywood," *The Velvet Light Trap* 52 (Fall 2003), 46.

10 Bertha Chin and Jonathan Gray, " 'One Ring to Rule Them All': Pre-viewers and Pre-Texts of the *Lord of the Rings* Films," *Intensities: The Journal of Cult Media* Issue 2: http://www.cult-media.com/issue2/Achingray.htm (accessed 31 March 2006).

11 Deborah Cartmell and Imelda Whelehan, "Harry Potter and the Fidelity Debate" in Mireia Aragay (ed.), *Books in Motion: Adaptation, Intertextuality, Authorship* (Amsterdam and New York: Rodopi, 2005), pp. 37–49.

12 I. Q. Hunter, "Tolkien Dirty: *Lord of the Rings* Sexploitation Films," paper given at "Tolkien 2005: 50 Years of *The Lord of the Rings*," Aston University, Birmingham, 13 August 2005; published as "Tolkien Dirty," in *The Lord of the Rings: Popular Culture in Global Context*, ed. Ernest Mathijs (London and New York: Wallflower Press, 2006), pp. 317–33.

13 On Tolkien as a proto-postmodern deep-ecologist, see Patrick Curry, *Defending Middle Earth: Tolkien, Myth and Modernity*.

14 On Tolkien as an author of World War I, see John Garth, *Tolkien and the Great War: The Threshold of Middle Earth* (London: HarperCollins, 2003).

15 Thompson, "Fantasy, Franchises," p. 46.

16 Smith and Matthews, *The Lord of the Rings*, p. 191.

17 Peter Krämer, *The New Hollywood: From* Bonnie and Clyde *to* Star Wars (London and New York: Wallflower, 2005), pp. 97–8.

18 Mark Cousins, *The Story of Film* (London: Pavilion Books, 2004), p. 378.

19 Tom Shone, *Blockbuster: How Hollywood Learned to Stop Worrying and Love the Summer* (London and Sydney: Simon and Schuster, 2004), pp. 303–4.

20 Ken Gelder, *Popular Fiction: The Logic and Practices of a Literary Field* (London: Routledge, 2004), pp. 142–57.

21 See, for example, the celebrated image of a ring-wearing Bush, captioned "Bush has the One Ring, Frodo has failed," archived at http://politicalhumor.about.com/library/images/blbushlordrings.htm (accessed 31 March 2006).

22 Justin Wyatt, *High Concept: Movies and Marketing in America* (Austin: University of Texas Press, 1994), p. 8. On the concept of post-classical film, see Peter Krämer, "Post-classical Cinema", in John Hill and Pamela Church Gibson (eds.), *The Oxford Guide to Film Studies* (Oxford: Oxford University Press 1998), pp. 289–309.

23 Warren Buckland, "A Close Encounter with *Raiders of the Lost Ark*: Notes on Narrative Aspects of the New Hollywood Blockbuster," in *Contemporary Hollywood Cinema*, ed. Steve Neale and Murray Smith (London: Routledge, 1998), p. 167.

24 Kristin Thompson, *Storytelling in the New Hollywood: Understanding Classical Narrative Technique* (Cambridge, Massachusetts and London: Harvard University Press, 1999), pp. 347–8.

25 Thompson, *Storytelling*, p. 8.

26 On the extended DVD versions, see Sue Kim, "Beyond Black and White: Race and Postmodernism in *The Lord of the Rings* Films," *MFS Modern Fiction Studies* 50.4 (Winter 2004), p. 887–9.

27 On the novel's and films' homoeroticism, see Anna Smol, " 'Oh . . . Oh . . . *Frodo*!': Readings of Male Intimacy in *The Lord of the Rings*," *MFS Modern Fiction Studies* 50.4 (Winter 2004), 949–79.

II

DEBORAH CARTMELL

Adapting children's literature

Inserted in Roald Dahl's *Charlie and the Chocolate Factory* (1964) is a "paragone," a poetic diatribe proclaiming the inestimable superiority of literature over television and the latter's responsibility for the present intellectual degeneration of the child in which Dahl's own voice can be heard loudly and clearly:

> HIS BRAIN BECOMES AS SOFT AS CHEESE
> HIS POWERS OF THINKING RUST AND FREEZE!
> HE CANNOT THINK – HE ONLY SEES![1]

The "paragone," the defense of the superior claims of one discipline over another, especially in terms of the visual and the verbal, has an extensive literature, from Plato to Sir Philip Sidney, and reappears in the twentieth and twenty-first centuries in the often competing and strained relationship between literature and film, and the covert paragone detectable in both forms. The most famous of all paragones, Ben Jonson's "Expostulation," an attack on his all too successful collaborator, the architect, Inigo Jones, is unnervingly prophetic of the current "he's only the author" syndrome (of Hollywood, where spectacle undeniably rules):

> O shows! Shows! Mighty shows!
> The eloquence of masques! What need of prose,
> Or verse, or sense, to express immortal you?[2]

Screen adaptation, on one level, grows out of the longstanding tradition of *ut pictura poesis*, a tradition that reflects on the mutual dependence and admiration of painting and literature. But where there is dependence and admiration, there is also incompatibility and jealousy. In the field of adaptation, the tension between the literary and the screen text is, possibly, most prominent in the area of children's texts, where concerns over film's moral influence and the threat to literacy have been prevalent since the inception of cinema. As George Bluestone observed in his pioneering work, the relationship between literature and film is simultaneously "overtly compatible" and "secretly hostile";[3] and, accordingly, this chapter will examine the competing, often overtly hostile relationship between film and literature by making explicit this implicit antagonism[4]. When it comes to adaptations of children's literature, the battle between film and literature seems to be at its most ferocious.

Collecting children's literary adaptations within a single work potentially reveals biases and preferences. Douglas Street's collection, *Children's Novels and the Movies* is arranged by classic children's stories and their film adaptations, thereby privileging the literary over the film text.[5] Adaptation studies tend to restrict themselves to classic literature with little or no regard for classic films – often, unbeknown to most, adaptations of little-known literary texts, or popular literature, betraying an unspoken assumption that the classic literary text is always preeminent. Consequently, this chapter considers three types of children's literary adaptations: adaptations of "classic" children's stories, adaptations of lesser known children's texts, and adaptations of popular children's fiction.[6] Surprisingly, given the number of adaptations of children's literature to screen, the area has attracted very little critical attention. Compared to the scarcity of literature on children's adaptations[7] at the time of writing, of the top thirty US moneymaking films, twenty-three were children's films and nine of these were adaptations of children's literature.[8] Although it's difficult to pin down what exactly constitutes children's literature, it can be distinguished from other literatures insofar as it is often more loved and better known. Children, unlike adults, love to re-read their favourite stories; and, correspondingly, in adapting these texts, there will be higher demands on fidelity. Obviously, the range of children's literature is enormous, from books designed to develop reading skills to those which appeal to both adults and a younger readership. This chapter will restrict itself to literature written for the older child.

Film adaptations of children's literature are divided here into films of "classic," "obscure" and "popular" texts. A "classic" children's book tends to inspire numerous film versions – every generation seems to have a film of *Peter Pan, Alice in Wonderland, Treasure Island*, and *Little Women*, for example. Lesser-known texts, however, tend to produce a single film and, if successful, the film becomes the ur-text in the minds of its viewers. It could be argued that *The Wizard of Oz* and *Mary Poppins* belong to this category. In this case, the film "makes" the literary text. In addition to classics and those arguably fated to obscurity without the movie, like *Mary Poppins* (the persistence of the novels, arguably, depends on the film), there is another category – adaptations of bestselling children's writing. In recent times these would be Enid Blyton, Roald Dahl and, of course, J.K. Rowling.

Significantly, the adaptations of these writers' works have been, on the whole, seen as inferior to the books. They have in no way threatened to overtake the book as the primary text in the minds of their audiences.

Classic adaptations

I have already remarked that literary texts adapted numerous times tend to have a classic status. To take one example, *Little Women* has had three major film adaptations (not to mention several television and stage adaptations, even an opera): George Cukor's 1933 film, starring Katherine Hepburn; Mervyn LeRoy's 1949 version with June Allyson as Jo and Elizabeth Taylor as Amy; and Gillian Armstrong's 1994 film, with Winona Ryder as Jo. Significantly, each deals with the Civil War (which forms a backdrop to the novel) and the tragic death of the third sister, Beth, in a manner suited to their different audiences. In LeRoy's postwar *Little Women*, closely based on Cukor's film (with the same scriptwriters), the Civil War is barely mentioned and Beth's death is not presented to us on screen; an audience recovering from the recent effects of World War II needs a different *Little Women*, one which will not re-awaken any unpleasant memories.

Although *Little Women* has not, and is not likely to have the "Disney treatment," undoubtedly, the Disney corporation has been the most prolific and lucrative twentieth-century adaptor of classic children's fiction, from fairytales to classic stories and novels. In most Disney films, fidelity to the text is openly flaunted; indeed, as is frequently observed, the ambition of a Disney adaptation is to usurp its source – no matter if it be a classic, obscure, or popular text – so that the film adaptation triumphs over its literary original, and, for most viewers, it is the film rather than the text that is the original.[9] Films were made for children from the beginning of cinema – five versions of Dickens's *A Christmas Carol* before 1915, an *Alice in Wonderland* in 1903,[10] but by far the greatest influence on the genre was Walt Disney whose surname has become a byword for a particularly conservative and lucrative form of children's cinema. Disney, starting with Mickey Mouse in 1928, also became involved in spin-offs, such as games, toys, and food, revolutionizing the children's cinema industry. As has been pointed out, Disney's gift wasn't for artistic impression but for the exploitation of the new technology[11] – underlying this is the "belief" that the film will overtake the literary text. According to Richard Schickel, Disney

> could make something his own, all right, but that process nearly always robbed the work at hand of its uniqueness, of its soul, if you will. In its place he put jokes and songs and fright effects, but he always seemed to diminish what he

touched. He came always as a conqueror, never as a servant. It is a trait, as many have observed that many Americans share when they venture into foreign lands hoping to do good but equipped only with know-how instead of sympathy and respect for alien traditions.[12]

A common feature of a Disney opening is the book becoming animated or Tinker Bell sprinkling fairy dust on the words of the opening credits, cunningly signifying that the transition from book to film enhances/enlivens/realizes and ultimately, improves the static words of the story. Clearly, Disney's visual language saturated the public and "his" Snow White became *the* Snow White, visually anchoring the character into an instantly recognizable figure.

Disney's visual style has been identified by Steven Watts as "sentimental modernism" in which:

- The real and unreal are combined.
- Tropes are refashioned from the Victorian period, exaggerating sentimentality and cuteness.
- Although images and experiences are broken down, rationality is always restored.
- The inanimate world is animated.
- High cultural signifiers are visually satirized.[13]

In terms of story, Disney films rely very much on the three-act classic Hollywood structure, "build/establish/resolve," as described by Linda Seger,[14] and contain values and themes that have been identified by Janet Wasko as:

- individualism and optimism
- escape, fantasy, magic imagination
- innocence
- romance and happiness
- good triumphing over evil.[15]

In addition to visual anchorage[16] was an ideological agenda that Disney brought to the stories, reflected in his founding role in the Motion Picture Alliance for the Preservation of American Ideals (the foundation of the Hollywood blacklist). It's no accident that the rise of Disney coincided with debates about the morality of the cinema and American values, and a very conservative view of the family is common to all these films. Disney's scant regard for his literary originals fueled debate about his influence on children – a letter by Frances Clarke Sayers to a Los Angeles newspaper articulates a growing number of concerns about Disney's threat to children's literature:

> I call him to account for his debasement of the traditional literature of childhood, in films and the books he publishes.

He shows scant respect for the integrity of the original creations of authors, manipulating and vulgarizing everything to his own ends.

His treatment of folklore is without regard for its anthropological, spiritual or psychological truths. Every story is sacrificed to the "gimmick" of animation.[17]

As mentioned previously, Disney doesn't merely adapt a narrative – he virtually steals it, making it *his* story, much to the disparagement of those who seek to preserve and revere the literary original. By visually satirizing cultural signifiers, Disney films reverse the high and low culture trajectory, insinuating that low culture is better than high. There are countless examples of the uneducated, "rough diamonds" (or versions of Rousseau's "noble savages") outwitting the so-called "posh" characters – the highly cultured Captain Hook versus the uneducated American Peter Pan, the British butler against the American alley cat in *The AristoCats*, the British tiger, Shere Khan, versus the American Mowgli in *The Jungle Book* are just some examples. In *Peter Pan*, the youngest Darling, Michael, is given an American accent, whereas his older siblings, John and Wendy, speak the Queen's English with the implication that the pure, natural, pre-lapsarian voice is that of an American.

Disney adaptations have been attacked for plundering and simplifying grand historical narratives, being responsible for the impoverishment of youth, and for closing the minds of their viewers through their insistence on closure – the endings of these films, repeatedly, resolve all the ambiguities and complexities of their literary sources. Finally, Disney movies often intimate to their viewers that film is better than literature. This is implied in the prefatory credits, with the book opening up into the film, the point at which "the magic begins." Disney films can be considered as the diametrical opposite of the "classic" or heritage film, narrowly defined as films that respect or revere the source text, producing what Andrew Higson calls, "a discourse of authenticity."[18] Unlike the heritage movie, Disney films, as indicated above, have no regard for fildelity and, indeed, challenge their literary sources by implicitly satirizing cultural pretension, including the highmindedness of the very texts the films are based on. The most highly rated films produced by Walt Disney (not including Disney enterprises) are as follows:

Votes

15,368	*Fantasia* (1940)
14,839	*Snow White and the Seven Dwarfs* 1937)
14,470	*Mary Poppins* (1964)
9,713	*Bambi* (1942)

9,386   *The Jungle Book* (1967)
7,184   *Dumbo* (1941)
7,158   *Pinocchio* (1940)
7,157   *Lady and the Tramp* (1955)
6,201   *101 Dalmatians* (1961)
6,074   *Sleeping Beauty* (1959)
5,885   *Cinderella* (1950)
5,096   *Peter Pan* (1953)
4,924   *Alice in Wonderland* (1951)[19]

This list reveals how successful Disney adaptations are as, in a number of cases, the film overtakes the source text as the "original" in most people's minds. Certainly this is the case of *The Lady and the Tramp, Pinocchio, Dumbo, The Jungle Book, 101 Dalmatians*, and, perhaps most notably, *Peter Pan*.

While, visually and structurally, these films have much in common, they're also strikingly similar in their ideological perspectives. On first glance, these films share common narrative ground, especially absent or neglectful fathers who must reassert themselves in some way in order for harmony to be restored. Oddly, as in Shakespeare's plays, mothers tend to be, on the whole, noticeable for their absence. The narrative is changed in ways which often promote "family values" by upraising or reinstating the father. *Peter Pan* is changed in Disney's 1953 film, so that Mr. Darling conforms to an ideal of fatherhood, having the final word in the film after having behaved badly at the beginning. This is at odds with J. M. Barrie's novel (1911) and play (first performed in 1904) which concludes with the ageing figure of Wendy and the turn-of-the-century topical suggestion that women are changing, whereas men are stuck in the past, incapable of accepting the passage of time. The successful adaptations of "classic" children's texts produced by Disney in the corporation's "Golden Age" tend to "lord" over the text, implicitly mocking the original's cultural pretentiousness by producing a popular and contemporary reading which, it is insinuated, is a preferable one. In the war between film and literature, film wins.

Adaptations of lesser read or "obscure" texts

It is often the case that a film can breathe life into a book and serve to raise awareness of its literary worth, enabling it to move from obscurity to "classic" status. It sometimes happens that a film, based on a little-known work, becomes itself the classic text. This is, arguably, the case with films like *The Wizard of Oz* (1939; based on L. Frank Baum's novel, 1900), *National Velvet* (1944; Enid Bagnold's novel, 1935), *Chitty Chitty Bang Bang* (1968;

Ian Fleming's novel, 1964), *The Neverending Story* (1984; Michael Ende's novel, 1979), *Bambi* (1942; Felix Salten's novel, 1926) and *Mary Poppins* (1964; P. L. Travers's novels). In these films, the source text is unknown to film-goers or known, largely, due to the success of the film.

In the 1960s, after much astute diversification into television and theme parks, the Disney company moved into live action films, with the most successful of these being *Mary Poppins* in 1964. Pamela Travers completed six books in the series and the film draws mostly from the first, but uses episodes and images from the next three. The film came out of the Disney studios in 1964 and, for anyone familiar with the books, much of the story is unrecognizable, although cameo appearances of major characters are carefully inserted at the beginning of the movie, presumably to appease devoted readers of P. L. Travers. Travers herself was not entirely happy with the film, especially disliking Mr. Banks tearing up the poem, written by the children, describing their ideal nanny, which occurs at the beginning of the film:

> All had to be sweetness and light and *cruelty* in order to get the sentimental outcome of the end. I pleaded with the Disneys not to let Mr. Banks tear up the poem. No good. And they never told me Mrs. Banks was to be a suffragette. I had suggested to Disney that it be set in Edwardian times – in that way it could never be out of date – but I never guessed he would gild the lily with Women's Suffrage.[20]

The major changes the film makes are the period in which it's set (Edwardian rather than 1930s), there are two children rather than four (five later on), the father is depicted as a hard-nosed patriarch and the mother, a superficial suffragette. Another major difference is in the character of Mary. In the books, she's an ambivalent figure, not as altruistic and kindly as the one famously portrayed by Julie Andrews. Finally, the figure of Bert (a minor character in the novels), complete with phony Cockney accent, is substantially enlarged to the second billing of the film. Typical of Disney's live action movies, the film mixes animation with "real people," and presents us with an unrealistic view of the world (there was no attempt to make the set realistic) as is clear from the opening sequence with the view of London which is instantly recognizable to film-goers. While Travers suggested the Edwardian period to Disney to give the film a sense of timelessness, she was distressed by the outcome. In spite of the striking precision of the date (it's 1910, "the age of men," as Mr. Banks gleefully asserts in his song) Disney has no desire to be historically accurate. The period he creates, however, is one which seems to be obsessed with childhood, children's fashion, and toys – rocking horses, dolls' houses, teddy bears. The nursery, depicted in the film, is an image of idyllic childhood. Like the 1960s when the film was made, the period may have been chosen as it is a time of radical change, especially in relation to gender roles. The centrality of male authority is at the crux of *Mary Poppins*, the film; George Banks's first song, as Brian E. Scumsky has observed, is about the family as an image of the British nation, the father is "Lord of the Castle." While smugly congratulating himself on his authority over the family, ironically the suffragette mother is trying to interrupt his song to inform him that his children have disappeared.[21] Nonetheless, he is still the focus of the family and is confronted and redeemed by both Mary and Bert at significant points of the film (revealingly, Mary is never seen to speak to Mrs. Banks, reflecting the inferior role of the mother).

The central pair, Mary and Bert, become, in the film, replacement parents – the bad parents are replaced by good ones, like fairy godparents, who arouse the responsibilities of the real parents. Bert literally rescues the children from the father in the bank sequence. In the end, the bad parents are reformed through the auspices of their counterparts. The suffragette banner is sacrificed for the tail of the kite, as a better family unit has been produced, one based, arguably, on American rather than British values. Indeed American Cockney Dick Van Dyke's Bert advises the quintessentially British and hierarchically obsessed Mr. Banks as to how to behave. Bert's ability to mix with all classes and his entrepreneurialism render him the quintessential American. The view of London, as Disney himself declared, is stagy and not accurate – it is an, unashamed, American construction of London which although quaint and cozy, fundamentally is seen to be in need of Americanizing, and/or democratizing.

Travers's novels are restructured into the archetypal Christian narrative of salvation, echoing Dickens's *A Christmas Carol* and films, like *It's a Wonderful Life* (1946), where a magical figure (or figures) descends on the world to save it from itself. Visually and morally, Mary Poppins is transformed from the cold and plain character of the novel. The soundtrack and songs make her almost angelic rather than the ambiguous figure she is in the book. What makes this an archetypal Hollywood adaptation of a children's text is its unashamed rewriting of the text in relation to conservative values regarding the composition of the family, coupled with its use of magic. It's easily translated into Disney's magical kingdom which subtly elevates the experience of viewing over reading, literature over film, popular culture over high culture, Americans over the British. The movement into the chalk picture, like the movement of Dorothy from black and white Kansas to the colorful world of Oz, is ultimately like moving from a "dull" book to the more immediate and exciting world of cinema. Indeed the magical episodes, meticulously explained on the DVD featurette, including sliding up the banister, tidying the nursery with a click of a finger, and tea on the ceiling, call attention to the world of cinema, which from its inception, has been associated with magic.[22] As Dorothy discovers in *The Wizard of Oz*, the wizard's magic (whose double as fantasist is the director himself) consists entirely of the projection of an image – the magic is film itself.

The legacy of Disney's triumph over the book can be felt in popular children's literature which seems to compete with film on its own terms. Arguably, Disney's dominance ended with the production of blockbuster films, in particular, *Jaws* (1975) and *Star Wars* (1977); their huge box office success, resulting in spin-offs and sequels which capitalize on a successful formula, transformed Hollywood cinema.

Adaptations of popular children's fiction

It is hardly surprising that lesser known literary texts are normally over-shadowed and/or overtaken by their film adaptation and that in adaptations, such as *Mary Poppins* or *The Wizard of Oz*, the balance of power resides with the film. This trajectory, however, is reversed in adaptations of popular children's writing, where the battle between the book and the film is, it would seem, at its most ferocious.[23] In the twentieth century, Enid Blyton was replaced by Roald Dahl after his enormous success with *Charlie and the Chocolate Factory* (published in America in 1964 and in the UK in 1967), as the most popular children's writer and he has been overtaken, of course, by J. K. Rowling. While there have been a number of adaptations of Blyton's works, it's fair to say that none stand out (excluding "Noddy"). Adaptations of *The Famous Five* (1996, 1978, 1970, 1969 and 1956) have sunk into oblivion. Although Dahl's *Charlie and the Chocolate Factory* has now two films to its name, most of Dahl's fiction has only found its way to film once and, as with the case of Blyton, the films have in no way overtaken the books in terms of popularity. This seems to be the normal fate of adaptations of popular children's literature in which, unlike in the previous categories, in the war between film and literature, the book wins hands down. Looking at Dahl's first big success, *Charlie and the Chocolate Factory*, the message is not just that the film is not as good as the book, but screen texts, on the whole, are seen to be vastly inferior to popular literature.

In the case of both Blyton and Dahl, it could be contended that the films cannot succeed because the books cater too much to a particular period, and have been regarded as "politically incorrect." Certainly, Dahl's writing can be seen as anti-authoritarian (attacking both adults and educational systems in novels such as *Danny the Champion of the World* [1975] or *Matilda* [1988], where school is more like a concentration camp than a nurturing refuge), anti-sentimental (the endings are sometimes cruel and seemingly unjust as in *The Witches* [1983] where the hero is turned into a mouse and left in this condition at the end of the novel), misogynistic (allegedly, women are often demonized, as in *The Witches*) and racist (the Oompa-Loompas in *Charlie and the Chocolate Factory* are virtually slaves, with Willy Wonka performing Nazi-like experiments on them).[24] Dahl's narratives are often regarded as dangerous, especially in their anti-authoritarianism, "not good for children," while in terms of their structure, they are often very conservative.

Although seeming not to play by the rules, Dahl's first successful novel, *Charlie and the Chocolate Factory*, comes out of the tradition that children's literature should be edifying, and teach a lesson. It is, essentially, a moral tale that "teaches" that virtue pays off (Charlie is rewarded, the other children are punished – the punishments fit the crimes). It's structured according to biblical stories of the chosen one reaching the promised land (the Chocolate Factory), with Cinderella (rags to riches) thrown in. Perhaps the most difficult part of the book to adapt is the final punishment. After the fearful fates of Augustus Gloop, Veruca Salt and Violet Beauregarde, we have the chastisement of the unimaginatively named Mike Teavee, which in terms of order, ought to be the worst of all. In the book, it's the longest and most complex.

> Oh, books, what books they used to know,
> Those children living long ago!
> So please, oh please, we beg, we pray
> Go throw your TV set away,
> And in its place you can install
> A lovely bookshelf on the wall.[25]

Dahl's "paragone," arguing for the inestimable superiority of books to television takes four pages in the novel; the Oompa-Loompas work themselves into a frenzy of irritation and frustration at the condition of today's children infected by too much television, which shrinks their intellect (and Mike is literally shrunk by the experience). Dahl thematizes the conflict between literature and screen, one which I've argued is particularly present in the area of popular children's literature and film.

Unsurprisingly, this episode is toned down and reduced in the 1971 film version, directed by Mel Stuart and starring Gene Wilder, as it would not do to demean screen entertainment in a screen entertainment (especially one destined to be repeated on television), or enter into a prolonged diatribe on the dumbing down effects of spectating rather than reading. Watching the 1971 film today, Mike Teavee comes across almost positively in his detailed knowledge of television, undoubtedly a future Media Studies lecturer. Rather than endeavor to degrade viewing and reassert the value of literature, the film implicitly declares its literary value through allusions to not only Dahl, but also classic English literature. Intertextual references to highbrow literature as well as popular entertainment are inserted throughout the film. Willy Wonka is a man, living in a magical kingdom (akin to Hollywood) who is, also, a lover of literature. Literary references in the film are listed under "trivia" in the Internet Movie Database,[26] including quotations from Shakespeare, "Where is fancy bred," "So shines a good deed" (*The Merchant of Venice*), "Sweet lovers love the spring time …" (*As You Like It*), "Is it my soul that calls me by my name?" (*Romeo and Juliet*), Keats, "A thing of beauty is a joy forever" (*Endymion*), and Oscar Wilde, "the suspense is terrible, I hope it will last" (*The Importance of Being Earnest*). Apparently, Roald Dahl hated the film.[27] While the novel is "anti-screen," the film seems to aspire to "literary cinema," by rewriting Willy Wonka as a figure inspired by grand historical narratives and the great tradition of English literature. Disturbingly, Wonka played by Johnny Depp in the 2005 film, directed by Tim Burton, as reviewers were quick to note, resembles Michael Jackson as much as he does Dahl's character; Mike Teavee's intelligence is deliberately censored by Johnny Depp's Wonka (who declares Mike's mumbling is unintelligible); and the words of the Oompa-Loompas' song are barely audible, spectacularly over-shadowed by a dazzling display of "shows" (to borrow Ben Jonson's phrase) with screens upon screens. Indeed, the film is packed with films within the film, including musical and visual tributes to filmic predecessors from *The Wizard of Oz* (the first view inside the factory) to *2001: A Space Odyssey*. Wonka's repression of Mike echoes Burton's of Dahl's; the television studio sequence shamelessly contradicts and silences Dahl's attack on media visual culture.

Dahl's successor, J. K. Rowling, blends the narrative styles and devices of her predecessors, Dahl and Blyton – the adventures of the famous three in a dark but fantastic world. While *Charlie and the Chocolate Factory* is "anti-screen," Rowling embraces film devices in her writing, but the adaptations of her novels elicit similar responses from her fans – the films are not as good as the book, indeed, films cannot surpass the pleasure of popular writing. A reviewer for *The Washington Post* sums up the general consensus that *Harry Potter and the Sorcerer's Stone* is doomed to be only a good copy: "the filmmakers haven't reshaped the story to suit the dramatic needs of the new medium. They didn't write a screenplay so much as cautiously string the book's chapters together like imitation pearls."[28] In hindsight, the caption advertising the film, "the magic begins" was ill judged as the film in no way bettered the original, as it seemed to anticipate, in the style of Disney. While the adaptations are increasingly taking more liberties with Rowling's writings, curiously, the books are regarded as both more magical and more filmic than the films.

While Mel Stuart's *Willy Wonka* can be described as "literary cinema," Rowling's novels are examples of what can be termed "cinematic literature." Rowling's popularity, I suggest, is, at least partially, down to the way the experience of reading draws from the passive experience of watching a film. The Harry Potter books seem to abide by the same conventions governing a "classic" Hollywood film. The first of the novels, for instance, is structured, like a Hollywood blockbuster (including the promise of sequels), with action sequences inserted at regular intervals. The experience of reading is modeled on the experience of watching a movie, with Harry's prominent glasses functioning like the lens of a camera and the writing can be described as cinematic. The visit to Mr. Ollivander's shop, for instance, is structured according to a series of quick edits:

> "Good afternoon," said a soft voice. Harry jumped. Hagrid must have jumped too, because there was a loud crunching noise and he got quickly off the spindly chair.
>
> An old man was standing before them, his wide, pale eyes shining like moons through the gloom of the shop.
>
> "Hello," said Harry awkwardly.
>
> "Ah yes," said the man. "Yes, yes. I thought Id be seeing you soon. Harry Potter." It wasn't a question. "You have your mother's eyes."[29]

Harry's eyes direct the gaze, with one picture being briskly replaced by another, as in a film. Rowling is constantly calling attention to "eyes." "Mr. Olivander moved closer to Harry. Harry wished he could blink. Those silvery eyes were a bit creepy."[30] In this instance, the narrative moves, like a camera, into close-up, then blurred focus, reflecting Harry's confused state. Indeed, although recalling a wide variety of other narratives, including Moses in the bulrushes and other myths of the chosen one, fairy stories, especially Cinderella, and boarding school tales, Rowling's main influence is undoubtedly the film that, arguably more than any other, changed the face of Hollywood: *Star Wars*. Harry shares a strange relationship with his nemesis, Voldemort, just like that of Luke Skywalker and Darth Vader. Harry, like Luke, discovers that he has a special ability; as Luke receives his saber from his mentor, Ben Obi-Wan Kenobi, Harry is given his wand (closely resembling the wand which "chose" Voldemort). The marketing of these novels is now almost identical to the marketing of a film – instead of lavish premieres, there are bookshop events to commemorate the release of a new installment.[31] And while the films of these books are becoming increasingly successful as adaptations, they don't, like a Disney film, threaten to overtake the experience of reading. In the battle between the book and the film, the book is, at present, the winner.

The relationship between a literary text and its film adaptation varies according to the status of the original, but the marriages are never equal, with one partner invariably, unwittingly, or deliberately, preying upon the other. In the area of children's literature and film, there is an inclination among fans and critics to privilege one over the other, and this can be at a cost to "classic" literature (how many children read *Alice in Wonderland* when they can see the film?) and to the benefit of contemporary children's fiction. But looking at adaptations of popular literature, the rivalry between the two can be detected in the growing tendency for children's literature to be more filmic, and film adaptations of popular literature to be more literary. The reflexivity apparent in both film and literature emphasizes both hostility and dependency, making the reading and spectating doubly complex and doubly pleasurable. As far as children's literature goes, most readers and spectators are bound to agree with Lewis Carroll's Alice who introduces the novel with what is, for her, a rhetorical question: "what good is a book without pictures?"

NOTES

1 *Charlie and the Chocolate Factory* (1964; rpt. London and New York: Penguin, 2001), p. 172.
2 *Ben Jonson: A Selection of His Finest Poems*, ed. Ian Donaldson (Oxford: Oxford University Press, 1995), pp. 1.139–41. See Judith Dundas, "Ben Jonson and the Paragone." *Sixteenth Century Journal* 9.4, (1978), 56–65.
3 *Novels into Film* (Los Angeles: University of California Press, 1957), p. 2. Kamilla Elliott also regards literature on film studies as evolving from earlier debates between poetry and painting and the frequent battle between words and images; see *Rethinking the Novel/Film Debate* (Cambridge: Cambridge University Press, 2003).
4 In *Literature and Film*, ed. Robert Stam and Alessandra Raengo (Malden, Massachusetts and Oxford: Blackwell, 2005), Robert Stam, in his introduction, lists eight sources of hostility to adaptation: disservice to the book; dichotomous thinking (merely assuming a rivalry exists); iconophobia; logophilia; anti-corporeality; the myth of facility; class prejudice; and parasitism. These sources are all one-sided, revealingly from the vantage of literature. Stam's book implies throughout that film needs defending when sitting beside literature and that hostility can only exist on the literary side. On the other hand, Robert Ray complains that literature and film remain in a pre-paradigmatic state as a result of their privileging the book over the film, to shore up literature's dwindling status due to the onslaught of film studies. (*How a Film Theory Got Lost and Other Mysteries in Cultural Studies* [Bloomington, Indiana: Indiana University Press, 2001], pp. 120–31).
5 *Children's Novels and the Movies* (New York: Ungar, 1983).
6 In *The Rough Guide to Kids' Movies* (New York and London: Penguin, 2004), Paul Simpson organizes children's cinema according to genre, such as "Action and Adventure," "Drama," "Musicals" or "Sci-fi." I've rejected such a division here, as this would lead to a prioritizing of film over literature.

7 Douglas Street's collection, *Children's Novels and the Movies*, seems to be the only book devoted to the subject of film adaptations of children's literature.

8 http://www.imdb.com (accessed 13 July 2005).

9 This is an extreme example of what Kamilla Elliott terms "the trumping concept of adaptation" (*Rethinking the Novel/Film Debate*, p. 174).

10 Douglas Street, *Children's Novels*, p. 10.

11 Janet Wasko, *Understanding Disney* (Oxford: Polity Press, 2001), p. 15.

12 *The Disney Version* (New York: Avon Books 1968), p. 191.

13 Steven Watts, *The Magic Kingdom: Walt Disney and the American Way of Life* (New York: Houghton Mifflin, 1997), pp. 104–5.

14 *The Art of Adaptation: Turning Fact and Fiction into Film* (New York: Henry Holt, 1992), pp. 82–3.

15 *Understanding Disney*, pp. 117–19.

16 See Paul Wells, pp. 201–2 in this volume.

17 Quoted in Schickel, *The Disney Version*, p. 299. Attacks on Disney for bludgeoning children with junk and debasing literary classics were countered by those who regarded Disney as an American Institution, an upholder of morality and family values. See Steven Watts, *The Magic Kingdom: Walt Disney and the American Way of Life* (Boston and New York: Houghton Mifflin, 1997), pp. 409–10.

18 *English Heritage, English Cinema: Costume Drama since 1980* (Oxford: Oxford University Press, 2003), p. 42.

19 As indicated on the Internet Movie Database http://www.imdb.com (accessed 13 July 2005).

20 Quoted in Brian Sibley, "How are They Going to make *That* into a Musical?: P. L. Travers, Julie Andrews and Mary Poppins," *A Lively Oracle*, ed. Ellen Dooling Draper and Jenny Koralek (New York: Larson Publications, 1999), pp. 51–62; p. 53.

21 "'All That is Solid Melts into the Air': The Winds of Change and Other Analogues of Colonialism in Disney's *Mary Poppins*," *The Lion and the Unicorn* 24 (2000) 97–109; p. 102.

22 See Robert Stam, *Literature Through Film: Realism, Magic and the Art of Adaptation* (Malden, Massachusetts and Oxford: Blackwell, 2005), p. 13.

23 "Popular" is defined here as literature that has been commercially but not "academically" successful.

24 Dahl, *Charlie and the Chocolate Factory*, p. 126.

25 Ibid., pp. 173–4.

26 http://www.imdb.com (accessed 7 March 2005).

27 http://www.imdb.com (accessed 7 March 2005).

28 Rita Kempley, "Harry Flies Off the Page: The Wizard Loses a Little of His Charm," *Washington Post* (Friday 16 November 2001), page C01, http://www.washingtonpost.com (accessed 7 July 2005).

29 *Harry Potter and the Philosopher's Stone* (London: Bloomsbury, 1997), p. 63.

30 Ibid., p. 63.

31 For an analysis of Rowling's cinematic style, see D. Cartmell and I. Whelehan, "Harry Potter and the Fidelity Debate," *Books in Motion, Adaptation, Intertextuality, Authorship*, ed. Mireia Aragay (Amsterdam and New York: Rodopi, 2005) pp. 37–49.

12

SARAH CARDWELL

Literature on the small screen: television adaptations

Practices, perceptions, and prejudices: film versus television adaptations

Since the birth of cinema, filmmakers have adapted an eclectic range of sources, including many and varied sub-genres of literature – from classic eighteenth- and nineteenth-century novels to "pulp" fiction, from thrillers to romances, from melodramas to ghost stories. The breadth and variety of film adaptations is clearly visible to most cinema-goers. When one speaks of television adaptations, in comparison, one tends to refer more particularly to prolific "classic serials": relatively faithful adaptations of classic, mostly nineteenth-century, works of literature. So-called classic serials have formed a flourishing and prominent genre on television since the earliest days of broadcasting, and have constituted a significant portion of television's dramatic output.

Television adaptations of classic novels are comparatively more promi- nent than adaptations of other kinds of sources, not necessarily because they outnumber them, but for two powerful reasons. First, they are more fre- quently advertised *as adaptations*, rather than being subsumed into other generic categories – compare *The Mayor of Casterbridge* (1978), *Middlemarch* (1994), and *Pride and Prejudice* (1995) which are clearly marked as classic-novel adaptations, with series such as *Miss Marple* (1985–1992), *Inspector Morse* (1987–2000), and *The Ruth Rendell Mysteries* (1987–2000), which are regarded primarily as detective serials, and only secon- darily (if at all) as adaptations. Second, classic-novel adaptations share a generic identity: they "look" similar to one another (or so it is claimed), so that their visibility is heightened, along with their tendency to be categorized straight- forwardly as adaptations.

The strong generic or group identity of television classic-novel adaptations has led, somewhat inevitably, to pejorative judgments from scholars and critics; as John Caughie notes, "academic television criticism ... has treated the classic serial with a certain disdain."[1] One of the most commonly held prejudices against these television adaptations is that they reflect television's tendency towards conservative, staid, and unimaginative programming in contrast with cinema's more vibrant, eclectic, and innovative offerings. It is argued that television returns again and again to the same core canon of texts, by Austen, Dickens, Eliot and the like and, moreover, adapts their works in familiar ways, employing generic norms that inhibit originality, imagination and individuality, and substituting recycled conventions and simplistic "translations" from novel to screen for truly innovative (re)interpretations of the sources. While film adaptations exhibit variety in their choice of sources, and directorial individuality and flair in their particular reinterpretations, television adaptations are often regarded as dull, formulaic products, further subsumed into categories with vaguely derogatory labels (heritage television, or costume drama, for example), rather than being regarded as potentially good, "serious" drama.

However, television's predilection for generically consistent classic-novel adaptations is not, on its own, sufficient evidence to uphold an accusation of a lack of imagination or enterprise. Rather, such artistic choices are better explained with reference to the medium-specific origins of television, and its arising technological, institutional, cultural, and formal features. One consequence of these distinctive features is that adaptation is particularly well suited to the medium; television's serial form, for example, is often better suited to adapting expansive classic novels than is cinema. It is this close "fit" between television and adaptation that partly explains the comparatively high rate of production of such programmes, and thus the establishment of a more clearly defined and longstanding genre of classic-novel adaptations than one encounters in the cinema.

This is not to underplay the creative and commercial connections and correlations that can be found between television and film adaptations, as selected historical instances reveal. In the 1980s and early 1990s, for example, at the height of the "heritage film," film adaptations such as *A Room with a View* (1985), *Maurice* (1987), and *Howards End* (1992) bore striking resemblances to their renowned televisual counterparts *Brideshead Revisited* (1981) and *The Jewel in the Crown* (1984). Similarly, the popularity of Raj epics such as *Jewel* and *Staying On* (1980) was echoed in the production of cinema-release films, *Heat and Dust* (1983) and *A Passage to India* (1984). Noticeably, in these cases of correspondence between cinema and television, it is not the case (as is sometimes assumed) that television "jumped on the bandwagon" and followed in the footsteps of pioneering filmmakers. *Brideshead* was the forerunner of Merchant Ivory's famous run of successful heritage films, and *Jewel* was contemporaneous with Lean's *Passage to India*. What is clear is that one can observe creative influences amongst and between filmmakers and television makers, especially once television technology had advanced beyond studio-based techniques.

That said, it is crucial that television adaptations are considered independently of film adaptations, and that the powerful influences of medium-specific technologies, institutions, and ideals are recognized as determinants of aesthetic practices. These medium-specific roots created the differences between film and television adaptations that may be perceived even today. Furthermore, the long-standing tradition of classic-novel adaptation within television underlines the value of considering this particular group of television adaptations as a genre or sub-genre that exhibits its own norms and conventions, which do not always correspond with those found in cinematic adaptations.

Classic-novel adaptations

Classic-novel adaptations are often termed classic serials, though this is a less accurate name, as there are some programs that fit within this "genre" which are not serials, and it is not the serials themselves that are necessarily regarded as classic, but their sources. It is more accurate, therefore, to use the term classic-novel adaptations. These programmes form a striking and coherent generic group, and their collective identity has been recognized in a concentrated range of academic writing that tends to highlight continuities and similarities across the texts.

The programs mostly tend to draw upon well-known literature of the nineteenth century, and sometimes of the eighteenth and early twentieth centuries. Until the mid 1990s, there was also a strong proclivity for *British* classic novels, reflecting the prevailing notion of "educating and informing" the public about British cultural heritage. Thus adaptations of Austen, Dickens, and the Brontës have proved particularly popular on British television: *Pride and Prejudice*, *Great Expectations*, and *Jane Eyre* have each been adapted five times, and *Wuthering Heights* six times. Interestingly, although British cinema has often spurned Hardy as a source, television has retained an interest in him: since 1950, there have been only three British cinematic Hardy adaptations (and two co-productions with other countries), but eleven television versions. This proclivity for broadcasters to favor nationally specific sources is mirrored across the Atlantic: Henry James is far more frequently adapted for American television than for television in other countries.

Some critics have alleged that all classic-novel adaptations look broadly the same, and that they iron out the significant differences between the source novels. This is an exaggeration. Instead, popular perceptions of the source novels' authors have had a great influence on the style and mood of the arising adaptations: while Austen's novels are mostly adapted into whimsical, lighthearted, gently ironic romances, Dickens adaptations have generally exhibited a darker tone and have rejected straightforward naturalism, bringing out the expressionistic qualities of the sources. But it is true, nevertheless, that adaptations of Dickens (and the Brontës) to some extent mark their differences from the conventions or norms of the group; Austen and, perhaps surprisingly, Hardy adaptations are more representative of television classic-novel adaptations, with their emphasis on high production values, their "heritage aesthetic," and their apparent nostalgia for a simpler rural past.

Compared with film adaptations, then, television adaptations have exhibited a greater interest in British classics. They have also placed a proportionately greater emphasis on dialogue, and on the slow development of characters and their interrelations. In order to make sense of this difference in approach, one must consider the early days of television.

The roots of television adaptation: early television to the 1970s

The technologies, institutions, and ideals of early television shaped classic-novel adaptations, and the impact of these factors lingers today within the genre.

The impact of medium-specific technologies on aesthetic practices

The technologies of television have always affected the stylistic choices that could be made by practitioners. At the most fundamental level, there are powerful historical reasons for the prominence of classic-novel adaptations within television. It is sometimes observed that television as a medium originated from a fascination with transmitting live moving images from one place to another, and that this fascination preceded considerations about what the technology might be used *for*. That is, at the point at which the technology to achieve this relay of moving images was invented, there had been little discussion about what precisely those images might be. Thus at first television was regarded as a valuable means of broadcasting live, "real" events, and although its dramatic potential was soon realized, there was a need to seek out ideas for dramatic content. Understandably, broadcasters turned to existing dramatic sources for inspiration: first, theatrical sources (play texts and theatrical performances) and then literary ones (novels and short stories). These provided broadcasters with ready-made material: good stories and credible characters. In 1930, before the BBC had established regular broadcasts, they screened Pirandello's play *The Man With a Flower in His Mouth*. In 1937, when national broadcasting had only just begun, the first live television drama to be broadcast was a literary adaptation: *Journey's End*, adapted from R. C. Sherriff's play. The first drama serial was also an adaptation: *Little Women*, which ran from December 1950 to January 1951. Adaptations from plays and from literary sources dominated television's schedules.

Early television had to contend with several technological limitations in comparison with contemporary film. First, it was almost entirely studio based, and the cameras were cumbersome, heavy, and difficult to move. This meant that changes of perspective and pace had to be created through vision mixing (cutting from one camera to another, in a three or four camera set-up), rather than through moving the cameras themselves, as in film. Moreover, the ability to record the material was not developed until 1947 (and very few of those recordings were kept, until the mid 1950s). A "repeat" was not a re-broadcasting of a previous recording, as it is today, but was an actual re-performance, as of a stage play, in which the actors reprised their roles. These conditions bore significant consequences for the aesthetics of programs: with no post-production editing, for example, it was difficult to gain the fine, subtle control over pace and movement that was within reach for a film editor. The combination of relatively still cameras, infrequent changes of *mise-en-scène* and lack of post-production editing led to an aesthetic that we would today consider staid and rigid, especially in contrast with contemporary cinema. Finally, the quality of sound and image were comparatively poor, undermining the potential for atmospheric demarcations on the soundtrack or intricate delineations of detail within the images.

Modes of performance were also influenced by these medium-specific conditions, leading to distinctively different methods of portraying characters from those found in film. The limited movement of characters meant that the actors were restricted to moving within a demarcated area, contributing to a "stagy" feel. Given the relative lack of physical and spatial movement available to the actors, and the limitations of the television camera in terms of cutting rapidly from one person to another in order to pick up tiny details of performance, verbal aspects of performance were of crucial importance. The screenwriter was regarded as the originator of the drama (in contrast with the director in cinema), and television established a tradition of valuing writing, and words, above other aesthetic aspects. (In this it also reflected its predecessor: radio.)

Interestingly, while some television programs fruitfully exploited later advances in technology that provided the opportunity for innovation, classic-novel adaptations conventionalized many of these early aesthetic traits and one can find them in adaptations up to and into the 1970s. The 1971 adaptation of

Persuasion, for example, is noticeably still and subdued in terms of camera-work, and lacking in stylistic flair. It is also conventionally "wordy," relying upon verbal communication to convey not just story but also theme, mood, and pace. In this, adaptations consciously echoed their sources (play texts and literature), which were literally "wordy." Despite the possibility for alternative modes of adaptation, many adaptors chose to persist with well-established televisual practices, retaining as many as possible of the words of the source text, reproducing dialogue and translating some descriptive passages into spoken words. Thus the desire for "fidelity" that is apparent in the aesthetic choices made in these classic-novel adaptations arose not just from an abiding sense of attachment to and respect for the original source, but also from the historical necessities and conventions of television production. This contrasts with film's early silent adaptations, which set aside words altogether and attempted to retell the stories in images. Television classic-novel adaptations have retained to this day a commitment to the careful and expressive use of verbal language, albeit alongside an expansion of the medium's audio-visual repertoire.

Given that a single set might form the location for an entire play or episode, early adaptations exhibited increased attention to details of setting and decor, compensating to some degree for a lack of shot variation and movement. One of the motivations behind such attention was an attempt to attain textual fidelity to the source, in the sense of accurately reproducing its historical and cultural moment, although unsurprisingly the programs inevitably reflect their contemporary contexts rather more than their sources' contexts. (Compare for example the aforementioned *Persuasion* of 1971 with the 1995 version, or the 1980 *Pride and Prejudice* with its 1995 counterpart.)

A strong emphasis on the importance of the spoken word and on detailed *mise-en-scène* compensated to some extent for the considerable limitations of early television. Moreover, such limitations must be offset against the medium's particular possibilities. First, the medium has a potential for intimacy that arises from its domestic setting and its consequent role within our everyday lives. Secondly, in terms of adaptations in particular, it has one significant advantage: the serial form. Caughie argues that

> If there is a classical form of television narrative, it may be the dramatic serial. While the television film emulates, to a greater or lesser extent, the form of the cinema feature film, and the single play derives its form from the theatre play, the drama serial, having failed to establish itself as a continuing tradition in cinema, now seems specific to television and radio.[2]

Cinematic films are ordinarily limited to around two hours; television serials can be much longer, enabling fuller, more slowly and complexly developed adaptations – especially of expansive books such as those classed as "great" literature. In this, television exhibits a closer relationship with nineteenth-century literature than does film, for much of the literature of that period was written and published in installments. When audiences gathered to hear Dickens read the latest installment of one of his tales aloud, they took part in a form of ongoing, communal engagement with the work that is most clearly approximated today by the audience of a television serial.

BBC Radio broadcast a regular Sunday evening serial, and this tradition was picked up by BBC Television. As mentioned previously, the first tele-vised drama serial was an adaptation (*Little Women*, 1950–1), which was followed by another adaptation: *The Warden*, adapted from Trollope, in 1951. That enduring favorite with adaptors, *Pride and Prejudice*, was first adapted for television in 1952. The potential for gradual, extended develop-ment across the duration of a serial can be seen in such long-running serials as *The Pallisers* (January to November 1974), adapted from six novels by Trollope, and *Clayhanger* (January to June 1976), from Arnold Bennett's novel; both serials ran for over twenty-six episodes. This is a form with which commercial cinema cannot compete. In this way, television adaptations are able not only to retain more of the source's narrative, but also to open out the details of the novel – its intricacies of plot, mood, and atmosphere, to build characters and our relationships with them more incrementally and care-fully, and to sustain a sense of contemplation.

The impact of institutions and ideals on aesthetic practices

Many of the stylistic conventions of classic-novel adaptations have their roots in television's early history and technology: sedate camerawork; an emphasis on words and on detailed *mise-en-scène*, as a means for attaining fidelity; and careful exploitation of the possibilities of seriality. But adaptations on televi-sion have also been influenced by prevailing ideas about television's (social) purpose. A Reithian notion of public service broadcasting (PSB) has been crucial in shaping adaptations. Lord John Reith was the first Director General of the British Broadcasting Corporation and is associated with its public service ideals: to inform, educate, and entertain; "Reithian" has become a shorthand for those ideals. PSB is a useful shorthand for those television channels which are state-funded, or funded by a licence fee, and whose remit is to some degree determined by the state, rather than the market. They are usually required to devote a percentage of their broadcasting to programs that further the public good, such as those that proffer education or information about important aspects of national and international culture. The remit of the BBC, which was the sole broadcaster until 1955, was to "educate, inform, and entertain." Adaptations were seen as a perfect way to achieve all these aims, bringing great literature (whether classic or contemporary, but especially the former) to the public. The sources most often chosen for adaptation support this analysis: acclaimed writers such as Austen, Hardy, Dickens, Eliot, and Tolstoy tend to be favored over those outside the canon. Moreover, despite massive changes in the landscape of television, the Reithian ideal still has currency today with broadcasters, critics, and audiences, especially when discussion turns to the role of the BBC (even if challenges to the licence fee pose a threat to such values).

Such PSB ideals should not be dismissed, especially if one is interested in exploring the specific aesthetic practices of television adaptation. The impact of broader ideals and purposes is too often overlooked when simplistic comparisons are made between cinema and television, and when television adaptations are accused of being more obsessed with fidelity and with a narrow range of British literature. Historically speaking, a television adaptation, unlike a film, cannot be regarded as mere entertainment. Its aim is not limited to being financially viable or even artistically successful; its accomplishments are also measured with reference to these broader conceptions of television's public role. This in part explains television adaptations' preoccupation with fidelity. If the public is to depend upon these representations of great literature for their educative and informative value, then the adaptations must provide a fair representation of the source novels. Thus the fidelity that has been encouraged by medium-specific features is endorsed by the ideals and institutions of the specifically televisual context.

Furthermore, given this emphasis on conveying accurate "content," the medium was required to remain just that: a means by which something, some pre-televisual event, could be accessed, just as it was when broadcasting original live events. Up to the 1970s, it was preferred that the medium itself remain invisible, or at least transparent, when adapting classic literature, and the relative stillness of the camera and corresponding lack of emphasis on "directorial style" such as that found in cinema enhanced this. In this way, adaptations developed as stylistically distinct from other television drama, where the form/content balance was struck differently, and where transparency was more often rejected in favor of formal experimentation, innovation, or reflexivity.

Consolidating and expanding the genre: classic-novel adaptations from the 1980s to the 2000s

By the 1980s, television had grown into what may be regarded as a multichannel environment (ITV had begun broadcasting in 1955, and Channel Four followed in 1982). Improvements in television technology, and the rise of videotapes and then DVDs, broadened television's aesthetic potential and meant that program makers could foresee endurance, even longevity, for their work. In addition, the opening up of the television market had a positive impact upon the development of television adaptations. Whilst the BBC had already established its reputation for reliable, well-produced adaptations of the classics, the commercial channel ITV made its mark with several innovative and successful adaptations, and indeed it was independent company Granada who was responsible for both *Jewel in the Crown* and the groundbreaking serial *Brideshead Revisited*.

Brideshead was shot on 16 mm, which enabled a greater variety of shots and camera movements, and allowed these "filmic" aspects to play as vital a role as the dialogue. Indeed, the serial's most significant achievement – the reproduction of the source novel's distinctively nostalgic tone – was attained through the careful integration of music, camerawork, dialogue, and performance, which in turn developed subtleties of pace, momentum, color, and tone. Again, the advantages of televisual serial form were fully exploited here, as the story was slowly and carefully unravelled, creating possibilities for reflection and contemplation on the part of the characters and the viewers.

The popularity and success of *Brideshead* revitalized the genre of classic-novel adaptations, and the 1980s saw a consolidation of the conventions that are now so familiar, and which include: high production values; "authentic," detailed costumes and sets; "great British actors"; light classical music; slow pace; steady, often symmetrical framing; an interest in landscapes, buildings, and interiors as well as characters; strong, gradually developed protagonists accompanied by entertaining cameo roles; and intelligent, "faithful" dialogue. These characteristics were not just repeated, but also deepened during the 1980s, as the genre became more familiar and program makers thus endeavoured to distinguish their work from others', through ever-increasing attention to the integration of stylistic details.

At the start of the 1990s, the genre was at risk of becoming stale. It seemed that the classic-novel adaptation might founder, as it appeared resolved to repeating the same fundamental conventions, like a stuck record. Another glut of Austen adaptations did little to alter this, although *Persuasion* (1992) stood out, combining fidelity to the dialogue and spirit of the source text whilst breaking away from norms of the genre and employing multi-strand narrative and even some hand-held camerawork. Andrew Davies's phenomenally successful *Pride and Prejudice*, in 1995, was saturated with the norms of the genre. Impressive and successful in its own right, this adaptation had an impact upon the viewing public that rivaled that of *Brideshead*, and revealed that the "multi-channel environment" did not disallow the kinds of mass television events that were possible in earlier eras. At the same time, though, the program marked a turning point. Having intensified every convention and exaggerated every code, it seemed that ensuing adaptations had nowhere to go. Interestingly, Davies himself (interviewed in this volume) was one of the first to recognize this, and true to his history of innovation and reinvention, he reshaped the genre yet again with his notable adaptations of *Moll Flanders* (1996) and *Vanity Fair* (1998), among others.

The efforts of program makers to revitalize classic-novel adaptations around the turn of the century can be seen in two areas in particular. First, there was a marked broadening in the range of source novels chosen for adaptation, in particular incorporating novels from outside Britain, such as *Madame Bovary* (2000), *Anna Karenina* (2000), *Doctor Zhivago* (2002) and *Crime and Punishment* (2002). Second, adaptations became stylistically more innovative, varied and reflexive. Thus we find the Brechtian deployment of direct address in *Moll Flanders*; the humorous undermining of generic norms in order to draw out buffoonish and satirical elements in *Vanity Fair*; the subtle yet sharp puncturing of generic expectations, especially nostalgic tone, in *The Tenant of Wildfell Hall* (1996); and the overturning of generic conventions in the experimental *Crime and Punishment*. Accompanying these changes are shifts in performance style, with acting becoming more varied across different adaptations. The reflexive styles of performance in much of Davies's work (such as *Moll Flanders* and *Vanity Fair*) are palpably distinct from the more naturalistic performances found in *The Tenant of Wildfell Hall*, for example.

Scholarship

Given the sheer range within the genre today, it is somewhat surprising that many critics and theorists continue to paint a very narrow picture of it. Adaptation theorists frequently overlook television altogether, and focus only on literature/film adaptations.[3] Current television scholarship tends to subsume adaptations into other categories, often regarding them simply as "costume dramas." Lez Cooke, for example, lumps together costume drama and classic-novel adaptations from the mid 1990s – at exactly the point at which the genre becomes more varied – with the justification that these programs are all a part of the "heritage export" which makes British programs like these so popular in other countries;[4] Robin Nelson also conflates the two.[5] Yet if there is a group of programs called "costume dramas," these include, alongside classic-novel adaptations, adaptations from popular novels, and original programs, and any seasoned viewer is able to recognize that these programs are distinct from one another. Costume dramas based on popular novels, such as Catherine Cookson adaptations (of which there was a glut in the 1990s), or original screenplays, such as *Upstairs Downstairs* (1971–5) and *House of Elliot* (1991–4) exhibit different emphases, scope, and values. Compared with their classic-novel counterparts, these programs place less emphasis on dialogue and rarely contend with issues of fidelity, and they intensify their use of melodramatic conventions, raising the emotional temperature through melodramatic music and performance styles. To subsume classic-novel adaptations into costume dramas is to over-simplify these televisual forms and underplay their differences.

Frequent and persistent recourse to notions of "heritage" also limits understanding of classic-novel adaptations. The heritage debate has long appealed to critics and theorists (myself included): Cooke writes about heritage television,[6] and Nelson argues that adaptations are concerned no longer with fidelity but with the nostalgic presentation of heritage.[7] But taken alone, this is too simplistic a view of the genre. It is true that the television classic-novel adaptation is closely related to the heritage film, but since the late 1990s in particular, it is simply not the case that the genre can be defined by its obsession with heritage – nor by a "nostalgic" tone – as is demonstrated by the exceptions named above.

Adaptations of contemporary and popular literature

While television classic-novel adaptations have historically had a high profile, this is not true of adaptations of contemporary and/or popular novels. These adaptations are relatively fewer, and they are much less visible, especially because many of them correspond quite easily to existing television genres and they thus find their place within pre-established forms, alongside non-adapted sources. In a sense, these are the "hidden" adaptations, which make little noise about their adapted status. For example, *Inspector Morse*, *The Ruth Rendell Mysteries*, and Catherine Cookson adaptations are commonly regarded not as adaptations but primarily as detective series, murder-mystery series, and romance, respectively. A similar logic applies with many science fiction adaptations: *The Time Machine* (adapted in 1949) is well known as a novel by H. G. Wells, but has been readapted so many times that it also forms part of a sub-genre of "time travel" films and programs. The 1954 television version of *Nineteen Eighty-Four*, despite the fame of its source, is usually explored as part of the history of science fiction television, rather than as an adaptation; even Jason Jacobs, in his excellent and detailed discussion of the program, limits his acknowledgment of its adapted status to a discussion of the comparative reception of the novel and the program.[8]

Adaptations of popular novels that are non-generic are rarer, but include adaptations as varied as those of R. F. Delderfield's *To Serve Them All My Days* (1980), Kingsley Amis's *The Old Devils* (1992), Hanif Kureishi's *The Buddha of Suburbia* (1993), Angela Lambert's *A Rather English Marriage* (1998), Mervyn Peake's *Gormenghast* (2000), Anthony Trollope's *The Way We Live Now* (2001), and Zadie Smith's *White Teeth* (2002). Of course these adaptations differ in terms of their success, but in opening up a range of genres, sources, perspectives, and voices, adaptations of contemporary and popular literature contribute to the breadth of television drama today.

Television and film adaptations today

Television adaptations have seen immense changes in their technological, institutional and creative contexts. Yet some fundamental features of early adaptations linger. Despite the broadening of the classic-novel adaptation canon, British television retains a penchant – and a reputation – for adapting great British classics and for working within some kind of public service remit; cinema, after the height of the heritage film, remains less clearly nationally specific. The issue of fidelity persists in the case of classic-novel adaptations, primarily because of the special status of these highly-regarded and much-loved sources. Yet while this is as true for film classic-novel adaptations as it is for television ones, still the latter exhibit a more overt historical commitment to fidelity, perhaps because of television's enduring PSB role. The consequences of this are that television produces some of the strongest, most sensitive adaptations of lengthy and/or complex novels, such as *Far From the Madding Crowd* (1998) and *Daniel Deronda* (2002). These two examples reveal that the modern competitive marketplace within television sometimes results in successful collaborations – the former is one in a long line of acclaimed BBC co-productions with the American PSB company WGBH Boston, and the latter was made by the producers of *Brideshead*: Granada, in collaboration with WGBH Boston and Mobil Masterpiece Theatre.

The historical legacy of television's establishment, consolidation, and development of the classic-novel adaptation should not be regarded as a hindrance, or as something which today's adaptors need to move on from, or away from. Of course, there will always be weak, formulaic and dull "generic products," but the presence of historically established traditions and structures also open up immense possibilities. Program makers are able to take a certain generic literacy for granted, and therefore have greater freedom to use generic shorthand, to play with and subvert formal conventions, and open up greater reflexivity within programs. These possibilities have been most clearly taken up in the adaptations of the late 1990s, especially in those scripted by Andrew Davies, who has made the genre his specialism, and is the closest it has to an auteur.

Davies's high profile draws attention to the fact that television still places a much stronger emphasis on writing than that found in the cinema, and despite technological and creative developments, and the notable increase in directorial flair within the medium, the screenwriter retains his status, and is comparable with the director in cinema. Not only does this allow an individual like Davies to build a career within television, it also means that he can endow this television genre with an artistic personality. Moreover, his work is the ultimate case-study for those interested in the progression of television adaptation: he has adapted popular and classic texts; he was a major contributor to the establishment of the genre of classic-novel adaptations; and he has always been eclectic in his choice of sources, but has become more interested in international sources in the late 1990s.[9]

Fidelity remains important – but it is also the case that notions of fidelity have altered. While in early adaptations it implied faithfulness to the words of the novel, in later adaptations, as television has developed stylistically, and greater expressive opportunities have opened up, fidelity has been reconfigured and adaptors have become more concerned with conveying the "spirit" of the source text. Adaptations have become more courageous and imaginative, and viewers seem more willing to accept changes to plot and dialogue if they perceive some underlying attempt to achieve fidelity to the style, tone, or spirit of the original. Perhaps this can be regarded as a shift in understanding: the affiliation to the source text remains, but it is possibly better conceptualized as a desire to show *respect* to that text, rather than to be *faithful* to it. In the early days of television, fidelity to the "content" – specifically the plot and the words – of the source was the dominant method through which an adaptor could express his or her respect for that former text; now with technological, cultural, and creative advances, there are many alternative ways. It also appears that adaptors have broadened their artistic impulses and updated the Reithian aim of educating and informing the audience to one of inspiring enthusiasm in the viewers for the source text and for the adaptation itself. This would explain why television adaptations today now rival the levels of variety and innovation that can be seen in cinematic versions.

While the small screen can suffer in contrast with the large screen (such as in the reception of the recent television version of *Doctor Zhivago*, in contrast with Lean's classic cinematic version), it can also fare well in comparison. The best television adaptations continue to use one of television's major strengths: its serial form – and exploit this in combination with a strong emphasis on writing high-quality dialogue, and the medium's greater capacity for intimate equality with the viewer. Thus lengthy, episodic, or picaresque novels often adapt more successfully to television: consider the feisty and fascinating television serial *Moll Flanders*, or the witty and reflexive television version of *Vanity Fair*, both of which overshadow the most recent cinematic versions (1996 and 2004).

This chapter opened with some of the more negative ways in which television adaptations have been characterized and dismissed. When examining television adaptation, one has the usual problem of a lack of archive material from before the 1950s, but this is less frustrating a barrier than having to counter common perceptions of the genre. Television scholars are able to get away with gross generalizations, most often derisive, which would not be tolerated in film studies. Characterizations of classic-novel adaptations, in particular, are frustratingly slow to change, and do not reflect the genre as it currently stands. Those of us who outlined the "genre" of classic-novel adaptations, drawing upon work on the heritage film, perhaps did not expect that these necessarily broad and tentative sketches would be perpetuated without further reflection, challenge, and refinement.[10] The "generic" approach has been extremely valuable in distinguishing television from film adaptations, and future studies may use it to delineate classic-novel adaptations from, for example, costume dramas. It has also steered television scholars away from simplistic comparative evaluations of adaptations with their source texts. But the generic approach should not replace a close attention to the distinctive qualities of individual texts, most of which do not fit straightforwardly within generic norms and boundaries. The generic context is only one of the contexts that have influenced television adaptations. It would be fruitful to move towards a greater understanding of and responsiveness to the particularities of the television medium, accepting its limitations and recognizing its special capacities, and to evaluate adaptations from within such a comprehension. It is also vital to recognize television's different historical purposes and principles. Television adaptations are not a branch of film adaptations but are a distinct medium-specific form.

NOTES

1 John Caughie, *Television Drama: Realism, Modernism, and British Culture* (Oxford Television Studies: Oxford University Press, 2000), p. 207.
2 Caughie, *Television Drama*, p. 205.
3 Three important recent publications in the field exemplify this tradition of excluding consideration of television adaptations, as their titles imply: Robert Stam and Alessandra Raengo's *Literature and Film: A Guide to the Theory and Practice of*

Film Adaptation (Malden, Massachusetts and Oxford: Blackwell, 2005); its companion volume, also edited by Stam and Raengo and published simultaneously by Blackwell, *A Companion to Literature and Film*; and Kamilla Elliott's *Rethinking the Novel/Film Debate* (Cambridge: Cambridge University Press, 2003). All three books extend their scope beyond adaptation studies, yet ignore television adaptations.

4 Lez Cooke, *British Television Drama: A History* (London: BFI Publishing, 2003), pp. 166–9.

5 Robin Nelson, "Costume Drama (Jane Austen adaptations)," in Glen Creeber (ed.) *The Television Genre Book* (London: BFI Publishing, 2001), pp. 38–41.

6 Cooke, *British Television Drama*, p. 83.

7 Nelson, "Costume Drama," p. 39.

8 Jason Jacobs, *The Intimate Screen: Early British Television Drama* (Oxford Television Studies: Clarendon Press, 2000), pp. 139–55.

9 Sarah Cardwell, *Andrew Davies*, The Television Series (Manchester: Manchester University Press), 2005.

10 Sarah Cardwell, *Adaptation Revisited: Television and the Classic Novel* (Manchester: Manchester University Press), 2002.

PART FOUR

Beyond the "literary"

13

PAUL WELLS

Classic literature and animation: all adaptations are equal, but some are more equal than others

There is little doubt even in the contemporary era when animation enjoys a high artistic, cultural, and popular profile, that the combination of high literature – "the classic" – and the "cartoon," still seems an unholy alliance. One wonders, for example, what director Brad Bird said to Poet Laureate, Ted Hughes, when preparing his adaptation of *The Iron Giant* (1999) – "Great poetic narrative Ted, but don't you think it's short on chases and custard pies?" This, of course, is to caricature both practices – literature as the embodiment of elevated "art" and animation as a vehicle only for comic events, slapstick, and spectacle. Neither is accurate, and in the case of *The Iron Giant*, Bird abandoned the more readily "animatable" and spectacular second half of Hughes's narrative to concentrate on the core relationship between a boy and a robot in a quasi-realist cartoon style. Nothing, then, should be taken for granted, and this discussion will seek to explore a range of perspectives on the relationship between classic literature and animation, and will extend a personal preoccupation on this matter. I have written elsewhere, for example, about the technical and aesthetic correspondence between literary practice and the animated form in the process of adaptation,[1] and I have also looked at the ways in which particular kinds of literary criticism may be applied to the analysis of animation, resulting in my own conception of the "subjective correlative."[2] Both these discussions will be drawn upon and reiterated again here, but the broad intention on this occasion is to explore literary texts for the mechanisms and methodologies which render them suitable for animation, and the ways, thereafter, that animation, in turn, reveals the core intentions, values, and aesthetic outcomes of those texts to best effect.

There remains a perennial concern about the success or otherwise of adapting literary texts in cinematic form *per se*. Producer Kevin Loader, for example, when taken to task by a *Sight and Sound* reviewer for insufficiently respecting the literary source in his adaptation of Ian McEwan's *Enduring Love*, suggests "any film based on a novel can only aspire to be a version of that novel" adding, "on stage after our screening at the London Film Festival Ian McEwan said that any writer releasing his novels to film-makers should witness a process of 'vandalisation,' before going on gener-ously to concede that Roger Mitchell and Joe Penhall (our director and screenwriter) had been the most urbane and intelligent of vandals."[3] Loader's overall point was to urge the film magazine to champion "screen story-telling" as something intrinsically different from literary narrative, and consequently, to judge it "unencumbered by literary expectation."[4]

John Glavin, in his Introduction to *Dickens on Screen*, takes this one step further in a clear, if provocative statement about the relationship between film and fiction, and the process of literary adaptation:

> Film, then, is not fiction's copy but another, and by no means a parallel Universe. To make a good film, or indeed any other sort of film, must mean inevitably to refuse, to disrupt, to subvert, the makings of fiction. We can even suggest a kind of counter-scale and claim that the more closely a film adapta-tion approaches its fictional predecessor the less it interests us as a film. Not only are film and fiction, then, by no means the same sort of thing, but by the end of the twentieth century, film had become the ground of fiction, all fiction, including fiction produced before the twentieth century.[5]

Glavin's position does not even prevaricate about the degrees of similarity between an adaptation and the original text. Film and fiction, he says, are different, that's that. Film must engage with fiction not on terms that speak to the integrity of the fiction, but in response to the different requirements of film. This, he adds, is largely because film is now the primary and omnipotent language of expression, perception, and understanding in civilization as we know it. This view, he endorses with the claims of Kenneth Tynan, who insists that human value and behavior is moulded by cinema, and that the past, with all its attendant (literary) fictions is now seen through the filter of cinematic language. For me, this argument is unpersuasive. While it is true that film may very well precede and perhaps even dictate a viewer's engagement with litera-ture, and influence the mental "illustration" we as readers create for ourselves as we interpret the text, the "cinematic" index at its heart is surely connected with a whole range of influences from visual culture, and not least those from the formative experiences of childhood, and the more complex and affecting aspects of our adult lives. Further, the perception of a text unencumbered by the lexicon of a known adaptation, must surely be related to the agency of the viewer and the visual codes and conventions that inform that person's percep-tion of the text, as well as the world that surrounds them.

Glavin's use of Tynan's authoritative voice is especially interesting, though, when he cites him suggesting that he was "certain that the full potential of the cinema will not be achieved until it concentrates on the development of *full length cartoons*," noting "what the cinema ought to be doing (and to have done) is to present coloured *images* of reality (or fantasy) designed by *artists*. At present – by using the camera merely to photograph *reality* – it is confirming itself to a function that is part newsreel and part photographed theater. In pure cinema there would be no real actors and no real background."[6] Casting aside the realm of questions that might arise from Tynan's perspectives on "realism" and "artists," to name but two issues, I wish to focus on his assertion concerning the "pure cinema" of "full length cartoons." Ironically, having established this as a critical benchmark by which the following chapters may be grounded, Glavin's collection then includes no analysis at all of cartoon adaptations of Dickens's novels and short stories, of which there are many (and which are mostly uninspiring), nor any evidence of how the perspectives which follow in a variety of chapters covering critical analysis, production processes, and pedagogic intent might align with this core concept. Of course, I am grateful to him for this, in the sense that while I have no intention of exploring Dickens as a particular exemplar of the "classic" text, I wish to engage with Tynan's assumption, and make further claims for the *specificity* it accords animation as a cinematic language of expression, a *particularity* which is intrinsically different from live action, and which inevitably scuppers Glavin's all encompassing view of the "cinematic" as the determining *lingua franca* of interpretation and understanding of the literary text, and real world lifestyles and attitudes.

I have previously used the concepts of "anchorage" and "relay" as a way of understanding how the detailed minutiae suggested in a literary text might have its most helpful representational ally in the very process by which animation itself is made.[7] The specific visual information required in the frame-by-frame creation of animated forms, and the design imperatives which inform it, necessitate an engagement with such minutiae as the prompt and catalyser of the image. It is not an act of record, but of interpretation, and has the advantage of not having to be mediated through the available "signs" of live actors, physical locations, material period costumes, etc. Therefore, the process towards completed animation works firstly as an act of primary drawn illustration, and secondly as a site for action predicated purely on that constructed in, and from the text; and *not* determined by the vagaries and demands of the film production process. Scrooge, for example, can be conceived as "Scrooge," and not Alistair Sim, Bill Murray, or Michael Caine in this guise.[8] It is perhaps no surprise, also, that more animated adaptations of *A Christmas Carol* have been made than any other Dickens text, as animation can more readily facilitate the supernatural scenarios (which, of course, are utilized in many of the live action versions as well, within the remit of special effects), and it is the most familiar of Dickens's stories. Even here, though, the animated adaptation can be "corrupted" by the presence of Mickey Mouse or Donald Duck – perhaps evidence of Glavin's omnipresence of the dominant cinematic mode – but when "pure," adapted from the text as a mode of illustration and story events, it is clearly the most effective and transparent translator of the original text, functioning readily as the operation of the "relay" between text and image, and the "anchorage" of meaning in the image from the text. Marina Warner substantiates this analogy in passing when suggesting "Sandro Botticelli's concentrated meditation on Dante's poem ['Inferno'] takes the ferocious tortures of the thieves stage by stage, almost like an animator drawing a sequence of cels today,"[9] effectively noting the visualization of events as an act of unfolding, developmental "change" – a determining "metamorphosis" that emerges out of the detailed minutiae of the action. It is simultaneously, though, an act of literal transformation which carries with it mythic and metaphoric possibility: "metamorphosis as divine fantasy, as vital principle of nature, as punishment, as reprieve, as miracle, as cultural dynamic, as effect of historical meetings and clashes, as the difference that lures, as lost idyll, as time out of time, as producer of stories and meanings."[10] It is inadequate, then, in the light of this notion to suggest that "anchorage" and "relay" are sufficient tools to delineate how this mode of "metamorphosis" is functioning in animated adaptation, and further tools are required to define the language of animation more closely, to corroborate its intrinsic use of the bi-function of metamorphosis as both a literal and metaphoric act.

To this end, I have explored a range of texts – mostly drawn from literary theorists – to demonstrate how the animated adaptation can be addressed as a mode of metamorphosis, embracing as many facets of the defining elements of "metamorphosis" as cited above, and corresponding with a further inter-rogation of the language of animation as a distinct form. Towards this end I have developed elsewhere[11] the concept of the "subjective correlative," employing the work of Sergei Eisenstein on Disney; the literary criticism of E. M. Forster and Virginia Woolf; Arthur Koestler's work on "creativity"; William Empson's definitions of "ambiguity"; poet and novelist Guillaume Apollinaire's conception of "the ideographic logic"; Donald Crafton's notion of "the self-figurative," and crucially, T. S Eliot's idea of the "objective correlative," as a set of tools by which to "read" an animated adaptation. Here I wish to reiterate those points, and to apply them to the notion of "adaptation as metamorphosis."

My own formulation of the "subjective correlative" effectively determines how and in what ways, and with what outcomes, the animator "transmutes" the literary source, by:

1 **Embracing and re-interpeting textual sources for "plasmatic potential"**
   This is based on film-maker and theorist Sergei Eisenstein's seminal definition of animation as "a rejection of once-and-forever allotted form, freedom from ossification, the ability to dynamically assume any form."[12]

2 **Enunciating the conflicts and tensions in the "serio-comic"**
   A reworking of Arthur Koestler's notion of the passage from "bathos" to "pathos," and the particular "modality" of expression which can make something serious or amusing, or both;[13] this is often, simultaneously, a tension between the literal and the abstract.

3 **Literally creating the process of interiority/exteriority as an illustrative outcome**
   Employing E. M. Forster's engagement with "Mickey and Minnie,"[14] and Virginia Woolf's critique of Dostoyevsky[15] this formulation uses the perspectives deployed in the description of "stream of consciousness" writing, and to note how this literary model echoes the process and outcomes in visualizing similar interior states in animation. Put simply, animation is especially suited to the depiction of dream states, thought processes, memories, fantasies, and emotional life.

4 **Using "ambiguity" as a mode of continuity and revelation**
   This is based on William Empson's notion that the English language is underpinned by deep ambiguity, leading him to observe, for example, that "English prepositions . . . from being used in so many ways and in combination with so many verbs, have acquired not so much a number of meanings as a body of meaning continuous in several dimensions."[16] Animation is, once again, particularly suited to using ambiguity and ambivalence to enrich the potential meaning of its text while condensing and minimizing its imagery.

5 **Adopting an "ideographic logic": an approach which literally pictorializes its own structure after the fashion of "concrete" poetry**
   While some animation does literally animate text and typography, the deployment of Apollinaire's notion is more in the spirit of his view that "psychologically, it is of no importance that this visible image be composed of broken language, for the bond between these fragments is no longer the logic of grammar but an ideographic logic, culminating in an order of spatial disposition totally opposed to discursive juxtaposition – it is the opposite of narration."[17] Crucially, animated texts, in being inherently self-reflexive "metafictions," simultaneously generate an "inner logic" of the animated world, and the spatial disposition of the adapted literary text. The stress in the process of creating the animation is pictorial (ideographic) first, and in this, captures the immediacy of the essence and textual detail of the literary source.

6 **Evoking a "self-figurative" perspective as an aesthetic outcome**
The "self-reflexiveness" of the animated form is intrinsically related to
Donald Crafton's notion of the "self-figurative" presence of the animator
in an animated film,[18] and is ultimately the key factor in the revision of
T. S. Eliot's concept of the "objective correlative": "The only way of expres-
sing in the form of art is by finding an 'objective correlative'; in other words,
a set of objects, a situation, a chain of events which shall be the formula of
that particular emotion; such that when the external facts, which must
terminate in sensory experience, are given, the emotion is immediately
evoked."[19] The presence of animator in the creative process of adaptation
effectively "subjectivizes" the "correlative" materials and resources of the
text. The animator is the explicit and present agent of "metamorphosis."

Such a "subjective correlative" then, defines a process which views any
"text" – linguistic or visual – as a model of transmutation which must
account for its execution ("plasmaticness"); its wit (the "serio-comic"); its
solipsism (the illustration of the "interior" creative premise – the space
when animation auteur and literary author simulate each other); its simulta-
neity of the literal and the abstract ("ambiguity"); its spatial discourse (the
"ideographic logic"); and its intended effect (the emotional outcome).
Consequently, it is my view that only animation can properly facilitate the
fullest proposition of the literary text, and evidence its defining theoretical
legacy within a modernist context. These propositions effectively work as a
"tool box" by which to deconstruct the specific relationship between animation and the classical literary text. To clarify these points, I wish to redress
Glavin's neglect of animated Dickens's texts by looking at the particular
example of *A Christmas Carol.*

Richard Williams's adaptation of Charles Dickens's celebrated Christmas
story, made in 1972, works within the parameters of the "subjective correlative," and is a ready endorsement of the "full animation" of the "Golden
Era" between 1928 and 1945 – at the moment when such application had all
but disappeared in the face of the more cost effective "limited animation"
used on television. A combination of Warner Bros. animators, including Ken
Harris, Chuck Jones, and Abe Levitow – who had already directed
Mr. Magoo's Christmas Carol (1962) – Disney alumni, George Nicholas
and Hal Ambro, and the British based Richard Purdum and Roy Naisbitt,
made the half-hour adaptation for American television, and it later won an
Oscar. Williams's sense of the "plasmatic potential" in the story is facilitated
by two key aspects. First he takes the opportunity to evoke Victorian London
through references to the pages of *The Illustrated London News,* and the
caricaturial work of John Tenniel, and John Leech, whose work he had also

successfully used in his animated sequences for Tony Richardson's *Charge of the Light Brigade* (1968). Secondly, the scale and extent of the "supernatural" imagery lends itself readily to animated metamorphosis. This particularly underpins the enunciative tension between Scrooge's lived and perceived reality – simultaneously literal and abstract – and part of the "wit" of Dickensian moral didacticism, via Williams's presentation of the story in the tradition of satirical caricature. The story, too, lends itself to a narrative and aesthetic ambiguity, in the sense that the whole episode of Scrooge's visitation by the ghosts of Christmas Past, Present, and Future could indeed be taking place in his head, his solipsism a stream of consciousness rendered visible as memory, projection, and selective thinking. The very "ambiguity" of Scrooge's status is compounded by the absent presence of the phantoms, who lead him through different spaces in time. The ideographic logic of the film is bound up in its use of metamorphoses of people and places as Scrooge must understand the changes he has experienced and learn to change from the embittered, inhuman soul he has become, and who he ultimately sees reflected in the spectral presences before him. The "inner logic" of the piece is bound up with Scrooge's alienation and the depressing series of animated "snapshots" which show his demise, his ambition and greed, and his own sense of loss, constantly juxtaposed with Williams's vigor in the depiction of human fortitude in the face of adversity, especially in the figures of miners, a lighthouse keeper, and sailors as they sing "God Rest Ye Merry, Gentlemen." Williams's knowledge of caricature recalls Hablot Knight Browne and George Cruickshank, the great Dickensian illustrators, who were the first to achieve a synthesis with the Dickens text because their visual imaginations, like Dickens's, had been shaped by the much deeper heritage and influence of William Hogarth. Williams's self-figuration is present in his use of animation to create an aesthetic that embraces all of this tradition – a tradition intrinsic to both this text and animation history – and which, simultaneously, make claims for the cartoonal form as a key associative language in combining the textual and visual arts by echoing their former relationship as text and illustration.

Having established the "subjective correlative" as one model of a critical "tool box" by which to unpack the adaptation process, I now wish to move beyond this formalist approach in the final aspect of this discussion, by embracing a wider *cultural* reading of animated adaptation. Geoffrey Wagner has suggested three categories of adaptation: "transposition" – "in which a novel is given directly on the screen with a minimum of apparent interference"; "commentary" – "where an original is taken and either purposely or inadvertently altered in some respect ... when there has been a different intention on the part of the film-maker"; and "analogy" – "which must represent a fairly considerable departure for the sake of making another work of art."[20] This categorization "by degree" is helpful in delineating the scale of intervention on the part of the adaptor, and in effect offers a view of the text either as a primary and unassailable source or merely a raw material for radical and potentially limitless re-working. At the heart of such a perspective remains the issue of fidelity in relation to the text, but as I hope I have demonstrated, "fidelity" is, perhaps ironically, most respected when subject to the multiplicity of approaches necessary in the facilitation, development, and application of the intrinsic language of animation, which both works *linearly* in the use of "metamorphosis" as its core methodology, and *laterally*, in its embrace of the number of levels implied in any one text. Useful here is Brian McFarlane's distinction between "transfer" and "adaptation proper"; he notes: " 'transfer' will be used to denote the process whereby certain narrative elements of novels are revealed as amenable to display in film, whereas the widely used term 'adaptation' will refer to the processes by which other novelistic elements must find different equivalences in the film medium, when such equivalences are sought or are available at all."[21] In many senses, animation is the facilitator of "equivalences" *par excellence*, and its mode of "transfer" simultaneously respectful and interrogative of "narrative".

I will pursue this perspective in an analysis of John Halas and Joy Batchelor's 1954 adaptation of George Orwell's *Animal Farm*, the first British full-length animated feature, which will function as a representative model of the ways in which an animated adaptation works within broader parameters of aesthetic and social influence.

Joy Batchelor, recalling the preparation of the film, writes:

> To turn this satire into an animated film was to face the issue of dramatising an animal story in which the characters must be as seriously portrayed as in a human story. No animal could be sentimentalised for the sake of the box office – the idea behind the story would not permit this. Once this story was selected, a new kind of cartoon film was to be made – a serious cartoon. A style of presentation in sound and image must be evolved to interpret this on the screen, and the essential incidents in the book planned out in dramatic shape and continuity. To effect this analysis, a breakdown chart was prepared, showing all the characters in their various relationships to the plot and to each other. It was obvious that certain animal and human characters, in which the book is naturally prolific (like Mollie, the vain and parasitic white pony), would have to recede into the background or be eliminated altogether, so that the animals and humans most concerned with developing the action and characterising the clash of interests could be kept in the foreground.[22]

Batchelor essentially identifies the "cardinal functions" – the key elements in the narrative which actually develop the story – and the "catalysers" – the focusing minutiae which ground the story in its milieu.[23] At the script development stage, this is a common practice in the adaptive process, but an animated film addressing this particular subject matter already has a number of issues to resolve which affect the adaptation at a cultural level. As Batchelor implies, to make a "serious" animated film was still unusual in the early 1950s, but only because "animation" was understood primarily as the work of the American cartoonal tradition, and most notably of the Disney studio. So-called serious animation had been made throughout the world since the beginning of cinema itself, from Ladislaw Starewich's *The Cameraman's Revenge* (1911) to Winsor McCay's *The Sinking of the Lusitania* (1918), to Fernand Léger's *Ballet Mécanique* (1924), to Lotte Reiniger's near full-length *The Adventures of Prince Achmed* (1926), but the dominance of Disney with the arrival of Mickey Mouse in *Steamboat Willie* (1928) all but relegated other forms of animation to near invisibility, and seeming irrelevance. With this dominance also came the overwhelming pre-eminence of the cartoon featuring animal characters in comic situations.[24] Jeff Rovin explains how and why this occurred :

> The number of drawings needed to produce an animated cartoon … dictated a "look" that was simpler than the illustrative technique used by Tenniel for *Alice's Adventures in Wonderland* or the realistic paintings of Beatrix Potter. Figures and expressions were caricatured and, freed from the more "realistic" treatment of animals in the past, writers came up with plots that were equally exaggerated. Moreover, because the comic and theatrical cartoon presentations were by necessity shorter, they tended to be gag driven rather than dependent on a great deal of plot. That made animal stories more comical than they'd been in the past, and in a world soon to be engulfed with world wars and a fiscal depression, funny animals became a beloved and much-needed respite … [C]artoons are now the accepted *lingua franca* of animals, the media of greatest impact and widest appeal.[25]

This series of events consolidated the cartoon in the public imagination as populated by "funny" animals. For *Animal Farm* to succeed in any way, the animation had to make the animals work successfully as believable characters, and for this to occur, the mode of caricature required was of a more realistic kind, and consequently, recalled the "animal" to animal animation for one of the first occasions in animation history. This involved long non-dialogue, non-anthropomorphized sequences of pure animal movement, seeing action from the point of view of the animals, creating the animal anthem from animal sounds, and scenes of brutality where animals kill other animals, as well as others of primal expression by animals which equate with "emotion."

The critic for *Cine Technician* stresses, "the theme is far from Disney, and the cruelties that occur from time to time are more realistic and shocking than any of the famous sadisms that have occurred in Disney films. The business of Napoleon bringing up puppies to be his own pack of killer dogs, the liquidators of those who oppose him is, for instance, bloodcurdling stuff. And the carting away of poor old Boxer is unrelieved agony."[26] It should be stressed, too, that when Napoleon asks the animals to consider their future, they only have visions of a hurtling butcher's block and hanging carcasses in an abattoir, an image far from the Disney vocabulary. Crucially, though, the same critic identifies an important point when he notes "The shock of straight and raw political satire is made more grotesque in the medium of the cartoon. The incongruities of recognisable horrors of some political realities of our times are emphasised and made more startling by the apparent innocence of the surrounding frame."[27] McFarlane's narrative "equivalences" are here bound up with several important aspects of animation as a specific "cultural" language as well as the "formal" one I described earlier. The very "innocence" of the form – purely implied through the historical determinism in the use of the medium – has the function of making the "transferred" elements of the text stand in a new relief, but more importantly, other elements of "equivalence" more emphatically suggest the "brutality" of human conflict and estrangement. The sense of the "grotesque" at the heart of this is significant. As Michael O'Pray has suggested, "the grotesque shares with caricature both the quality of exaggeration and also the characteristic blend of the humorous and the horrific," adding, "the grotesque is thus a sign of resistance, a symbolic destruction of official culture."[28] Again, though, this is as much a part of the capacity for animation to simultaneously "amplify" or "dilute," at once potentially exaggerating a form by virtue of the freedoms within its language, or reducing it by virtue of its complete artifice and illusionism. *Animal Farm* benefits from the innate tension between the expectations of "the cartoon" and the complex dynamics of the "narrative" and its challenging themes. The notion of "animation as metamorphosis" functions here as a mediation between the innocence of Disneyesque populism (with all its attendant gaucheness and sentimentality) and Orwellian politics (not merely in relation to the story operating as a metaphor of the Russian Revolution, but debates about animals and their treatment), a major ideological shift achieved by the re-configuring of both the animated *langue* itself, and the implications of the text. Halas and Batchelor recognized this fine balance. Batchelor notes, "the scene with Benjamin and Boxer, where Boxer was hurt was also a very difficult one, because it was terribly emotional and [we] had only drawings to go by, no help from living actors. It had to be very carefully handled to avoid slipping over from tragedy to tragic-comedy."[29] Significantly, though, this was not only important because of the need to authenticate the narrative, but to enhance the seriousness of the message within the broader context of the Cold War. Like Orwell's original work, written in 1946, the film was exploited for a wider political need. It is in this sense that the film needs further attention, as the cultural "formation" of "animation" was clearly specifically used as a social tool.

Halas and Batchelor had made *The Shoemaker and the Hatter* explaining the Marshall Plan in 1949. Its writer, Philip Stapp, had connections in the United States, and knew Louis De Rochemont, the producer of the "March of Time" newsreels at Paramount, from their shared time in the Navy. De Rochemont was to produce *Animal Farm*, with the strong likelihood that the film was actually funded by the CIA, who sought to make peacetime propaganda in the guise of entertainment, to support the ideological currencies of Cold War politics. As Karl Cohen has suggested "the CIA's Office of Policy Co-ordination, which directed covert government operations, had two members of the Psychological Warfare Workshop staff obtain the screen rights to the novel ... Mrs. [Sonia] Orwell signed after [the CIA] agreed to arrange for her to meet her hero, Clark Gable."[30] Through the highly regarded De Rochemont, a British animation company could be approached, working much more cheaply than their American counterparts and without the complications of engaging with an increasingly politically active, and allegedly left-wing animation industry in the States. Though Halas and Batchelor had already considered making *Animal Farm*, and had indeed begun preparatory treatments, American funding with its correspondent "creative" interventions ensured the project was completed, even though it went through some nine versions. The most controversial aspect was the change from Orwell's original ending: the film merely shows the continuing corruption of the pigs, and the resolution of the animals in mounting another revolt. Though Halas always claimed that this was to create a more universal, humanitarian fable with an anti-totalitarian position, enabling the audience to take some degree of relief and reassurance from the film, such an ending, of course, did suit CIA anti-communist objectives. I wish to argue, however, that the ending itself is less important than the ways that "animation" has facilitated more than what is "transferred," and created an "equivalence" of Orwell's core intentionality.

As Raymond Williams has remarked:

> In *Animal Farm* [Orwell's] strong and liberating intelligence transforms a bitter perception into an active and stimulating critique. Beyond the details of the local analogy, and paradoxically beyond the more fundamental despair, this lively awareness connects and informs. Even the last sad scene where the excluded animals look from man to pig and pig to man and cannot tell which is which, carries a feeling that is more than disillusion and defeat. Seeing that they are the same because they act the same, never mind the labels and formalities, is a moment of gained consciousness, a potentially liberating discovery. In its small

scale and within its limited terms, *Animal Farm* has a radical energy which goes far beyond its occasion and has its own kind of permanence.[31]

Williams could easily be speaking here of Halas and Batchelor's film. Still, some fifty years later, the film affects in a way that demonstrates the "radical energy" of animation to provoke a level of "gained consciousness." One only need to take a cursory glance from the Fleischers' version of *Gulliver's Travels* (1939) to *Animal Farm* (1954) to Svankmajer's *Alice* (*Něco z Alenky*) (1988) to Selick's *James and the Giant Peach* (1995) to Zemeckis's *The Polar Express* (2004) to see how animation as a technique in itself has adapted its aesthetics to facilitate the continuity of the "radical energy" at its heart, and to perpetuate a "gained consciousness" through, and about classic literary texts. Simultaneously, animation foregrounds its own intrinsic difference and yet produces the common imagery that unites the reader's imagination with their own consciousness of the writer's text, uniquely bringing insight and understanding to the experience, needs, and intentions of both.

NOTES

1 See P. Wells, "'Thou Art Translated': Analysing Animated Adaptation" in D. Cartmell and I. Whelehan (eds.), *Adaptations* (London and New York: Routledge, 1999), pp. 199–213.
2 See P. Wells, "Literary Theory, Animation and the 'Subjective Correlative': Defining the Narrative 'World' in Brit-Lit Animation" in *Animated Worlds*, ed. S. Buchan (London: John Libbey, 2005).
3 K. Loader, "Watching in the Dark," *Sight & Sound* 14. 12 (NS, December 2004), 80.
4 Ibid., p. 80.
5 J. Glavin (ed.), *Dickens on Screen* (Cambridge and New York: Cambridge University Press, 2003), p. 4.
6 Quoted in Glavin (ed.), *Dickens on Screen* p. 6. See J. Lahr (ed.), *The Diaries of Kenneth Tynan* (London and New York: Bloomsbury, 2002), p. 100, 21 July entry.
7 See Wells, "Thou Art Translated."
8 These actors featured in *Scrooge* (1951), *Scrooged* (1988), and *The Muppet Christmas Carol* (1998). This issue is being increasingly problematized, however, by the presence of named and promoted "stars" as the voice talent in major animated films. Crucially, though, for the most part, audiences (and most particularly, children) still think of the characters as, e.g. "Shrek," not Mike Myers, or "Woody," not Tom Hanks. Interestingly, in relation to this point, PIXAR's leading director, John Lasseter has noted:

> The casting of the actors is something we are considering as we are developing the storyboard. We cast for not how big a star they are, but how good an actor they are – how well their natural voice fits in with the character persona that we are trying to put across. We also hope to get actors who are quite good at ad-libbing. Working on a feature that takes four years to make; it is like telling the same joke every week for that time, it gets awfully old. We try to look for

spontaneity as much as we can. In casting an actor, we oftentimes take a line of dialogue from a movie or a TV show that they have been in, take away the picture, and put in a drawing or image of the character that we are interested in them playing, and it is remarkable because sometimes when you take away the physical image of these really great actors there is something really lacking – it is flatter than you would expect – but other times it really comes alive with just that voice, and we go with those actors. (Interview with the author, October 2001.)

9 Marina Warner, *Fantastic Metamorphoses, Other Worlds* (Oxford: Oxford University Press, 2002), p. 38.

10 Ibid., p. 79.

11 See P. Wells, "Literary Theory."

12 Quoted in J. Leyda (ed.), *Eisenstein on Disney* (London and New York: Methuen, 1988), p. 21.

13 See A. Koestler, *The Act of Creation* (London: Pan Books, 1970).

14 See E. M. Forster, "Mickey and Minnie" in *The American Animated Cartoon*, ed. D. Peary and G. Peary (New York: E. P. Dutton, 1980), pp. 238–40.

15 Virginia Woolf, "More Dostoyevsky," *Books And Portraits*, ed. M. Lyon (London: Triad Granada, 1979), p. 142.

16 W. Empson, *Seven Types of Ambiguity* (London: Peregrine, 1961), p. 5.

17 Quoted in E. Leslie, *Hollywood Flatlands: Animation, Critical Theory and the Avant Garde* (London and New York: Verso, 2002), p. 23.

18 See D. Crafton, *Before Mickey: The Animated Film 1899–1928* (Chicago and London: University of Chicago Press, 1993), p. 11.

19 T. S. Eliot, "Hamlet" in *Selected Prose of T. S. Eliot*, ed. F. Kermode (London and Boston: Faber & Faber, 1980), p. 45.

20 G. Wagner, *The Novel and the Cinema* (Rutherford, New Jersey: Fairleigh Dickinson University Press, 1975), pp. 222–6.

21 B. McFarlane, *Novel to Film: An Introduction to the Theory of Adaptation* (Oxford: Clarendon Press, 1996), p. 13.

22 J. Batchelor, "Scriptwriting for Animation," unpublished paper, The Halas & Batchelor Collection, Lewes, p. 8.

23 R. Barthes, "Introduction to the Structural Analysis of Narratives" in *Image–Music–Text*, trans. S. Heath (Glasgow: Fontana/Collins, 1966), p. 89.

24 See discussion of Disney in Chapter 11 in this volume.

25 J. Rovin, *The Illustrated Encyclopaedia of Cartoon Animals* (New York: Prentice Hall, 1991), p. v.

26 Author unnamed, "All Animals are Equal – but Some are More Equal than Others," *Cine Technician*, January 1955, p. 7.

27 Ibid., p. 7.

28 M. O'Pray, "Surrealism, Fantasy and the Grotesque: The Cinema of Jan Svankmajer" in, *Fantasy and the Cinema*, ed. J. Donald (London: BFI, 1989), pp. 256–8.

29 A. E. Jenkins, "A Film Technician's Notebook," *Cine Technician* (May 1955), 70.

30 K. Cohen, "The Cartoon That Came In From The Cold," *The Guardian* (7 March 2003), 8.

31 R. Williams, *Orwell* (London: Fontana, 1971), p. 74.

14

ANNETTE DAVISON

High fidelity? Music in screen adaptations

Adaptation from page to screen turns a novel into a soundtrack. In that respect it hands the text over to the composer as much as to the scriptwriter.[1]

The discussion of music rarely plays a major role in novels. In many cases, it is not mentioned at all. Nevertheless, in screen adaptations music is likely to play a significant role: it may be commissioned solely for the adaptation; a collection of pre-existent (or newly composed) tracks may be compiled; or, a producer may choose a combination of both. While our attention may not always be directed towards it, music in films and television programs *always* affects our experience of the image and narrative in some way, even when not consciously attended to. Think of John Williams's score for Steven Spielberg's 1975 adaptation of Peter Benchley's novel *Jaws*, for example.

Film and television scoring is both a product and a practice of the "long" twentieth century: an aesthetic and pragmatic response to the development of specific technologies and cultural forms. Of course, music itself is both a cultural product and a cultural practice. As such, musical composition, performance, and reception are subject to the more general transformations of society and culture over time, and those experienced by composers, performers, and listeners. In this way, the discussion of music in classic novels offers intriguing insights into the changing character of perceived relationships between music and society, as an exploration of the BBC's 1995 serial adaptation of Jane Austen's *Pride and Prejudice* (1813) demonstrates. A discussion of the use of pre-existent music in the screen adaptation of Thomas Mann's 1912 novella *Death in Venice* follows. First, however, an introduction to music's potential on screen is necessary.

Music in film and television drama

The effects of music as part of a filmed dramatic experience are powerful and diverse. They include, but are not limited to: producing mood; increasing, decreasing, or maintaining an experience of temporality; offering indications of, or amplifying, characters' emotions or feelings; indicating the geography, culture, or era in which a scene is set, and against which characters' musical preferences may be judged; encouraging an audience toward particular interpretations of narrative elements; and generating a sense of unity. In addition, and perhaps most basically, the continuity of individual musical cues can direct audience attention away from discontinuities in the image caused by the cuts between shots, due to the shifts between camera angles.

As a result of scoring and other classical cinematic or televisual conventions, audiences are encouraged to form an engagement with the fictional world of the action, and to perceive that world as a real and coherent entity. Indeed, it has been argued that mainstream scoring practices are closely allied to what various film theorists and historians have called "classical cinema."[2] In this context, "classical scoring" is defined as the set of structural conventions originally institutionalized as a set of filmmaking practices in the 1930s and 1940s that were united in the aim of heightening the fictive reality of a film's narrative.[3] The mixing and audiovisual editing of these scores and soundtracks were organized around these same conventions, including the privileging of dialogue, the synchronization of music and action, the use of music as continuity and to "control narrative connotation."[4] These classical practices persist in mainstream cinema, although the musical languages used are sometimes different. Indeed, pop songs can also function according to these conventions and practices, and generate many of the same effects, albeit in different ways.[5]

Historically, music has enjoyed an association with text (e.g. lyrics, libretti, conversation), with images (e.g. record/CD sleeve art), and with moving pictures, whether they be cultural products (e.g. religious and state ceremonies, opera, music videos, television advertisements), or part of an individual's life (e.g. use of personal stereos, radios in the home or car). Musical materials have absorbed cultural and personal meanings through these associations, and they guide our interpretations of the music used in films and television dramas, whether consciously heard and interpreted, or not. Anahid Kassabian addresses the distinction between recognizing and interpreting *cultural* musical codes on the one hand, and having *personal* associations with particular pieces of music, on the other.[6] Kassabian is particularly interested in the processes of identification experienced by film audiences, and highlights that "engagements [between filmgoers and film scores] are conditioned by filmgoers' relationships to a wide range of musics both within and outside of their filmgoing practice."[7] Thus, in addition to the engagements offered by classical scoring (which pop scores and compilation soundtracks may share), due to the often powerful associations that individuals develop in relation to particular pop songs, genres, or singers *outside* of the cinematic experience (associations with, for example, people or periods in one's life, relationships, events), Kassabian suggests that the use of pop in films enables audience members to bring their personal histories to bear on their relationship with a film.[8] By contrast, classical scoring composed for a specific film is usually involved in closing down, or narrowing interpretative possibilities through its attempt to engage audience members in a process of "assimilation," to encourage them to inhabit a subject-position that might otherwise appear unfamiliar. Audience members do not need to be musically "literate," i.e. possess the ability to compose, or analyze music in specifically musical terms, they need only musical "competence," i.e. the ability to decode musical meaning typically gained through basic acculturation: exposure to dual- or multi-media cultural products, such as nursery rhymes, operas, films, adverts, songs, or whatever.[9] Evidence from experiments conducted with Western listeners suggests a high level of competence in decoding the meaning of such musical cues.[10]

In analyzing the relationship between a film's narrative and its score, Claudia Gorbman proposes a useful distinction concerning the apparent source of film music that is also relevant to adaptation studies. Music seemingly generated within the film's action, or "diegesis," which characters within the scene can hear, is designated diegetic music, while music produced outside of the film's diegesis, which characters in the scene do *not* have access to is classified as non-diegetic (or extra-diegetic) music.[11] In the following section, I focus on some of the effects of non-diegetic scoring. In the main, these effects are reliant upon music's capacity for signification, and the audience's capacity to decode it.

Music in *Pride and Prejudice*

"I consider music as a very innocent diversion . . ."

(Mr. Collins, *Pride and Prejudice*, Chapter 18)

As was expected of her (and all middle- and upper-class girls and young women in Regency England), Jane Austen took piano lessons. Women of these classes were not expected to work: a leisured life was proof of their families' ability to provide for them. They were expected to demonstrate certain accomplishments, however, to display the benefits of an education of sorts, though it was very different to that lavished on boys, who did not – in general – learn to play the piano. In Chapter 8 of Austen's *Pride and Prejudice*, Charles Bingley and Mr. Darcy discuss the "extent of accomplishments," with Darcy stating that he "cannot boast of knowing more than half a dozen" women who are "really accomplished." Mr. Bingley provides an account of the requirements necessary to live up to Darcy's classification:

> A woman must have a thorough knowledge of music, singing, drawing, dancing, and the modern languages, to deserve the word; and besides all these she must possess a certain something in her air and manner of walking, the tone of her voice, her address and expression, or the word will be but half deserved.

The value of such accomplishments, i.e. "as [commodities] in the marriage market," were well understood in the period.[12] As Arthur Loesser notes in his social history of the piano, of these commodities, musical performance "was a favourite because it could be shown off best while actually being accomplished."[13] In discussing women's skills at the piano at this time, James Parakilas notes that "Their playing always 'places' them – defines their upbringing and their character – in the eyes of men as well as of older women, and even in their own eyes"[14] … and those of Jane Austen.

In the late eighteenth century, possession of a piano demonstrated wealth and position.[15] Innovations in the development of the instrument offered social opportunities that earlier keyboard instruments, such as the spinet and the clavichord, could not furnish; the hammer action of the pianoforte enabled the production of a much greater dynamic range. Not only did this affect the music written for the instrument, it also meant that the piano could be used for social occasions such as the playing of music for dancing, as well as more intimate gatherings. In a period well before radios or gramophone players, when professional concerts in England were held generally only in London or Bath, amateur music-making offered opportunities for young people not available elsewhere: in particular, legitimated (i.e. chaperoned) contact with members of the opposite sex. This might include dancing and listening to or performing music. Although pianos were firmly planted in the world of the home – and thus also under the watchful eye of older relatives[16] – musical performance provided "a socially sanctioned medium to communicate feelings the interaction [of the sexes] may inspire within the bounds of propriety."[17] Examples of this within Austen's work include descriptions of the musical couplings of characters at the piano as veiled allusions to their more sensuous leanings, though constrained by polite society, as in her descriptions of John Willoughby and Marianne Dashwood's joint performance in *Sense and Sensibility*, and the discussion of a piano in *Emma* between Frank Churchill and Jane Fairfax, that disguises a discussion of their affections.[18]

It is generally agreed that Jane Austen's novels offer a faithful account of the importance of musical performance in the lives of young women of the period, and the many subtleties of the situation.[19] For instance, it does not do to play *too* well: in *Pride and Prejudice*, Elizabeth Bennet's musical abilities are described as "pleasing, though by no means capital" (Chapter 6). Yet her performances are considered more agreeable than those of her bookish younger sister, Mary; a better player, but one with "neither genius or taste," who chooses – inappropriately – to entertain polite society with "long concertos."[20] Mary's performance of two songs after supper at the Netherfield Ball has Elizabeth in agony, for her sister "was not fitted for such a display; her voice was weak and her manner affected." In the BBC's 1995 serial adaptation of the novel, Mary's assiduous skills in performance are contrasted with the easy confidence and musicality of her sister, Elizabeth, the modesty of Georgiana Darcy, and the (apparently) superior breeding of Miss Bingley and Mrs. Hurst. The distinction is made most obvious when, after Mary's solemn and mannered performance of a Handel song at the Netherfield Ball and her father's censure of the second song, Mrs. Hurst produces a dazzling and exuberant performance of Mozart's Rondo "Alla Turka."[21]

Carl Davis composed the original music for the series, chose and performed the music played by the young women in the story, and arranged the music selected for the balls.[22] The size and sound of the bands for the balls (a smaller, more coarse sounding three-man-band for the Assembly Rooms at Meryton; a larger, more sophisticated group for Netherfield) were used to indicate the wealth and superior standing of the Bingleys.[23] Although music features in a number of key scenes in *Pride and Prejudice*, Austen makes little reference to specific pieces. For the women's performances, Davis chose music that would have been available, theoretically at least, in 1810, at around the time that Austen was revising the earlier, *First Impressions*, into *Pride and Prejudice*: works by Handel, Haydn, Mozart and Beethoven.[24] Austen's own library of music (much of it copied out in her own hand) contains songs, short pieces, and transcriptions of works by Handel and Haydn, a Gluck aria, and a march by Mozart (though misattributed to his pupil Thomas Attwood).[25] In the main, however, as might be expected, her library comprises popular tunes of the day, Celtic airs, and music by composers then popular and fashionable, but whose names have since fallen from the canon: Ignaz Pleyel, Domenico Corri, William Boyce, Thomas Arne, James Hook, and Frantisek Kotzwara (composer of the then highly popular *Battle of Prague*).[26] As Mary Burgan highlights in her study of "Women and Music in Nineteenth-Century Fiction," "charming" works that didn't require technical virtuosity were sought-after: " 'salon' music, simple ballads and sacred songs, or simplified transcriptions of more difficult pieces."[27] Davis's research and subsequent musical choices represent a largely successful attempt to present this musical world with fidelity, applying only a little poetic license to amplify the subtle distinctions presented through the characters' relations with music.

Loesser's explanation of what made musical performance a favorite among accomplishments – "it could be shown off best while actually being accomplished" – describes well the powerful impact of these scenes in the BBC's adaptation of the novel. Where we have the opportunity to experience the joy and agony of these performances through Austen's, and her characters' words and emotions when reading the novel, here we are given the opportunity to experience them at first hand, with access to all the excitement and pain generated by the shot/reverse-shot sequences that draw our attention to the characters' responses to these performances.[28] The scene in which music perhaps adds most to the adaptation while retaining its faithfulness to the novel is the choreographed conversation between Elizabeth and Mr. Darcy that takes place at the Netherfield Ball (Chapter 18; Episode 2, 30.59–36.08 [min.sec.]). The couple move elegantly together; their graceful execution of the dance hinting at their suitability in love. This interpretation is enhanced by the (forced) conversation brought about by Elizabeth's dissatisfaction with Mr. Darcy's incapacity for small talk, and polite society's expectation of it. The momentary separations of the couple caused by the choreography of the dance builds tension in our reception of their verbal sparring, while the harmonized sophistication of their motions contradicts it.

In addition to the diegetic music in this adaptation, Davis's original score for the series fulfills many of the same functions as classical scoring. Rather than the symphonic sound of many scores for classical cinema, Davis limited his forces to eighteen players for larger scenes and, in the case of more intimate scenes, modelled them on a Beethoven septet popular at the time, to capture the "sense of a small town in 1813."[29] In addition, he chose to feature the distinctive sound of a fortepiano – the eighteenth- and nineteenth-century precursor to today's piano – prominently within his score, thus underlining the important role of the instrument in the lives of the novel's protagonists. Melvyn Tan, a foremost fortepianist, played the part, most notably in the music for the opening and closing credits. Stylistically, Davis's score captures a sense of the style of the Classical era and refers to musical topics – such as "hunting" and the "learned style" (the latter used in association with Lady Catherine de Bourgh) – that musicologist Kofi Agawu argues were well understood by audiences of the time. Occasionally, the score also exhibits some of the spontaneity and passion of a later, Romantic musical sensibility.[30]

Davis's scoring techniques are predominantly those employed in classical scoring. That is, an abundance of semiotic information is conveyed through musical signs or codes: through tempo, register, rhythm, orchestration, key, and harmony of the music, by means of the melodic structure of the themes (or fragments thereof), and by making alterations to these elements. Such musical codes inflect the audience's reception of what is seen on the screen.

Davis highlights the importance of the opening credits music in this, to set the scene: with no dialogue or sound effects "it's the main chance the composer has to make a statement" and "sharpen the audience's expectations of what's about to come."[31] With the credits music for *Pride and Prejudice*, Davis's aim was to capture "the essence of the book": to "address the two themes" of "sense and sensibility [that] run through all Jane Austen's books."[32]

The music begins with a lively preparatory-type phrase that incorporates a hunting motif and behaves as a clarion call to the viewer, with Tan's scalic passages on the fortepiano scurrying nimbly through the sequence's rests and sustained passages (1a). Here Davis portrays the novel's "wit and vitality, its modern feel," while the "slight hunting refrain ... echoes one of the main drives of the book, the hunt for husbands!," and links to the second part.[33] This comprises a longer, more lyrical theme that consists primarily of ascending phrases in sequence, which Davis associated with "marriage and affairs of the heart" (1b).[34] Where the first theme (1a) remains clearly rooted to the tonic (around which the scalic passages dance), the second (1b) makes a more harmonically dynamic move away from the tonic to the dominant, and then returns to the tonic. In the image, we see a hand at work on a piece of embroidery. A selection of richly textured fabrics and fashion items are captured in close-up, and these provide the steadily swirling background to the titles. Heard in combination with the needlework, Tan's dexterous and even performance of the many scalic passages in the sequence seems to entwine the titles for the key actors together.

A good deal of Davis's score for the series is generated from the development and transformation of this two-part theme composed for the credits, along with material from a small number of additional motifs, such as a pseudo-stately though, ultimately, comic bassoon figure associated with Mr. Collins, and the more regal dotted-rhythm motif that distinguishes Lady Catherine. Economy in musical material, such as that found here, can create a strong sense of unity in a score. Too much novelty, and attention may be drawn towards the music as an element in its own right, whereas the recurrence and variation of familiar themes (and familiar song forms) offers variety within constraints. A brief discussion of some of the cues heard in Episode 5 (Chapters 44 to 49) highlights this economy of material and illustrates the variety of music's effects on screen. The episode begins with a visit to Elizabeth by the Darcys (and Bingley) in Lambton, and ends with the discovery of Lydia and Wickham in London, and Elizabeth's growing fondness for Darcy.

Music's ability to offer continuity is demonstrated early on. During the Darcys' visit to Elizabeth in the parlour of the Inn at Lambton, she and her party are invited to dine with them the following day. The cut from the Inn to a mid-close-up of Mr. Darcy at Pemberley the next evening is elided by a musical bridge signalled by Georgiana's request to hear Elizabeth play, to which Elizabeth replies "If you insist upon it, yes, you shall." The line is followed almost immediately by a music cue: the end of Elizabeth's performance of Mozart's "Voi che sapete" from *Le Nozze di Figaro* (04.31–05.11). Georgiana then plays (from 06.04), but a dissonant chord struck at Miss Bingley's mention of Mr. Wickham returns Elizabeth to the piano, under the appearance of needing to turn Georgiana's pages: Mr. Darcy's gratification at the discretion and compassion of this act leads him to look upon her even more favorably (signified by the reverse-shots of his looks to Elizabeth). Shortly after their eyes meet (06.55), the orchestra begins to underscore Georgiana's performance of Beethoven (06.59–07.40). A similar cue – though this time an orchestral arrangement of the Mozart aria – begins after Darcy defends Elizabeth in the face of Miss Bingley's criticism (09.13). We see him striding through his house, smiling, and – through a flashback – recalling Elizabeth's rescue of Georgiana. This Mozartian cue continues across the cut to the next morning, when it is then transformed into a sprightly version of theme 1b in the major, as Darcy rides to Elizabeth at Lambton with alacrity (to 10.38).

However, before Mr. Darcy's arrival at Lambton, Elizabeth learns of Lydia's elopement through Jane's letters. The reading of the letters is underscored by vigorous minor key versions of theme 1a, which also provide continuity as the action is cut between Lambton and dramatizations of the elopement. All subsequent news of the couple's flight is heard in conjunction with minor key versions of fragments of the same theme (1a). Versions of fragments of theme 1b, also now in the minor, are heard alongside Mr. Darcy's subsequent search for the couple and the exhausted return of Mr. Bennett home to Longbourne following his futile searches in London. The arrival and departure of Mr. Collins is heralded by a return of the bassoon figure, though this time subdued and in the minor. In this way, transformations of the original themes reflect changes in mood, the emotions of the protagonists, yet also a correspondence with the speed and excitement of the action, all brought about by developments in the narrative. The familiarity of these themes, and of the orchestral arrangements of music performed by the young women, assists in camouflaging the intrusion of this music, which, logically speaking, could reveal the artifice of this fictional world.

Using pre-existent music

In other scenarios the familiarity of the music chosen may have a rather different effect, particularly if the music is pre-existent, as is the case with the Adagietto from Gustav Mahler's Symphony No. 5 featured, almost exclusively, by Luchino Visconti in his 1971 film adaptation of Thomas Mann's novella, *Death in Venice*. Broadly speaking, film scoring is composed after visual sequences have been filmed and edited, thus avoiding the need to re-compose music cues when changes are made during image editing. However, when a pre-existent musical work is featured as part of a film score (not, importantly, when being performed or played back as source music, e.g. on a radio), the relationship between the image and the music changes: here the autonomy of the music is prioritized, with the image often cut *to the music*.

As Claudia Gorbman notes, the reception of audio-visual information is most usefully understood in terms of "mutual implication": at times our interpretation of the image and/or narrative is guided by the music, on other occasions, our interpretation of the score may be driven by the image and/or the narrative. This has particular relevance for the use of pre-existent music, since attributes associated with one or other element may be transferred to another, and influence its reception. Thus, in the case of Mahler's Adagietto and *Death in Venice*, for instance, the seriousness and integrity associated with the high cultural status of Mahler's music may inflect our interpretation of the drama.

Excerpts from the Adagietto are heard five times in the film, including over the opening and closing credits. The first occasion signals the protagonist's arrival in Venice, and the measured appearance of dawn is matched by the gradual flowering of the Adagietto's opening: gently arpeggiated harp figures and a sustained chord in the lower strings are hesitantly joined by an anacrusis in the upper strings that leads to a suspension on the first beat of the bar, resolved on the second. This deferred resolution wrong-foots the security of the downbeat, creating a sense of timelessness. Later, the scene is unsettled by a fortissimo chord in the minor, again with suspensions (at the end of bar 46): the emphatic solemnity of this chord seems out of kilter with the peaceful voyage of the ship into Venice. The clash may foreshadow Aschenbach's fate, but it seems more likely that the conflict is caused by preserving the integrity of the Adagietto over a match between the music and the action. By contrast, when the same extract is heard at the end of the film, the chord signals the moment of Aschenbach's death; here the association seems more fitting.

The third extract occurs at the moment at which the composer's fate is sealed: having glimpsed into the abyss of the Dionysian (signified by the presence of the young Polish boy – Tadzio), Aschenbach accepts the seduction with complicity. His decision to leave Venice is overtaken by an overwhelming desire to stay in order to remain in the company of the boy, whom the composer believes embodies the Platonic Ideal of Beauty, and whose existence undermines the careful Apollian approach Aschenbach has taken towards creativity throughout his life. Tadzio exposes him to the creative potential of the Dionysian. Having travelled tardily to the train station, the misdirection of his luggage allows Aschenbach to cancel his plans and return to the hotel. The extract begins as Aschenbach takes the vaporetto to the station: here the music seems to underline his sadness at leaving the city. It is interrupted as he buys his ticket and the loss of his luggage is reported. He shouts at the stationmaster to recover his trunk at once. The music returns as he sits down on a bench at the station and smiles smugly to himself at his wit to use the situation to his advantage. By contrast to his earlier vaporetto ride, the return trip to the hotel is buoyant: it's astonishing how Aschenbach's elation appears to transform the character of the Adagietto from sombre to celebratory.

Some have argued that Visconti's use of Mahler's music demonstrates that music does not in itself express emotion or meaning. Rather, "[it] is the context that provides the meaning, and the context includes the perception of the viewer."[35] Certainly, whether music can ever be heard "innocently" or "solely in reference to itself" any more is debatable. Thus, when analyzing film music cues, labeling can be problematic: it is reliant on our individual experience of cultural codes and personal associations. And yet, the characteristics of each music cue also behave as a form of interpretative constraint, privileging certain potential meanings over others. In the case of Mahler's Adagietto, its signifying capacity is at least partly channeled by the expressive qualities generated by the abundance of suspensions, harmonic ambiguity, and modulation.

Of course, some film directors have made a point of placing particularly well-known songs, or other musical works in contexts that conflict with their accepted interpretations. Music is promiscuous: on the one hand, once attached to a particular visual scenario, it will often feel like it has *always* been there and cannot be imagined otherwise; on the other, its meaning is greatly dependent on the context of this attachment in combination with the history of its other multi-media (and/or personal) associations. We may develop strong associations with particular songs, or scores, primarily as a result of their placement in films, which may in turn affect our relationship with those songs/scores outside of the cinema. Clearly, soundtrack albums have a role to play here.

As with re-reading the original text, soundtrack albums offer us the opportunity to re-live our experience of a film or television programme, but here via its music. For Baz Luhrmann's *William Shakespeare's Romeo and Juliet* (1996) two soundtrack albums were produced: a compilation that features the wide range of pop/rock genres heard in the film, and thus enables the album to appeal to a broad demographic; and the orchestral score by Nellee Hooper, Marius de Vries, and Craig Armstrong. Unusually among soundtrack albums, the cues on the latter album are presented in the order in which they appear in the film, with film dialogue segues between cues, thus offering a very particular form of continued engagement with the film.[36]

In adaptations of novels in which music plays a primary role, a soundtrack album offers an opportunity to experience the original in a different medium.[37] For example, Nick Hornby's 1995 novel *High Fidelity* name-drops its way through literally hundreds of songs, artists, and albums in a variety of genres: "punk, blues, soul, and R&B, a bit of ska, some indie stuff, some sixties stuff – everything for the serious record collector."[38] The novel concerns the protagonist's journey from "you are what you like" (musically speaking), to a grudging acceptance that record collections do not necessarily "make the man," or woman. And yet, the novel's success is partly dependent on presenting the musical taste of a fictional thirty-something pop aficionado as something to be coveted, i.e., as cultural capital.[39] In this respect, the novel functions as an imaginary compilation tape for its readers: a situation that a soundtrack album could – and did – exploit.

In this chapter I have highlighted that the analysis of music and musical culture discussed in literature can reveal much about the dynamic character of the relationship between music and society (or societies) through time, and may well differ according to sex, class, gender, race, and so on. I have offered an introduction to some of the functions that scoring performs in the adaptation of literature to screen, of which a primary goal is to create an engagement between the audience and the fictional world of the on screen drama. Music is also used to confirm the locale and the era in which the action takes place, presenting characters' emotions or musical preferences, providing unity and continuity, and offering extra-diegetic commentary. Music's ability to achieve all this, and more, is reliant on a number of factors: its ontology as a time-based medium; its signifying potential as a cultural product (and that of film scoring as a cultural practice); and its capacity to slip seamlessly between the many different narrational levels employed in filmmaking.[40] Although its presence may evade our attention completely at times, film music plays an important, and indeed transformative role in the adaptation of literature on screen.

NOTES

1 Erica Sheen, "'Where the Garment gapes': Faithfulness and Promiscuity in the 1995 BBC *Pride and Prejudice*," in *From Page to Screen: Adaptations of the Classic Novel*, ed. Robert Giddings and Erica Sheen (Manchester: Manchester University Press, 2000), p. 23.

2 Claudia Gorbman, *Unheard Melodies: Narrative Film Music* (London and Indianapolis: BFI and University of Indiana Press, 1987), pp. 70–3.

3 Thus here "classical" does not refer to the symphonic forces associated specifically with music of the Classical period of European art music history (c. 1750–1820), nor with those associated with "classical music" *per se*.

4 Kathryn Kalinak, *Settling the Score: Music and the Classical Hollywood Film* (Madison: University of Wisconsin Press, 1992), p. xv.

5 See Jeff Smith, *The Sounds of Commerce: Marketing Popular Film Music* (New York: Columbia University Press, 1998), pp. 154–229.

6 Though, of course, these categories need not be mutually exclusive.

7 Anahid Kassabian, *Hearing Film: Tracking Identifications in Contemporary Hollywood Film Music* (London: Routledge, 1992), p. 2.

8 Recent music sociology suggests that such associations are generated not only by pop music, but by musical works of any genre that hold particularly strong associations for individuals. See Tia deNora, *Music in Everyday Life* (Cambridge: Cambridge University Press, 2000).

9 Kassabian, *Hearing Film*, pp. 15–36.

10 See particularly Philip Tagg and Bob Clarida, *Ten Little Tunes* (New York: Mass Media Music Scholars' Press, 2003).

11 In practice, the classification of diegetic or non-diegetic is not always straightforward. In addition, in terms of score/soundtrack production, the relationship between music and *image* (rather than music and *narrative*) takes precedence in the film and music industries, with a distinction based on whether or not musicians are seen on screen (this incurs different scales of payment).

12 Mary Burgan, "Heroines at the Piano: Women and Music in Nineteenth-Century Fiction," in *Victorian Studies* 30.1 (Autumn 1986), p. 61.

13 Arthur Loesser, *Men, Women and Pianos: A Social History* (New York: Simon and Schuster, 1954), p. 268.

14 James Parakilas, *Piano Roles: Three Hundred Years of Life with the Piano* (New Haven and London: Yale University Press, 1999), p. 96.

15 As the means for the mass production of the instrument developed and ownership of a piano became more accessible, the exclusivity associated with the instrument diminished.

16 In *Pride and Prejudice* (Chapter 31), Elizabeth Bennet plays the piano for Lady Catherine de Bourgh, Mr. Darcy, and Colonel Fitzwilliam while visiting Rosings. Despite professing a great love of music ("There are few people in England, I suppose, who have more true enjoyment of music than myself, or a better natural taste"), Lady Catherine proceeds to talk over Elizabeth's performance. While teasing Mr. Darcy, Elizabeth stops playing, drawing the attention of Lady Catherine. At her request to know the subject of their discussion, Elizabeth begins to play again.

17 Jodi Lustig, "The Piano's Progress: The Piano in Play in the Victorian Novel," in *The Idea of Music in Victorian Fiction*, ed. Sophie Fuller and Nicky Losseff (Aldershot: Ashgate, 2004), pp. 83–104; p. 88.

18 Lustig, "The Piano's progress."

19 For more detail, see Lustig, "The Piano's Progress"; Loesser, *Men, Women and Pianos*, pp. 267–79, Parakilas, *Piano Roles*, pp. 96–103; and Patrick Piggott, *The Innocent Diversion: A Study of Music in the Life and Writings of Jane Austen* (London: Cleverdon, 1979).

20 As "the only plain one in the family, [Mary] worked hard for knowledge and accomplishments, [and] was always impatient for display." Jane Austen, *Pride and Prejudice*, Chapter 6.

21 Episode 2 (of 6). The Rondo "Alla Turka" is from Mozart's Piano Sonata No. 11 in A major, K. 331.

22 The dances were chosen in collaboration with choreographer Jane Gibson.

23 Sue Birtwistle and Susie Conklin, *The Making of Pride and Prejudice* (London: Penguin and BBC Books, 1995), p. 62.

24 Carl Davis, in a radio interview with Andrew Ford for ABC Radio National in Australia on 14 February 2004. Transcript available at http://www.abc.net.au/rn/music/mshow/s1093566.htm (accessed 22 May 2005).

25 See Piggott, *The Innocent Diversion*, pp. 131–54.

26 Ibid., pp. 131–54.

27 Mary Burgan, "Heroines at the Piano: Women and Music in Nineteenth-Century Fiction," p. 57.

28 Think, for example, of Elizabeth's performance of Mozart's "Voi che sapete" (often translated as 'Tell Me of Love'), from *Le Nozze di Figaro* (*The Marriage of Figaro*), at Pemberley, and Mr. Darcy's obvious admiration of her accomplishments (Episode 5, 0.04.31). In the opera, Cherubini's aria is addressed to the Countess and Susanna concerning the nature of love. He wishes to know whether the strange and wonderful feelings he has might be love. Clearly, for those who know the context of this aria, there is added frisson in terms of its presence in this scene in the series. Erica Sheen profitably connects the opera's "[preoccupation] with the rendering visible of concealed infidelities" with Jane Austen's Wickham plot-line. Sheen, "Where the Garment Gapes," p. 25.

29 Davis, cited in Birtwistle and Conklin, *The Making of Pride and Prejudice*, p. 66.

30 Sheen suggests that Davis alludes to Wagnerian musical language (specifically to *Der Ring des Nibelungen* and *Tristan und Isolde*), and perhaps also Wagnerian ambition, at the end of Episode 5, at the moment that Elizabeth tells of her fear that she may never see Mr. Darcy again. The threat of "immersion" this music engenders was salvaged by its occurrence at the end of an episode: "you could simply go away and take a cold shower." Sheen, "Where the Garment Gapes," p. 27.

31 Davis, cited in Birtwistle and Conklin, *The Making of Pride and Prejudice*, p. 64.

32 Davis, cited in ibid., p. 65.

33 Davis, cited in ibid., p. 65.

34 Davis, cited in ibid., p. 65.

35 Michael Chanan, "Mahler in Venice?", in *Music and Musicians* (June 1971, revised 2000). Available online at: http://www.mchanan.dial.pipex.com/mahler%20in%20venice.htm (accessed 22 May 2005).

36 Typically, a score's cues are re-ordered to create a sequence that is dynamic in musical terms alone. Additionally, most film soundtrack albums do not include all of the music cues that were heard in the film.

37 Of course, some film adaptations foreground particular songs or tracks, often memorably, whether or not they feature in the original text. Quentin Tarantino's 1997 adaptation of Elmore Leonard's *Rum Punch* (1992), as *Jackie Brown*, is a good example. See Ken Garner, " 'Would You Like to Hear Some Music?': Music in-and-out-of-Control in the Films of Quentin Tarantino," in *Film Music: Critical*

Approaches, ed. K. J. Donnelly (Edinburgh: Edinburgh University Press, 2001), pp. 188–205.

38 Nick Hornby, *High Fidelity* (London: Indigo, 1996), p. 38.

39 This term was developed by French sociologist, Pierre Bourdieu, and describes a distinction between wealth that is economic, and a form of wealth that is cultural and organized according to social class and education. Cultural capital is the knowledge we develop through our education and our background, from which social status is bestowed. However, Simon Frith and Sarah Thornton argue that Bourdieu's hierarchies of taste operate not only in terms of the distinction between high art and popular culture, but that hierarchies also exist *within* these categories. Pierre Bourdieu, *Distinction: A Social Critique of the Judgement of Taste*, trans. Richard Nice (London: Routledge and Kegan Paul, 1984); Simon Frith, *Performing Rites: Evaluating Popular Music* (Oxford: Oxford University Press, 1998), p. 35, and Sarah Thornton, *Club Cultures: Music, Media and Subcultural Capital* (Cambridge: Polity Press, 1995), pp. 1–25.

40 See Edward Branigan, *Narrative Comprehension and Film* (London: Routledge, 1992), for a more detailed discussion of the different narrational levels involved in filmmaking.

15

JAN BAETENS

From screen to text: novelization, the hidden continent

What is the common feature of books such as *King Kong* (Delos W. Lovelace), *La Dolce Vita* (Lo Duca), *Les Vacances de Monsieur Hulot* (Jean-Claude Carrière), *Les 400 coups* (François Truffaut and Marcel Moussy), *Jabberwocky* (Ralph Hoover), *Basic Instinct* (Richard Osborne), *The Full Monty* (Wendy Holden), *Saving Private Ryan* (Max Allan Collins) or *eXistenZ* (Luther Novak)? Are they (unknown) books adapted into (famous) movies, following the old saying that only bad literature can be turned into good cinema? Quite the contrary: all these books are novelizations, i.e. novels based on previous and normally "original" filmic texts (I will come back later to the question on the meaning of the word "text").

Within the field of film and literature studies, novelizations represent an ignored field, whose quantitative importance (since there exists a real novelization industry) and qualitative diversity (since "novelization" has many meanings depending on various national and linguistic traditions in which it appears) has never been fully acknowledged. Today, however, this situation seems to be changing rather rapidly. First, economically speaking, novelizations have become more visible, following the generalization of "cross-media narrative" in contemporary Hollywood storytelling and hence the subsequent multiplication of novelized films. In fact, each major Hollywood film that is not based itself upon a previous novel or play tends to be transformed into a novel (among other types of commercial tie-ins, of course). But there is also a second reason, which is more academic and which has to do with the crisis of traditional adaptation studies in the film and literature field. The critical questioning of most of the theoretical and methodological underpinnings of adaptation studies are both cause and effect of the new interest in novelization.

On the one hand, the crisis of the classical adaptation paradigm, with for instance its belief in the sharp and clear distinction between the (literary) "original" and the (cinematographic) "copy," makes room for cultural practices that no longer obey this ideal scheme: in the case of novelization, literature ceases to be both the source and the prestigious other of film (although it is not always clear whether they really "follow" the movie, since many novelizations are based on the screenplay and made by ghost-writers who never see one single shot of the movie itself while doing their job. A novelization is definitely different from a book adapted to the screen; most novelizations are also rather unsophisticated, to put it mildly, for the very simple reason that literary sophistication, which is not totally absent from the field, as we will see later on, is simply not what is primarily at stake in most of the novelizations.) Put in more radical terms, novelization questions the importance of the source–target relationship and the very issue of literary connoisseurship.

On the other hand, the study of novelization itself enhances the critical *aggiornamento* of the adaptation paradigm, since it brings to the fore many aspects that help to sharpen some of the critiques addressed to it. A good illustration of the "strategical" importance of novelization is that it tends to be used today as a kind of container-concept in which one gathers all types of narratives and narrative forms that have always surrounded film, ranging "from the catalogue to the trailer."[1] Yet in spite of this new context, novelization still remains a kind of hidden continent,[2] whose various features deserve more close attention, for they are in many regards highly representative of the new approach of cinema as embedded in a complex set of intermedial hybrid structures. In this chapter, I will sketch some historical and cultural aspects of the genre (assuming that novelization is one single genre, which may not be accepted by everyone), consider some global tendencies that can be found throughout most types of novelization, and finally try to rearticulate, in brief, what is at stake for the broader field of film and literature studies.

Novelization in time and space

It is tempting to define novelization with respect to what we know of contemporary Hollywood novelization, i.e. as commercial and standardized tie-ins of real or would-be blockbusters, put on display as 200-page pocketbooks in bookshops or newsstands in airports during a very limited period, written by almost anonymous authors (often ghost-writers, some specializing in this type of writing) whose sole function is to rewrite in continuous, smooth, and banal prose the last version of the screenplay. While following the screenplay as closely as possible, the aim is to address the broad audience of occasional readers who might be interested in getting or staying in touch with the movie they have just seen (or just missed) and the characters (or rather the stars) whose images illustrate the front cover of these books.

Such a definition is very helpful in situating a large part of what can be considered novelization, and even more in helping us understand why the genre continues to be either completely ignored or despised by literary scholars and film theoreticians, not only by those who never read this type of literature, but also by those who produce it and who often refuse to sign it with their own name.[3] As far as I know, the concrete readership of novelizations has never been researched, neither quantitatively nor qualitatively: we do not really know who buys and/or reads these books, just as we can only guess what motivates these customers and what may be the social relevance of their reading (this absence is the more strange since cultural and popular studies have familiarized us with all types of cultural-anthropological research on "illegitimate" genres such as romance, porn, comics, photonovellas, soap operas, and so on). Yet, the identification of novelization as a genre with the sub-genre of the contemporary Hollywood novelization would miss some important points. Indeed, this narrow definition exposes us to a double risk of decontextualization: first by dehistoricizing the genre (novelization, even in Hollywood, has not always been what it is now, supposing one may say that it has always been there, which is far from being the case); second, by neutralizing the cultural complexities and differences within the genre itself (there are, for instance, cases of novelizations that belong to what Pierre Bourdieu would call the "restricted market" of the literary field, i.e. to the high-art segment of books written by and for those who struggle for the symbolic domination of the canon). For all these reasons, it is necessary to get a larger picture of what might be called novelization.

Roughly speaking novelization is as old as film itself. If one accepts that each narrative based on a filmic source-text can be considered a form of novelization, it is even possible to trace the history of the genre to the catalog descriptions of the very first films sold by Lumière and Edison.[4] But often, the very beginnings of the genre are linked with the serial or installment movies, such as in France, the films made for Pathé by the famous director Louis Feuillade.[5] Published in serial form before their reprint in book form, these novelizations raise fascinating questions about the merging of literature, cinema, and the intermediate form of scriptwriting, as well as questions on authorship, since much of this work, despite the strong personality of Feuillade, was collaborative. The readership for novelizations and serials completed each other in many ways, the novelization offering the opportunity to pick up with the story if one had missed an installment or wanted to be able to follow the story if it wasn't possible to see the movies themselves (for instance for those living in more rural areas).

With the emergence of the feature film, the narrative streamlining of cinema, and the triumph of the studio system, novelizations did not of course disappear, but their formal and cultural status changed rather dramatically. As Charles Musser argues, Hollywood novelizations should be seen as part of a new set of genres that represent the other side of the movie industry's cannibalization of the written word: novelizations are to be situated somewhere in between the better known new forms of writing that are the fan magazines, which often contain some forms of shorter novelization, and the Hollywood novel, which in some cases comes very close to it.[6]

Although still targeting a more popular audience, some established publishing houses in Europe, where the same type of novelizations were of course also produced, attempted in those years to provide readers with new and somewhat culturally upgraded forms of novelization.[7] The aim of these books was, on the whole, to offer what seemed to be missing in the movies themselves: the dialogue, during the last years of the silent era, and a strong narrative framework after that. Novelizations of the former type tend to be more "wordy" (logically, characters talk more than they are allowed to do in silent films, where the dialogue had to appear in autonomous shots). Novelizations of the latter type tend to generalize the formula of the first-person narrator (a literary equivalent of the filmic voice-over, which was not popular at all during the first years of the talkies, and which were heavily inspired by theatrical models). The lack of success of these novelizations must have been very disappointing, since most publishers rapidly closed the specialized series they had launched. Yet in spite of this commercial failure, novelizations have never been totally absent, and one notices that the eagerness to novelize pops up regularly during the years of "classic" moviemaking (between the beginning of the talking movies and the great economic shifts of the New Hollywood system in the mid to late 1970s, after *Jaws* and *Star Wars*).

In the meantime, several avant-garde movements, in the first place Surrealism, had launched various attempts to invent new forms of writing directly inspired or influenced by cinema, whose status is not always clear: whereas some texts had the ambition to recreate within the field of literary writing the newly discovered aesthetics of film montage, others tried to give a more literary twist to the emerging genre of scriptwriting, while the position of a third group remained somewhat ambiguous, oscillating between the literary reworking of filmic language and the filmic realization of literature. Some strange forms of novelization came out of this creative chaos: novelization in verse, a form that would not really be exploited in mainstream poetry writing on cinema, in which other themes and aspects (mainly the movie star on the one hand and cinema-going on the other) would become rapidly dominant.[8] There are also novelizations of screenplays that were never actually produced (although it is certainly arguable whether the very concept of novelization can be used for this type of work). Surrealism might have been on the point of realizing completely new forms of novelization, yet its dynamics in this field collapsed with the introduction of the talking movies, which stopped abruptly the commitment of the Surrealists to film, not only because of their nostalgia for the silent era and its visual audacities but also (and probably even more so) because of their incapacity to go on making films themselves (the shift from silent to talking movies had increased the production costs to such an extent that the private sponsors of Surrealist cinema were no longer willing or able to finance these commercially problematic projects).

A fourth type of novelization came to the fore during the decade of the so-called "film-as-writing" movement after World War II, represented for instance in France by the critic Alexandre Astruc, who coined in 1948 the concept of "caméra-stylo." The idea of filmmaking as writing fostered the outbreak of the auteur theory, with its strong emphasis on authorship as the expression of a director, so that a work (and even a work of art) is no longer totally controlled by the writer's "vision." Once again, the status of the novelizations of these years is complex, not to say paradoxical. It was indeed precisely during the era that announced the succession of literary writing by cinematographic writing that new forms of novelization were invented and that cinematographic "authors" were strongly encouraged to publish books. These were not only in the form of shooting scripts (which became suddenly a literary genre, the prestige of a director being measured by the number of technical shooting scripts he or she managed to get out in print) or in that of the interview book (a new genre invented by the "cinephiles" of those years, who considered the long interview as the major channel of the author's "vision"[9]), but also in that of the creative, novelistic reworkings of their own movies. These were the great years of the "ciné-roman," neither shooting scripts nor traditional novels, and it is perfectly legitimate to consider the specific contribution of the authorship years to the genre of the novelization.

Fifth and last (at least in this short historical sketch) is the contemporary Hollywood novelization. Technically speaking, this model seems at first sight the most simple of all, since most of the time it follows the shooting script in a rather docile way, the novelizers being no "real" "authors," but ghost-writers hired to execute one of the side-products of the multimedia production line that the making of a Hollywood movie has become since the generalization of the Spielberg-Lucas cinema, catering for a mostly juvenile audience, and using the movie as no more than the starting point of broader marketing strategies targeting the non-theatrical outlets as well as the multimedia diversification of branded ideas and characters. Yet here too, such a rapid and overly moralizing approach would miss the innovative aspects of this type of novelization, whose commercial agenda has given birth to creative forms of what might be called "continuative" novelizations – i.e. novelizations that rather than trying to reproduce the content and the flavor of a movie, reuse its characters and fictional universe in order to multiply and broaden its content matter (the case of *Star Trek* is the first to come to mind). Moreover, and I will return to this, the novelization form has proven very successful in the empowerment of contemporary audiences, which have managed, thanks also to new technologies such as the internet, to appropriate the genre in order to express, in often very seductive and disrupting ways, subcultural sensibilities. In other words, what seemed to be nothing more than one more channel of global capitalist brainwashing has seen its form and meaning redefined and "repurposed" by all types of users.

The internal stratification of the genre

Obviously, the chronological survey sketched above has no other ambition than to offer a first idea of the internal diversity of the genre, which the recent explosion of Hollywood novelizations and the systematic worldwide translation and uniform marketing of these books indicate. Just as a closer look at the history of the genre has helped to nuance the current domination of one single type, a more detailed analysis of the novelization will help to question its simplistic linear development.

Indeed, the story of the genre is synchronous. Novelization types do not simply supersede or replace each other; most of the time older forms either go on living in themselves or continue to exert a more or less hidden influence on newer forms. It may even occur that older forms come back in unexpected ways. A good example of this case is the recent hype of soap novelizations, which definitely represent a "new" variation on the "old" installment or serial forms, while borrowing several features of more recent evolutions in feature serialization, such as the tendency toward "continuation" rather than toward merely narrating actual shooting scripts. To study novelization is to become attentive to these sedimentations, which leave room enough for all kinds of anachronisms in the temporal logic of the genre (the genre itself being perhaps, as I will try to argue later, a peculiar example of creative cultural anachronism). In the context of film studies, where we are gradually becoming conscious of the (postmodern) shift from narrative cinema to what this type of cinema was believed to have left behind, namely the non-narrative cinema of attractions, such anachronisms are perhaps more crucial to the understanding of the medium's complexities than teleological speculations on the essence of film and the "natural" link between filmmaking and storytelling.

Second, and it is now high time to articulate this more explicitly, the very history and definition of novelization, both as a formal structure and as a cultural practice, cannot be separated from the national and linguistic contexts in which it comes to appear. Here too, the analogy with film itself, where the role of national traditions cannot be denied, there can only be a "world" or "globalized" approach to the genre, in which several models compete and interact without ever merging in one single model. Even if many cultural and linguistic areas do not invent new types of novelization by themselves, local features will always determine the specific use of the general models. The fashionable novelization of soap operas in the 1990s, for instance, which seems at first sight to reflect rather passively the penetration of post-Dallas and post-Dynasty "clones," has not been the same at all in the various countries or areas in which it took place, if only for the very specific relationships each (Western) state allowed or created between private and public television and media concerns. What is certainly different in each cultural context is the genre's chronology, both in its linear and its stratified or non-synchronous forms, and this observation should always prevent us from making too hasty generalizations.

Third, a more subtle study of novelization should start mapping the socio-cultural tensions within the field. These tensions are strong, much stronger than in other comparable fields, given the absolute gap that seems to exist between the two extreme positions. On the one hand, there is the novelization which is, for good or bad reasons, considered a strictly commercial product, a mere "thing" with no cultural superego, so to speak, which does not differ from other types of merchandizing. On the other hand, there are some attempts to originate high-art occurrences of the genre (the fact that they are very rare make them only the more valuable from a symbolic point of view). These high-art novelizations differ in almost all aspects from their commercial counterparts. That they have a different type of author (an "author," not simply some ghost-writer, studio employee, or subcontractor), a different type of publisher (more mainstream, with a catalogue of "real" books), a different target audience (preferably readers who do not confess a specific love of cinema), a different style (more sophisticated), and so on, should of course not come as a surprise. What may be more intriguing is the fact that these books *do* and simultaneously *do not* novelize the same movies as do their commercial anti-models. Indeed, one cannot fail to notice that high-art novelizations often do have a very strong preference for very traditional, even Hollywood movies. At this level, the difference is almost negligible. Yet at the same time, what is rewritten by high-art novelizations is never the movie that has come recently to the theater: "real" authors always focus on either older movies (one guesses the movies that impressed them a lot when they were adolescents) or genres (and one knows the importance of this parameter in auteur theory, the "vision" of a director being revealed by his/her capacity to interpret in a personal manner the impersonal constraints of a genre). So Robert Coover rewrites a whole range of genres in his *A Night at the Movies*, while Tanguy Viel, author of *Cinéma*, rewrites in 1999 the Joseph Mankiewicz 1972 movie *Sleuth*.[10] Curiously, novelizations in verse seem to stick less to this cinephile nostalgia.[11] The major difference between both types is – and this too should come as no surprise – their degree of self-consciousness. Commercial novelizations narrate unmediated stories; what is narrated is not presented as seen on screen, whereas high-art novelizations systematically narrate mediated stories. What is narrated is presented as something that is projected on a screen (the importance of this crucial difference will be made more explicit later in this chapter).

Fourth and last, the internal differentiation of the field can only increase when one starts realizing that the boundaries between novelization and other types of narrative appear as blurred as they may seem sharp between the two opposite cases of commercial and high-art novelization. Initially, this is because novelization cannot, of course, be limited to the sole field of film novelization. Other non-novelistic media have been, are being, or will be novelized, from the theater to the videogame (to take one example of a medium "older" and one of a medium "younger" than film). And as already mentioned, because it is often not easy to exclude from the umbrella-concept of novelization, a certain number of practices that have never been labeled, as such, but which are nevertheless convincing examples of narrative recreations of cinematographic source-texts (long summaries included in essays, for instance, aiming at providing the readership with detailed information on the film under discussion in the pre-video era, when it was often difficult, not to say practically impossible to have an actual access to the visual material).[12]

Some generic features

Despite the internal variety of the genre, novelization does obey a series of prototypical genre features, with the two notions of anti-adaptation and anti-remediation. To qualify novelization as *anti-adaptation* may seem a strange proposal, since at first sight, the mechanism that converts a film into a novel is not fundamentally different from what happens when making the step from a book into a film. Yet the very observation of what most novelizations produce as their output clearly demonstrates that there is no real analogy between the two operations. Whereas the result of the filmic adaptation of a book can be anything, to the extent that some of these adaptations make such free use of their source material that the "original" becomes almost or totally unrecognizable,[13] novelizations distinguish themselves, some counterexamples notwithstanding, as narrations which remain very close to the storyline of the novelized movie. The reason for this systematic convergence has nothing to do with the cultural respect due to the original (this would be absurd, since in many cases the films that are novelized have no canonical status, nor do they have the ambition to achieve this status). It has also not systematically to do with the legal constraints that limit the freedom of the novelizers (although many ghost-writers are given a very precise and detailed contract, which prevents them from letting go of the original storyline and characters). The decisive criterion is, on the contrary, the fact that the commercial novelization is not obliged to do what even very commercial filmic adaptation cannot escape: the switching of one medium to another. When adapting a book into a movie, one cannot but transform words into images, even if the book has already a very graphic style, or seems to be conceived from the very beginning as a virtual screenplay. Yet when adapting a movie into a novel, such a shift is often avoided, since the material that is transformed is less the movie than the script, that is a text having the same semiotic features as the expected written output. It is the absence of this "semiotic gap" that explains why so many novelizations are so close to the movie, and even why it seems so difficult to do something else, while in the case of the filmic adaptation of a book, nothing seems so difficult as to remain faithful to the book, hence the very understandable and, I think, legitimate valorization of the fidelity issue, which is not necessarily to be considered a symptom of the inferiority of "vulgar" cinematographic language to more "prestigious" literary language, but the expression of a challenge to which many artists are not indifferent. Since fidelity is, for good semiotic reasons, absolutely impossible, it becomes very exciting to pursue such a diabolic endeavor. Whatever may be the concrete conclusions that novelizers and their readers draw from this situation, the fact is that novelization cannot be treated as simply the "other side" of filmic adaptation. In that sense, it should be possible to call it a form of anti-adaptation.

It is without doubt less problematic to consider novelization a form of anti-remediation. If, as argued by Bolter and Grusin, the dynamics of media history in Western culture is determined by the craving for increased realism, i.e. of the transparency of the signs of representation, and the replacement of old media by new ones that give the user an increased, although always imperfect and therefore always temporary, feeling of "presentness" of the represented,[14] the very existence of the novelization genre is something that goes thoroughly against the grain of history. Indeed, the remediation of the old media of the novel by the newer media of cinema has become a kind of cliché that is shared by both the professionals (not only the media theoreticians but also the critics and the writers themselves, who feel helpless when confronted with the power of the image) and the public (who has made film, with pop music, the major artistic expression of the twentieth and twenty-first centuries). Novelization is moreover not a type of writing that makes an extensive use of literary/visual techniques and is therefore an historic "monster." Its dramatically anachronistic status should force us to rethink more than one stereotypical belief about the relationship between media.

Anti-remediation and anti-adaptation are, of course, two features that do not complete each other by coincidence. If novelization is such a bad candidate for Bolter and Grusin's remediation theory, it is, in the first place, because of the very lack of any fundamental media change. While the reworking of a cinematographic screenplay into a printed novel may entail quite a lot of technical and formal transformations, it does not alter the essentially verbal status of the source text (this would be the case if the source text was something like a storyboard, yet this is not what normally happens since most novelizations are elaborated on the basis of the verbal screenplay, not on that of the graphical storyboard). And if, vice versa, novelization often seems so weak, so uninventive an adaptation, it is also because of the rewriter's conviction that he or she is working within a medium that is not able to compete with the rhetorical and emotional force of the visual narrative of the movie.

Yet at the same time, the derogatory description of novelization, at least at a lexical level, that has been followed above, fails to take into account some essential observations which the abstract viewpoint of media theory may overlook but which the more anthropological perspective of cultural theory cannot emphasize enough: the fact that novelization exists, that it seems a prosperous genre, that the novelizing drive in Western society appears to be an important factor in our contact with film as a social practice. Novelizations clearly demonstrate two things: first, that a cultural form like this can no longer be treated in binary terms, second, that our use of the genre suggests that contemporary media culture forces us to exceed each simple comparison between autonomous media. If novelization, despite being so terribly old-fashioned compared to the newer media it cannot pretend to remediate, nevertheless exists, not just as a secondary by-product for marginal users, but as part of the global and cross-media package that we still call a movie today, but which resembles more a merchandized collective experience than a "thing" in the traditional meaning of the word, then the genre may enhance our understanding of the failure of binary relationships in media theory. What novelization displays, among many other objects and practices, is the shift from independent media to media environments.

Here, it is no longer the sole logic of remediation of a medium by another that is at work, but the very logics of multiplication, for instance by infinite reduplication or permanent adaptation from one medium into another, of whatever seems capable of meeting the needs or the expectations of an audience, sometimes in a very unexpected manner. In this wider process, novelization has its role to play and this part can no longer be separated from or opposed to that of the medium it successfully or unsuccessfully remediates. This is why it is not enough to state that the art of the novel is becoming an implicit art of novelization, for it is well known that more and more authors write books whose main ambition is to be turned into a movie.[15] One should logically go a step further and add that, as a corollary, all movies are now conceived in such a way that their novelization can become part of their global media form.

The confusion that is frequently taking place between the book as source-text of the movie (in the case of an adaptation) and the book as one of the commercial tie-ins of the film (in the case of novelization) is highly revealing in this respect: when confronted with "the book of the film," we no longer know which came first, the book or the movie, and we no longer know which reading strategy to adopt. To put things even more radically, when reading *tout court*, are we not all trying to imagine what a filmic adaptation of a book could look like? But things work the same the other way round. In a theater, do we not think already of what the DVD-version will bring to us, do we not already have in mind ideas about the cover of its novelization, do we not already dream of the continuations that we are going to co-author on one of the websites launched by the fans of the movie's videogame?

Beyond adaptation studies

Despite being probably the most despised and certainly the least studied aspect of film as social and cultural practice, novelization does bring to the fore a certain number of crucial issues in the film and literature field. The most obvious contribution of the genre is, of course, its critique of traditional adaptation studies. The practice of novelization undoubtedly fortifies the stance of all those who no longer accept the issues of priority, hierarchy, and fidelity in discussions on the relationships between book and film. Yet novelisation does not only enhance the critique of adaptation studies, it helps us to abandon all binary approaches of cinema and literature. Instead of comparing books and films, even in a spirit of equality and without taking into account questions of priority and cultural value, novelization forces us to consider cinema and literature in the global (mass) media structure of our time and to tackle the various ways in which media complete and contaminate each other, without losing their specific features. Novelization, therefore, is less an agent of simplification than of complexification, since it foregrounds the internal hybridization of contemporary media, both literary and cinematographic. At the same time, it points towards the very limits of such a poly-centering approach, since the genre also meets countless issues of copyright and ownership, which strongly diminish the manoeuvring space of the novelizer.

NOTES

1 As the subtitle of the *XII International Film Studies Conference of Udine-Gorizia* (8–10 March 2005) put it.
2 See for instance the chapter by Robert Stam that provides the theoretical frame-work of a recent collection on film and literature (Stam and Raengo (eds.), *A Companion to Literature and Film* [Malden, Massachusetts and Oxford: Blackwell, 2005]). Only a few lines are devoted to the issue of novelization, and although the evaluation of the genre is no longer despising (which would of course have been in complete contradiction of Stam's own "Bakhtinian" agenda), the very under-representation of any novelizing practices are symptomatic of the persistent reduction of "literature *and* film" to "literature *into* film." A different sound can be heard in this volume's editors' "Introduction" to the book *Adaptations* (ed. Cartmell and Whelehan [London and New York: Routledge 1999]).
3 A good inside testimony is given by John August in 2004: http://johnaugust.com/archives/2004/where-to-find-natural-born-killers-novelization.
4 Of course this term was also used before the advent of film for novelized plays.
5 If Feuillade's *Fantômas* films can be considered "normal" adaptations, several of his later films were scripted, shot, and serialized almost simultaneously. Francis Lacassin, *Feuillade* (Paris: Seghers, 1964).
6 Musser's article takes as an example the two Hollywood novels by Horace McCoy, *They Shoot Horses, Don't They?* (1935) and *I Should Have Stayed Home* (1938), which he analyses very convincingly as (implicit) novelizations of *42nd Street* (Lloyd Bacon, 1933) and *Gold Diggers of '33* (Mervyn LeRoy, 1933). Stam and Raengo (eds.), *A Companion to Literature and Film*, pp. 229–57.
7 The main sources of information here are the books by Alain and Odette Virmaux, *Le Ciné-Roman* (Paris: Edilig, 1984) and Jeanne-Marie Clerc, *Cinéma et Littérature* (Paris: Nathan, 1993), although neither of them really focuses on the genre of novelization itself.
8 See for instance Philip French and Ken Wlaschin (eds.), *The Faber Book of Movie Verse* (London: Faber, 1993).
9 As we all know, the mother of all interview books is still the unchallenged Truffaut *Hitchcock* book (Paris: Gallimard, 1993), itself a continuation of books such as *La Politique des auteurs*.
10 More immodestly, the author of this chapter has proposed in 2005 his remake in verse of Jean-Luc Godard's *Vivre sa vie* (1962) in *Vivre sa vie: Une Novellisation en vers du film de Jean-Luc Godard* (Paris-Bruxelles: Les Impressions Nouvelles, 2005).
11 French and Wlaschin (eds.), *Faber Book of Movie Verse*.

12 A famous example here is Stanley Cavell's book on the screwball comedy, *The World Viewed* (Cambridge, Massachusetts and London: Harvard University Press, 1979), in which the author theorizes his own way of retelling the pictures.

13 See for example Amy Heckerling's *Clueless*, "based on" Jane Austen's *Emma*.

14 Jay David Bolter and Richard Grusin, *Remediation: Understanding New Media* (Cambridge, Massachusetts: MIT University Press, 1999).

15 The beginnings of this shift, which reflects of course the changing power relations between literature and cinema, are often situated in the late twenties, with the encounter of the hard-boiled detective writer and the Hollywood studios.

16

DEBORAH CARTMELL AND IMELDA WHELEHAN

A practical understanding of literature on screen: two conversations with Andrew Davies

Andrew Davies is, undoubtedly, one of the most successful and prolific writers and adaptors for television and cinema; included in his oeuvre are *A Very Peculiar Practice* (1986, 1988), *Pride and Prejudice* (1995), *Tipping the Velvet* (2002), *The Way We Live Now* (2001), *Bridget Jones's Diary* (1996), and *Bleak House* (2005). Although best known for his work in television and cinema, Andrew Davies is also a writer for both adults and children and has written for the stage and radio. He spoke to Deborah Cartmell and Imelda Whelehan twice; over lunch in Birmingham and in a public conversation at De Montfort University, Leicester. Speaking about authorship, fidelity, audiences, casting, and his past and current projects, Davies offers insight into his distinctive "televisual" aesthetic.

Interview with Andrew Davies 11 October 2004, Deborah Cartmell and Imelda Whelehan

DC: To what extent do you look at previous adaptations when adapting a text?

AD: The answer is I used to avoid watching other people's adaptations, lest I get influenced by them, but since I watch an awful lot of television I generally found that I'd seen the previous adaptation years ago. And it's possible to have a false memory syndrome about these things, and actually forget about something that somebody else did and think it's my own idea. These days, I make myself watch the old adaptations, so at least if I plagiarize them I'm doing it consciously. But usually when it comes to it, I find I don't want to. An interesting example is *Bleak House*, which I'm working on at the moment. I really admired the 1982 adaptation when I saw it before and I thought I couldn't possibly improve on it – but when I saw it again, I found I wanted to do it very differently, with much more pace and intercutting. But there was one moment which was just so striking that I felt I had to rip it off; or to put it more respectably, offer a kind of homage to the earlier adaptation, that's the death of Jo, the crossing sweeper. Where, in the book, Dickens comes out with this bit of angry poetry: "Dead, your Majesty. Dead, my lords and gentlemen. Dead, Right Reverends and Wrong Reverends of every order" and so forth, and they actually had Jarndyce saying that aloud in that earlier adaptation. It's just so powerful I wanted to do it again, and did. But that's a rare exception – in fact I can't remember ever doing that before. An example of unconscious plagiarism is a big dog I introduced into the Netherfield garden to play with Elizabeth, having completely forgotten that Fay Weldon did the same in her adaptation ten years earlier. No one spotted it, so far as I know.

IW: You've talked a bit about how much freedom you've had and you said nowadays you actually have a lot of freedom in choosing texts for adaptation.

AD: Yes, sometimes I suggest novels to the broadcaster, but it's mostly the other way round, you know, that's what they think of as one of their skillful areas, selecting the book, and as it were, you're marrying the book to the writer. *He Knew He Was Right* [2004] is one that I suggested to them and I've just been suggesting this Alan Hollinghurst novel which is on the Booker prize shortlist, *The Line of Beauty*.[1] And that probably will happen, so it's a very fortunate situation to be in.

IW: So there isn't a typical brief that you're presented with really – you're providing the ideas?

AD: More often it will be the other way round. Like *Bleak House*. I didn't suggest that and I was reluctant to do it, partly because I admired the earlier one so much, partly because I'm not sure how much of a Dickensian I am really, so we're certainly finding out! His minor characters are just so full of vitality and can be very funny – Guppy and Smallweed are two of my favorites. And Tulkinghorn makes a great villain – a villain who is sure he's in the right. It's the heroines who are so dismayingly soppy and unrealized.

DC: Is Esther's disfigurement going to be very minor?

AD: Not at first! Yes she'll have to have the spots, but they'll fade! Apart from that, I've dropped her smugness, all her toe-curling nicknames (Dame Durden and all that), played up her quickness and intelligence, made it clear what a damaged child she is – first told she would have been better never born, and then being groomed for sex by Jarndyce ... Was that what she really wanted? Probably not, but since he says it, she thinks, maybe, it will be all right. It's quite a dodgy area, but an interesting one to explore. Dickens raises it, in a way, but shies away from it, as usual ... Why did he [Jarndyce] not get married before? Why does he settle on a child? Of course, she's grown up by the time he actually pops the question, but by then she's so obliged to him, isn't she? Somebody was trying to talk me into the notion, and I think he's probably right, that all that stuff about Jarndyce going off to the Growlery really implies that he's going off to masturbate about Esther. But I didn't go so far as to include a masturbation scene!

DC: Denholm Elliott is my vision of Jarndyce. He's so nice you believe him.

AD: He's also quite tortured because he's managed to pull himself back from the brink of what happens to Richard, and what happened to his uncle, so there's always this abyss of depression and madness he can fall into. But he is cushioned by his wealth – he has no need to go to law. I think Dickens should have rigged the plot a bit differently in that way somehow. He didn't have to make it so easy on Jarndyce.

DC: How do you cope with the voice, especially given that Dickens himself is one of the main characters?

AD: Good point. Can't do that really. You can do something about the way he sees it – visually.

DC: But the helplessness I think comes across.

AD: It's that kind of frustration really that leads to, you know, putting Dickens's words in Jarndyce's mouth, but you can't do that very often.

DC: I guess it is a question of how much the author intrudes into what you do. There seems to me a tendency to be less faithful to a literary text in the late 1990s and today, but somehow to authenticate the narrative by using authorial presence in some way. Mary Shelley's *Frankenstein*, or Bram Stoker's *Dracula*, for instance.

AD: Doing it in the title?

DC: Or including bits of the author's biography in the film [as in *Little Women*, 1994]. It makes it seem more authentic, but in fact it's less authentic as it's not like the book at all. But you seem to want to distance yourself as much as possible from the author.

AD: Well, it's partly because one of the backgrounds I've come from is quite academic, and the great thing when I was coming of age, as it were, was don't trust the writer, trust the text. It's naïve and silly to regard the novels or poems or whatever as being a clue to the true nature of the author, what matters is what they manage to get down on paper. It might be truer than they thought it was. *Sons and Lovers* is a good example. Lawrence wrote it so truly that even though you know he wanted you not to sympathize with the father, you do, and you think, "fucking hell, the mother is a big problem," and "actually you're not very nice either." You know there's a chapter called something like "The Judgement on Miriam," or something like that. He has a shag with Miriam and he doesn't know anything about sex and so her response is disappointment and he blames her. But he wrote it well enough so that you can make a completely different judgment from the one that the author did. In the same way, Dickens is writing about a man who for some reason, can't deal with grown-up women, so what he'd like to do is groom this girl.

DC: By giving Jarndyce Dickens's words, you're associating Dickens with that darker side.

AD: No, Jarndyce is fine with regards to some questions in life, like don't get involved with lawyers, or it's better for a chap to have a profession where he can make his own living, respect himself, rather than hoping for hand-outs. That's all very good. But I think, no, he does regard women in a different way from men, he seems to think girls are sort of special which I think probably Dickens also thought, and this is not taking into account any of the biographical stuff, because we all know that however Dickens idealized and sentimentalized women, in real life he treated them appal-lingly. No doubt the two things are related. But this thing he's got going on with Esther (who am I talking about, Dickens or Jarndyce? Both probably). He's completely in control really; she depends on him for everything, and the only reason he would want to get married to her, I would think, is that he wants to have sex with her.

IW: Have you looked at the two films of *Little Dorrit* – there's a similar problem encountered there, isn't there? Perhaps the challenge isn't risen to there. She remains innocent, he remains asexual.

AD: I think they were just so boring. It was an interesting concept, having one film with her in it and one film with her not in it. But actually to go through with it for six hours! It would have been much better to have just written it down as an idea as one way of doing *Little Dorrit*, but it probably wouldn't work, and it didn't. I was very cross at the time because I rather wanted to adapt *Little Dorrit* myself, but thought I couldn't go back to it for about ten years – about ten years is about time really. I'd probably do it now. But she never managed to get any sort of drama out of it. The one thing I liked was that blue dress.

DC: There is a feeling that we have to preserve the text, but also make sure that the author is still intact at the end of it all, that you have some respect for them. But as you say about Lawrence, it's really hard to do that.

AD: He's still such a good writer, wonderful writer. An adaptation particularly is a kind of reading of the book. It's not like the final reading of the book. Rather, it's what I thought or we thought at that time. I might come back in twenty years – if I'm still here – and have another go.

DC: You're unique in that you're known as an adaptor. You've actually created a whole niche, haven't you, when you think about Huxley or someone like that, they adapted novels,[2] but they weren't primarily known for that, and you're a writer as well but I can't think of anyone else who is like that, who is so well known for this.

AD: I think it's odd as well. But I've just fallen into it gradually. I'm not quite sure how I acquired this extra visibility, which is certainly no handicap to my career. So for television adaptations, I generally get first refusal, which is a delightful position to be in. If it's a movie adaptation then there will be a lot of people ahead of me, of whom Tom Stoppard and Christopher Hampton would be two. Both of them are exceptionally skilled ... I thought Christopher Hampton's adaptation of *Les Liaisons Dangereuses* was absolutely fabulous. Stoppard does masses, you know. He often doesn't get a big credit for it.

IW: He hasn't got that association. People don't look at the credits and think about him in the way they do with you.

AD: Well, with movies it's the director who gets the attention, apart from the stars.

IW: But people will associate you with *Bridget Jones's Diary* as well won't they?

AD: No not really. I wouldn't think so. It'll be the actors, I would think. They probably don't even know who directed it … Richard Curtis, yes, because he's made that "rom com" genre his own.

IW: I think you were picked out as being involved in the production of the film because of the whole Darcy thing, of course.[3]

AD: Well it was. That was why they got me involved really, because they weren't quite sure at that stage what kind of film they wanted to make. I think I told them what they wanted to hear, which was that all this stuff about the urban family was just a sideline, and was not actually very interesting, except for people who were actively in the urban family. When Bridget got a boyfriend, she wouldn't exactly abandon the urban family, but it would no longer be her first priority. And the film had to be a romantic comedy, I told them, with classic Beatrice and Benedick structure, and Darcy had to be more like Mr. Darcy, and so my contribution to the script was a restructuring of what had been there previously. And then Richard Curtis came in and rewrote every scene, really without disturbing the structure of the scenes, but it is quite odd working on one of those things where it's almost like being in a factory. You're sort of one of three stations on the track and the car passed through the bit where it's put all together and then it moves on and they may strip everything out, reupholster it, respray it and then it goes out.

IW: Did you feel that you didn't recognize it at the end?

AD: Yes, I recognized the book in it, and my structure, and the relationship to *Pride and Prejudice* and so on, and a few of the lines here and there, but not a tremendous lot. I still haven't seen the finished one, the second one, and it's coming out in November so it's about time they gave me a look at it really – it's too late to say anything now [it was released in 2004].

DC: Do you have any say in who plays what?

AD: No. A bit in television. If I make suggestions, they will take some notice of it. Usually when I'm writing the thing, I don't think of a particular actor, but I sometimes come up with an idea when I've finished the script. I always know who *wouldn't* be right. But I must say, writing this version of *Bleak House*, it's been difficult to rid my mind of the images of some of the people who played in the last adaptation: Diana Rigg, and Peter Vaughan in particular.

IW: Did we touch on this issue whether it matters if you very much respect the text that you're adapting?

AD: Yeah. It does and there is also a kind of politics of this whole thing. I suppose the writer I respect most, in terms of sheer professionalism, is Jane

Austen. Everything works out right. Mostly, you don't notice how crappy these plots are until you try to adapt them, but you don't ever have to worry about hers. Everything happens according to the right season and the timing is perfect, like the time it takes to get from x to y is always right. And so apart from that point of view, I respect her very much, but also she had a small output, and the books are enormously well known by the people who admire her. Unless you come up with something that is manifestly better, which is exceptionally difficult because she is so good, you stick pretty close to it. I restrain myself to writing the scenes that she didn't write, really, because she chose not to take the liberty of writing scenes with men on their own or men with other men. I thought that could help such a lot, especially since I was writing such a pro-Darcy adaptation in *Pride and Prejudice*. If they saw him suffering or just doing something very physical, the audience would treat him more like a real person, and not just have Elizabeth's view, where she only sees him when he's in a bad mood all dressed up in evening dress.

And to the question "would I adapt anything for which I didn't have very much respect?" I have done that, for particular reasons. *House of Cards* – that Michael Dobbs political novel – just had a great thriller plot, but the characters were not awfully well drawn. The dialogue was hopeless and he kind of missed a trick, I thought, not pulling the girl detective any closer into the villain. Thinking of Robert McKee, the scriptwriters' guru,[4] another thing I remembered from his course, was always put sex on the spine of the story. Now, in the book, she's having an affair with the assistant editor of the paper, which just goes nowhere. The spine of the story is Urquhart's rise to power, and her story is finding the truth about him and destroying him and, so I thought, well, that's where the sex has to be. But he's more than old enough to be her father! All the better – she can call him Daddy while they're doing it! The ending of the book has her confronting him with the truth and he hurls himself off the roof of the Palace of Westminster. But when I got to that point I realized that "my" Urquart would never do that. He would throw her off instead. So he did. And so I completely changed the ending.

IW: So you completely restructured it?

AD: Yes as I saw it and I was encouraged to do so by Michael Wearing who was the executive producer of it and who, when he gave it to me, said "it's an interesting little book. It's not very good, needs a bit of tweaking, think Jacobean," so I gave him all these soliloquies which were inspired by Olivier in *Richard III*, really, and lots of other things. And the director took up all that Jacobean stuff, and in terms of the lighting, all kinds of darks and lights ...

IW: Back to the question of first principles, are you saying that you don't have a set of first principles in adapting a literary text?

AD: No, I don't, because I like to think one can do different books in different ways, so that what I do do is that if I haven't read it before or if I'm rereading it from a long time back, I just try to have quite an innocent reading of it the first time and just see what appeals to me, what doesn't, what I'd like to highlight, what I'd like to disguise, what I'd like to get rid of, just on the basis of what interests me. And obviously what interests me will also have a lot to do with "the way we live now" – and what kind of relevance different parts of the book have, or don't have, because some bits will seem really interesting and vital and some bits, won't.

And then the next thing would be just the nitty-gritty thing – try and decide how many episodes and how they would divide up. And while all this is going on, I'd be gradually coming towards some notion as to what dramatic style to use. Basically, I mean, you're hoping to have mostly dramatic scenes, but is it going to be all like that or are you going to use any voice-over? If it's a first person narrative, there's often a temptation to use a first person voice-over (it's in *Tipping the Velvet* for example). But then, I've always been taken by first person to camera and occasionally I'll do that.

I did it in *He Knew He Was Right*, partly because a lot of it was so internal, especially for the hero, what he's going through; and I didn't want to do it as a voice-over because I think that's a bit like you're excluded and you're overhearing him. I thought it would be a lot more fun if he actually talked to us about it and, when he started, I thought it was a bit unfair on his wife so she's going to have some and then I thought, actually, there's all these other people who have got a point of view. So it finished up with about half a dozen people having bits of "to camera" stuff, with varying success. In *Bleak House* I'm doing a straight dramatization, except that the thing is we're doing it in half hours. I deliberately tried to make it, in some ways, like a soap.

IW: Is it because you know when it is being scheduled [after *Eastenders*]?

AD: Partly that, yes. And it's been discussed, right from the beginning, to go in that slot, so there will be a lot of children in the audience, and we want a dramatic style that doesn't seem too unfamiliar or uncomfortable to them, so it's short scenes, relatively simple language. In the old days, classic serials used to go out at Sunday teatime. We don't want it to be cozy like that, but we do want to draw in a wider audience than the traditional costume drama audience.

IW: So that older kids . . .?

AD: A lot of kids stay up until then . . . If it's a big success, they'll be allowed to stay up, they'll be getting culture as well as entertainment!

There's an awful lot of characters to keep a grip on but then again, there are in soaps, too. And very short scenes.

DC: There's so much of the text that you have to explain. How do you do it?

AD: You can do so much with looks and glances. My daughter when she was 8 or 9 used to watch quite a bit of adult drama with me. She was always quite into it. It always surprised me that although a lot of the stuff that went on was way beyond her experience, she was always very good at picking up who you were supposed to like and who you don't like, who you trusted and who you didn't trust. She's a script editor in Drama now.

Second interview: 23 February 2005, De Montfort University

DC: You have said that the thing that you are probably going to be best known for in your whole career is putting Mr. Darcy in a wet shirt. As brilliant as it was and as much as we all enjoyed it, do you actually regret this? Does it overshadow, perhaps, your other achievements?

AD: No. How can I regret bringing so much pleasure to so many women! It's probably the only way I will ever be able to do it. And it was an accident actually because I wanted him to dive in totally naked which was part of my scheme for getting the leading characters out of their posh tight restricting clothes as often as possible, but for some reason, perhaps because it would have been a very tedious and an elaborate striptease anyway, he didn't dive in naked, he dived in with his shirt on and so gave us this scene. And I didn't realise how erotic it was going to be. But I think the kind of serious lesson from all this is that when it is in a visual medium it's those visual things that stick in the mind most, just as in the book you remember the dialogue and the descriptions and the interior feelings and so on as conveyed in words. In the series my own favorite one is those glances across the piano that tell us he is in love, but that wet shirt moment is really the first time Elizabeth has seen Darcy as natural man, as it were. She has always been thrust into rooms with this rather daunting, beautifully turned-out guy and here he is all wet and tousled and mysteriously more fascinating than ever, or suddenly fascinating, especially with his huge grounds spread out behind him and his wonderful house. No I don't mind at all about Darcy's wet shirt. I am quite happy!

IW: You have been working on *Brideshead Revisited* and *Bleak House*. With *Bleak House* we know you have finished with it and it has started filming. Did you want to perhaps say a few words about that?

AD: I'll take them one at a time. *Bleak House*: I have never done a Dickens before. I was extremely chary about taking it on because I am sure that there are quite a few people in this audience who saw the 1980s adaptation with Denholm Elliott and Diana Rigg in it, which was to my mind a really, really terrific adaptation. I watched that again with some trepidation thinking, you know, am I going to be able to do anything that approaches the excellence of that and rather to my relief I found that it did seem to play rather slowly and that though Denholm Elliott and Diana Rigg were absolutely magnificent and unlikely ever to be done better, though we hope as well, other aspects weren't very good. The awful heroine, Esther Summerson, she's awful in the book. Dickens did not to my mind really succeed with her and it was a great pleasure to abandon Esther's first person narration which is so kind of smug and self-regarding, while trying to seem not so, and Esther herself is such a bore and a prig. So I thought we could probably do something with this and kind of tweak her a little bit so that she is not quite so sick-making and also her little pal Ada as well. We thought the really nice thing about Ada was she was just crazy about Richard so we made them like two teenagers in love. I think two things about it that are kind of different and new: one is that it is the longest adaptation in terms of hours that has been seen on the BBC for quite a long time, so it is eight whole hours; we started off with ten but then shrank it. It is in half-hour episodes and it is going out earlier in the evening, about eight-thirty, and hoping to attract a young audience and perhaps a more popular audience, hoping that what's left of the *Eastenders* audience will carry on watching *Bleak House*. It seemed a wonderful thing at first, but with *Eastenders* going down the tubes I am not so sure how good an idea it is! So they have started filming it but you won't get to see it until November [2005]. Yes and I have written a script for *Brideshead Revisited* as a movie, but it was going to go into production this year, but it's now postponed until next year for the usual reasons, which are funding and casting. When they get that right we will see my version of *Brideshead*, I hope.

DC: We have spoken a lot about Dickens in the past and I get the impression from your *Bleak House* that you are rewriting Dickens for a contemporary audience.

AD: I am always disinclined to look in biographies for stuff to help. The Elizabeth Jane Howard [*Falling*, broadcast 6/3/05] was a kind of exception in a way because that story was based on a true experience which she recounts briefly in her autobiography, so I was obviously looking in that for any clues although there weren't any really; all the best stuff is in the novel. I wouldn't say I am hugely trying to change Dickens because it's a huge book, *Bleak House*, and there is plenty of stuff in it to choose from. I suppose to a large extent I choose and perhaps build up and highlight the elements of the book that I think are most likely to appeal to a modern audience and soft-pedal the rest. With *Bleak House* there was a particular problem that I have referred to already, that you just can't avoid because she is the heroine and if you have got a strong feeling that the audience are going to find her, especially kids of the same age as Esther, impossibly smug and priggish. We have got to look for elements, without cheating the book too much, that are there, and so the element that I looked for was that she is actually very good at practical solutions, but she also starts from a position that, in fact, more and more kids start from today, in that she doesn't know who her parents are exactly and she is kind of looking for a mum in a hopeless kind of way, never expecting to find her. She has got a very low self-image at the beginning of the book because she is constantly being told that she is her mother's disgrace and that it would have been better if she had never been born. But she finds out that she is very good at practical solutions, people stand around dithering and she thinks of the common sense way of solving it and it works, and she finds that actually people regard her very favorably and she has got quite sharp judgments about character that she seems to see through people, like the dreadful Skimpole, much more quickly than anybody else. I kind of sharpened up all that bit, you see, so that elements were already in Esther. I built up but kind of ignored all this, oh God, all those dreadful nicknames that they give her – Dame Durden and our little mother and all that bollocks. I couldn't bear it. So those are the kind of changes that I make; the other very difficult thing is trying to sort out that plot of *Bleak House* which is murderously complicated and in parts doesn't quite work as one often finds when one gets to adapting something. So that's what I do.

IW: We spoke to you a few months ago and you said that there was one writer who was almost perfect to adapt and that was Jane Austen. I wondered if you could say why she is so perfect to adapt and then perhaps tell us if there is anyone who ranks closely to Austen?

AD: Well, yes, one of the reasons why Austen is so delightful to adapt, and there are many, is that thing I just said about Dickens. When you get down to it, you find that the plot doesn't quite work: that is true of Trollope, it's true of Thackeray it's true of, no, George Eliot's plots do work, but the plot of *Middlemarch* is so intricate that although one could understand it, it was impossible to convey it in a television adaptation. Whereas in Jane Austen, everything works and not only just the plot, but if she said the apple trees were in blossom, you would be bang in the right month, all those kind of things work perfectly. A second reason is that her dialogue is so sharp and witty and dramatic, you can just copy it out and one does that quite a lot. It just needs a bit of pruning because it was a slower time and people had time for longer sentences, but it is so sharp and witty and it's so funny and also, she is so dramatic, she builds up her drama. She sets up her little jokes and time bombs and big dramatic surprises and then she pays them off at just the right moment, you know, like great comedy writers are supposed to do. There's all that, oh yes, and quite often somebody like Pasternak is the worst example of somebody who never writes the scene that is almost obligatory that you really want him to write; Jane Austen always gives it to you, you know, you always get those big things; Lady Catherine, Darcy's proposal, she dramatizes it properly and so makes the adaptor's work very easy and pleasant. So that's why she is the best.

IW: So no-one ranks near Austen?

AD: No-one comes close. No-one comes close. Although you know all those great writers are great fun to do. Some of Trollope is – Trollope *is* patchy. You get some wonderful bits, some wonderful scenes, other bits mysteriously not. When I did *The Way We Live Now* [2001], for example, the guy who turns out to be the main character, Melmotte, this fascinating villain who sort of sits at the center of the plot like a fat old spider in the web, in the book he hardly says anything except when he is bawling out his children and at board meetings he says: "everything's under control, next question please," that kind of thing, and I thought that if he's the star of the show, he's got to say more than that, so I wrote him a few big speeches because I thought he was like that guy Gordon Gecko in *Wall Street*, I mean, not exactly like him, but "greed is good" – all that kind of thing – so I wrote him some speeches about how unbridled ruthless capitalism was very good for the world and was going to save us all and everybody would have a share etc. Anyway, I am sort of rambling; the point is it's so arrogant isn't it? Because they are such great writers and so much better than me, but I do think that some of them need a bit of help.

DC: I am wondering if there is any writer you wouldn't adapt – who you wouldn't touch with a barge pole.

AD: I wouldn't be too keen on Virginia Woolf, I have to say. No I don't think I would, but I did once see a very good adaptation of *To The Lighthouse* by Hugh Stoddart and I watched it and I thought so that's what that was about, was it? But no, she's one I would avoid, and Henry James, I have never been tempted. Oh yes and the Brontës for another reason really, it's not that they are unadaptable it's just that I think they are all mad! It's an awful thing to say, but with the exception of *Jane Eyre*, which I would have a crack at, I think there is something about them. They just didn't get it. They just didn't understand what the world was like and they were trying to write about the world and all they could write about was what was going on in their own heads, so it's more like poetry than novels really. I know there's a grim shocked silence here! I know there are probably some big Brontë fans, but anyway, I can't help it, that's what I think!

DC: I'm going to ask you about D. H. Lawrence.

AD: Ah, D. H. Lawrence! Yes, do you know when I was about 19 he was my God and my girlfriends had a terrible time and I gradually thought that again maybe he didn't get it, in some sort of way. I still think they are fascinating but I think it's a big problem adapting them now. Somebody did a *Sons and Lovers* quite recently [2003] and the hero Paul was quite a sort of chirpy working-class lad which really kind of isn't the novel is it? But there again it's just another adaptor taking a few liberties and improving things. But no, I don't think I would like to do a D. H. Lawrence. In fact, I have turned down *Women in Love* again quite recently.

IW: I'm going to ask you a big question now. The 1990s was really the heyday of the resurgence of literary adaptations particularly of the nineteenth-century novel, latterly perhaps some eighteenth-century novels. How do you think approaches have changed because of that increasing popularity? What sort of things come up now?

AD: They're in a bit of a tricky or ambiguous situation at the moment, these adaptations. It was something that's always had a following but not a huge following and I think it was *Pride and Prejudice* that did it, because it got a very big audience, I think ten or twelve million, which was not the hugest audience in those days but a very, very good drama audience, and that was the point at which ITV started taking an interest in it and thinking, well, if that's the sort of audience we can get, we can do some classics too. But they would not do risky or little-known ones. They would do big, big titles and even better if they have got sort of slightly raunchy associations with them like *Moll Flanders* [1996] which was another one of mine which was hugely successful on ITV. I think ITV have rather gone off them now because the audience for all dramas, and in fact all terrestrial television, has come off and costume drama is the most expensive of all kinds of drama to produce. The BBC will continue to do it because it is one of the things that people expect the BBC to do and the governors will have to make sure we churn out at least one a year, which is good for me. So I think that's the situation at the moment, and in terms of style and so on, I think the kind of pace of drama, the expectations of the audience (being able to guess things and wanting to cut out a scene sooner because they've already got a sense of what's coming next) are increasing tendencies. Although this *Bleak House* is eight hours, it's a very, very fast eight hours. I put more plot into it, more sub-plots and more action than usually comes in, you know. Most of everybody's favorite minor characters are in there.

IW: You said that one Janeite gave you seven out of ten for *Pride and Prejudice* and that you ought to be pleased with that, she told you. Do you think now you can get away with more liberties, people are used to accepting that adaptation is about rethinking and reinterpretation?

AD: I think, yes, they do. There is one chap who persecutes me occasionally through the pages of the *Independent* from an old-fashioned purist point of view, saying if the book's worth doing why not exactly do the book and there's a very long argument to be had about that which I won't have now. In general and surprisingly, people like the Jane Austen Society and the George Eliot Society have been very generous and very understanding and the Trollope Society, too, who are a bit of a frightening lot. But the Jane Austen Society are very much, as you would imagine them, the George Eliot Society are mostly tremendous Nuneaton patriots and there is something charmingly local about them, but the Trollope Society have got a lot of oldish chaps who used to be in the army, huge old guys about seven foot tall in beautiful Savile Row suits and they have got a Trollope Society tie and they all wear it, but they are all right as well, once you get over your initial terror.

DC: If you are not too terrorised by the Janeites or the Trollope Society, you do tend to be known for costume drama, although you did do one *Othello* [2001] that was updated to a contemporary setting. Have you ever been tempted to update Jane Austen, for instance, to do a contemporary adaptation of *Emma* like *Clueless* for instance?

AD: I think I'm a bit old probably to do a teen adaptation now but it's something that I often recommend other people to do, you know, when I have screen writing students and so on. I think *Sense and Sensibility* would be a great candidate, you know, two girls, they might be sisters, they might just be best friends. One of them picks dreadful men with a kind of unerring talent and there would probably be more men, I would think, but one in particular who is, you know, like a dark destroyer kind of thing and her friend who can see all that happening to her and who is stuck with this sort of dull guy, who is not only dull but he has got other interests as well which is a terrible cheek really. But there's a very good story there and she's just such a wonderful model for how to work the plot out and *Clueless* was brilliant I thought. But yes, I think the other good teen pictures that were based on things were mostly based on Shakespeare, weren't they? Excellent idea, I think, but, you know, somehow not for me. Let somebody else do that.

NOTES

1 This won the Booker Prize, 2004. Davies's adaptation was broadcast by the BBC in 2006.
2 Aldous Huxley, among other things, adapted *Pride and Prejudice* (1940), discussed in Chapter 5 in this volume.
3 See discussion of "Darcymania" in Chapter 5 in this volume.
4 Andrew Davies attended a course given by Robert McKee.

FURTHER READING

Agawu, Kofi. *Playing with Signs: A Semiotic Interpretation of Classical Music.* Princeton: Princeton University Press, 1991.

Andrew, Dudley. *Concepts in Film Theory.* Oxford, London, Glasgow: Oxford University Press, 1984.

Arnheim, Rudolf. *Film as Art.* Berkeley: University of California Press, 1957.

Austen, Jane. *Pride and Prejudice.* Oxford: Oxford University Press, 1998.

Aycock, Wendell, and Michael Schoenecke (eds.). *Film and Literature: A Comparative Approach to Adaptation.* Lubbock: Texas Tech University Press, 1988.

Baetens, Jan. "Novelization, a contaminated genre," *Critical Inquiry* 31-4 (Autumn 2005), 43–60.

　Vivre sa vie. Une novellisation en vers du film de Jean-Luc Godard. Paris-Bruxelles: Les Impressions Nouvelles, 2005.

Baetens, Jan, and Marc Lits. *La Novellisation: Du film au livre/Novelization: From Film to Novel.* Leuven: Leuven University Press, 2004.

Bakhtin, Mikhail. *Speech Genres and Other Late Essays,* Caryl Emerson and Michael Holquist (eds.). Austin: University of Texas Press, 1986.

　"Discourse in the Novel," 1934/5. Bakhtin, *The Dialogic Imagination,* Caryl Emerson and Michael Holquist (trans.). Austin: University of Texas Press, 1992, pp. 257–422.

Balázs, Béla. *Theory of the Film: Character and Growth of a New Art* (1948). Trans. from the Hungarian by Edith Bone. New York: Dover Publications Inc., 1970.

Ball, Robert Hamilton. *Shakespeare on Silent Film: A Strange Eventful History.* New York: Theatre Arts Books, 1968.

Barber, Lynn. "Jolly Good Fellowes." *The Observer* (28 November 2004).

Barr, Charles. "Introduction: Amnesia and Schizophrenia." *All Our Yesterdays: 90 Years of British Cinema,* Charles Barr (ed.). London: British Film Institute, 1986, pp. 1–29.

Barthes, R. *Image–Music–Text,* S. Heath (trans.). Glasgow: Fontana, Collins, 1966.

Baudrillard, Jean. *Simulacra and Simulation.* Sheila Faria Glaser (trans.). Ann Arbor: University of Michigan Press, 1994.

Bell, E., L. Haas, and L. Sells (eds.). *From Mouse to Mermaid: The Politics of Film, Gender, and Culture.* Bloomington: Indiana University Press, 1995.

Belsey, Catherine. "Shakespeare and Film." *Literature/Film Quarterly* 11 (Spring 1983), 152–7.

Benchley, Peter. *Jaws.* London: Deutsch, 1974.

Benjamin, Walter. *Understanding Brecht*. London: Verso, 1973.
"The Work of Art in the Age of Mechanical Reproduction: Third Version." *Selected Writings*, Volume IV: 1938–1940, Howard Eiland and Michael W. Jennings (eds.), Edmund Jephcott et al. (trans.). Cambridge, Massachusetts: Harvard University Press, 2003, pp. 251–83.

Bhabha, Homi. "Introduction: Narrating the Nation." *Nation and Narration*, Homi Bhabha (ed.). London: Routledge, 1990, pp. 1–7.

Birchard, R. S. *Cecil B. DeMille's Hollywood*. Lexington: The University Press of Kentucky, 2004.

Birtwistle, Sue, and Susie Conklin. *The Making of Pride and Prejudice*. London: Penguin and BBC Books, 1995.
The Making of Jane Austen's Emma. London: Penguin, 1996.

Bluestone, G. *Novels into Film*. Berkeley: University of California Press, 1957.

Bolter, Jay David, and Grusin, Richard. *Remediation: Understanding New Media*. Cambridge, Massachusetts: MIT University Press, 1999.

Bordwell, D. *Narration in the Fiction Film*. London: Routledge, 1986.

Bourdieu, Pierre. *Distinction: A Social Critique of the Judgement of Taste*, Richard Nice (trans.). London: Routledge and Kegan Paul, 1984.

Boyum, Joy Gould. *Double Exposure: Fiction into Film*. New York: New America Library, 1985.

Branigan, Edward. *Narrative Comprehension and Film*. London: Routledge, 1992.

Braudy, Leo, and Marshall Cohen (eds.). *Film Theory and Criticism*. 6th ed. New York: Oxford University Press, 2004.

Brecht, Bertolt. "The Film, the Novel, and Epic Theatre." *Brecht on Theatre*, John Willett (ed.). New York: Hill & Wang, 1964, pp. 47–51.
Journals 1934–1955, John Willett (ed.), Hugh Rorrison (trans.). London: Methuen, 1993.

Brooker, Will. *Using the Force: Creativity, Community and 'Star Wars' Fans*. London: Continuum, 2002.

Buckland, Warren. "A Close Encounter with *Raiders of the Lost Ark*: Notes on Narrative Aspects of the New Hollywood Blockbuster." *Contemporary Hollywood Cinema*, Steve Neale and Murray Smith (eds.). London: Routledge, 1998.

Burgan, Mary. "Heroines at the Piano: Women and Music in Nineteenth-Century Fiction." *Victorian Studies* 30.1 (Autumn 1986), 51–76.

Burnett, R. G., and E. D. Martell. *The Devil's Camera: Menace of a Film-Ridden World*. London: Epworth, 1932.

Cardwell, Sarah. *Adaptation Revisited: Television and the Classic Novel*. Manchester: Manchester University Press, 2002.
Andrew Davies. The Television Series. Manchester: Manchester University Press, 2005.

Cartmell, D., I. Q. Hunter, H. Kaye, and I. Whelehan, (eds.). *Pulping Fictions: Consuming Culture Across the Literature/Media Divide*. London: Pluto, 1996.
Trash Aesthetics: Popular Culture and its Audience. London: Pluto Press, 1997.
Sisterhoods. London: Pluto Press, 1998.
Alien Identities. London: Pluto Press, 1999.
Classics in Film and Fiction. London: Pluto Press, 2000.

Cartmell, D., I. Q. Hunter, and I. Whelehan (eds.). *Retrovisions: Reinventing the Past in Film and Fiction*. London: Pluto Press, 2001.

Cartmell, Deborah, and Imelda Whelehan. "Harry Potter and the Fidelity Debate." *Books in Motion: Adaptation, Intertextuality, Authorship*, Mireia Aragay (ed.). Amsterdam and New York: Rodopi, 2005, pp. 37–49.

Cartmell, D., and I. Whelehan (eds.). *Adaptations: From Text to Screen, Screen to Text*. London: Routledge, 1999.

Caughie, John. *Television Drama: Realism, Modernism, and British Culture*. Oxford Television Studies. Oxford: Oxford University Press, 2000.

Cavell, Stanley. *The World Viewed*. Cambridge, Massachusetts: Harvard University Press, 1979.

Chanan, Michael. "Mahler in Venice?" *Music and Musicians* (June 1971 revised 2000). Available online at: http://www.mchanan.dial.pipex.com/mahler%20in%20venice. htm (accessed 22 May 2005).

Chance, Jane. "Is There a Text in This Hobbit? Peter Jackson's *Fellowship of the Ring*." *Literature/Film Quarterly* (2002: 2), 79–85.

Charney, Leo. *Empty Moments: Cinema, Modernity, and Drift*. Durham, North Carolina: Duke University Press, 1998.

Chin, Bertha, and Jonathan Gray. "'One Ring to Rule Them All': Pre-viewers and Pre-Texts of the *Lord of the Rings* Films." *Intensities: The Journal of Cult Media* Issue 2. http://www.cult-media.com/issue2/Achingray.htm

Chow, Rey. "A Phantom Discipline." *PMLA* 116.5 (2001), 1,386–95.

Christensen, Inger. *Literary Women on the Screen: The Representation of Women in Films Based on Imaginative Literature*. Bern: Peter Lang, 1991.

Clerc, Jeanne-Marie. *Cinéma et littérature*. Paris: Nathan, 1993.

Coats, Paul. *Film at the Intersection of High and Mass Culture*. Cambridge: Cambridge University Press, 1994.

Coelsch-Foisner, Sabine. "Reading Rosamunde Pilcher from a Consumer Perspective." *Consumer Cultures: Journal for the Study of British Cultures*, Jürgen Kramer (ed.) 11.2 (2004), 155–67.

Collick, John. *Shakespeare, Cinema and Society*. Manchester: Manchester University Press, 1989.

Collins, Jim. *High-Pop: Making Culture into Popular Entertainment*. Oxford: Blackwell, 2002.

Cook, P., and P. Dodd (eds.). *Women and Film: A Sight and Sound Reader*. London: Scarlet Press, 1996.

Cooke, Lez. *British Television Drama: A History*. London, BFI Publishing, 2003.

Coover, Robert. *A Night at the Movies*. New York: Linden Press /Simon & Schuster, 1987.

Corrigan, Timothy. *Film and Literature: An Introduction and Reader*. New Jersey: Prentice Hall, 2000.

Crafton, D. *Before Mickey: The Animated Film 1899–1928*. Chicago and London: University of Chicago Press, 1993.

Cunningham, Michael. *The Hours*. London: Fourth Estate, 1999.

Curry, Patrick. *Defending Middle Earth: Tolkien, Myth and Modernity*. London: HarperCollins, 1998.

Dahl, Roald. *Charlie and the Chocolate Factory*, 1964. London and New York: Penguin, 2001.

Dallen, J. Timothy and Stephen W. Boyd. *Heritage Tourism*. Harlow: Pearson, 2003.

Dardis, Tom. *Some Time in the Sun: The Hollywood Years of Fitzgerald, Faulkner, Nathanael West, Aldous Huxley, and James Agee*. New York: Scribner's, 1976.

Deleuze, Gilles. *Cinema 2: The Time Image*. Hugh Tomlinson & Robert Galeta (trans). London: Athlone, [1985] 1989.

DeNora, Tia. *Music in Everyday Life*. Cambridge: Cambridge University Press, 2000.

Desmond, John M. and Peter Hawkes. *Adaptation: Studying Film and Literature*. Boston: McGraw, 2006.

Dick, Philip K. *Minority Report*. London: Gollancz, 2002.

Doane, Mary Ann. *The Desire to Desire: The Woman's Film of the 1940s*. Basingstoke: Macmillan, 1987.

"Film and the Masquerade: Theorising the Female Spectator." *Hollywood: Critical Concepts in Media and Cultural Studies*, Volume IV, Thomas Schatz (ed.). London: Routledge, 2004, p. 102.

Dollimore, Jonathan, and Alan Sinfield (eds.). *Political Shakespeare: New Essays in Cultural Materialism*. Manchester: Manchester University Press, 1985.

Donald, James, Anne Freidberg, and Laura Marcus (eds.). *Close Up, 1927–1933: Cinema and Modernism*. Princeton: Princeton University Press, 1998.

Easthope, Antony. *Englishness and National Culture*. London and New York: Routledge, 1998.

Eisenstein, Sergei. *Film Form: Essays in Film Theory*. New York: Harcourt, Brace, and World, 1949.

Eliot, T. S. "Hamlet." *Selected Prose of T. S. Eliot*, Frank Kermode (ed.). London and Boston: Faber & Faber, 1980.

Elliott, Kamilla. *Rethinking the Novel/Film Debate*. Cambridge: Cambridge University Press, 2003.

Ellis, J. *Visible Fictions*. London: Routledge, 1982.

Ely, M. L. "The Untold Want: Representation and Transformation Echoes of Walt Whitman's *Passage to India* in *Now, Voyager*." *Literature/Film Quarterly* 29.1 (2001), 43–52.

Empson, W. *Seven Types of Ambiguity*. London: Peregrine, 1961.

Forster, E. M. "Mickey and Minnie." *The American Animated Cartoon*. D. Peary and G. Peary (eds.). New York: E. P. Dutton, 1980, pp. 238–40.

French, Philip, and Ken Wlaschin. *The Faber Book of Movie Verse*. London: Faber, 1993.

Frith, Simon. *Performing Rites: Evaluating Popular Music*. Oxford: Oxford University Press, 1998.

Garner, Ken. "'Would You Like to Hear Some Music?': Music in-and-out-of-Control in the Films of Quentin Tarantino." *Film Music: Critical Approaches*, K. J. Donnelly (ed.). Edinburgh: Edinburgh University Press, 2001, pp. 188–205.

Garth, John. *Tolkien and the Great War: The Threshold of Middle Earth*. London: HarperCollins, 2003.

Genette, Gérard. *Palimpsests: Literature in the Second Degree*, Channa Newman and Claude Doubinsky (trans.). Lincoln and London: University of Nebraska Press, 1997.

Paratexts: Thresholds of Interpretation, Jane E. Lewin (trans.). Cambridge: Cambridge University Press, 1997.

Gervais, David. *Literary Englands: Versions of "Englishness" in Modern Writing*. Cambridge: Cambridge University Press, 1993.

Gibson, Pamela Church. "Fewer Weddings and More Funerals: Changes in the Heritage Film." *British Cinema of the 90s*, Robert Murphy (ed.). London: British Film Institute, 2000, pp. 115–24.

Giddings, R., K. Selby, and C. Wensley. *Screening the Novel: The Theory and Practice of Literary Dramatization*. London: Macmillan, 1990.

Giddings, Robert, and Keith Selby. *The Classic Serial on Television and Radio*. London: Palgrave Macmillan, 2001.

Giddings, R., and E. Sheen (eds.). *The Classic Novel: From Page to Screen*. Manchester: Manchester University Press, 2000.

Gikandi, Simon. *Maps of Englishness: Writing Identity in the Culture of Colonialism*. New York: Columbia University Press, 1996.

Glavin, J. (ed.). *Dickens on Screen*. Cambridge and New York: Cambridge University Press, 2003.

Gledhill, C., et.al. *Reinventing Film Studies*. London: Hodder Arnold, 2000.

Gorbman, Claudia. *Unheard Melodies: Narrative Film Music*. London and Indianapolis: BFI and University of Indiana Press, 1987.

Greenfield, Lia. *Nationalism: Five Roads to Modernity*. Cambridge, Massachusetts: Harvard University Press, 1992.

Gripsrud, Jostein. " 'High Culture' Revisited." *Cultural Theory and Popular Culture: A Reader*, John Storey (ed.). Athens, Georgia: University of Georgia Press, 1998, pp. 536–7.

Harper, Sue. *Picturing the Past. The Rise and Fall of the British Costume Film*. London: British Film Institute, 1994.

Harrington, John. *Film and/as Literature*. Englewood Cliffs, New Jersey: Prentice-Hall, 1977.

Hewison, Robert. *The Heritage Industry: Britain in a Climate of Decline*. London: Methuen, 1987.

Higson, Andrew. *Waving the Flag: Constructing a National Cinema in Britain*. Oxford: Oxford University Press, 1995.

  English Heritage, English Cinema: Costume Drama since 1980. Oxford: Oxford University Press, 2003.

Hollows, J., et. al. (eds.). *The Film Studies Reader*. London: Arnold, 2000.

Horak, Jan-Christopher (ed.). *Lovers of Cinema: The First American Film Avant-Garde, 1919–1945*. Madison: University of Wisconsin Press, 1995.

Hornby, Nick. *High Fidelity*. London: Indigo, 1996.

Horton, Andrew, and Stuart Y. McDougal (eds.). *Play it Again, Sam: Retakes on Remakes*. Berkeley: University of California Press, 1998.

Howkins, Alun. "Rurality and English Identity." *British Cultural Studies: Geography, Nationality, and Identity*, David Morley and Kevin Robins (eds.). Oxford: Oxford University Press, 2001, 145–56.

Hunter, I. Q. "Tolkien Dirty." *Lord of the Rings: Popular Culture in Global Context*, Ernest Mathijs (ed.). London and New York: Wallflower Press, 2006.

Hutcheon, Linda. *The Politics of Postmodernism*. London: Routledge, 1989.

Jacobs, Jason. *The Intimate Screen: Early British Television Drama*. Oxford: Oxford Television Studies, Clarendon Press, 2000.

Jameson, Fredric. *The Cultural Turn: Selected Writings on the Postmodern*. London: Verso, 1998.

Jenkins, A. E. "A Film Technician's Notebook." *Cine Technician* (May 1955), 70.

Jenkins, H. *Textual Poachers: Television, Fans and Participatory Culture*. London: Routledge, 1992.

Jorgens, Jack. *Shakespeare on Film*. Bloomington: Indiana University Press, 1977.

Kalinak, Kathryn. *Settling the Score: Music and the Classical Hollywood Film*. Madison: University of Wisconsin Press, 1992.

Kaplan, E. Ann. *Motherhood and Representation: The Mother in Popular Culture and Melodrama*. London: Routledge, 1992.

Kassabian, Anahid. *Hearing Film: Tracking Identifications in Contemporary Hollywood Film Music*. London: Routledge, 2001.

Kawain. Bruce F. *Faulkner and Film*. New York: Frederick Ungar, 1977.

Keil, C. *"From the Manger to the Cross*: The New Testament Narrative and the Question of Stylistic Retardation." *Une invention du diable? Cinéma des premiers temps et religion*, R. Cosandey, A. Gaudreault, T. Gunning (eds.). Sainte-Foy: Les Presses de l'Université Laval, 1992, pp. 112–20.

Klein, Michael and Gillian Parker. *The English Novel and the Movies*. New York: Unger, 1981.

Kline, T. Jefferson, *Screening the Text: Intertextuality in New Wave French Cinema*. Baltimore: Johns Hopkins University Press, 1992.

Koestler, A. *The Act of Creation*. London: Pan Books, 1970.

Kreitzer, L. J. *The New Testament in Fiction and Film*. Sheffield: Sheffield Academic Press, 1993.

Kristeva, Julia. *Desire in Language: A Semiotic Approach to Literature and Art*, Leon. S. Roudiez (ed.); Thomas Gora, Alice Jardine and Leon S. Roudiez (trans.). New York: Columbia University Press, 1980.

Kumar, Krishan. *The Making of English National Identity*. Cambridge: Cambridge University Press, 2003.

Lacassin, Francis. *Feuillade*. Paris: Seghers, 1964.

Lahr, J. (ed.). *The Diaries of Kenneth Tynan*. London and New York: Bloomsbury, 2002.

Landy, Marcia. *Cinematic Uses of the Past*. Minneapolis: University of Minnesota Press, 1997.

(ed.). *The Historical Film: History and Memory in Media*. New Brunswick, New Jersey: Rutgers University Press, 2001.

Langford, Paul. *Englishness Identified: Manners and Character 1650–1850*. Oxford: Oxford University Press, 2000.

Lanier, Douglas M. " 'Art thou base, common, and popular?': The Cultural Politics of Kenneth Branagh's *Hamlet.*" *Spectacular Shakespeare: Critical Theory and Popular Cinema*, Lisa S. Starks and Courtney Lehmann (eds.). Madison, New Jersey: Fairleigh Dickinson University Press, 2002, pp. 149–71.

LaPlace, Maria. "Producing and Consuming the Woman's Film: Discursive Struggle in *Now, Voyager.*" *Home is Where the Heart is: Studies in Melodrama and the Woman's Film*, Christine Gledhill (ed.). London: BFI Books, 1987.

Leitch, Thomas. "Twelve Fallacies in Contemporary Adaptation Theory." *Criticism* 45.2 (Spring 2003), 149–71.

Leonard, Elmore. *Rum Punch*. New York: Delacorte, 1992.

Leslie, E. *Hollywood Flatlands: Animation, Critical Theory and the Avant Garde*, London and New York: Verso, 2002.

Leyda, J. (ed.). *Eisenstein on Disney*. London & New York: Methuen, 1988.

Lindvall, T. *The Silents of God: Selected Issues and Documents in Silent American Film and Religion, 1908–1925*. Lanham, Maryland and London: The Scarecrow Press, 2001.

Loesser, Arthur. *Men, Women and Pianos: A Social History*. New York: Simon and Schuster, 1954.

Lothe, J. *Narrative in Fiction and Film: An Introduction*. Oxford: Oxford University Press, 2000.

Lucas, John. *England and Englishness: Ideas of Nationhood in English Poetry, 1688–1900*. Iowa City: University of Iowa Press, 1990.

Lustig, Jodi. "The Piano's Progress: The Piano in Play in the Victorian Novel." *The Idea of Music in Victorian Fiction*. Sophie Fuller and Nicky Losseff (eds.). Aldershot: Ashgate, 2004, pp. 83–104.

Macdonald, Gina and Andrew (eds.). *Jane Austen on Screen*. Cambridge: Cambridge University Press, 2003.

Magliozzi, R. S. *Treasures from the Film Archives: A Catalog of Short Silent Fiction Films held by FIAF Archives*. Metuchen, New Jersey and London: The Scarecrow Press, 1988.

Mann, Thomas. *Death in Venice and Other Stories*. Joachim Neugroschel (trans.). Harmondsworth: Penguin Books, 1999.

Mast, Gerald, Marshall Cohen, et al. (eds.). *Film Theory and Criticism: Introductory Readings*. Oxford: Oxford University Press, 1992.

Mayne, Judith, *Private Novels, Public Films*. Athens, Georgia: University of Georgia Press, 1988.

McCabe, Susan. *Cinematic Modernism: Modernist Poetry and Film*. Cambridge: Cambridge University Press, 2005.

McFarlane, Brian. *Novel to Film: An Introduction to the Theory of Adaptation*. Oxford: Clarendon Press, 1996.

McMillen, W. "A Century of Lew Wallace and a Half Century of Ben-Hur." *The Mentor* (May 1927), pp. 33–35.

Miles, Peter. *Cinema, Literature and Society*. London: Croom Helm, 1987.

Monaco, James. *How to Read a Film*, 3rd edn. Oxford: Oxford University Press, 2000.

Monk, Claire. "The British Heritage-Film Debate Revisited." *British Historical Cinema: The History, Heritage and Costume Film*, Claire Monk and Amy Sargeant (eds.). London and New York: Routledge, 2002, pp. 176–98.

Nelmes, Jill. *An Introduction to Film Studies*, 3rd edn. London: Routledge, 2003.

Nairn, Tom. *The Break-up of Britain*. London: New Left Books, 1977.

Naremore, James (ed.). *Film Adaptation*. London: The Athlone Press, 2000.

Neale, Steve. *Genre and Hollywood*, London and New York: Routledge, 2000.

Nelson, Robin. "Costume Drama (Jane Austen adaptations)." *The Television Genre Book*, Glen Creeber (ed.). London: BFI Publishing, 2001.

Nicol, Allardyce. *Film and Theatre*. London, Bombay, Sidney: George G. Harrap & Company, 1936.

O'Pray, M. "Surrealism, Fantasy and the Grotesque: The Cinema of Jan Svankmajer." *Fantasy and the Cinema*, J. Donald (ed). London: BFI, 1989, pp. 256–8.

Orr, John. *Cinema and Modernity*. Cambridge: Polity Press, 1993.

Orr, John, and Colin Nicholson, (eds.). *Cinema and Fiction: New Modes of Adapting, 1950–1990*. Edinburgh: Edinburgh University Press, 1992.

Parakilas, James, et al., *Piano Roles: Three Hundred Years of Life with the Piano*. New Haven and London: Yale University Press, 1999.

Parill, Sue. *Jane Austen on Film and Television: A Critical Study of the Adaptations*. Jefferson, North Carolina: McFarland, 2002.

Paxman, Jeremy. *The English: A Portrait of a People*. London: Penguin, 1999.

Pearce, Joseph. *Tolkien: Man and Myth*. London: HarperCollins, 1998.

Pearson, Roberta, and William Uricchio. *Reframing Culture: The Case of the Vitagraph Quality Films*. Princeton: Princeton University Press, 1993.

Pidduck, Julianne. *Contemporary Costume Film: Space, Place and the Past*. London: British Film Institute, 2004.

Piggott, Patrick. *The Innocent Diversion: A Study of Music in the Life and Writings of Jane Austen*. London: Cleverdon, 1979.

Prouty, Olive Higgins. *Pencil Shavings: Memoirs*. Cambridge, Massachusetts: The Riverside Press, 1961.

Now, Voyager, 1941. New York: The Feminist Press, 2004.

Pucci, Suzanne, and James Thompson (eds.). *Jane Austen and Co.: Remaking the Past in Contemporary Culture*. Buffalo: State University of New York Press, 2003.

Ray, Robert. *How a Film Theory Got Lost and Other Mysteries in Cultural Studies*. Bloomington: Indiana University Press, 2001.

Reynolds, P. (ed.). *Novel Images: Literature in Performance*. London: Routledge, 1993.

Richardson, Robert. *Literature and Film*. Bloomington: Indiana University Press, 1969.

Rosebury, Brian. *Tolkien: A Cultural Phenomenon*. London: Palgrave Macmillan, 2003.

Ross, Harris. *Film and Literature, Literature as Film*. London: Greenwood, 1987.

Rothwell, Kenneth. *A History of Shakespeare on Screen*, 2nd edn. Cambridge: Cambridge University Press, 2004.

Rovin, J. *The Illustrated Encyclopaedia of Cartoon Animals*. New York: Prentice Hall, 1991.

Rowling, J. K. *Harry Potter and the Philosopher's Stone*. London: Bloomsbury, 1997.

Sakai, Naoki. *Translation and Subjectivity. On "Japan" and Cultural Nationalism*. Minneapolis: University of Minnesota Press, 1997.

Samuel, Raphael. *Theatres of Memory*. London and New York: Verso, 1994.

Schickel, Richard. *The Disney Version*. New York: Avon Books 1968.

Scumsky, Brian E. " 'All That is Solid Melts into the Air': The Winds of Change and other Analogues of Colonialism in Disney's *Mary Poppins*." *The Lion and the Unicorn* 24 (2000), 97–109.

Seger, Linda. *The Art of Adaptation*. New York: Holt, 1992.

Sheen, Erica. "'Where the Garment Gapes': Faithfulness and Promiscuity in the 1995 BBC *Pride and Prejudice*." *The Classic Novel: From Page to Screen*, Robert Giddings and Erica Sheen (eds.). Manchester: Manchester University Press, 2000, pp. 14–30.

Shippey, Tom. *J. R. R. Tolkien: Author of the Century*. London: HarperCollins, 2001.

"Another Road to Middle Earth: Jackson's Movie Trilogy." *Understanding The Lord of the Rings: The Best of Tolkien Criticism*, Rose A. Zimbardo and Neil D. Isaacs (eds.). New York: Houghton Mifflin, 2004, pp. 233–54.

Sibley, Brian. "How are they Going to Make *That* into a Musical? P. L. Travers, Julie Andrews, and Mary Poppins." *A Lively Oracle: A Centennial Celebration of P. L. Travers*, Ellen Dooling Draper and Jenny Koralek (eds.). New York: Larson, 1999, pp. 51–62.

Simpson, Paul. *The Rough Guide to Kids' Movies*. New York and London: Penguin, 2004.

Sinyard, Neil. *Filming Literature: The Art of Screen Adaptation*. London: Croom Helm, 1987.

Skeggs, B. (ed.). *Feminist Cultural Theory: Process and Production*. Manchester: Manchester University Press, 1995.

Smith, Jeff. *The Sounds of Commerce: Marketing Popular Film Music*. New York: Columbia University Press, 1998.

Smith, Jim and J. Clive Matthews. *The Lord of the Rings: The Films, The Books, The Radio Series*. London: Virgin Books, 2004.

Smol, Anna. "'Oh ... Oh ... Frodo!': Readings of Male Intimacy in *The Lord of the Rings*." *MFS Modern Fiction Studies* 50.4 (Winter 2004), 949–79.

Spiegel, A. *Fiction and the Camera Eye: Visual Consciousness in Film and the Modern Novel*. Charlottesville: University Press of Virginia, 1976.

Stam, Robert. *Literature through Film: Realism, Magic and the Art of Adaptation*. Malden and Oxford: Blackwell, 2005.

Stam, Robert, and Alessandra Raengo (eds.). *A Companion to Literature and Film*. Malden, Massachusetts and Oxford: Blackwell, 2005.

    Literature and Film: A Guide to the Theory and Practice of Film Adaptation. Malden, Massachusetts and Oxford: Blackwell, 2005.

Story, John. *Inventing Popular Culture*. Oxford: Blackwell, 2003.

Street, Douglas (ed.). *Children's Novels and the Movies*. New York: Ungar, 1983.

Taylor, Gary. *Reinventing Shakespeare: A Cultural History from the Restoration to the Present*. Oxford: Oxford University Press, 1991.

Thompson, Emma. *The Sense and Sensibility Diaries*. London: Bloomsbury Press; New York: Newmarket Press, 1996.

Thompson, Kristin. *Storytelling in the New Hollywood: Understanding Classical Narrative Technique*. Cambridge, Massachusetts and London: Harvard University Press, 1999.

    "Fantasy, Franchises, and Frodo Baggins: *The Lord of the Rings* and Modern Hollywood." *The Velvet Light Trap* 52 (Fall 2003), 45–62.

Thornton, Sarah. *Club Cultures: Music, Media and Subcultural Capital*. Cambridge: Polity Press, 1995.

Troost, Linda, and Sayre Greenfield (eds.). *Jane Austen in Hollywood*. Lexington: University Press of Kentucky, 1998, 2001.

Truffaut, François. *Hitchcock*. Paris: Gallimard 1993.

Viel, Tanguy. *Cinéma*. Paris: Minuit. 1999.

Vincendeau, G. (ed.). *Film/Heritage/Literature: A Sight and Sound Reader*. London: BFI Publishing, 2001.

Virmaux, Alain and Odette. *Le Ciné-Roman*. Paris: Edilig, 1984.

Voigts-Virchow, Eckart (ed.). *Janespotting and Beyond: British Heritage Retrovisions since the Mid-1990s*. Tübingen: Narr, 2004.

Wagenknecht, E. *Movies in the Age of Innocence*. Norman, Oklahoma: Oklahoma Press, 1962.

Wagner, G. *The Novel and the Cinema*. Rutherford, New Jersey: Fairleigh Dickinson University Press, 1975.

Warner, Marina. *Fantastic Metamorphoses, Other Worlds*. Oxford: Oxford University Press, 2002.

Wasko, Janet. *Understanding Disney*. London: Polity, 2001.

How Hollywood Works. London: Sage, 2003.

Watts, Steven. *The Magic Kingdom: Walt Disney and the American Way of Life*. New York: Houghton Mifflin, 1997.

Wells, P. "Literary Theory, Animation and the 'Subjective Correlative': Defining the Narrative 'World' in Brit-Lit Animation." *Animated Worlds*, S. Buchan (ed). London: John Libbey, (2006).

Williams, R. *Orwell*. London: Fontana, 1971.

Wood, Michael. "Modernism and Film." *The Cambridge Companion to Modernism*, Michael Levenson (ed.). Cambridge: Cambridge University Press, 1999, pp. 217–32.

Wright, Elizabeth. *Postmodern Brecht. A Re-Presentation*. London: Routledge, 1989.

Wright, Patrick. *On Living in an Old Country: The National Past in Contemporary Britain*. London: Verso, 1985.

Wyatt, Justin. *High Concept: Movies and Marketing in America*. Austin: University of Texas Press, 1994.

INDEX

(Note: All films and TV productions are marked in bold)

Cambridge companions to ...

AUTHORS

Edward Albee *edited by Stephen J. Bottoms*

Margaret Atwood *edited by Coral Ann Howells*

W. H. Auden *edited by Stan Smith*

Jane Austen *edited by Edward Copeland and Juliet McMaster*

Beckett *edited by John Pilling*

Aphra Behn *edited by Derek Hughes and Janet Todd*

Walter Benjamin *edited by David S. Ferris*

William Blake *edited by Morris Eaves*

Brecht *edited by Peter Thomson and Glendyr Sacks* (second edition)

The Brontës *edited by Heather Glen*

Frances Burney *edited by Peter Sabor*

Byron *edited by Drummond Bone*

Albert Camus *edited by Edward J. Hughes*

Willa Cather *edited by Marilee Lindemann*

Cervantes *edited by Anthony J. Cascardi*

Chaucer, *second edition edited by Piero Boitani and Jill Mann*

Chekhov *edited by Vera Gottlieb and Paul Allain*

Coleridge *edited by Lucy Newlyn*

Wilkie Collins *edited by Jenny Bourne Taylor*

Joseph Conrad *edited by J. H. Stape*

Dante *edited by Rachel Jacoff* (second edition)

Charles Dickens *edited by John O. Jordan*

Emily Dickinson *edited by Wendy Martin*

John Donne *edited by Achsah Guibbory*

Dostoevskii *edited by W. J. Leatherbarrow*

Theodore Dreiser *edited by Leonard Cassuto and Claire Virginia Eby*

John Dryden *edited by Steven N. Zwicker*

George Eliot *edited by George Levine*

T. S. Eliot *edited by A. David Moody*

Ralph Ellison *edited by Ross Posnock*

Ralph Waldo Emerson *edited by Joel Porte and Saundra Morris*

William Faulkner *edited by Philip M. Weinstein*

Henry Fielding *edited by Claude Rawson*

F. Scott Fitzgerald *edited by Ruth Prigozy*

Flaubert *edited by Timothy Unwin*

E. M. Forster *edited by David Bradshaw*

Brian Friel *edited by Anthony Roche*

Robert Frost *edited by Robert Faggen*

Elizabeth Gaskell *edited by Jill L. Matus*

Goethe *edited by Lesley Sharpe*

Thomas Hardy *edited by Dale Kramer*

Nathaniel Hawthorne *edited by Richard Millington*

Ernest Hemingway *edited by Scott Donaldson*

Homer *edited by Robert Fowler*

Ibsen *edited by James McFarlane*

Henry James *edited by Jonathan Freedman*

Samuel Johnson *edited by Greg Clingham*

Ben Jonson *edited by Richard Harp and Stanley Stewart*

James Joyce *edited by Derek Attridge* (second edition)

Kafka *edited by Julian Preece*

Keats *edited by Susan J. Wolfson*

Lacan *edited by Jean-Michel Rabaté*

D. H. Lawrence *edited by Anne Fernihough*

David Mamet *edited by Christopher Bigsby*

Thomas Mann *edited by Ritchie Robertson*

Christopher Marlowe *edited by Patrick Cheney*

Herman Melville *edited by Robert S. Levine*

Arthur Miller *edited by Christopher Bigsby*

Milton *edited by Dennis Danielson* (second edition)

Molière *edited by David Bradby and Andrew Calder*

Nabokov *edited by Julian W. Connolly*

Eugene O'Neill *edited by Michael Manheim*

George Orwell *edited by John Rodden*

Ovid *edited by Philip Hardie*

Harold Pinter *edited by Peter Raby*

Sylvia Plath *edited by Jo Gill*

Edgar Allan Poe *edited by Kevin J. Hayes*

Ezra Pound *edited by Ira B. Nadel*

Proust *edited by Richard Bales*

Pushkin *edited by Andrew Kahn*

Philip Roth *edited by Timothy Parrish*

Shakespeare *edited by Margareta de Grazia and Stanley Wells*

Shakespeare on Film *edited by Russell Jackson* (second edition)

Shakespearean Comedy *edited by Alexander Leggatt*

Shakespeare on Stage *edited by Stanley Wells and Sarah Stanton*

Shakespeare's History Plays *edited by Michael Hattaway*

Shakespearean Tragedy *edited by Claire McEachern*

Shakespeare's Poetry *edited by Patrick Cheney*

George Bernard Shaw *edited by Christopher Innes*

Shelley *edited by Timothy Morton*

Mary Shelley *edited by Esther Schor*

Sam Shepard *edited by Matthew C. Roudané*

Spenser *edited by Andrew Hadfield*

Wallace Stevens *edited by John N. Serio*

Tom Stoppard *edited by Katherine E. Kelly*

Harriet Beecher Stowe *edited by Cindy Weinstein*

Jonathan Swift *edited by Christopher Fox*

Henry David Thoreau *edited by Joel Myerson*

Tolstoy *edited by Donna Tussing Orwin*

Mark Twain *edited by Forrest G. Robinson*

Virgil *edited by Charles Martindale*

Edith Wharton *edited by Millicent Bell*

Walt Whitman *edited by Ezra Greenspan*

Oscar Wilde *edited by Peter Raby*

Tennessee Williams *edited by Matthew C. Roudané*

Mary Wollstonecraft *edited by Claudia L. Johnson*

Virginia Woolf *edited by Sue Roe and Susan Sellers*

Wordsworth *edited by Stephen Gill*

W. B. Yeats *edited by Marjorie Howes and John Kelly*

Zola *edited by Brian Nelson*

TOPICS

The Actress *edited by Maggie B. Gale and John Stokes*

The African American Novel *edited by Maryemma Graham*

The African American Slave Narrative *edited by Audrey A. Fisch*

American Modernism *edited by Walter Kalaidjian*

American Realism and Naturalism *edited by Donald Pizer*

American Women Playwrights *edited by Brenda Murphy*

Australian Literature *edited by Elizabeth Webby*

British Romanticism *edited by Stuart Curran*

Canadian Literature *edited by Eva-Marie Kröller*

The Classic Russian Novel *edited by Malcolm V. Jones and Robin Feuer Miller*

Contemporary Irish Poetry *edited by Matthew Campbell*

Crime Fiction *edited by Martin Priestman*

The Eighteenth-Century Novel *edited by John Richetti*

Eighteenth-Century Poetry *edited by John Sitter*

English Literature, 1500–1600 *edited by Arthur F. Kinney*

English Literature, 1650–1740 *edited by Steven N. Zwicker*

English Literature, 1740–1830 *edited by Thomas Keymer and Jon Mee*

English Poetry, Donne to Marvell *edited by Thomas N. Corns*

English Renaissance Drama, second edition *edited by A. R. Braunmuller and Michael Hattaway*

English Restoration Theatre *edited by Deborah C. Payne Fisk*

Feminist Literary Theory *edited by Ellen Rooney*

The French Novel: from 1800 to the Present *edited by Timothy Unwin*

Gothic Fiction *edited by Jerrold E. Hogle*

Greek and Roman Theatre *edited by Marianne McDonald and J. Michael Walton*

Greek Tragedy *edited by P. E. Easterling*

The Irish Novel *edited by John Wilson Foster*

The Italian Novel *edited by Peter Bondanella and Andrea Ciccarelli*

Jewish American Literature *edited by Hana Wirth-Nesher and Michael P. Kramer*

The Latin American Novel *edited by Efraín Kristal*

Literature of the First World War *edited by Vincent Sherry*

Literature on Screen *edited by Deborah Cartmell and Imelda Whelehan*

Medieval English Theatre *edited by Richard Beadle*

Medieval Romance *edited by Roberta L. Krueger*

Medieval Women's Writing *edited by Carolyn Dinshaw and David Wallace*

Modern American Culture *edited by Christopher Bigsby*